YOUTH, PORNOGRAPHY, AND THE INTERNET

Dick Thornburgh and Herbert S. Lin, *Editors*

Committee to Study Tools and Strategies for Protecting
Kids from Pornography and Their Applicability
to Other Inappropriate Internet Content

Computer Science and Telecommunications Board
National Research Council

NATIONAL ACADEMY PRESS
Washington, D.C.

NATIONAL ACADEMY PRESS • 2101 Constitution Avenue, N.W. • Washington, D.C. 20418

NOTICE: The project that is the subject of this report was approved by the Governing Board of the National Research Council, whose members are drawn from the councils of the National Academy of Sciences, the National Academy of Engineering, and the Institute of Medicine. The members of the committee responsible for the report were chosen for their special competences and with regard for appropriate balance.

This study was supported by Grant No. 1999-JN-FX-0071 between the National Academy of Sciences and the U.S. Departments of Justice and Education; Grant No. P0073380 between the National Academy of Sciences and the W.K. Kellogg Foundation; awards (unnumbered) from the Microsoft Corporation and IBM; and internal funds of the National Research Council. Any opinions, findings, conclusions, or recommendations expressed in this publication are those of the authoring committee and do not necessarily reflect the views of the organizations or agencies that provided support for this project.

International Standard Book Number 0-309-08274-9

Library of Congress Control Number 2002110219

THE NATIONAL ACADEMIES

National Academy of Sciences
National Academy of Engineering
Institute of Medicine
National Research Council

The **National Academy of Sciences** is a private, nonprofit, self-perpetuating society of distinguished scholars engaged in scientific and engineering research, dedicated to the furtherance of science and technology and to their use for the general welfare. Upon the authority of the charter granted to it by the Congress in 1863, the Academy has a mandate that requires it to advise the federal government on scientific and technical matters. Dr. Bruce M. Alberts is president of the National Academy of Sciences.

The **National Academy of Engineering** was established in 1964, under the charter of the National Academy of Sciences, as a parallel organization of outstanding engineers. It is autonomous in its administration and in the selection of its members, sharing with the National Academy of Sciences the responsibility for advising the federal government. The National Academy of Engineering also sponsors engineering programs aimed at meeting national needs, encourages education and research, and recognizes the superior achievements of engineers. Dr. Wm. A. Wulf is president of the National Academy of Engineering.

The **Institute of Medicine** was established in 1970 by the National Academy of Sciences to secure the services of eminent members of appropriate professions in the examination of policy matters pertaining to the health of the public. The Institute acts under the responsibility given to the National Academy of Sciences by its congressional charter to be an adviser to the federal government and, upon its own initiative, to identify issues of medical care, research, and education. Dr. Harvey V. Fineberg is president of the Institute of Medicine.

The **National Research Council** was organized by the National Academy of Sciences in 1916 to associate the broad community of science and technology with the Academy's purposes of furthering knowledge and advising the federal government. Functioning in accordance with general policies determined by the Academy, the Council has become the principal operating agency of both the National Academy of Sciences and the National Academy of Engineering in providing services to the government, the public, and the scientific and engineering communities. The Council is administered jointly by both Academies and the Institute of Medicine. Dr. Bruce M. Alberts and Dr. Wm. A. Wulf are chairman and vice chairman, respectively, of the National Research Council.

iv

Preface

Youth, pornography, and the Internet. The combination of these elements is a subject on which individuals from all walks of life—parents, teachers, librarians, school administrators, library board members, legislators, judges, and other concerned citizens—have thoughts and strong opinions. Those with products and services to sell are also interested in and concerned about the subject. Some from the online adult entertainment industry fear that efforts to restrict the access of children to certain kinds of sexually explicit material on the Internet will impinge on what they see as legitimate business opportunities to market their products and services to adults. Those with technology-based protection systems to sell hope to capitalize on what they see as a growing market for solutions to the problem, however that may be defined.

Views in this subject area are highly polarized. Because strongly held values are at stake, the political debate is heated, and often characterized by extreme views, inflammatory rhetoric, and half-truths. Against the backdrop of intense lobbying in the halls of Congress and many local school and library board meetings in communities across the country, a document assembling in one place the different dimensions and pros and cons of approaches that might be taken to address the problem can help to conduct the debate over "what to do" in a more informed manner.

Thus, one purpose of this report is to provide a reasonably complete and thorough treatment of the problem and potential solutions that airs all sides. In addition, different communities or groups of readers are likely to be interested in different aspects of this report.

- Parents will be interested in its description and assessment of a reasonably comprehensive set of tools and strategies for protecting their children on the Internet from exposure to inappropriate sexually explicit material (and other inappropriate material for that matter), many of which can be deployed in their homes. Furthermore, to the extent that parents understand the advantages and disadvantages of these various tools and strategies, they can engage their legislators and local administrative bodies more effectively.

- Adults responsible for children and youth in other settings—school, libraries, after-school programs, camps, and so on—will be interested in this description and assessment as well for classroom and other purposes, but also in the political and organizational issues that surround the use of these various tools and strategies. Those responsible for education broadly construed will also be attentive to the issues related to material that is improperly or incorrectly identified as inappropriate for children and youth.

- The information technology (IT) sector is likely to be interested in finding business opportunities for helping parents and others deal with the issues as they see fit, while many commercial interests in the IT sector and in other corners are concerned about the possibility of regulation.

- Law enforcement agencies may be interested in this report to help clarify their roles and responsibilities in both preventive and tactical operations, and may benefit from the report's overview about existing law in this area. The judiciary, especially at the local level, may find perspective and understanding that can be useful in trying and hearing cases touching on the subject matter of this report.

- Policy makers will be interested in all of these dimensions of the issue, and must decide how to weigh them in their attempts to formulate appropriate policy. Further, much of this report points to legal, economic, technical, and social realities that affect how legislation and regulation might actually play out.

ORIGIN OF THIS STUDY

In November 1998, the U.S. Congress mandated a study by the National Research Council (NRC) to address pornography on the Internet (Box P.1). In response to this mandate, the Computer Science and Telecommunications Board (CSTB), responsible within the National Academies for issues at the nexus of information technology and public policy, engaged the NRC's Board on Children, Youth, and Families (BOCYF) to form a committee with expertise diverse enough to address this topic. The resulting committee was composed of a diverse group of people, including individuals with expertise in constitutional law, law enforcement, libraries and library science, information retrieval and representa-

Box P.1
Legislative Language That Led to This Study

In Public Law 105-314, the Protection of Children from Sexual Predators Act of 1998, Title IX, Section 901, the U.S. Congress passed the following legislation:

SEC. 901. STUDY ON LIMITING THE AVAILABILITY OF PORNOGRAPHY ON THE INTERNET.

(a) IN GENERAL—Not later than 90 days after the date of enactment of this Act, the Attorney General shall request that the National Academy of Sciences, acting through its National Research Council, enter into a contract to conduct a study of computer-based technologies and other approaches to the problem of the availability of pornographic material to children on the Internet, in order to develop possible amendments to Federal criminal law and other law enforcement techniques to respond to the problem.

(b) CONTENTS OF STUDY—The study under this section shall address each of the following:

(1) The capabilities of present-day computer-based control technologies for controlling electronic transmission of pornographic images.

(2) Research needed to develop computer-based control technologies to the point of practical utility for controlling the electronic transmission of pornographic images.

(3) Any inherent limitations of computer-based control technologies for controlling electronic transmission of pornographic images.

(4) Operational policies or management techniques needed to ensure the effectiveness of these control technologies for controlling electronic transmission of pornographic images.

(c) FINAL REPORT—Not later than 2 years after the date of enactment of this Act, the Attorney General shall submit to the Committees on the Judiciary of the House of Representatives and the Senate a final report of the study under this section, which report shall—

(1) set forth the findings, conclusions, and recommendations of the Council; and

(2) be submitted by the Committees on the Judiciary of the House of Representatives and the Senate to relevant Government agencies and committees of Congress.

Based on this language and as noted in the text, the statement of task was negotiated with the Department of Justice in ways that would lead to a report that placed the issue of concern in context and would provide a range of useful alternatives for constituencies affected by this issue. The charge below guided the work of the Committee to Study Tools and Strategies for Protecting Kids from Pornography:

The project, requested by the U.S. Congress, seeks to frame the problem in an appropriate social, legal, educational, technological, and ethical context; present what is and is not scientifically known about the impact on children of exposure to sexually explicit material; and provide information useful to various decision-making communities (e.g., parents, the information technology industry, school boards, librarians, and government at all levels) about possible courses of action across educational, legislative, law enforcement, and technological fronts. While it does not present explicit recommendations about actions that should be taken, it does provide findings and conclusions that result from committee deliberations.

tion, developmental and social psychology, Internet and other information technologies, ethics, and education.

CSTB, with input from BOCYF, developed a proposal that was responsive to the legislative mandate. As a result of discussions with the Department of Justice's Office of Juvenile Justice and Delinquency Prevention, the Department of Education, and various private companies in the information technology industry, the study's statement of work was adjusted to include non-technological strategies as well as technology options for protection and to address "pornography" as the primary systematic focus of the study's exploration of inappropriate content, with other areas addressed as appropriate for context-setting purposes, explored incidentally rather than systematically.

Further, the negotiated statement of work noted that the final report would place the issue of concern in context, provide a range of useful alternatives for constituencies affected by this issue, and explicate the foundation for a more coherent and objective local and national debate on the subject of Internet "pornography," but would avoid making specific policy recommendations that embed particular social values in this area.

METHODOLOGY AND CAVEATS

As with most controversial issues, the reality of both problem and solution is much more complex than the rhetoric would indicate. To complement the expertise of its members and to understand the issue more effectively, the committee took a great deal of testimony over the course of its study. In its plenary sessions, it heard testimony from some 20 parties with differing points of view and expertise; these parties are identified in Appendix A (which provides the agendas of the various plenary sessions). It held two workshops to explore both technical and non-technical dimensions of the issue; summaries of these workshops were published prior to the publication of this report.[1]

Members of the committee also visited a range of communities across the United States to hear firsthand from the various constituencies—not the least of which were the children involved. Thus, the committee conducted seven site visits from April through June 2001 in a variety of

---

[1]See National Research Council and Institute of Medicine, 2001, *Nontechnical Strategies to Reduce Children's Exposure to Inappropriate Material on the Internet: Summary of a Workshop*, Board on Children, Youth, and Families and Computer Science and Telecommunications Board, Joah G. Iannotta, ed., National Academy Press, Washington, D.C.; and Computer Science and Telecommunications Board, 2002, *Technical, Business, and Legal Dimensions of Protecting Children from Pornography on the Internet: Proceedings of a Workshop*, National Academy Press, Washington, D.C.

geographical locales: Austin, Texas, on April 3-4; Greenville, South Carolina, on April 17-18; Salt Lake City, Utah, on April 26-27; San Diego, California, on May 2-3; Blacksburg, Virginia, on May 8-9; Coral Gables, Florida, on May 30-June 1; and Redding, Shelton, Bristol, Kent, and Hamden, Connecticut, on June 1-2.

Finally, the committee issued a call for white papers and received about 10 (all of which are posted on the project Web site at <http://www.itasnrc.org>). The committee noted the existence of other work and reports on the subject, such as the final report of the COPA Commission,[2] the report of the House Committee on Commerce on the Children's Online Protection Act,[3] *Safeguarding the Wired Schoolhouse* from the Consortium on School Networking,[4] and various efforts supported by the Bertelsmann Foundation (e.g., *Protecting Our Children on the Internet*[5]). And, because the committee was, by design, composed of individuals with varying expertise and perspectives on the issues, the committee learned from itself—through argument and discussion. As a result of this process, it is fair to say that every committee member came to understand the issue differently than when he or she first joined the study—and left behind any notion that an instant solution could be found.

This study is not a comprehensive study of safety on the Internet, nor even one on safety for children on the Internet. The primary emphasis of this study is on approaches to protect youth from pornography—or more properly, sexually explicit material deemed inappropriate for minors—though the relevance of these approaches to some other kinds of material deemed inappropriate receives some attention as well. This emphasis does not reflect a consensus of the committee that inappropriate sexually explicit material is—or is not—the most important safety issue on the Internet for children, but rather the fact that such material was a central element in the legislative mandate to the committee.

This study is not a study on the impact of exposure to such material, nor does it come to a consensus on this question. Committee members had, and continue to have, a variety of different views. Committee members do share common views about the undesirability of exposing children to some kinds of sexually explicit material, but they do not share

---

[2]The COPA Commission was established as part of the Child Online Protection Act, discussed in Chapter 4. Information on the COPA Commission can be found online at <http://www.copacommission.org>.

[3]H.R. No. 105-775.

[4]Consortium for School Networking. 2001. *Safeguarding the Wired Schoolhouse*. Available online at <http://www.safewiredschools.org/pubs_and_tools/white_paper.pdf>.

[5]Jens Waltermann and Marcel Machill, eds. 2000. *Protecting Our Children on the Internet*. Bertelsmann Foundation Publishers, Gutersloh, Germany.

views about other kinds of sexually explicit material. But coming to consensus on a world view regarding all sexually explicit material was not the task given to the committee, and the consensus on the material contained in this report—which focuses on things that communities can do to help themselves—indicates that such agreement is not necessary for making informed decisions.

Note also that this report mentions a variety of companies, products, services, and Web sites. These references are for illustrative purposes only, and their mention should not be taken by readers as an endorsement in any way.

SCOPE AND PURPOSE OF THIS REPORT

This report surveys the technical, legal, law enforcement, educational, and economic dimensions of the problem of coping with materials and experiences on the Internet that are inappropriate for children. In addition, it describes a range of social and educational strategies, technology-based tools, and legal and regulatory approaches that can help children to use the Internet more safely. Thus, this report provides a framework within which responsible adults can develop their own approaches—embodying their own values—for the children in their care.

This study does not make recommendations about what communities should do about the problem. Although this study explicates the factors that can enter into choices about appropriate approaches to protecting kids from inappropriate sexually explicit material on the Internet, the choice of any particular approach implies a particular weighting of these various factors, and hence embeds a particular value choice, which the committee was not charged to make. Rather, the study emphasizes the information needed to conduct a reasoned discussion among those seeking to decide what to do. Any given community's decision will be shaped by the values it brings to that decision-making process.

ACKNOWLEDGMENTS

Many people contributed to this complex study and comprehensive report. The committee took testimony from many individuals at its plenary sessions and at site visits. The site visits in particular were valuable precisely because they gave committee members a sense of life "in the trenches," allowing them to put into appropriate perspective the input received during plenary sessions and contributed in white papers. (Appendix A provides the agendas of all meetings and site visits.)

Talking to children about their perceptions and reactions to sexually explicit material on the Internet is obviously a sensitive and delicate undertaking, and the committee is deeply grateful to those individuals and schools that allowed their students, teachers, and administrators to speak freely with committee members and staff.

These site visits would not have been possible without the assistance of people at each locale. The committee and staff would like to acknowledge the following individuals:

• In Austin, Jeanette Larson, youth services manager, Austin Public Library, provided numerous leads regarding whom to contact to arrange focus group sessions. Many thanks also to Randy Strickland for brokering sessions with students and teachers at John Connally High School in Pflugerville, Texas; Sulema Vielman, for sessions with librarians at Cepeda Branch Library, Austin, Texas; Julia Cuba of the Girl Scouts Lone Star Council for her advice; and Angela Knott-Fryer of Settlement Home.

• Arrangements in Greenville were facilitated by Norman Belk, immediate past president of the South Carolina Library Association, and Beverly White, executive director, Education Technology Services, the School District of Greenville County. The committee is also grateful to Rosia Gardner of Mauldin Middle School, Simpsonville, South Carolina; Michael Evans, branch manager of the W. Jack Greer Library of Mauldin; Sheila Bradley and Rodney C. Thompson of the Phillis Wheatley Association, Greenville; and Ginger Stuart, interim principal, Greenville Senior High Academy of Academic Excellence.

• The committee thanks Chip Ward, assistant director, and Nancy Tessman, director, of the Salt Lake City Library, for their willingness to host sessions, make contacts, and suggest leads to staff. It also thanks Laura Hunter, director of content, Utah Education Network; Paula Houston, obscenity and pornography complaints ombudsman, Office of the Attorney General; Clint Spindler, principal, Tooele Junior High School, Tooele, Utah; and Sandra Shepard, principal, Tooele High School, Tooele, Utah, for their contributions to the site visit.

• In San Diego, Suzanne Hess of El Cajon Library in El Cajon and Charlie Garten, director of technology in the Poway Unified School District, were pivotal in organizing library and school sessions. The committee also thanks Paul Robinson, Rancho Bernardo High School; Walter Desmond, Lincoln High School, San Diego; and Andrea Skorepa, director, Florencia Gomez, youth service director, and Teresa Murillo, computer lab coordinator at Casa Familia in San Ysidro, for hosting focus group sessions.

• Sincere thanks are extended to Peggy Meszaros, director of the Center for Information Technology Impacts on Children, Youth, and Families at the Virginia Polytechnic Institute and State University, for her extensive help in identifying and arranging focus groups in Blacksburg, Virginia. The committee also thanks Gary McCoy, principal of Blacksburg Middle School; Mary Fain, principal of Blacksburg High School; and Andrew Michael Cohill, director of Blacksburg Electronic Village, for their contributions to the site visit.

• In Coral Gables, Florida, the committee appreciates the assistance of Anne Thompson, program commissioner of the National PTA; Karin Brown, president of Miami-Dade County PTA; Joyce Corces, Coral Gables High School; Alexander Rodriguez-Roia, Boys and Girls Club of Miami; and Jenine Gendron, Fischler Graduate School of Education and Human Resources, Nova Southeastern University, Ft. Lauderdale.

• In Connecticut, the committee appreciates the assistance of Arlene Liscinsky, treasurer of the Connecticut State PTA, for the Shelton visit; Therese Duncan, vice president for legislation of the Connecticut State PTA, for the Kent visit; Deborah Walsh, president of the Connecticut State PTA, for the Hamden visit; and Beverly Bobroske, president of the Connecticut Association of Boards of Education, for the Bristol visit.

Most of all, the committee appreciates the parents and students for their frank participation in the focus group sessions that took place during the site visits.

In the initial stages of project development, David Eisner from America Online was instrumental in convening representatives from the online industry to discuss the project. As a result of these meetings, the NRC came to understand the concerns of this community in greater detail.

The committee members also extend their appreciation to the numerous presenters who briefed them during the project. Of particular interest was a special session at the committee's December 2000 workshop with community teams. Team members were charged with listening to the expert presentations and then applying what they had learned, as well as their own experience, to a hypothetical scenario. Committee members engaged community teams as they reported their thoughts about application. The purpose of this activity was to provide information to the committee regarding how the expert but largely theoretical testimony might be interpreted and applied in practical terms by education and library professionals working in the field. For their participation in this activity, the committee thanks Paulette Armstrong, Carol Bird, Stephen Boyles, Trina Brown, Andy Carvin, Deb Elder, Marjorie Geldon, William Giddings, Wayne Hartschuh, Marge Medd, David Milhon, Irene E. Millett, Sandra Patton, Jeana Pulis, Mike Westmoreland, Arthur Wolinsky, and in particular, for their enormous contribution to orchestrating the community teams, Sara Fitzgerald and Keith Krueger of the Consortium for School Networking.

The committee also appreciates the hundreds of suggestions and constructive criticism provided by the reviewers of an early draft of this report. That input helped the committee to sharpen its message and strengthen its presentation.

Within the NRC, the lead unit on the project was the Computer Science and Telecommunications Board. However, the committee received a high level of support from members and staff of the Board on Children, Youth, and Families—and specifically calls attention to the critical roles played by Joah Ianotta, research assistant for BOCYF, in developing the summary of the first workshop on non-technical strategies, and by Gail Pritchard, previously staff officer for CSTB, and Mickelle Rodriguez, former senior project assistant, in organizing the site visits under very trying conditions.

Finally, grateful thanks are offered to Microsoft, IBM, and the Kellogg Foundation, whose financial support for this project was essential in rounding out the sponsorship of the Departments of Justice and Education. CSTB's sponsors enable but do not influence its projects.

A PERSONAL NOTE FROM THE CHAIR

The National Academies are well known for producing authoritative reports on controversial subjects. It is the hope of the committee that this report will be seen as comprehensive and authoritative, but I believe it is bound to disappoint a number of readers. It will disappoint those who expect a technological "quick fix" to the challenge of pornography on the Internet. It will disappoint those who suggest that an aggressive law enforcement effort is all that is necessary to shut down pornography purveyors of all types. It will disappoint parents, school officials, and librarians who seek surrogates to fulfill the responsibilities of training and supervision needed to truly protect children from inappropriate sexual materials on the Internet. And it will disappoint free speech absolutists who maintain that children have an unrestricted right to access whatever materials they choose to read or view in today's society.

Many of the members of this committee, including its chair, brought to our task somewhat simplistic views of the challenges implicit in our charge. My own views were shaped by a career in law enforcement during which time I learned that the issue of children and pornography is highly political and emotionally volatile. As a parent and a grandparent, I also feel that I have a personal stake in this issue.

I think it is fair to say that all committee members recognize that we finish our task enriched by the welter of material developed for our use and by the exchanges that took place among us. Most of us are somewhat chastened, I suspect, by adherence to our earlier views. For, in truth, as our report spells out in great detail, there are no easy answers to the questions posed to our society by the proliferation of sexually explicit materials and their ready availability to children, particularly through the modern miracle we know as the Internet.

Today our society is awash in graphic, sexually explicit materials that are widely available in nearly every medium of communication—print, audio, and video—and in nearly every imaginable setting from home and school to overnight lodging. Much of the material with which this report is concerned was clearly violative of the obscenity laws a decade or so ago, but seldom are prosecutions brought in this 21st century.

The ubiquitous nature of the Internet poses special challenges for those concerned with this phenomenon. According to the U.S. Census, two-thirds of U.S. school-age children had home access to a personal computer in 2000.[6] And, most of these computers provide access to the Internet. These figures are even higher when school-provided access is added, and 90 percent of our children have Internet access in either homes or school.

The rapid growth in the availability of Internet images during the last decade has posed two specific problems in the conduct of this study. First is the private nature of Internet usage. Parental and teacher or librarian supervision is not nearly as easy when children seek or are inadvertently exposed to sexually explicit materials on the Internet as when such images are available in books or on the family television set. "Policing" by responsible adults is much more difficult when the Internet is involved.

Moreover, the fact that the Internet is a worldwide method of communication creates two special problems for law enforcement—even when the subject matter is what has been traditionally outlawed as obscene. U.S. Supreme Court decisions defining what is "obscene" depend, among other things, on the development of "community standards" against which the offending materials may be measured. What is the "community" for a medium that is worldwide in its reach? In addition, as the report notes, much of the pornography available on the Internet in the United States has its origins outside our borders and beyond the reach of law enforcement officials here. These are truly vexing challenges to even the most capable of modern criminal investigators and prosecutors.

The breadth of background and experience of the members of this committee was a significant advantage in pursuing our charge. Likewise, the process undertaken by the committee was designed to seek out and wrestle with the many issues implicit in that charge. We sought to order

---

[6]See U.S. Census Press Release. 2001. "9-in-10 School-Age Children Have Computer Access; Internet Use Pervasive, Census Bureau Reports." September 6. Available online at <http://www.census.gov/Press-Release/www/2001/cb01-147.html>.

our inquiry in a way that ensured that we heard from all sides and representatives of every interested point of view. Our field trips took us to communities across the country so that we might learn firsthand the views of parents, teachers, children, community leaders, and law enforcement officials. We also sought out experts in child development and child psychology, those intimately familiar with the technology of the Internet, and representatives of the adult entertainment industry themselves. I am satisfied that no potential sources of information or opinion were neglected, even if certainty on many points remained elusive.

In the final analysis, I believe that this report advances our understanding of the problems of children's access to inappropriate sexual materials on the Internet. But much work remains to be done. As noted, it is essential that unresolved legal issues be put to rest. An observation to the effect that "we know obscenity when we see it" will no longer suffice. We live under the rule of law, and prosecutors and courts must attempt to resolve these problems, however difficult that may be.

In addition, it is by no means clear that enough research has been carried out in this important area. Social science research into the effects of children viewing sexually explicit materials has not been carried out because of ethical considerations (although one must wonder if such reluctance doesn't speak to the reality of the harm itself). The computer industry has produced some of the largest personal fortunes in American history. Yet it has been curiously reluctant to commit its massive resources to leading-edge research and development efforts in this area.

Although, as the report emphasizes, responsibility for meeting this challenge truly begins at home, we must exert ourselves as a society to provide every possible support mechanism to parents concerned about this threat to their children's well-being. No concerned parent, however responsible and determined, should be left to his or her own devices in dealing with such a truly global challenge.

It may be that some members of the committee itself complete their assignment somewhat disappointed in our accomplishments. But, in life, the important tasks are never easy ones. If this task is deemed to be important for the future of our society and our children, our comprehensive study of the multitude of issues involved in protecting children from pornography on the Internet may prove to be a building block for future efforts that can provide workable answers to the difficult questions inherent in such a study.

If this study has succeeded even in part in its undertaking, credit is due to the remarkable and talented men and women who contributed so much of their valuable time, thought, and effort to this unique and daunting task. They set themselves to this difficult task in the best traditions of searching inquiry which have always characterized this great nation.

Special thanks are due to Dr. Herbert Lin, whose tireless efforts kept us on track and whose skills at managing a sometimes fractious group were admirable indeed.

Dick Thornburgh, *Chair*
Committee to Study Tools and Strategies for Protecting Kids from Pornography and Their Applicability to Other Inappropriate Internet Content

April 2002

Acknowledgment of Reviewers

This report has been reviewed in draft form by individuals chosen for their diverse perspectives and technical expertise, in accordance with procedures approved by the National Research Council's Report Review Committee. The purpose of this independent review is to provide candid and critical comments that will assist the institution in making its published report as sound as possible and to ensure that the report meets institutional standards for objectivity, evidence, and responsiveness to the study charge. The review comments and draft manuscript remain confidential to protect the integrity of the deliberative process. We wish to thank the following individuals for their review of this report:

Danni Ashe, Danni's Hard Drive,
Libby Black, Boulder Valley School District,
Frederick P. Brooks, University of North Carolina,
Robert Corn-Revere, Hogan and Hartson LLP,
David Finkelhor, University of New Hampshire,
Elizabeth D. Liddy, Syracuse University,
Eleanor Maccoby, Stanford University,
Michael Miller, PC Magazine,
Anita M. Pampusch, Bush Foundation,
Michael Puma, The Urban Institute,
William J. Raduchel, AOL Time Warner,
Sally G. Reed, Norfolk Public Library,
Carol Lynn Roddy, Ohio Public Library Information Network,
Paul Rothstein, Fried, Frank, Harris, Shriver, and Jacobson,

Lynne Shrum, University of Georgia,
Jane M. Spinak, Columbia Law School,
Bruce Taylor, National Law Center for Children and Families,
Jody Townsend, Colorado PTA,
Joseph Turow, University of Pennsylvania,
Willis H. Ware, RAND Corporation,
Ellen Wartella, University of Texas at Austin,
Gio Wiederhold, Stanford University, and
Nancy Willard, University of Oregon.

Although the reviewers listed above provided many constructive comments and suggestions, they were not asked to endorse the conclusions or recommendations, nor did they see the final draft of the report before its release. The review of this report was overseen by Lyle Jones, University of North Carolina, and Eugene Volokh, UCLA Law School. Appointed by the National Research Council, they were responsible for making certain that an independent examination of this report was carried out in accordance with institutional procedures and that all review comments were carefully considered. Responsibility for the final content of this report rests entirely with the authoring committee and the institution.

Contents

PART III

APPENDIXES

YOUTH, PORNOGRAPHY, AND THE INTERNET

Executive Summary

The Internet is both a source of promise for our children and a source of concern. The Internet provides convenient access to a highly diverse library of educational resources, enables collaborative study, and offers opportunities for remote dialog with subject-matter experts. It provides information about hobbies and sports, and it allows children to engage with other people on a near-infinite variety of topics. Through online correspondence, their circles of friendship and diversity of experience can achieve a rich and international scope. [Section 1.1]

Yet press reports have suggested to many that their children are vulnerable to harm on the Internet. While only a small fraction of material on the Internet could reasonably be classified as inappropriate for children, that small fraction is highly visible and controversial.[1] If the full educational potential of the Internet for children is to be realized, such concerns must be reasonably addressed. [Section 1.1]

At the request of the U.S. Congress in 1998, the Computer Science and Telecommunications Board of the National Research Council assembled a committee with expertise in many fields. Based on a wide range of information sources as well as the committee's own expertise,

---

[1]For purposes of this report, "material" refers to that which may be seen or read (e.g., images, movies, or text on a Web page), while "experiences" are interactive (e.g., talking to a stranger through instant messages or chat rooms). E-mail sent or received that is essentially advertising is "material," while a sequence of interactive e-mails corresponds to "experiences."

this report seeks to frame the problem in a legal, educational, techno-logical, social, and societal context and to provide information useful to various decision-making communities—e.g., parents, the information technology industry, school boards, librarians, and government at all levels—about possible courses of action to help children be safer in their use of the Internet.

DEFINITIONAL CONSIDERATIONS IN PROTECTING CHILDREN FROM INTERNET PORNOGRAPHY

The term "pornography" lacks a well-defined meaning. To be sure, broad agreement may be found that some materials are or are not "porno-graphic," but for other materials, individual judgments about what is or is not "pornography" will vary. In recognition of this essential point, the report uses the term "inappropriate sexually explicit material" to under-score the subjective nature of the term. [Sections 1.2, 4.1]

The term "child" is also problematic. From birth to the age of legal emancipation covers a very wide developmental range. What is inappro-priate for a 6-year-old to see may not be inappropriate for a 16-year-old to see, and in particular, older high school students have information needs for education that are very different from those of elementary school students. [Section 5.1 and Table 5.1]

Finally, "protection" is an ambiguous term. For example, does "pro-tection" include preventing a child from obtaining inappropriate material (sexual or otherwise) even when he or she is deliberately seeking such material? Or, does it mean shielding a child from inadvertent exposure? Or, does it entail giving the child tools to cope effectively with exposure to inappropriate material if he or she should come across it? These sce-narios pose conceptually different problems to solve. [Section 8.2]

All of these ambiguities complicate enormously the debate in com-munities about the nature of the problem and what might or should be done about it.

SEXUALITY IN MEDIA

The fact that children can sometimes see—and even sometimes seek out—images of naked people is not new. However, compared to other media, the Internet has characteristics that make it harder for adults to exercise responsible supervision over children's use of it. A particularly worrisome aspect of the Internet is that inappropriate sexually explicit material can find its way onto children's computer screens without being actively sought. Further, it is easy to find on today's Internet not only images of naked people, but also graphically depicted acts of heterosexual and homosexual intercourse (including penetration), fellatio, cunnilingus, masturbation, bestiality, child pornography, sadomasochism, bondage, rape, incest, and so on. While some such material can be found in sexually explicit videos and print media that are readily available in hotels, video rental stores, and newsstands, other sexually explicit material on the Internet is arguably more extreme than material that is easily available through non-Internet media. [Section 1.2]

The Internet also enables many strangers to establish contact with children. While many interactions between children and strangers can be benign or even beneficial (e.g., a student corresponding with a university scientist), strangers can also be child predators and sexual molesters. Face-to-face contact with such individuals may be traumatic and even life-threatening for a child; for this reason, Internet-based interaction (which includes chat rooms, instant messages, and e-mail dialogs, and which could involve the transmission of sexually explicit material as one component) that can lead to face-to-face contact poses a greater potential danger to children than does the passive receipt of material—even highly inappropriate material—per se. The anonymity and interaction-at-a-distance of using the Internet prevent a child from using cues that arise from face-to-face interaction to help judge another's intent (e.g., gestures, tone of voice, age). [Sections 1.3 and 5.5]

THE LEGAL CONTEXT

The legal context for sexually explicit material is driven by the First Amendment to the Constitution, and three categories of sexually explicit material are subject to government regulation. *Obscenity* is sexually explicit material that violates contemporary community standards in certain specified ways. (How the appropriate "community" is defined is a matter of great uncertainty, especially in an Internet context.) *Child pornography* is material that depicts a child engaged in a sexual act or "lewd" exhibition of his or her genitals. Obscenity and child pornography enjoy no First Amendment protection. A third category of sexually explicit material that is not obscene and not child pornography can be *obscene for minors*, such material may be regulated for minors but must be freely available to adults. [Section 4.1]

NEW TECHNOLOGY, DIFFERENT ECONOMICS

Searching the Internet for information is generally enabled by "search engines" that accept a few user-typed terms and return to the user links to Web pages that refer to those terms. A search engine can be used to find information on science, sports, history, and politics, as well as sexually explicit material. Furthermore, because of ambiguities in language (e.g., "beaver" has both sexual and non-sexual connotations), a search will sometimes return links to material that is not related to what the user is trying to find. In some cases, that unrelated material will contain sexually explicit content when it was not sought. [Section 2.3 and Box 2.3]

A second common use of the Internet is to communicate with others. However, the Internet is designed in such a way that it transports bits of information without regard for the meaning or content of those bits. Thus, Internet traffic can contain a letter to one's aunt, a chat about sports, a draft manuscript for a report, or sexually explicit images. Furthermore, controlling traffic demands special effort at the sending and/or receiving points. [Section 2.1 and Box 2.2]

The Internet is also a highly anonymous medium. Such anonymity can be advantageous for a teenager who finds answers on the Internet to questions that he or she is too embarrassed to ask an adult. It can also be disadvantageous, in that someone can conduct antisocial or criminal activities (e.g., child sexual solicitation) with less fear of identification and/ or sanction than might be true in the physical world. [Sections 2.1, 2.3]

Information technology drives the economics of information on the Internet. Because information can be represented in digital form, it is very inexpensive to send, receive, and store. Thus, for a few hundred dollars to cover the cost of a digital camera and a Web site, anyone can produce sexually explicit content and publish it on the Web for all to see. Furthermore, because the Internet is global, regulatory efforts in the United States aimed at limiting the production and distribution of such material are difficult to apply to foreign Web site operators. [Section 2.1]

Sources of inappropriate sexually explicit material on the Internet are commercial and non-commercial. The commercial source is the online adult entertainment industry, which generates about a billion dollars a year in revenue from paying adults. (For comparison, the adult entertainment industry as a whole generates several billion dollars a year—perhaps as much as $10 billion.) According to the best information available to the committee, U.S. business entities in the industry support around 100,000 sites (globally, there are about 400,000 for-pay adult sites). Globally, sexually explicit Web pages constitute a few percent of the 2+ billion publicly accessible Web pages as of this writing. [Section 3.1]

For many online adult entertainment firms, profitability depends on drawing a large volume of traffic in a search for paying customers, and many seek revenue through the sale of advertising that typically makes no effort to differentiate between adults and children. Further, the aggressive marketing campaigns that firms need to stand out in a highly saturated market—where margins are inherently low and traffic is therefore critical to economic survival—inevitably reach both minors and adults. The exposure of minors to such material is thus a side effect of the effort to reach large numbers of paying customers. [Section 3.2]

To date, public debate has focused largely on commercial dimensions of inappropriate sexually explicit material on the Internet. But there are many non-commercial sources of inappropriate sexually explicit material on the Internet, including material available through peer-to-peer file exchanges, unsolicited e-mail, Web cameras, and sexually explicit conversation in chat rooms. Solutions that focus only on commercial sources will therefore not address the entire problem. [Section 5.4]

THE IMPACT OF SEXUALLY EXPLICIT MATERIAL ON CHILDREN

Perhaps the most vexing dimension of dealing with children's exposure to sexually explicit material on the Internet is the lack of a clear scientific consensus regarding the impact of such exposure. Nonetheless, people have very strong beliefs on the topic. Some people believe that exposure to certain sexually explicit material is so dangerous to children that even one exposure to it will have lasting harmful effects. Others believe that there is no evidence to support such a claim and that the impact of exposure to such material must be viewed in the context of a highly sexualized media environment. [Chapter 6]

It is likely that individuals on both sides of the issue could reach agreement on the undesirability of exposing children to depictions of the most extreme and most graphic examples of sexual behavior, in the sense that most individual parents on each side would prefer to keep their children away from such material. The committee concurs, in the sense that it believes that there is some set of depictions of extreme sexual behavior whose viewing by children would violate and offend the committee's collective moral and ethical sensibilities, though this sentiment would not be based on scientific grounds. However, protagonists in the debate would be likely to part company on whether material that is less extreme in nature is inappropriate or harmful: such material might include information on sexual health, the depiction of non-traditional "scripts" about how people can interact sexually, and descriptions of what it means to be lesbian or homosexual in orientation. [Sections 7.3, 7.4]

Extreme sexually explicit imagery to create sexual desire on the one hand, and responsible information on sexual health on the other, are arguably unrelated and, many would contend, easily distinguished. But much content is not so easily categorized. While some extreme sexually explicit material meets legal tests for obscenity (and therefore does not enjoy First Amendment protection), less extreme material may not—and material described in the previous paragraph, lingerie advertisements, and models in swimsuits generally do enjoy First Amendment protection, at least for adults and often for children. [Section 7.3]

In short, sexually oriented content that falls outside the realm of extreme sexually explicit imagery is likely to be the source of greatest contention, and there are arguments about whether such content would be subject to regulatory efforts aimed at reducing the exposure of minors to material that is or may be sexual in nature. [Section 7.3]

PATHS OF EXPOSURE

Children may be exposed to inappropriate Internet material or experiences through a variety of channels, including Web pages, e-mail, chat rooms, instant messages, Usenet newsgroups, and peer-to-peer file-sharing connections. Furthermore, the exposure may be sought by the child (i.e., deliberate) or unsought by the child (i.e., inadvertent), and there are many forms of each kind of exposure. An example of deliberate exposure occurring is when a child searches for sexually explicit terms in a search engine and clicks on the links returned. An example of inadvertent exposure occurring is when a child receives unsolicited e-mail containing sexually explicit material or links to such material. [Section 5.4]

IDENTIFYING INAPPROPRIATE MATERIAL

Three methods can be used to identify inappropriate material. Whether machine or human, the agent that makes the immediate decision about the appropriateness of content can do so based on its specific content, rely on a tag or label associated with the material, or examine the source of the material (or a combination of these factors). [Section 8.1]

In practice, the volume of material on the Internet is so large that it is impractical for human beings to evaluate every discrete piece of information for inappropriateness. [Box 2.6] Moreover, the content of some existing Web pages changes very quickly, and new Web pages appear at a rapid rate. Thus, identifying inappropriate material must rely either on an automated, machine-executable process for determining inappropriate content or on a presumption that everything that is not explicitly identified by a human being as appropriate is inappropriate. An approach based on machine-executable rules abstracted from human judgments inevitably misses nuances in those human judgments, which reduces the accuracy of this approach compared to that of humans, while the presumption-based approach necessarily identifies a large volume of appropriate material as inappropriate. [Section 2.3]

All mechanisms for determining if material is appropriate or inappropriate will make erroneous classifications from time to time. But note that such misclassifications are fundamentally different from disagreement over what is inappropriate. Misclassifications are mistakes due to factors such as inattention on the part of humans or poorly specified rules for automated classification. They will inevitably occur, even when there is no disagreement over the criteria for inclusion in various categories. In contrast, disagreements over what is appropriate result from differences in judgment—Person A says, "That material is inappropriate" and Person B says of the same material, "That material is not inappropriate." Both of these issues exacerbate the problem of putting into place a systematic way to protect children. [Box 12.1]

CONCEPTS OF PROTECTION

Whether protection is based on law, technology, or education, it generally involves some combination of the following concepts: [Section 8.6]

- *Restricting a minor to appropriate material* through techniques that give a minor access only to material that is explicitly judged to be appropriate;
- *Blocking inappropriate material* through techniques that prevent a minor from being exposed to inappropriate material;
- *Warning a minor of impending exposure to inappropriate material or suggesting appropriate material,* leaving him or her with an explicit choice to accept or decline a viewing;
- *Deterring the access of minors to inappropriate material* by detecting access to such material and imposing a subsequent penalty for such access;
- *Educating a minor about reasons not to access inappropriate material* in order to inculcate an internal sense of personal responsibility and to build skills that make his or her Internet searches less likely to turn up inappropriate material inadvertently;
- *Reducing the accessibility of inappropriate material* so that inappropriate material is harder for minors to find;
- *Reducing the appeal of deliberate contact with inappropriate material* by making access to the material (and only such material) more difficult, cumbersome, and inconvenient; and/or
- *Helping a minor to cope with the exposure to inappropriate material* that will most likely occur at least occasionally with extended Internet use.

All of these concepts have costs and benefits. Any party seeking to decide on an appropriate mix of approaches based on these concepts must consider the extent and nature of physical, emotional, developmental, social, ethical, or moral harm that it believes arises from exposure to inappropriate material or experiences. Greater costs may be justifiable if the presumed harm is large and highly likely, or if young children rather than youth in late adolescence are involved. [Section 14.4]

Differing institutional missions must also be considered. A public school serves the primary purpose of providing academic instruction for individuals that have not attained the age of majority. By contrast, a public library serves the primary purpose of providing a broad range of information to the entire community in which it is based, including children and adults, and the information needs of the community—taken as a whole—are generally much more diverse than those of children and youth in school. Thus, it is not surprising that schools and libraries have different needs and might take different approaches in seeking to protect children and youth from inappropriate Internet material and experiences. [Section 8.4]

APPROACHES TO PROTECTION

Public Policy

Public policy to affect the supply of inappropriate sexually explicit material can operate to make such material less available to children. For practical and technical reasons, it is most feasible to seek regulation of commercial sources of such material—because these seek to draw attention to themselves (and non-commercial sources generally operate through private channels). Public policy can provide incentives for the adult online industry to take actions that better deny children's access to their material and to some extent to reduce the number of providers of such material. [Chapter 9]

Public policy can go far beyond the creation of statutory punishment for violating some approved canon of behavior to include shaping the Internet environment in many ways. For example, public policy can be used to reduce uncertainty in the regulatory environment; promote media literacy and Internet safety education (including development of model curricula, support of professional development for teachers on Internet safety and media literacy, and encouraging outreach to educate parents, teachers, librarians, and other adults about Internet safety education issues); support development of and access to high-quality Internet material that is educational and attractive to children in an age-appropriate manner; and support self-regulatory efforts by private parties.

Social and Educational Strategies

Social and educational strategies are intended to teach children how to make wise choices about how they behave on the Internet and to take control of their online experiences: where they go; what they see; what they do; who they talk to. Such strategies must be age-appropriate if they are to be effective. Further, such an approach entails teaching children to be critical, skeptical, and self-reflective of the material that they are seeing.

An analogy is the relationship between swimming pools and children. Swimming pools can be dangerous for children. To protect them, one can install locks, put up fences, and deploy pool alarms. All of these measures are helpful, but by far the most important thing that one can do for one's children is to teach them to swim. [Section 10.3]

Perhaps the most important social and educational strategy is *responsible adult involvement and supervision.* [Section 10.4] *Peer assistance* can be helpful as well, as many youth learn as much in certain areas from peers or near-peers (e.g., siblings) as they do from parents, teachers, and other adult figures. [Section 10.5] *Acceptable use policies* in families, schools, libraries, and other organizations provide guidelines and expectations about how individuals will conduct themselves online, thus providing a framework within which children can become more responsible for making good choices about the paths they choose in cyberspace, thereby learning skills that are relevant and helpful in any venue of Internet usage. [Section 10.6]

Internet safety education is analogous to safety education in the physical world, and may include teaching children how sexual predators and hate group recruiters typically approach young people, how to recognize impending access to inappropriate sexually explicit material, and when it is risky to provide personal information online. *Information and media literacy* provide children with skills in recognizing when information is needed and how to locate, evaluate, and use it effectively, irrespective of the media in which it appears, and in critically evaluating the content inherent in media messages. A child with these skills is less likely to stumble across inappropriate material and more likely to be better able to put it into context if and when he or she does. [Section 10.8]

The greater availability of *compelling, safe, and educational Internet content* that is developmentally appropriate, educational, and enjoyable material on a broad range of appealing or helpful topics (including but not limited to sex education) would help to make some children less inclined to spend their time searching for inappropriate material or engaging in inappropriate or unsafe activities. Greater availability entails both the development of new appropriate content, as well as portals and Web sites designed to facilitate easy access to existing appropriate content. [Section 10.9]

Public service announcements and media campaigns could help to educate adults about the need for Internet safety and about the nature and extent of dangers on the Internet. Such campaigns are best suited for relatively simple messages (e.g., "be aware of where your child is on the Internet" and "ask for parental controls when you subscribe to an Internet service provider"). [Section 10.10]

Social and educational strategies focus on the nurturing of personal character, the development of responsible choice, and the strengthening of coping skills. Because these strategies locate control in the hands of the youth targeted, children have opportunities to exercise some measure of choice—and as a result some children are likely to make mistakes as they learn to internalize the object of these lessons. [Section 10.11]

These strategies are not inexpensive, and they require tending and implementation. Adults must be taught to teach children how to make good choices on the Internet. They must be willing to engage in some-times-difficult conversations. They must face the trade-offs inevitable with pressing schedules of work and family. And these strategies do not provide a quick fix. But in addition to teaching responsible behavior and coping skills for when a child encounters inappropriate material and experiences on the Internet, they are relevant to teaching children to think critically about all kinds of media messages, including those associated with hate, racism, senseless violence, and so on; to conduct effective Internet searches for information and to navigate with confidence; and to make ethical and responsible choices about Internet behavior—and about non-Internet behavior as well. [Section 10.11]

Technology-Based Tools

A wide array of technology-based tools are available for dealing with inappropriate Internet material and experiences. *Filters*—systems or services that limit in some way the content to which users may be exposed—are the most-used technology-based tool. [Section 12.1]   All filters suffer from both false positives (overblocking) and false negatives (underblocking). However, filters can be highly effective in reducing the exposure of minors to inappropriate content if the inability to access large amounts of appropriate material is acceptable. Teachers and librarians most commonly reported that filters served primarily to relieve political pressure on them and to insulate them from liability (suggesting that filter vendors are more likely to err on the side of overblocking than on underblocking). In addition, filters reduced the non-productive demands on teachers and librarians who would otherwise have to spend time watching what students and library patrons were doing. Note also that filters can be circumvented in many ways, the easiest way being to obtain unfiltered Internet access in another venue (e.g., at home).

Monitoring of a child's Internet use is another technology-based option. [Section 12.2] Many monitoring options are available (e.g., remote viewing of what is on a child's screen, logging of keystrokes, recording of Web pages that he or she has visited)—and each of these options can be used surreptitiously or openly. Surreptitious monitoring cannot deter deliberate access to inappropriate material or experiences, and raises many concerns about privacy (for example, in a family context, it raises the same questions as reading a child's diary or searching his or her room covertly). Furthermore, while it probably does provide a more accurate window into what a child is doing online compared to the lack of monitoring, it presents a conflict between taking action should inappropriate behavior be discovered and potentially revealing the fact of monitoring.

The major advantage of monitoring over filtering is that it leaves the child in control of his or her Internet experiences, and thus provides opportunities for the child to learn how to make good decisions about Internet use. However, this outcome is likely only if the child is subsequently educated to understand the nature of the inappropriate use and is reinforced in the desirability of appropriate use. If, instead, the result of detecting inappropriate use is simply punishment, the result is likely to be behavior motivated by fear of punishment—with the consequence that when the monitoring is not present, inappropriate use may well resume. Clandestine monitoring may also have an impact on the basic trust that is a foundation of a healthy parent-child relationship.

Age verification technologies (AVTs) seek to differentiate between adults and children in an online environment. [Section 13.3] A common AVT is a request for a valid credit card number. Credit cards have some meaningful effectiveness in separating children from adults, but their effectiveness will decline as credit-card-like payment mechanisms for children become more popular. Other AVTs can provide higher assurance of adult status, but often at the cost of greater inconvenience to at least some legitimate users.

A number of other technology-based tools are discussed in the main report.

OVERALL CONCLUSIONS

Contrary to statements often made in the political debate, the issue of protecting children from inappropriate sexually explicit material and experiences on the Internet is very complex. Individuals have strong and passionate views on the subject, and these views are often mutually incompatible. Different societal institutions see the issue in very different ways and have different and conflicting priorities about the values to be preserved. Different communities—at the local, state, national, and international levels—have different perspectives. Furthermore, the technical nature of the Internet has not evolved in such a way as to make control over content easy to achieve. [Section 14.1]

There is no single or simple answer to controlling the access of minors to inappropriate material on the Web. To date, most of the efforts to protect children from inappropriate sexually explicit material on the Internet have focused on technology-based tools such as filters and legal prohibitions or regulation. But the committee believes that neither technology nor policy can provide a complete—or even a nearly complete—solution. While both technology and public policy have important roles to play, social and educational strategies to develop in minors an ethic of responsible choice and the skills to effectuate these choices and to cope with exposure are foundational to protecting children from negative effects that may result from exposure to inappropriate material or experiences on the Internet. [Section 14.3]

Technology can pose barriers that are sufficient to keep those who are not strongly motivated from finding their way to inappropriate material or experiences. Further, it can help to prevent inadvertent exposure to such materials. But, as most parents and teachers noted in their comments to the committee, those who really want to have access to inappropriate sexually explicit materials will find a way to get them. From this point, it follows that the real challenge is to reduce the number of children who are strongly motivated to obtain inappropriate sexually explicit materials. This, of course, is the role of social and educational strategies. [Section 14.4]

As for public policy, the international dimension of the Internet poses substantial difficulties and makes a primary reliance on regulatory approaches unwise. Absent a strong international consensus on appropriate measures, it is hard to imagine what could be done to persuade foreign sources to behave in a similar manner or to deny irresponsible foreign sources access to U.S. Internet users. [Section 14.4]

This is not to say that technology and policy cannot be helpful. Technology-based tools, such as filters, provide parents and other responsible adults with additional choices as to how best to fulfill their responsibilities. Law and regulation can help to shape the environment in which these strategies and tools are used by reducing at least to some extent the availability of inappropriate sexually explicit material on the Internet, for example, by creating incentives and disincentives for responsible business behavior. Moreover, developments in technology can help to inform and support policy choices, and public policy decisions necessarily affect both technology and the nature and shape of parental guidance. In concert with appropriate social and educational strategies, both technology and public policy can contribute to a solution if they are appropriately adapted to the many circumstances that will exist in different communities. In the end, however, values are closely tied to the definitions of responsible choice that parents or other responsible adults wish to impart to their children, and to judgments about the proper mix of education, technology, and policy to adopt. [Section 14.3]

Though some might wish otherwise, no single approach—technical, legal, economic, or educational—will be sufficient. Rather, an effective framework for protecting our children from inappropriate materials and experiences on the Internet will require a balanced composite of all of these elements, and real progress will require forward movement on all of these fronts. [Section 14.3]

PART I

1

Introduction

The Internet is both a source of promise for our children and a source of concern. The promise is of Internet-based access to the information age—and the concern is over the possibility that harm might befall our children as they use the Internet. Realizing the promise in all its richness requires that adults put these concerns into perspective and also take responsible steps to address them. The purpose of this report is to help put the risks of Internet use by children into perspective and to provide a balanced assessment of different approaches that can help parents and other responsible adults to deal constructively with the risks that children face on the Internet, using as its primary illustrative example protecting kids from inappropriate sexually explicit material on the Internet.

1.1 THE INTERNET: SOURCE OF PROMISE, SOURCE OF CONCERN

Many policy makers, teachers, parents, and others concerned with education reform believe that the Internet has the potential to enhance and transform K-12 education. For example, the report of the Web-based Education Commission, released in March 2001, asserted that "the Internet is making it possible for more individuals than ever to access knowledge and to learn in new and different ways" (Box 1.1).

NOTE: Appendix B contains a list of acronyms and a glossary that the reader may wish to consult.

Box 1.1
Views of the Web-based Education Commission
on the Internet and K-12 Education

The following excerpts are reproduced, respectively, from the Foreword and from Section 1 of *The Power of the Internet for Learning:*

> For education, the Internet is making it possible for more individuals than ever to access knowledge and to learn in new and different ways. At the dawn of the 21st Century, the education landscape is changing. Elementary and secondary schools are experiencing growing enrollments, coping with critical shortages of teachers, facing overcrowded and decaying buildings, and responding to demands for higher standards. . . . The Internet is enabling us to address these educational challenges, bringing learning to students instead of bringing students to learning. It is allowing for the creation of learning communities that defy the constraints of time and distance as it provides access to knowledge that was once difficult to obtain. . . .
>
> The Internet is perhaps the most transformative technology in history, reshaping business, media, entertainment, and society in astonishing ways. But for all its power, it is just now being tapped to transform education. . . . The Internet is bringing us closer than we ever thought possible to make learning—of all kinds, at all levels, any time, any place, any pace—a practical reality for every man, woman, and child. The World Wide Web is a tool that empowers society to school the illiterate, bring job training to the unskilled, open a universe of wondrous images and knowledge to all students, and enrich the understanding of the lifelong learner. . . .   Web-based education is just beginning, with something of far greater promise emerging in the middle distance. Yet technology, even in its current stage of development, can already allow us to realistically dream of achieving age-old goals in education: to center learning around the student instead of the classroom, to focus on the strengths and needs of individual learners, [and] to make lifelong learning a reality. . . . The Internet is a tool that can help us empower every student and elevate each individual to new levels of intellectual capacity and skill.

SOURCE: *The Power of the Internet for Learning: Moving from Promise to Practice.* 2001. Report of the Web-based Education Commission to the President and Congress of the United States. March. Available online at <http://interact.hpcnet.org/Webcommission/index.htm>.

Increasingly, school-age children have the ability to reach the Internet, driven by the steadily increasing fraction of U.S. classrooms and schools connected to the Internet over the past 5 years and the growing presence of networked information technologies in the home and elsewhere.[1] By the fall of 2000, 98 percent of public schools in the United States had access to the Internet, compared with 35 percent in 1994.[2] In addition,

---

[1]Anne Cattagni and Elizabeth Farris. 2001. *Internet Access in U.S. Public Schools and Classrooms: 1994-2000.* NCES 2001-071. U.S. Department of Education, Office of Educational Research and Improvement. U.S. Government Printing Office, Washington, D.C.

[2]School connections to the Internet have been supported by a variety of federal programs, of which the federal E-rate program and the technology programs operated by the Department of Education have been most important. For more information on the E-rate program, see <http://www.sl.universalservice.org/> and on the Department of Education programs, see <http://www.ed.gov/Technology/edgrants.html>.

dial-up connections were used by 74 percent of public schools with Internet access in 1996, but in 2000, only 11 percent of public schools relied on such connections, with the remainder using faster dedicated-line Internet connections. In the classroom, only 3 percent of instructional rooms were wired for Internet access in 1994; by 2000, 77 percent of instructional rooms were connected to the Internet. In public libraries, Internet access is nearly ubiquitous, with over 95 percent of all library outlets with an Internet connection in 2000 and an average of 8.3 workstations per connection. Over half of these outlets have high-speed connectivity.[3] And around 17.7 million children had access to the Internet from their homes by late 1999.[4]

Such changes are hardly a surprise. Though these adoption curves substantially trail the overall price reduction curves for computing capability (unit capacity halves in price every 18 months), data storage (unit capacity halves in price every 12 months), and bandwidth (unit capacity halves in price every 9 months), it is likely that Internet access for homes and schools will be the norm in the future.

For children, the Internet generally eliminates many constraints of time and space encountered in the physical world and, as such, fundamentally broadens children's access to information and experiences. For example, the Internet provides convenient access to an almost unlimited and highly diverse (if usually unverified) library of information resources that can be used for educational purposes. It enables collaborative education and study, and it provides opportunities for remote engagement with subject matter experts. It provides information about hobbies and sports. Finally, it allows children to engage with other people on a near-infinite variety of topics and interests. Through online friendships and pen pals, their circles of acquaintance and diversity of experience can be vastly enlarged across state and national boundaries.

At the same time, fueled by press reports and some personal experience, children's easy access to the Internet raises concerns in parents and communities about less productive or safe aspects that may result from their Internet use. One frequently stated concern relates to the easy Internet availability of "pornography," but public concerns are not confined to this area (as Section 1.3 discusses further).

Success in dealing with such concerns is arguably a necessary (but not sufficient) condition for fully exploiting the social and educational poten-

---

[3]See <http://www.nclis.gov/statsurv/2000plo.pdf>.

[4]See <http://cyberatlas.internet.com/big_picture/demographics/article/0,,5901_390941, 00.html> for a summary of the Grunwald study. The full study (Grunwald Associates, 2000, *Children, Families, and the Internet 2000*, Burlingame, Calif.) is available online at <http://www.grunwald.com/survey/index.htm>.

tial of the Internet for children. For example, a study from the Annenberg Public Policy Center found that parents in the United States are deeply fearful about the Internet's influence on their children while at the same time believing that the Internet has important and positive educational potential.[5] Ridiculing such fears as if they were a sign either of techno-cultural unsophistication or of insufficient dedication to the First Amend-ment—as is often done—is not helpful.

Given the nature of the Internet and how children and other people use it, it is likely that most children will be exposed to some inappropriate material or experiences by virtue of their mere access to the Internet. This is certainly true if no actions are taken to prevent such exposure, but the National Research Council's Committee to Study Tools and Strategies for Protecting Kids from Pornography and Their Applicability to Other Inap-propriate Internet Content concluded during its investigation that there is no set of actions that will eliminate this risk entirely.

Many policy makers at federal, state, and local levels (including mem-bers of the U.S. Congress, state legislators, school boards, and local librar-ies) have sought solutions that focus primarily on the availability to chil-dren of pornography on the Internet. With some exceptions, the central element of these solutions is a filter, based on technology that is intended to allow objectionable content to be blocked. However, the overall prob-lem has many facets—technological, social, psychological, legal, emo-tional, moral—and so, too, does any particular proposed approach to solution.

1.2 A CRITICAL DEFINITIONAL ISSUE: WHAT IS "PORNOGRAPHY"?

The term "pornography" has no well-defined meaning. Despite the fact that individuals use the term as though it does and behave as though there is a universal understanding of what is and is not covered by the term, judgments about the precise dividing line between the "porno-graphic" and the "non-pornographic" vary widely. (And, as with any public issue, a large fraction of the public will not particularly care about the nuances of any given definition.) Indeed, it was Supreme Court Jus-

---

[5]Joseph Turow. 1999. "The Internet and the Family: The View from Parents, the View from the Press." Annenberg Public Policy Center, University of Pennsylvania, Philadel-phia. This is not to say that concerns about the Internet are limited to the potential negative influence on children. For example, many adults, including parents, worry about a loss of privacy associated with Internet use. Moreover, attempts to differentiate children from adults—one aspect of protecting children from inappropriate material on the Internet—may have privacy implications as well.

tice Potter Stewart who observed, "I can't define it [obscenity], but I know it when I see it." Furthermore, the same image or text can have different meanings and interpretations depending on context. For example, *Lady Chatterly's Lover* has been considered pornographic in some contexts and good literature in others.

Recognizing these ambiguities, the committee chose to use the term "sexually explicit material," which is material—textual, visual, or aural—that depicts sexual behavior or acts, or that exposes the reproductive organs of the human body. Sexually explicit material may be used for many purposes—education, art, entertainment, science, personal sexual gratification or fantasy, and so on. From common usage, "pornography" might be seen as material that is intended to create sexual arousal or desire, and usually involving sexually explicit material.[6]

For expository and analytical purposes (and to prevent passages from being misinterpreted or taken out of context), this report uses the term "inappropriate sexually explicit material" in many places where it might have used "pornography." The use of the term "inappropriate sexually explicit material" manifestly raises the issue of "inappropriate by whose definition," a basic point that must be kept in mind in all discussions relating to this topic.

Public concern and controversy in this area arise from the fact that on today's Internet, it is easy to find graphically depicted acts of heterosexual and homosexual intercourse (including penetration), fellatio, cunnilingus, masturbation, bestiality, child pornography, sadomasochism, bondage, rape, incest, and so on. Although some such material is comparable to sexually explicit videos and print media that are easily available in hotels, video rental stores, and newsstands, other sexually explicit material on the Internet is more extreme than that which is easily available through non-Internet media. Furthermore even the most graphic of these images can find their way onto children's computer screens without being actively sought, which makes this medium different from most other media.

Because the committee found that many people are unaware of the kinds of sexually explicit material that can be found on the Internet, it

---

[6]Of course, "intent" is itself ambiguous, because it may refer to intent on the part of the creator of the material, or intent on the part of the viewer of the material. Under this usage of the term, an individual may believe that clinical discussions of sexual behavior and advertisements for contraceptives or lingerie are "pornographic" because some people respond to such material in a sexual manner, even if those materials were not produced with such a result in mind. A second issue (with this definition) arises in the likely event that a young child does not become sexually aroused after being exposed to such material.

pondered how best to illustrate the range of material described above.[7] After deliberation, the committee decided that the best way to illustrate such material would be to invite the reader of this report to use a general-purpose Internet search engine to search on terms such as "sex," "orgy," "bondage," "cum," or "rape" coupled with terms such as "pics," "avi," and "jpg." If the search engine's filter for adults-only content is turned off, the search engine will return in the first several links a variety of Web sites containing the content listed above.[8] This process will illustrate the content available, as well as the ease with which it is available when it is deliberately sought out.

1.3 OTHER TYPES OF INAPPROPRIATE MATERIAL AND EXPERIENCES

Youth have been exposed to materials of concern through many different kinds of media—print (books, comic books, or magazines), television, movies, billboards, and telephones, as well as the Internet. Correspondingly, U.S. society has long been concerned about the types of information to which youth are exposed. Frequently, such concern focuses on information related to sexual matters, from the facts and biology of human reproduction to graphic portrayals of unusual sexual activity. But in addition to inappropriate sexually explicit material, there are other types of material that various parties regard as inappropriate, some of which several students and parents told the committee were more upsetting or objectionable than sexually explicit material. These include:

• Hate speech and overt racism: material extolling the inherent or moral superiority or inferiority of a particular race, ethnic group, or sexual orientation; racial epithets; or religious bigotry. (Note that Europeans

---

[7]One alternative was to include actual screen shots of such material in the report. However, the inclusion of such material would inevitably become the primary focus of this report, rather than any of the committee's analytical work. A second alternative was to provide specific Web sites that are good examples of the material described. However, inclusion of such sites in a National Academies' report would give them undue prominence, and the committee did not want to be in the position of increasing the exposure that such sites receive.

[8]The reader may also find it instructive to turn the filter "on" to see how one type of filtering works. In this case, the search results will be different, but some sexually explicit material is likely to appear. As discussed in Chapter 12, filters seek to block certain kinds of material from appearing (or, equivalently, do not return links to those kinds of material) but cannot perform this task perfectly. Note that the results from filters embedded into search engines are not necessarily those that would be obtained from other types of filters.

may regard such material as being of more concern than sexually explicit material, a point that underscores the cultural dimensions of concern.[9])

- Violent speech and imagery, including but not limited to

—Graphic images of blood and gore (without medical purpose), resulting from the application of weapons to the human body. These images may be photo-realistic or cartoon-like, and may also involve animals and/or avatars.

—Depictions of violence to the human, such as people being shot, stabbed, or beaten up.

—Information on the use and construction of weapons, explosives, and other tools of violence.

Media violence has been a prominent social concern for many years, especially given that the presence of violent media content is largely unregulated. In the case of media violence, the debate centers on concerns that exposure to such content is one factor leading to childhood aggression. However, the broadcast of obscene, indecent, and profane language is regulated by law,[10] and so sexual content has been more heavily regulated than violence on the public air waves.

- Expressions of extreme nationalism or extreme political views: for example, materials from violent conspiracy theorists, and materials extolling the inherent superiority or inferiority of certain nations or national groups.
- Materials recruiting new members into non-traditional religious groups or cults.
- Information on drugs, alcohol, tobacco, gambling, and the means to gain access to them.
- Scientific concepts such as evolution and the "Big Bang" theory for the creation of the universe.

Of course, this short list does not begin to exhaust the type of materials that some individuals may regard as inappropriate for children. Disentangling this relativism from the necessity of action cannot be made easy by the mere introduction of technical means, because technology cannot divine human intent or judgment (a point addressed further in Chapter 2). Further, different individuals even within a given community may have very different sets of concerns.

---

[9]See <http://www.pewinternet.org/reports/toc.asp?Report=36>. This point is further explored in Computer Science and Telecommunications Board, National Research Council, 2001, *Global Networks and Local Values*, National Academy Press, Washington, D.C.

[10] 18 U.S.C. 1464.

As for inappropriate Internet experiences, the committee concluded that the potential harm from interacting one-on-one with strangers on the Internet is a far greater threat to children than the potential harm of simply viewing inappropriate images on the Internet.[11] The likelihood that such interactions will lead to actual meetings between children and strangers, with the obvious attendant dangers, although relatively small, should not be overlooked because of the potentially very serious consequences of such meetings.

This theme recurred repeatedly in committee discussions with many of the parents and children at site visits, and it served to place into perspective the concerns expressed about sexually explicit material. Indeed, for these parents, the risk of predators who seek to entice children into such encounters is an especially serious danger for children compared with merely viewing inappropriate material, and the Internet creates opportunities for molesters to meet potential victims in a setting where none of the ordinary visual and location clues of the physical world apply. Table 1.1 describes differences in the nature of the child's interaction on the Internet between passive and interactive exposures to inappropriate material.

Some polling data reflect these concerns to a certain extent. For example, a survey by the Pew Internet and American Life Project[12] indicated that while parents generally agree that for the most part the Internet is a good thing or at least has a neutral impact on their own children, they have many concerns about the Internet and they struggle to protect their children from the worst elements of the online experience without keeping children from its benefits. They are concerned that their children will be stalked or harassed online (parents of girls are more concerned than parents of boys about these matters). While only a very small proportion of strangers who contact children via the Internet are likely to be sexual predators, they are understandably concerned about such interactions given the possibly severe consequences. They are also concerned about what their children might see or read online (parents of younger children are more concerned about this than parents of older children). And many worry that the Internet may lead some young people to do dangerous or harmful things.

---

[11]The committee does not intend to say that interactions with all strangers are dangerous. For example, the "strangers" may be students at the same age level in another school, or participants in a moderated chat room, or the sender of a large-group mailing list that does not support two-way interaction. In such cases, the interaction may be reasonably safe. But it is the potential danger raised by interacting one-on-one with unknown adults that is the committee's primary concern.

[12]See <http://www.pewinternet.org/reports/toc.asp?Report=36>.

TABLE 1.1 Differences in the Nature of the Child's Interaction: Passive Versus Interactive Exposures

	Passive Interaction	Interactive Interaction
Source of "threat"	The material itself	The predator
The nature of possible danger involved	Psychological or emotional harm	Physical as well as psychological or emotional harm
Time scale of exposure	Short (minutes for a one-time exposure) to long (years for long-term media consumption)	Long (weeks or months)

1.4 A BROAD SPECTRUM OF OPINION AND VIEWS

Parents have a long-recognized responsibility to care for their children and to raise them in a manner consistent with their own values, and they can feel that exposure to certain materials found on the Internet reduces their ability to carry out their parental responsibilities. As argued by one parent,[13]

> How I train my children and what moral values I impart to them doesn't do much good if they're simply walking by a computer in the reference area while an adult male is accessing hard-core pornography, which has been a very common occurrence at our library. What gives the library or anyone else that right, especially in a public institution, to take away the innocence of my child? We get frequent phone calls from distraught parents . . . who are being responsible parents with their children in the library and suddenly being exposed to the most vile material.

While the definition of "hard-core pornography" and the frequency of adult males using library facilities to access such material are open to debate, sentiments such as those reflected above can be powerful motivators for political action. On the other side, another parent wrote the following:[14]

> Be it books, or the Internet, or movies, or music, it's our job as parents to teach children what we believe is acceptable and not acceptable, our values, morals. . . . By the time they're old enough to read or cruise the Internet, they're old enough to know your basics of right or wrong. My

---

[13]Michelle Yezerski, director, Citizens for the Protection of Children. See <http://netwinds.com/library/yezerski-meeks.htm>.

[14]Deb McNeil, parent, Benton, New York. See <http://www.csmonitor.com/durable/1999/06/01/p11s1.htm>.

advice is to set perimeters in cyberspace [and] then trust their judgment—which you instilled.

In addition, the United States has seen in recent decades increasing
cultural and social heterogeneity, and opinions on how to protect children from inappropriate sexually explicit material on the Internet vary
widely. Such diversity was reflected in the testimony to the committee
as well.

Because the varying definitions of pornography, the nuances of public concern about pornography, and their implications for action defy
consensus, effective approaches that deal with pornography in ways that
honor democracy and a pluralistic society must allow for, indeed empower, varying community judgments (and in the case of the Internet, a
possible community with no geographic bounds on the one hand and
individual family judgments on the other), a point that is common to
dealing with any of the wide range of material that some people might
regard as inappropriate.[15]

There is also considerable variability in views of the Internet as compared to views of other media. In one group are those who believe that
even though the Internet is a medium unlike any others, the ethical and
moral codes, cultural norms, and laws that govern behavior on the Internet should be generally the same as those that govern behavior and
interactions in the physical world.[16] For example, in the non-networked
world, such techniques include movie ratings, special (restricted) sections
of video and book stores, opaque wrappings over the covers of adult
magazines, reports to law enforcement officials of suspected child por-
nographers by photo processing lab personnel, special hours or channels
for transmission of certain types of cable TV shows, and so on. Parties in
this group suggest that the problems of minors and Internet pornography
are no different than those in other media, and they see no reason for
different goals or types of regulation in the Internet domain.

In another group are those who believe that because the Internet is a
medium unlike any other, the ethical and moral codes, cultural norms,
and laws that govern behavior on the Internet should be different from
those that govern behavior in other media.[17] This second group is itself

---

[15]Differences in such judgments are also illustrated in Computer Science and Telecommunications Board, National Research Council, 2001, *Global Networks and Local Values*.

[16]See, for example, Jack L. Goldsmith, 1998, "Against Cyberanarchy," *University of Chicago Law Review*, Fall.

[17]See, for example, David R. Johnson and David G. Post, 1996, "Law and Borders—The
Rise of Law in Cyberspace," *Stanford Law Review* 48: 1367.

divided. Some believe that the social and societal problems posed by the Internet differ qualitatively from—and are worse than—their physical world analogs, so that special regulation is warranted, including mandatory filters on school or library computers and prohibitions on certain content on the Internet that may be freely available elsewhere. Others believe that although the problems with respect to the Internet may not necessarily be worse than in the physical world, special attention and regulation in the Internet domain are warranted anyway, especially where Internet access becomes an economic or educational necessity. In this case, the desire for regulation to cope with problems with respect to the Internet arises because the Internet is a new medium that offers opportunities for solutions that did not emerge from society's solutions to the analogous problems in the physical world.[18]

Still others argue that the Internet is so different that regulations from the physical world should not apply at all. Indeed, in the formulation of the project that is the subject of this report, a variety of cyber-libertarians and industry representatives argued that the project should be scoped as narrowly as possible, and preferably should not be undertaken at all, because any attention to these issues would simply point—inappropriately, from their perspective—to targets for government regulation.

There are also differing and mutually incompatible approaches to defining what is objectionable. One approach is based on the notion that individual communities—including individual families—have the right (and obligation) to define what is objectionable. A second approach, rarely stated but often implicit as the motivating force behind certain policy positions, is the idea that a particular definition of objectionable—namely one supported by specific advocates with a specific social agenda—is appropriate for all communities.

Then, there is a question about the agendas of some people who object to "pornography" and sexually explicit material. While it is likely that agreement could be reached among people of varying perspectives on the undesirability of minors being exposed to certain types of "hardcore" material, there is profound disagreement about a great deal of other material related to sexuality, including nudity, homosexuality, art, material about sexually transmitted diseases, bestiality as it relates to animal rights, abortion and contraception, sex education, and so on. Because many of those who raise the most vocal objections to hard-core material also object to many other types of material related to sexuality, those with

---

[18]For more discussion of this point, see Computer Science and Telecommunications Board, National Research Council, 1994, *Rights and Responsibilities of Participants in Networked Communities*, National Academy Press, Washington, D.C. This report also addresses some of the perspectives raised in the preceding few paragraphs.

different views fear that the objections to hard-core material expressed by the most vocal may be at least in part a cover for an agenda that will eventually restrict these other types of material as well.

Some parents are silent about the issue of "Internet pornography" and do not appear to be very active in attempting to keep their children away from these materials or in protecting their children on the Internet. Silence and inactivity may reflect a sense that the Internet presence of adult-oriented sexually explicit material is simply not much of an issue for them, or may indicate a lack of knowledge about the quantity and type of material available or about how to keep their children from it. Or, it may signal resignation and an attitude that the availability of such material is yet another side effect of modernity, much as the smokestacks that were once regarded as symbols of progress. It might also indicate a principled position—that it is insulting to suggest that they should have to solve the problem, that such material should not be available so profusely in the first place, or that regulation of such material is itself inappropriate. Or, it might indicate that parents trust that their children will not search for sexually explicit materials online, or that they know what to do and are able to handle themselves should they encounter such materials.

A point on which most parties agree—implicitly if not explicitly—is that the Internet is a medium in which to preserve policy ground that they have gained in other domains and to advance their policy goals further if possible. That is, the Internet presents both new risks (for losing ground) and new opportunities (for gaining ground). Thus, familiar policy battles are re-fought, clothed in new rhetoric and updated with new facts, but reflecting the same differences in values and goals that characterized similar disagreements associated with more traditional media.

1.5 FOCUS AND STRUCTURE OF THIS REPORT

The committee's deliberations revealed a degree of complexity not apparent from the usual political debate. Nevertheless, a number of themes recurred frequently. These themes are sketched in the sections above, are addressed in greater detail in chapters to follow, and are summarized in Box 1.2 to provide a road map for the reader.

Part I of this report examines the issue along several dimensions and in context. This chapter (Chapter 1) provides an initial framing of the issue. Chapter 2 describes the rapidly changing technological environment primarily as it relates to sexually explicit material. Chapter 3 addresses the economic dimensions of the issue. Chapter 4 focuses on the relevant legal and regulatory regimes. Chapter 5 discusses children and their knowledge of, exposure to, and use of the Internet. Chapter 6 addresses the scientific research base regarding the impact on children of

Box 1.2
Themes Pervasive Throughout the Report

Each of the following themes becomes apparent in the discussion and analysis presented in Chapters 2 through 13. They are presented here to provide the reader with signposts for material to come.

On Inappropriate Material

- The term "pornography" often serves as a proxy in the political debate for a wide range of ill-defined sexually explicit material and does not have a formal legal definition.

On Minors and Culture

- Minors span a wide developmental range that varies with age, and the age of a minor has considerable influence on the impact that exposure to sexually explicit material will have on that minor as well as on the approaches that are appropriate for protection.
- Community standards regarding sexual depictions both explicit and implied appear to have changed in the direction of greater tolerance at least over the last decade.
- Many children know far more about information technology than their parents, teachers, and other adults responsible for their care and well-being, a situation that reverses the traditional gap in knowledge between adults and children.

On Law

- The First Amendment protects from government action speech on the Internet as well as in other media.
- Material that is obscene or that constitutes child pornography enjoys no First Amendment protection.
- Definitions of material that is obscene (or that is "obscene with respect to minors") vary from community to community, and so whether material is legally obscene or legally obscene with respect to minors cannot be ascertained from its content alone.
- Sexually explicit materials that are "obscene with respect to minors" may be regulated for minors, but not in a way that denies access to adults.
- Because of the relative dearth of obscenity prosecutions in recent years, there is considerable uncertainty about the nature of sexually explicit material that could be successfully prosecuted as legally obscene.
- The global reach of the Internet greatly complicates the challenge of restricting content providers or Internet service providers.

On Technology and Economics

- The online adult entertainment industry exists because of demand from adults but is only one source of sexually explicit material.
- The anonymous interactions possible through the Internet make it very difficult to differentiate between adults and minors.

(continues)

Box 1.2 (continued)

• The low cost of entry and decentralized management of the Internet mean that a large number of Internet "publishers" or content providers is inevitable. The result, in general, is often a wide variety of sources of generically similar content (so that there are many sources of similar sexually explicit material).

On Protection

• Technology alone cannot protect Internet-using youth at a level that eliminates the need for responsible adult supervision and education.
• Multiple approaches for protection are generally appropriate, but social and educational strategies are foundational in helping a child learn to make good decisions about Internet usage and to cope effectively with inappropriate material should he or she come across it.
• The specific combination of approaches that should be used to protect children depends on the values of the child's parent or guardian and the community of which these parties are members.

exposure to sexually explicit material. Chapter 7 examines some of the non-scientific considerations involved in this issue.

Part II assesses a variety of generic approaches to protecting children from exposure to inappropriate material on the Internet. Chapter 8 poses general considerations regarding what "protection" means. Chapter 9 focuses on legal and regulatory approaches. Chapter 10 addresses social and educational strategies that seek to educate individuals to use the Internet safely, to make good decisions about content to be viewed, to reduce their exposure to inappropriate material, and to mitigate the consequences, if any, of viewing inappropriate material. Chapter 11 provides a perspective on technology-based tools for protection, and Chapters 12 and 13 focus on a variety of specific tools for use by end users and other parties.

Part III consists of a single chapter (Chapter 14) that addresses communities of action that must coordinate their use of different tools, strategies, and legal and regulatory approaches. Further, it recaps key findings and conclusions and shows relationships among several threads whose discussion has started in Chapter 1, and it outlines where a richer and deeper knowledge base would help to address the issue of protecting children from inappropriate material on the Internet.

Because this report is quite long, several chapters also include a number of tables with some summary observations that provide an orientation to the material of the report.

2

Technology

Suppose that a student is assigned to do a report for school on animals that build things, and he selects beavers as his primary topic. Connecting to the Internet through a computer at home, he goes to an online search engine, where he tries to search the Internet for information about "adult beavers." The search engine returns links to a large number of Web pages. When he clicks on a certain link, he is surprised when he finds a sexually oriented Web site intended for adult use.

This scenario—or one similar to it—is one of the most common that underlies parental concerns about children using the Internet. This chapter addresses the technological dimensions of this "reference scenario" and some of the things that can be done to protect against it.

2.1 AN ORIENTATION TO CYBERSPACE AND THE INTERNET

2.1.1 Characteristics of Digital Information

In the reference scenario, the student is seeking information (content) on beavers—a kind of animal. All information on the Internet is represented in bits—electronic strings of 1's and 0's that are later interpreted according to some algorithm to produce a representation that is meaningful to human beings. Digital information has properties very different from those of the information that a student might retrieve in a book. For purposes of this report, the salient aspects of this digital representation of information are the following:[1]

---

[1]More discussion can be found in Computer Science and Telecommunications Board, National Research Council, 2000, *The Digital Dilemma: Intellectual Property in the Information Age*, National Academy Press, Washington, D.C.

• *Reproducible.* Unlike a physical book or photograph or analog audio recording, a digital information object can be copied infinitely many times, often without losing any fidelity or quality.

• *Easily shared.* Because information is easily copied, it is also easy to distribute at low cost. Digital information can be shared more easily than any type of analog information in the past. In the physical world, broadcasting information to groups has serious costs and hence requires a certain wherewithal and commitment. Technologies such as e-mail and Web sites allow broadcasting to many people at the touch of a single button.

• *Flexible.* A variety of different types of information can be represented digitally: images, movies, text, sound. Digital information can even be used to control movement in the physical world through digitally controlled actuators.

• *Easily modified.* Digital representations of information can be easily manipulated. It is trivial to modify an image—say, changing hair color from blond to red, adding a few notes to a musical score, or deleting and adding text to a document. So, for example, a naked body can be affixed to a head of a child, words modified from their original intent and music "borrowed" freely, and even virtual "people" created, all without leaving a visible trace of these manipulations.

• *Difficult to intercept.* Because no physical object is necessarily associated with a digital information object, interdiction of digital information is much more difficult than interdiction of a physical object carrying information. In other words, there is no book, no magazine, no photo that can be intercepted by physical means.

2.1.2 The Nature of the Internet Medium and a Comparison to Other Media Types

In the reference scenario, the student relies on the Internet. The preceding discussion about digital information is important, but the nature of the Internet itself also makes it quite unlike other more traditional media such as television, film, print, and the telephone. Thus, it is useful to describe certain key features of the Internet medium and to compare it to some other, more traditional media.

• *The Internet supports many-to-many connectivity.* A single user can receive information and content from a large number of different sources, and can also transmit his or her content to a large number of recipients (one-to-many). Or a single user can engage with others in a one-to-one mode (one-to-one). Or multiple users can engage with many others (many-to-many). Broadcast media such as television and radio as well as print are one-to-many media—one broadcast station or publisher sends to many recipients. Telephony is inherently one-to-one, although party lines and conference calling change this characterization of telephones to some extent.

• *The Internet supports a high degree of interactivity* (Box 2.1). Thus, when the user is searching for content (and the search strategy is a good one), the content that he or she receives can be more explicitly customized to his or her own needs.[2] In this regard, the Internet is similar to a library in which the user can make an information request that results in the production of books and other media relevant to that request. By contrast, user choices with respect to television and film are largely limited to the binary choice of "accept or do not accept a channel," and all a user has to do to receive content is to turn on the television. The telephone is an inherently interactive medium, but one without the many-to-many connectivity of the Internet.

• *The Internet is highly decentralized.* Indeed, the basic design philosophy underlying the Internet has been to push management decisions to as decentralized a level as possible. Thus, if one imagines the Internet as a number of communicating users with infrastructure in the middle facilitating that communication, management authority rests mostly (but not exclusively) with the users rather than the infrastructure—which is simply a bunch of pipes that carry whatever traffic the users wish to send and receive. (How long this decentralization will last is an open question.[3]) By contrast, television and the telephone operate under a highly centralized authority and facilities. Furthermore, the international nature of the Internet makes it difficult for one governing board to gain the consensus necessary to impose policy, although a variety of transnational organizations are seeking to address issues of Internet governance globally.

• *The Internet is intrinsically a highly anonymous medium.* That is, nothing about the way in which messages and information are passed through the Internet requires identification of the party doing the sending.[4] One

---

[2]Customization happens explicitly when a user undertakes a search for particular kinds of information, but it can happen in a less overt manner because customized content can be delivered to a user based, for example, on his or her previous requests for information.

[3]Marjory S. Blumenthal and David D. Clark. 2001. "Rethinking the Design of the Internet: The End to End Arguments vs. the Brave New World," in *Communications Policy in Transition: The Internet and Beyond*, B. Compaine and S. Greenstein, eds. MIT Press, Cambridge, Mass.

[4]It is true that access to the Internet may require an individual to log into a computer or even to an Internet service provider. But for the most part, the identity of the user—once captured for purposes of accessing the Internet—is not a part of information that is automatically passed on to an applications provider (e.g., a Web site owner). More importantly, many applications providers—for entirely understandable business reasons—choose not to require authentication. (Strong authentication in general requires an infrastructure that is capable of providing a trusted verification of identity—and in the absence of such an infrastructure, strong authentication is an expensive and inconvenient proposition for the user. This point is discussed at greater length in Section 2.3.2.)

Box 2.1
Interactivity of the Internet

The Internet provides bidirectional capability between communicating parties that can be equally rich in both directions. The Internet's interactivity can be used:

• *To search for information.* In this application, the user sends a little information (to specify what he or she is seeking), and can receive in return a lot of information from many sources (many-to-one communication). Typical applications include using search engines and broadcasting requests for particular kinds of information.

• *To interact with other people on a peer-to-peer basis* (one-to-one communication). In this application, information exchanges tend to be more symmetric. Typical applications include using e-mail and instant messaging. For example, a youth may encounter a friendly, or a dangerous, adult. A friendly adult might be an expert who provides good answers to sexual questions or real-time coaching on how to handle a bad online experience; a dangerous one might be one who seeks to lure the child into an improper sexual encounter. Or a child may gather with other children to share sexually explicit material among themselves, or to discuss matters related to sexuality.

• *To broadcast information to wide audiences* (one-to-many communication). In this case, the amount of information that the user sends out is relatively large, and the volume of what is returned is typically small. Typical applications include broadcasting unsolicited e-mail (spam) to large, undifferentiated audiences with an invitation to view an adult-oriented site or setting up a Web site on which the user posts sexually explicit pictures taken on last week's vacation.

The interactivity of the Internet and its capability of supporting real-time interaction is a major differentiator from other media such as film, books, video, and radio that offer passively consumed content. Users of these latter media view or listen to the content offered, and how the media experience unfolds is determined by only one user choice—whether or not to continue viewing or listening. The Internet, as well as much of modern computer-based information technology such as CD-ROM-based video games and Nintendo, expands the range of user choices. Thus, while it is possible to use the Internet to consume media content passively (and many do use it in such a manner), it also allows the user to interact with other parties, and the number of modes of interaction today is large and still expanding.

Such interaction implies a dynamically constructed media experience, and thus one can "talk" with people in a chat room, send instant messages on a one-to-one basis with anyone, post and read messages on computer bulletin boards on any imaginable topic, exchange e-mail on a one-to-one or a one-to-many basis with anyone, assume fictional "roles" in games and other experiences, and join communities with others that revolve around a shared interest or passion. The information content exchanged in these interactions can be text, images, video clips, sound recordings, or real-time video or sound.

The interactivity of the Internet is very attractive and useful for many purposes. For example, in an educational context, the Internet allows students to collaborate over large geographical distances and to engage with subject-matter experts in a wide variety of fields. But interactivity on the Internet also enables "children talking to strangers," an action that raises concerns for many parents. Without the normal cues available in the physical world (e.g., gestures, voice tone, facial expression, age), children are especially vulnerable to being preyed on by people who are not what they claim to be.

important consequence of the Internet's anonymity is that it is quite difficult to differentiate between adult and minor users of the Internet, a point whose significance is addressed in greater detail in Chapter 4. A second consequence is that technological approaches that seek to differentiate between adults and minors (discussed in Chapter 13) generally entail some loss of privacy for adults who are legitimate customers of certain sexually explicit materials to which minors do not have legitimate access.

• *The capital costs of becoming an Internet publisher are relatively low,* and thus anyone can establish a global Web presence at the cost of a few hundred dollars (as long as it conforms to the terms of service of the Web host). Further, for the cost of a subscription to an Internet service provider (ISP), one can interact with others through instant messages and e-mail without having to establish a Web presence at all. The costs of reaching a large, geographically dispersed audience may be about the same as those required to reach a small, geographically limited audience, and in any event do not rise proportionately with the size of the audience.

• *Because nearly anyone can put information onto the Internet, the appropriateness, utility, and even veracity of information on the Internet are generally uncertified and hence unverified.* With important exceptions (generally associated with institutions that have reputations to maintain), the Internet is a "buyer beware" information marketplace, and the unwary user can be misinformed, tricked, and seduced or led astray when he or she encounters information publishers that are not reputable.

• *The Internet is a highly convenient medium,* and is becoming more so. Given the vast information resources that it offers coupled with search capabilities for finding many things quickly, it is no wonder that for many people the Internet is the information resource of first resort.

2.1.3 Internet Access Devices

In the reference scenario, the student uses a computer to access the Internet. While today a personal computer is the most common way to connect to the Internet, devices for accessing the Internet are proliferating. Entire businesses have begun to spring up in order to ready content and delivery of information for a host of other devices. These devices include:

• Handheld organizers like Palm and Handspring—typically these devices contain built-in wireless modems and use services like OmniSky;
• Cell phones with built in Web access;
• WebTV™ and Internet access devices that are used on TV sets and customized to MSN and AOL and whose deployment began in 2001;
• Blackberry RIM and wireless paging devices;

- Standalone Internet machines like the Compaq Ipaq and mail-stations;
- Kiosks designed for surfing the Internet and typically used in public spaces;
- Game machines like Sega, Nintendo, Microsoft's Xbox. Today's gaming technology (e.g., Sony's Playstation) increasingly uses the Internet to provide users with multi-player communities in which a user can compete against and/or cooperate with other like-minded individuals. Software is generally available on CD-ROMs, and the widespread availability of CD-ROM writers makes the possibility of non-vendor-produced games and activities a realistic one. Game-playing applications are also increasingly available for use on various Web sites, sometimes for free. Note that such games often contain violent material.

In addition, many commercial establishments frequented by children, including coffee shops, department stores, and fast food restaurants, will have customer-usable Internet access points. Broadband Internet access—needed for efficient transmission of images and movies—will also grow in the future, though with some uncertainty about how fast it will be deployed. Specialized Web access devices will cost much less than today's computers (a few hundred dollars each rather than several hundred or thousand dollars). Wireless Internet access is also expected to grow in popularity, though the feasibility of transmitting high-quality images through wireless links remains an open question.

These devices and business trends suggest increasingly ubiquitous access to the Internet. Note also an important social point—wireless access and access "anywhere" enable users, including children, to escape many forms of local supervision (e.g., someone looking over his or her shoulder), and individuals will not be as dependent on school, libraries, and work to provide Internet access. Consequently, approaches to Internet protection and safety for children that depend on actions whose effect is limited to a single venue will be increasingly ineffective.

2.1.4 Connecting to the Internet

In the reference scenario, the student connects to the Internet. In general, access to cyberspace is provided by one or more Internet service providers (ISPs). For children, Internet connections are available via:

- *Personal Internet service.* In this case, a party subscribes to a consumer-oriented ISP, and gains access to the Internet through as many places as the provider can provide access ports. Such services are generally responsible for home access. There are many variations in the offerings from ISPs and many different fee structures as well. Note that an individual child may be using a family account, a personal account associated with a family account, or a friend's personal Internet service.

• *School and/or library Internet service.* A student (or faculty member or staff person) or a library patron uses school or library facilities to obtain Internet access. In general, schools and libraries obtain Internet service for their students and patrons through business-oriented ISPs, and a whole host of classroom ISPs have been brought to the market.

• *Public terminals.* An individual pays "by the minute" for Internet access at a public terminal, which may be located in a coffee shop or an airport, or through a wireless service.

In addition to Internet connections, some ISPs offer other services designed to enhance the user's experience. Proprietary services (including parental controls to help manage the online experience of children) and content are offered by a number of online service providers. These services and content are available only to those who subscribe to those online service providers. In other cases, services are available to some non-subscribers (for example, the instant message (IM) services of some ISPs can provide IM service to those who do not subscribe to those ISPs).

Moreover, various online service providers develop—and seek to develop—reputations about the kinds of content that they may offer. For example, a service provider may bill itself as being "family-friendly" and thus provide access only to Web sites that it regards as appropriate. The denial of access to all Web sites not on the provider's "family-friendly" list is a proprietary service that the online provider offers that is unavailable to others who do not subscribe to it.

ISPs offer dial-up or broadband access to the Internet. The majority of at-home access is today achieved through dial-up connections—a user's computer dials an ISP phone number and connects to the ISP through an ordinary modem. However, broadband access, generally through DSL (digital subscriber lines) from phone companies or cable modems from cable TV companies, is growing because of the higher-bandwidth connections offered. Higher bandwidth is relevant because some kinds of material contain many more bits than others. Text, for example, typically contains many fewer bits than do images, and images contain many fewer bits than movies have. Thus, viewing of graphics-intensive material online through a low-bandwidth connection is often very tedious and tries the patience of all but the most dedicated users.

ISPs also require their subscribers to abide by certain terms of service, violation of which is grounds for termination of the service contract with a subscriber. An individual subscriber to an ISP is bound directly by the terms of service of that ISP. An individual who obtains Internet service through an intermediary is bound by the terms of service imposed by the intermediary, which may (or may not) be stricter than those that bind the ISP and the intermediary. Note also that ISPs vary across a wide range in the extent to which they enforce their terms of service. A typical provision in the terms of service of many ISPs might forbid a user from posting sexually explicit material under most conditions.

ISPs make decisions about content that they will carry. In particular, many ISPs do not allow access to every Usenet newsgroup (e.g., they may not carry newsgroups that carry a large volume of child pornography).[5] For subscribers to these ISPs, the newsgroups that are not carried can be difficult to find and are for many practical purposes non-existent.[6]

Finally, ISPs are funded by subscription and/or by advertising. Subscription entails periodic payment by the user to the ISP for access privileges. Advertising entails payments by advertisers to the ISP for the privilege of displaying ads, and thus the user must be willing to accept the presence of ads in return for access privileges.

2.1.5 Identifying Devices on the Internet: The Role of Addressing

Every computer or other device connected to the Internet is identified by a series of numbers called an IP address.[7] The domain name system is a naming system that translates these computer-readable IP addresses into human-readable forms, namely domain names. Thus, a domain name is a name that identifies one or more IP addresses. A canonical domain name has the form "example.com."

Every domain name has a suffix corresponding to a top-level domain (TLD), in this example .com. Until October 1, 2001, the most common top-level domains allowed for Internet use have been .net, .org, .com, .edu,

---

[5]Usenet is a worldwide distributed discussion system consisting of a set of newsgroups with names that are classified hierarchically by subject. "Articles" or "messages" are "posted" to these newsgroups by people on computers with the appropriate software— these articles are then broadcast to other interconnected computer systems via a wide variety of networks. Some newsgroups are "moderated"; in these newsgroups, the articles are first sent to a moderator for approval before appearing in the newsgroup. For more information, see Chip Salzenberg, "What Is Usenet?," available online at <http://www.faqs.org/faqs/usenet/what-is/part1/>.

[6]There are Web sites through which one can read Usenet newsgroups even if the ISP has decided not to carry certain newsgroups, thus circumventing the ISP's selection policy.

[7]The IP address of a device provides a unique address to which and from which messages can be routed. A typical IP address has the form a.b.c.d, where a, b, c, and d are numbers from zero to 255. The mapping between domain name and IP address is managed by devices known as domain name servers. More information is given in a Computer Science and Telecommunications Board report on domain name systems that is currently in preparation. Note also that IP addresses may be mapped dynamically to devices, so today, a user's computer would have one IP address and tomorrow it might have a different one.

.gov, and .mil. In addition, a number of two-letter country suffixes have been recognized. As this report goes to press, a number of other top-level domains have been approved: .biz, .info, .pro, .coop, .aero, .museum, and .name. (How many other TLDs will eventually be available is an open question, and the issue of the number and type of TLDs is highly charged politically and economically.) As a rule of thumb, the non-country suffixes indicate something about the nature of the party with which the site is affiliated. For example, example.museum is likely operated by a museum; example.gov is operated by a government agency.

The domain name is a key element of routing traffic across the Internet. For example, a typical e-mail address is of the form "John.Doe@example.com." The address of a typical Web site has the form "www.example.com." The Web site address is generally part (or all) of a uniform resource locator (URL) that identifies a particular Web page that can be found on a Web site. Thus, www.example.com/page1 might refer to a page on the example.com Web site.

2.1.6 Functionality of the Internet

In the reference scenario, the student used a search engine to search the World Wide Web for information about beavers. Search engines are only one aspect of the functionality that the Internet offers, and as the Internet matures, new functions based on new applications and technologies are constantly being introduced. Some of the more important applications of the Internet are described below and are summarized in Table 2.1.

- The *World Wide Web* (WWW) refers to the set of all the information resources that can be accessed via the hypertext transfer protocol (HTTP). Loosely speaking, it is the set of all Web pages that can be addressed by a request of the form "http: URL."[8] Today, the publicly accessible World Wide Web consists of over 2 billion Web pages,[9] though there is a great deal of uncertainty in any estimate of Web size. Web pages are associated with particular hosts (though not every host has a Web page), and many Web pages themselves include links to other Web pages. The Web is based on a client-server model—a user (client) specifically requests a Web page from a host (server).
- *Search engines* help to organize, classify and return information based on a query, and those who surf the Web typically rely on various

---

[8]Most browsers handle addresses without a preceding "http:" as though it was present. Also, some Web pages are accessible only through the "https:" protocol.

[9]For example, as of November 2001 the Google search engine had indexed 1.6 billion Web pages. As of April 2002, it had indexed 2.1 billion Web pages.

TABLE 2.1 Selected Internet Applications and Their Implications for Exposing Children to Inappropriate Sexually Explicit Material and Potentially Dangerous Experiences

Channel	Key Points
Web pages	Identified by and accessed through knowledge of the uniform resource locator (for example, http://www.random_sex_site.com, http://www.just_fine_kids_site.com) Can display still images, text, and movies Generally the channel used today by the adult online industry Can be found by typing the URL into a browser or clicking on a link (links can be embedded in instant messages, e-mail, and so on; included in other Web pages; or found through a search engine)
E-mail	Requires knowledge of a user's e-mail address Can contain (or carry) text, images, links to Web pages; can be used to initiate two-way dialog as well as to deliver information and files Sender's e-mail address can be faked (or be misleading) Is the route for unsolicited commercial e-mail (spam)
Chat	Generally text-based, and conducted in a "chat room"; text can contain links to Web pages Can be public (accessible to anyone) or private (by invitation only) Content of chat and online identities of participants are visible to everyone participating in the chat room Chat rooms are an online equivalent of CB radio Used to initiate, establish, and maintain online relationships
Instant messages	One-on-one dialog, and private Text-based, but can contain links; images and voice can sometimes be transmitted as well Initiation of instant message requires knowledge of user name "Buddy lists" allow user to know who is online at the same time as the user
Usenet	Populated by some 30,000 newsgroups of specialized topics; newsgroups function essentially as online bulletin boards on which users can post anything they wish, often anonymously Many newsgroups contain sexually explicit material, and some are oriented primarily toward such material; sexually explicit content on Usenet newsgroups is often more extreme than those on adult-oriented Web sites Cost of content distribution is borne by Internet service provider that carries newsgroups with content rather than by publisher or receiver Sexually explicit Usenet newsgroups serve as conduits for advertising of adult-oriented Web sites and as a medium in which sexually explicit content can be exchanged among users Internet service providers make choices about what Usenet newsgroups to carry; some carry the full line, and others carry only a subset (e.g., all except those devoted to child pornography)
Peer-to-peer connections	Connection between two users that is made directly without mediation through a central server Purpose of peer-to-peer connection is typically for file-sharing (of any kind of content, including sexually explicit content) Not generally anonymous (because connections are peer-to-peer, each user must have an Internet address with which to interact) Cost of distribution is borne by the Internet service provider rather than the end users

---

Box 2.2
How Search Engines Work

Search engines help users find information on the Internet stored in Web pages. Typically, a user will type some words (the "search query") into a search engine, and the search engine will return a number of "links" on its results page. To reach any of these results, the user clicks on the link, which transfers the user away from the search engine and into the uniform resource locator (URL) corresponding to that link.

A search engine works by matching the user's query against an index of Web pages (documents) on the Internet that it has stored in a database. An index is necessary because with over 2 billion pages on the Internet, a real-time search of all of them when someone makes an information request would be prohibitively expensive and time-consuming. An index allows a search to be completed in a much smaller amount of time (seconds rather than days or weeks), though at the cost of some incompleteness and inaccuracy (because pages may have changed or been added since the index was created).

No search engine indexes (or even could index) all of the pages on the Web, and each search engine indexes a different set of pages. For this reason, and because of the dynamic nature of the Web, all search engines are inherently "incomplete," and the contents of their indexes (and thus search results) differ from one another.

A search engine builds its index of Web pages by sending out a "spider" to retrieve the pages from Web sites. Spiders retrieve only static pages, not pages that are hiding as databases or are dynamically generated. Most spiders also obey the robot.txt file on a Web site; if the file says, "Do not index this site," they do not index that site. They can store millions of words and hundreds of thousands of sites.

A paper published in *Nature* in 1999 estimated the types of material indexed, excluding commercial sites. "Scientific and educational" sites were the largest population. Health sites, personal sites, and the sites for societies (scholarly or other) are all larger than the percentage estimated for pornography; i.e., a few percent of Web pages contained material that could reasonably be characterized as adult-oriented, sexually explicit material.[1]

For a more detailed description of how search engines index Web pages, interpret queries, and search their databases, see Appendix C.

---

[1]Steve Lawrence and Lee Giles. 1999. "Accessibility of Information on the Web," *Nature* 400: 107-109.

---

types of search engines to find the information they are seeking. Box 2.2 describes how search engines work. Search engines rely on technologies of information retrieval, as discussed in Section 2.2. Given the enormous volume of information on the Web, users in general do not know where to find the information they seek. To cope with this situation, search engines have been developed to help users find the addresses of information residing on the Web. While no data have been collected on this point, it is probably fair to say that search engines enable the finding of most information that people access on the Internet.

- *E-mail* refers to messages that are sent electronically from one user to another (or to many others) and read at a time of the recipient's choosing. E-mail can carry attachments that can be other information objects, such as images, movies, audio recordings, and so on. E-mail can also be used as a direct marketing tool ("spam") analogous to third-class postal mail (also known as junk mail). The use of e-mail requires knowledge of a recipient's e-mail address.

- *File sharing* refers to a process in which devices controlled by end users (i.e., "peers") interact directly with each other to transfer files between them, rather than interacting through a central server. In some file-sharing networks, a central server holds a publicly accessible index to the files available from end users (but not the files themselves). End users then transfer the files between themselves.[10] Other peer-to-peer file-sharing networks eliminate even the centralized server index function. Users of these systems are connected to a network of other parties (rather than to a centralized index), and a query from one user goes to an immediate circle of possible respondents. If not satisfied, the query then goes from those respondents to other respondents. Furthermore, such queries are highly anonymous, though file transfers between end users are not. Although peer-to-peer interaction is most often performed in a user-to-user mode, there is no reason that in principle a single user could not establish peer-to-peer connections to a large number of other users and thus function in a "server-like" mode for those users.

- *Usenet newsgroups* are a broadcast medium in which anyone anywhere with a computer can be a transmitter. Typically groups form around shared social interests. Thus, the Usenet becomes the place for discussion among self-selecting groups interested in specific topics. The volume carried by Usenet newsgroups is substantial (over 50 gigabytes per day on more than 10,000 newsgroups).[11] Anyone can "post" a message on any Usenet newsgroup (perhaps anonymously—see Section 2.3), governed only by his or her own judgment in ascertaining the relevance of the message to the nominal topic of that newsgroup. Newsgroups are named as described in Box 2.3.

---

[10]This mode of file sharing first gained widespread publicity with the Napster network, an online service that facilitated the sharing of digital music files among users. The files themselves—the information content of interest to end users—always remained on client systems and never passed through a centralized server (such as one that would host a Web page). Instead, the server gave end users the ability to search for particular files of interest and to initiate a peer-to-peer transfer between the users willing to share (and receive) files without the payment of a fee, even when the files constituted legally protected intellectual property. Napster is important for this discussion because there is no particular reason that the files in question must be digital music files—and indeed, extensions of the Napster protocol can handle other types of files.

[11]Personal communication, Dan Geer, president of Usenet.

Box 2.3
Characteristics of Usenet Newsgroups

Naming

Naming of newsgroups is hierarchical and of arbitrary depth. Naming of Usenet newsgroups mirrors the spirit of how computer and other network end points are named within the Internet as a whole, which Usenet predates. Hence

- [comp.org.usenix] is the computer professional organization USENIX,
- [comp.os.linux.announce] is announcements concerning a computer operating system named LINUX,
- [rec.travel.africa] is about recreational travel to Africa,
- [alt.sex] is about sex in general, whereas
- [alt.sex.wanted.escorts] is an obvious specialization,
- [net.config] is about configuring networks,
- [alt.drugs.mushrooms] is about mushrooms as sources of drugs,
- [misc.health.diabetes] is advice on diabetes and health, and
- [ne.politics] is wars of words around New England politics.

By technocratic convention, some parts of the hierarchy are static and new groups can only arise by consensus voting (groups improperly created do not get carried). Conversely, other parts of the hierarchy (notably "alt") are wide open to the creation of new groups and subgroups, all under the banner of anti-censorship. Not surprisingly, the alt-newsgroups contain large amounts of sexually explicit content of all varieties.

Moderation

Some groups are "moderated," which means that postings are routed to moderators, people who either approve and forward or deny and delete prospective postings. This is enormously thankless work, and first-rate moderation often requires load sharing among several people working as one. Because unmoderated groups are available to all, the "spam" problem that bedevils e-mail is vastly worse in Usenet. Ironically, the parts of Usenet devoted to communications about sexual matters are so overwhelmed with advertisement that they have been effectively censored inasmuch as no useful discussion can take place within them due to the volume of junk.

Sexually Explicit Content

Usenet newsgroups in the "alt" hierarchy come and go. On one day in 2001, an examination of Usenet on one server of one ISP showed:

- 287 Usenet discussion groups in the alt.sex.* hierarchy, most of which were (in principle) text groups and which contained an aggregate of 30,541 postings in a recent 3-day interval (which overcounts the number of original posts because many are repeatedly cross-posted to multiple groups);
- 469 postings in one sample group, alt.sex.anal, appearing in the 3-day interval, of which 102 appeared by their own headline description to be involving children;
- 27 Usenet groups in the picture-oriented alt.binaries.erotica.* hierarchy, containing an aggregate of 6,469 postings in the 3-day interval (again without regard to duplicate cross-postings); and
- 198 Usenet groups in the picture-oriented alt.binaries.pictures.* hierarchy, of which 57 (of the 198) appeared to be sex related and which contained an aggregate of 46,417 postings in the 3-day interval (again without regard to duplicate cross-postings).

Similar results for availability, volume, quality, repetition, and ease of access apply to other channels in like manner.

- *Internet relay chat (IRC) and chat rooms.* These are popular real-time interactive services on the Internet that function as the equivalent of CB radio, where one person talks on a channel and anyone listening on that channel can hear and respond. IRC and chat rooms allow users to exchange text-only messages in real time with other people all over the world. IRC "channels" and chat rooms can be public (so that they can be found by others wishing to join the conversation) or private (so that they are invisible to the general public and special knowledge of the channel's or chat room's name is needed to join). IRC and chat rooms require a user to take active (initiating) steps to join an ongoing conversation. In addition, some chat rooms or channels on the Internet are monitored by employees or volunteers for language and content and behaviors, but most are not. (These monitors sometimes have the ability to force particular users out of a conversation.)

There are many variants of chat rooms. Chat rooms can be based on interests—movies, sports, hobbies—or can be just a place to meet people. Some of the latest technologies are found in the online gaming community where people assume digital visual representations called avatars. Avatars can then interact with each other in cyberspace. The chat then has a visual animated component. MUDs and MOOs are complex online games relying mainly on text interactions while relatively new games like Microsoft's *Age of Empires* and Electronic Arts' *The Sims Online* utilize visual representations to create fantastic communities for role playing.

- *Instant messaging services* allow a two-way, real-time, private dialog between two users These services include such well-known entities as AOL's Instant Messenger and Yahoo's Messenger. A user initiating a message sends an invitation to talk to another (specific) user who is online at the same time. Unlike IRC, no channel-seeking initiating step is required on the part of the recipient to become part of such a conversation.[12] Instant messaging also allows someone to carry on multiple private conversations simultaneously. Instant messaging is very popular today for both professional and personal use, because unlike in chat rooms, one tends to talk to people whom one already knows. Note also that IMs are

---

[12]Buddy lists are an important element of IM services. A buddy list contains the online names of "buddies" of a given user and indicates when one or more come online. When the user knows that "sue123" is online, she can send "sue123" an instant message and start a conversation. Thus, buddy lists facilitate online real-time communication among people who know each other's online names. Most IM services also offer a blocking option that enables a user who receives an IM from someone to block it. This option is used when a user receives an IM from someone with whom the user does not want to communicate (e.g., a stranger, or a friend with whom one is on the "outs").

often used in conjunction with chat rooms or other online activities—a user in a chat room can send an IM to someone else in the chat room (because he or she sees the other party's screen name or "handle"), thus establishing a private communication. Once limited to text-only interactions, IM services are increasingly sophisticated. For example, some IMs can support direct voice interactions and exchanges of music or image files. Other IM services allow a user to block selected other parties from contacting him or her, thus increasing the difficulty of harassment.

• *Videoconferencing applications* are growing. Web cameras and streaming media depend on the increasing availability of broadband Internet connections to allow the high-quality real-time transmission of audio and video content. Today's Internet videoconferencing suffers from many of the same problems as Internet telephony, most notably poor quality (low resolution as well as "jitter" in the moving images). A popular consumer videoconferencing application is CU-SEE-ME, a very inexpensive videoconferencing tool originally developed at Cornell University for educational applications and now used to support a wide variety of video applications. Chat rooms are often forums in which Web cameras are used to send pictures in real time.

• *Streaming media, video, and audio* are allowing people to watch movies like broadcasts over the Web as well. A movie that is now available through pay-per-view cable TV may readily become available through the Internet (a phenomenon known as digital convergence), perhaps augmented by the availability of an online chat room for discussion of that content with one's friends and/or an electronic commerce site where one can purchase products or services illustrated in the movie.

• *Internet telephony* allows two-way real-time voice communication to be established without records of such communications appearing on family telephone bills. A variety of standards now in place facilitate the interoperability of Internet telephony products, which would otherwise be hampered by proprietary specifications and protocols. However, because the Internet was not designed to support real-time operations, the quality of such connections remains an issue, though progress is being made in this area. Internet telephony products enable Internet users to establish real-time voice contact without the need for a telephone, and even today, voice connections (of somewhat low fidelity) can be established through certain types of instant message and in some chat rooms.

In addition to these functions, there are a variety of Internet applications for facilitating Web activity (Box 2.4). The use of these applications is often free, and they are important because they reduce the costs and difficulty of establishing a (non-commercial) Web presence and of gener-

---

Box 2.4
Internet Applications for Facilitating Web Activity

A number of companies provide free e-mail accounts that are accessible from anywhere on the World Wide Web. Because they are free, many savvy consumers have set these accounts up to do their more general e-mail (for instance to get information from companies), while they reserve their private e-mail address for a much closer circle of friends and colleagues.

A second service available from service providers is free storage. A company will provide some limited amount of storage online (25 megabytes is a common number), and the user can make that storage space accessible to anyone that he or she chooses. Online storage can be used to host a Web site or as a private online "drop" for any kind of digitized electronic content. A variant on free storage services is free Web page hosting—a user receives a limited amount of disk space to construct a publicly accessible Web page, with content restricted only by the terms of service to which the user agrees in return for the free service.[1]

A third service is that of the "online community." Services that promote online communities help to bring like-minded individuals into electronic contact and interaction with each other. The Internet service providers promoting these communities provide directories, search engines, chat rooms, and an organization to help facilitate these electronic affinity groups.

---

[1]Note that free services often have characteristics that may make them less desirable than for-pay services. For example, a business owner who is concerned about high reliability and availability of resources is likely to want a service that provides frequent file backup, a feature that is unlikely to be available from a free storage provider.

---

ating communities of shared interest—in sports, in science, and in trading of sexually explicit materials.

Finally, a variety of peripheral devices are also relevant to a discussion of Internet functionality. The availability of devices to convert sound into digital form, to digitize existing images, and to record still and video imagery enables individuals to generate digital content inexpensively and in private. Digital cameras, Web cameras, and camcorders are dropping in price and the pictures they take increasing in quality, and virtually anyone can publish videos to the Web or can participate in or set up videoconferences at very low cost.[13] Thus, while one might have had

---

[13]A 2001 video advertisement from Sony Europe for its Vaio line of notebook computers (which can have a Webcam built into them) depicts a man working at home on his Vaio notebook computer (with the Webcam). An adult female whom he obviously knows enters the room, greets him, strips to her underwear in another room, and starts behaving with him in a very sexually aggressive manner. The advertisement closes with several businessmen on the other end of a video conference looking at their screen in surprise seeing the woman on top of the man. The advertisement is sexually suggestive but depicts no overt sexual activity or nudity.

difficulty in the past in taking a picture of a couple having sex (because of the difficulty in having the film developed), today a digital camera enables one to do the same in complete privacy.

2.1.7 Cost and Economics of the Internet

On the Internet, the cost of handling information is rapidly decreasing. From a message sender's point of view, electronic messages cost next to nothing to create, exactly nothing to duplicate, and virtually nothing to send, and—given the anonymity of the Internet—inexpensive bandwidth imposes none of the costs normally associated with responsibility, prudence, or probity, leading to problems such as unsolicited commercial e-mail (also known as spam). Bandwidth is inexpensive enough that most ISPs and services recognize that it is cheaper to "send everything" through its pipes than to determine if a message or information is inappropriate, unwanted, or unrequested by the receiver.

Furthermore, because digital information can be so freely reproduced, it is essentially impossible to rely on mechanical difficulty or expense of reproduction to curtail the availability of anything to anyone. Once released onto the Internet, content is next to impossible to ban—whether that content involves a political manifesto, sensitive classified information, company trade secrets, one's medical records, or child pornography.[14]

Finally, the Internet contains an enormous volume of material that changes rapidly. The sheer mass of this material means that it is economically prohibitive to review every publicly accessible item for its inappropriateness or lack thereof.

The economics described above suggest that if it costs virtually nothing to provide content to everyone, then an entirely free market will seek to make all possible content available to everyone. The implications of such economics are further discussed in Chapter 3.

2.1.8 A Global Internet

The Internet transcends the physical boundaries of local communities and national borders alike, thus expanding the universe from which con-

---

[14]This is not to say that all content on the Internet remains accessible, but in practice attempts to ban certain information content result in efforts by those interested in such information to copy and distribute it. Thus, while the personal medical records of John Doe may not be of particular interest, and if posted today may disappear without a trace tomorrow, the reason is that no one except John Doe is likely to be interested in such records. However, if the personal medical records of the President of the United States were posted on the Internet, it would be virtually impossible for the most determined efforts of the White House to erase them and to eliminate all access to them.

tent of various kinds can be drawn. Of particular relevance is that many other nations have different views about visual depictions of sexuality and the human body. For example, images of frontal nudity are found in mainstream print media in many parts of Europe, and publication or broadcast of such images raises little concern or outcry there. Thus, material not seen as "pornographic" by those providing it (e.g., content providers in Europe) may be perceived as such by those viewing it in a different cultural context (e.g., by some viewers in the United States).

A further consequence of the Internet's international nature is that only with great difficulty (and many would argue that it is impossible) can laws passed in one jurisdiction affect the behavior of parties in other jurisdictions that are not generally subject to such laws.[15] Thus, to the extent that sexually explicit material of any kind—or any other type of material, for that matter—is available from overseas sources, laws that seek to restrict U.S. content providers from making such material available to U.S. citizens will fail to restrict it in practice.[16]

2.1.9 The Relative Newness of the Internet

Amidst all of the attention given to the Internet and dot-com phenomena, it is helpful to recall that the Internet has been a part of the national consciousness for less than a decade (since the mid-1990s). Ten years is an enormously long time compared to the time scale of technology change, but it is quite short on the time scale of social, economic, and legal change. Given that the array of pre-Internet social, economic, and legal and regulatory practices to balance competing societal interests developed over a time scale of many decades (and in some cases, centuries), it is not surprising that the Internet has offered something of a vacuum into which many parties seeking quick advantage have moved.

For example, the practice of adult-oriented Web sites using addresses that are based on common words or that are similar to those of non-adult businesses draws many people to sites that they had not intended to visit. Branding histories have not been established that allow users to differentiate between reliable and unreliable information. Certain practices that are acceptable in the real world—such as direct marketing—may cross

---

[15]Of course, such a claim is valid only to the extent that content providers and ISPs are numerous and dispersed internationally. If the number of ISPs is small enough (as could happen through attrition or mergers and acquisitions in one jurisdiction), they become likely targets for regulation, as regulatory efforts can be concentrated rather than dispersed.

[16]On the other hand, sources that appear to be foreign may in fact be under the jurisdiction of U.S. law. For example, the mere fact that a domain name has a country suffix such as .ru or .jp does not necessarily mean that its owner is located in Russia or Japan. Indeed, in this hypothetical example, such parties may well reside in California or Iowa.

over into the unacceptable in cyberspace because they are increasingly voluminous and often seen as more intrusive as well.

Perhaps the most important consequence of the relative newness of the Internet is the generation gap in knowledge between parent and child. It may be that as today's children become parents themselves, their familiarity with rapid rates of technological change will reduce the knowledge gap between them and their children, and mitigate to some extent the consequences of the gap that remains.

2.2 TECHNOLOGIES OF INFORMATION RETRIEVAL

As suggested in the reference scenario in which a student seeks information on adult beavers, information retrieval is an important part of what people do on the Internet. By virtue of its vast scope, the Internet is a route for obtaining a range and variety of material to which one would most likely not otherwise have easy access—such materials include history, science, entertainment, games, medical information, and religious information, as well as materials that adults deem inappropriate for children. If children are treated as adults on the Internet, children may come across such materials.

Searching for information on the Internet is different from searching for information in, for example, a library in the physical world. Typically, an individual might search for information using an Internet search engine. A common initial search strategy—used by many inexperienced individuals—is to type one or two keywords and then to examine the sites that are returned. For a word such as "sex," a search engine might return information on sex education sites, a set of biology notes on sex, and adult-oriented Web sites. By contrast, a user of a physical library might rely on the content labeling in various classification systems, such as those of the Library of Congress and the Dewey Decimal systems. On the Internet, this absence of reliable content labeling confounds specificity in searching. Further, the scale of a "Web catalog" (i.e., the volume of information accessible through popular search engines) is much larger than that of most library catalogs of holdings, and Web search engines often do not provide adequate categorization of Web pages contained in their databases. Finally, the most important distinction between the physical library and the Internet is the fact that all physical libraries exercise some editorial discretion in acquiring materials, whereas the Internet is a venue in which the publications of any party are available and retrievable without editorial restriction.

Information retrieval systems support people in finding information in large databases of information objects (whether in the form of text, images, video, or other media) that is relevant to their problems or situations. Internet search engines, where the database is the Web, are a typical example of such systems, as are libraries, where the database is the collection. To accomplish their goals, information retrieval systems must:

- Represent the content of the information objects (what the objects are *about*), through a process called *content representation* or *content analysis*;
- Represent the person's information "need," through a process called *problem* or *user representation*;
- Match the representations of information objects and information problem, to retrieve those objects that are most likely to be useful to the searcher (*search techniques*); and
- Provide an interface between the user and the other components of the system to support the user's interaction with those components and with the information objects.

Filtering systems, discussed at greater length in Sections 2.3.1 and 12.1, work like information retrieval systems in reverse; that is, they are concerned not with retrieving desirable information, but rather with making sure that undesirable information is not retrieved. However, their essential operations remain the same: they must represent the content of the information objects; they must represent relevant characteristics of the user; they must match object representations with user representations to eliminate undesirable objects; and they must provide a means for users to specify or otherwise indicate what is not desired.

The essential problem with information retrieval (and filtering) is that all of these processes are inherently *uncertain*. With respect to content analysis, what an information object is about can be many things for many people. The problem is intrinsically difficult, even for humans: one person may think a picture shows a starry sky; another may interpret it as a symptom of mental ill-health; and a third is interested only in the brush technique. Similarly, one user may find a particular page of text obscene; to a second it is merely embarrassing; and to the third, it contains important health-care information. Also, even representing what text is about is fraught with uncertainty. Most words mean many things (polysemy); most concepts can be expressed in many ways (synonymy).

Images are a particularly difficult recognition challenge for computers. Computers seek to recognize an image by analyzing the relationship of the pixels in it (color tone, contrast, and so on). While it is often possible to tell whether a picture has nearly naked people in it, images of the California desert and apple pies are also sometimes identified as pictures with naked people by today's image recognition software.[17] And

---

[17]D.A. Forsyth and M.M. Fleck. 1999. "Automatic Detection of Human Nudes," *International Journal of Computer Vision* 32(1): 63-77.

image recognition technology is for the most part incapable of distinguishing minors from adults (and hence cannot identify child pornography with any reliability). At the same time, using words that may be found alongside images provides additional information that can help identify sexually explicit images properly.

With respect to representing the user (or what the user desires or desires not to see) the problems are similarly difficult. Users are in general unable to specify precisely that which they do not know but may be searching for, nor are they (or a computer algorithm, or another person) able to specify precisely the characteristics of that which they should not see. The matching process is thus itself inevitably uncertain, since the representations on which it depends cannot be complete and certain.

Because information retrieval and information filtering are probabilistic, any search engine will find material that is irrelevant to the user's needs and fail to find material that is relevant. Similarly, any filter will inevitably allow the passing of some undesirable material, and will filter out some desirable material. Any attempt to avoid errors of the first type will lead to an increase in errors of the second type, and vice versa.

These points are discussed in greater detail in Section 2.3.1 and in Appendix C.

2.3 TECHNOLOGIES RELATED TO ACCESS CONTROL AND POLICY ENFORCEMENT

As more people—and children—connect to the Internet, problems such as exposure to inappropriate material and experiences assume a higher profile. One logical conclusion might be that if technology helped to create these problems, technology can help to solve them. While the committee does not believe that technology is yet the foundation of good solutions to these problems (and may never be), technologies nevertheless do have useful roles to play. Below is a brief discussion of technologies that may be relevant.

2.3.1 Filtering Technologies

Filtering technologies allow Internet material or activities that are deemed inappropriate to be blocked, so that the individual using that filtered computer cannot gain access to that material or participate in those activities. Typically, material is determined to be inappropriate on the basis of its source, its content, or the labels that have been associated with it. Determination of inappropriate content can be accomplished by computer-based methods, by a combination of computer-based methods and human judgment, or by human judgment alone. This section addresses automatic and human plus automatic methods, since the size of the Internet effectively prevents use of human judgment alone (Box 2.5). (In the case of methods based on a combination of human plus automatic techniques, a human rater examines Web sites that a preliminary machine-performed analysis has identified for human examination, and makes a judgment call about whether the site is inappropriate, and if so, determines the objectionable category into which the page falls.)

Filtering technologies can be applied in several ways. One is by the establishment of so-called "black lists," which are lists of sources that have been deemed to be inappropriate, and that the user is prevented from accessing. Another is by the establishment of "white lists," which are lists of sources that have been deemed appropriate, and thus are the only sources that the user is allowed to access. These two methods require a priori identification of the bad (good) sites, which are then incorporated into the filtering software, which stands between the user's Internet access tool and the Internet itself. Bad sites for black lists can be identified through any of the technologies described below. Also, in a priori determinations of inappropriate content, the categorization judgment is usually made days, weeks, or even months in advance of the user's request for the Web site—a point that is significant in light of the fact that the content of Web sites typically changes over time.

A third means of applying filtering technologies occurs in real time, that is, at the time that the user is actually interacting on the Internet and when the information in question is flowing directly to the user. In this case, there may be no a priori blocking of specific sites or sources; rather, the content or other characteristics of retrieved items are analyzed prior to display, and on this basis it is determined whether they should be displayed to the user. This real-time method can also be used in reverse; that is, it can be used to analyze the user's request, and on this basis decide whether the request should be allowed, or disallowed. Although conducted in real time, this method nevertheless requires a priori specification of indicators of content which determine that that source has inappropriate content. Finally, only real-time content monitoring is useful for monitoring and selective blocking of outgoing information, such as blocking certain text from appearing in e-mail (e.g., a phone number).

Note that if a requested Web site is determined to be inappropriate, there are several options for how much material from that site should be blocked. For example, all material on that site might be blocked (everything on www.example.com). Or only a certain directory might be blocked (www.example.com/directory1 might be blocked, while www.example. com/directory2 might not be blocked). Or a particular page within a directory might be blocked (e.g., www.example.com/directory1/picture1.jpg).

Box 2.5
Human Scrutiny of Every Site to Be Blocked?

The Web is so large that it is impossible for a human being to have scrutinized every possible Web page that a viewer might access. However, filter vendors often claim that some human being has examined every one of the sites blocked by their filter and identified it as inappropriate.

On the face of it, such a claim is not necessarily inconsistent with the first statement about the size of the Web. But the sheer size of the Web means that the screening process involved must involve a mix of automated and human process. In particular, the only method that makes sense for large-scale screening is for some automated process to nominate sites for blocking, and for an individual to evaluate the nominated sites.

Can the claim of human examination for every site be substantiated? One assumption on which the claim rests is that blocked sites are revisited on the time scale on which the content of a site is likely to change. If the revisit rate is inadequate to keep up with such changes, a site that may have been properly blocked when it was first added to the list may remain blocked even if the site's new content would not be deemed inappropriate (overblocking).

A more serious issue is that human evaluation of a site is a labor-intensive process. The critical variable is how long it takes for a human being to evaluate a Web page. Finkelstein and Tien[1] estimate 1 minute per page as a reasonable overall estimate for sustained work. This estimate is quite plausible if the page contains a significant amount of textual material that must be read (as would be the case for hate speech, for example), but is likely high by a factor of 5 or 10 for pages that contain images of the kind typically found on adult Web sites. Assuming about 200 workdays per year, an individual doing page evaluation alone might be able to evaluate somewhere between 0.1 million and 1 million pages per year.

These figures suggest that an effort of 10 person-years is needed to create a comprehensive list of a million sites to be blocked (including both text and images)—while an effort on the order of a person-year is required if the primary target is sexual images of the sort found on adult Web sites.

Reliable software to identify possibly inappropriate sites could reduce the effort required considerably. That is, the software—set to minimize underblocking—would propose candidate sites for human evaluation, and the resulting higher level of overblocking would propose sites for which human decision making is essential. Moreover, technology could be used to filter out duplicates, reducing further the overall number of sites that would require human decision making.

See also the discussion in Finkelstein and Tien, "Blacklisting Bytes"[2]

---

[1] Seth Finkelstein and Lee Tien, 2000, "Blacklisting Bytes," white paper submitted to the Committee on Tools and Strategies for Protecting Kids from Pornography and Their Applicability to Other Inappropriate Internet Content. Available online at <http://www.itasnrc.org> and at <http://www.eff.org/Censorship/Censorware/20010306_eff_nrc_paper1.html>.

[2] Finkelstein and Tien, 2000, "Blacklisting Bytes."

Filtering by Internet Domain Names and Addresses

Filtering by Internet domain names and addresses is typically accomplished by examination of the name of the Web site that is requested by the user or returned to the user, in the case of real-time filtering. The name of a Web site (or page on a Web site) is specified by a uniform resource locator (URL). A given URL, for example, http://www.example.com/directory1/picture1.jpg, is usually checked against this list in a number of ways.

In the case of a priori filtering, the URL is checked against a preexisting list of inappropriate names generated by the filter vendor. All parts of the URL are compared to a list of words or terms that have been previously found to be associated with sites containing inappropriate material, or that are believed are likely to be associated with inappropriate material. For example, www.hotmama.com is likely to refer to an adult Web site.[18] The .xxx domain (discussed in Section 13.1) is based on this notion.

This method can be used to permit access, as well as to prevent access. For instance, a site in the .gov domain would in general be considered highly unlikely to contain inappropriate material, as would a site with the name of a museum. In the case of real-time filtering, access would be denied (allowed) based on the comparison; in the case of a priori filtering, the URL would probably be forwarded to a human evaluator, who would determine whether it should be placed on the black list.

A related method is to examine the links that are made from a site and to a site. Because many adult Web sites are linked to each other, a referral to a known adult site A that is present on Web site B provides reason to assume that B is also an adult site.

A second method is to check the IP address of the Web site—in this (made-up) case, 203.12.34.12. If this address is on a list of inappropriate IP addresses, access is blocked. This approach is helpful when a Web site has only an IP address and no domain name associated with it.

A complication in this analysis of page names is that different hosts can share the same IP address through a process known as IP-based virtual hosting, which is a way of assigning multiple domain names to the same IP address. IP-based virtual hosting is made possible by the fact that the HTTP protocol passes the URL containing the requested domain name to the site at the given IP address, and the software at that IP address maps the domain name to the appropriate portion of the server. Thus, an entry in the domain name server need not point to a unique address, and a given IP address does not specify a Web site unambiguously. Thus, www.porn-company.com and www.safe-for-kids.com might share the

---

[18]As of October 26, 2001, this Web site presented a blank page. But it may not be blank in the future.

same IP address (e.g., 204.1.23.3), even though each of these names, when entered into a browser, would reach the correct sites. A list that designated 204.1.23.3 as containing inappropriate material would block both domain names.

Filtering by Textual Analysis

Filtering by textual analysis makes use of information retrieval representation technologies discussed in Section 2.2 and Appendix C. The basic concept is to examine all of the text that is on the site or page that is being considered (or in the search request), and to determine whether that text is indicative of inappropriate content.

The most naïve method of doing this is to compare the individual words of the text or request to a list of words that are strongly associated with inappropriate content. For example, the site might be deemed inappropriate if any of a number of keywords is found (e.g., "orgy," "cum," "bomb," "gun," "marijuana," and so on). When such words are found, access is blocked, or the site is flagged for possible inclusion on a black list.

However, many words have more than one meaning (for instance, "beaver" can have both sexual and nonsexual meanings); furthermore, the context in which words appear has a great effect on their appropriateness (for instance, the word "breast" can appear in a cancer information site, as opposed to an adult-oriented, sexually explicit site). More sophisticated text analysis techniques that are available to address these problems can, for instance, identify phrases (e.g., "beaver dams" or "breast cancer") in order to determine appropriateness more precisely.

Another method of textual analysis that is used for filtering is text classification or categorization (see Appendix C). This technique analyzes the text as a whole, taking account of such characteristics as frequency of occurrence of various words, co-occurrence of pairs or other combinations of words, and other statistical parameters of the text. Text classification is first applied to a so-called training collection of texts that are already known to be either appropriate or inappropriate, in order to discover regularities in the statistical properties of appropriate texts and inappropriate texts. The same technique is then applied to texts retrieved from the Web, and their statistical characteristics are used to classify them as either appropriate or inappropriate.

Filtering by Image Analysis

Almost all sexually explicit material on the Internet is associated with images. As indicated in Section 2.2 and Appendix C, analysis of images to determine if they are inappropriate is a very hard problem, if it is to be done accurately. Nevertheless, there are some techniques that can provide clues to the potential inappropriateness of an image.[19] For instance, it is possible to identify large expanses of what is likely to be flesh in an image, and it is also possible to determine whether an image is likely to be of one or more people. Also, it is possible to have a set of canonical or usual inappropriate images, against which images on a Web site can be compared. However, all of these techniques are highly error-prone and therefore are most often used in combination with other indicators of potential inappropriateness as described below.

Filtering by Labels

All Web pages have associated with them information that describes various characteristics of the page and that is typically hidden from the user. For example, HTML or XML tags within the body of a page can encode various rules that determine how information is structured on the page. This low-level information can be used to compare the page's structure against a set of structures commonly associated with inappropriate pages. At a somewhat higher level, Web sites have associated with them information about the site or page as a whole. Such metadata can be used to determine the appropriateness (or not) of a site. Metadata is not directly viewable by the user, a feature that has been exploited by many inappropriate (and even some appropriate) sites in order to bias search results toward themselves.

For instance, due to the nature of search engines, the more times a word that is used in a query appears in a site, the higher up in retrieval rankings that site will be placed. Thus, extended repetition of commonly used search terms in the metadata, which have no relationship to the actual content of the site itself, will result in that site's being retrieved and placed highly in the results when those terms are used.

This methodology can, however, also be used for filtering purposes, in the following ways. The terms in the metadata can be compared to the words in the text of the page, and if those in the metadata are markedly dissimilar from those in the page, that page is suspect. Also, the fact of unusual repetition of words in the metadata can be used as a clue for filtering.

---

[19]A brief summary concerning the technology of screening for sexually explicit images can be found in James Ze Wang, Jia Li, Gio Wiederhold, and Oscar Firschein, 1998, "System for Screening Objectionable Images," *Computer Communications Journal* 21(15): 1355-1360, and papers referenced therein.

The most straightforward method of labeling for filtering is labeling to indicate the nature of the content of the Web page or site. This can be accomplished either by third parties who label sites according to some established set of categories that indicate their content, or by the producer of the site. This is, in effect, the human version of the statistically based automatic text classification described above. The filter then works by establishing which categories of sites are allowed to be presented, reading the appropriate label in the metadata, and refusing all sites that are either on a black list of categories, or not on a white list.

A common framework for labeling is the Platform for Internet Content Selection (PICS—Box 2.6). In the domain of television, the V-chip is a filter that is based on labeling. (Movies and video games also have labels

---

Box 2.6
The Platform for Internet Content Selection

The Platform for Internet Content Selection (PICS) is a framework for the support of content-rating systems. PICS provides standards that facilitate self-rating and third-party rating of content. Self-rating is performed by the content providers, who label the content they create and distribute. Third-party rating enables multiple, independent labeling services to associate additional labels with content created and distributed by others. Services may devise their own labeling systems, and the same content may receive different labels from different services.

A content provider wishing to include a PICS-compliant label with its content first chooses a rating vocabulary to use, such as ICRA or RSAC-i. A provider will describe the content to be rated in terms of this vocabulary (usually generated by filling out an online questionnaire about that content). The output of that questionnaire is metadata with the appropriate, standardized, machine-readable descriptors, which is then placed into the metadata portion of a Web site. A third-party rater uses much the same process, except that the metadata is associated with the URL at which the content is found and placed into a database residing in a "label server."

PICS is part of a larger effort being managed by the World Wide Web Consortium on metadata, that is, data associated with Web content that represents information about that content in a way that is easy for machines to deal with. Metadata is intended to facilitate searching, helping authors to describe their documents in ways that search engines, browsers, and Web crawlers can understand.

SOURCE: See <http://www.w3.org/PICS>; Paul Resnick, 1997, "Filtering Information on the Internet," *Scientific American*, March; and Jim Miller and Paul Resnick, 1996, "PICS: Internet Access Controls Without Censorship," *Communications of the ACM* 39(10): 87-93. For opposing views on the desirability of PICS, see Simson Garfinkel, "Good Clean PICS: The Most Effective Censorship Technology the Net Has Ever Seen May Already Be Installed on Your Desktop," <http://hotwired.lycos.com/packet/garfinkel/97/05/index2a.html>; Lawrence Lessig, 1997, "Tyranny in the Infrastructure," *Wired* 5.07(July), <http://www.wired.com/wired/5.07/cyber_rights.html>; and Jonathan Weinberg, 1997, "Rating the Net," *Hastings Communication and Entertainment Law Journal* 19(2): 453.

(i.e., ratings) that often appear before a program is televised or a game is played, but these are not machine-readable. Further, these labels are intended to provide advice to consumers rather than to enable techno-logical denial.)

Filtering Using Combinations of Methods

All of the technologies of filtering that are discussed above have in-herent uncertainties associated with them, which lead them to make er-rors both of commission (misinterpreting a site as inappropriate) or omis-sion (not identifying an inappropriate site). However, the sources of error in each of the techniques are different. Thus, by combining the various techniques, the level of error can be reduced. For example, if image analysis indicates the high probability of a naked person but textual analy-sis does not indicate any of the words usually associated with adult-oriented material, analysis of the associated URL finds the domain .gov, and the metadata indicates that the owner of the site is the National Gallery of Art, the filter would be justified in predicting that the site should not be regarded as containing adult-oriented, sexually explicit material, despite the evidence from image analysis. Such methods show promise in improving filter performance.

Trade-offs in Filtering

As mentioned above, filtering is subject to two kinds of error: errors of commission, also known and referred to in this volume as Type I er-rors, or as *overblocking*, and errors of omission, also referred to as Type II errors, or *underblocking*. In the information retrieval literature (see Ap-pendix C), these kinds of errors are associated, respectively, with the performance measures of precision and recall. The first type of error—overblocking—occurs when a site that is appropriate is filtered, i.e., is deemed inappropriate and therefore denied to the user. The second type of error—underblocking—occurs when a site that is in fact inappropriate is deemed appropriate, and therefore permitted to the user.

Due to the nature of filtering, these two types of errors are inevitable. It is possible to adjust the method of filtering such that the occurrence of one type of error is reduced; however, reducing one type of error will always result in increasing the other type of error. For instance, one can reduce underblocking by setting the standard for what is inappropriate at a very low level (e.g., denying access to all sites or refusing all queries that contain the word "adult" or the word "sex"). This might result in many sexually explicit sites being successfully filtered, but it will clearly also result in a concomitant increase in overblocking, since many obviously appropriate sites will also be filtered.[20] In some settings (e.g., in doing research), it is desirable to minimize overblocking. In other settings (e.g., in households that are highly risk-averse), it is desirable to minimize underblocking. But it is not possible to minimize both simultaneously. Note also that even a low rate of overblocking will still cause a large number of pages to be blocked, simply because most of the content on the Web consists of innocuous content.

Quantitatively estimating the rates of these two types of errors, or the rate of success in blocking and not blocking, depends on knowledge (or estimation) of four numerical parameters, as indicated in Box 2.7.

Placement of Filters

Filters can be installed in a variety of places. Some ISPs use filters to screen the content they pass onto their subscribers. The major Internet browsers (Internet Explorer and Netscape) support label-based filtering. Some search engines provide users with the option to perform filtered searches. Third-party commercial software vendors sell stand-alone filters that can be installed on a personal computer or into a local area network serving an organization (e.g., a school or a library system). See Section 12.1.1 for a more detailed discussion of this issue.

2.3.2 Technologies for Authentication and Age Verification

The process of authentication involves assessing the validity of an assertion about the identity of a user.[21] (Note that a separate issue relates to the identification of a specific piece of software or hardware being used (Box 2.8). When only a specific individual is using that software or hardware, the authentication problem is reduced to that of identifying the specific software or hardware in use. But in general, multiple users of a given software or hardware system must be assumed.[22])

---

[20]This is a real example from a filtering system that was encountered at one of the site visits.

[21]In this report, the term "identity" is used in its colloquial sense, namely for the biological life form—the human being—in question. Security specialists often refer to identity more generally as a collection of information about an individual. For more discussion, see CSTB's forthcoming study on authentication technologies, with project information available at <http://www.cstb.org/web/projects/authentication>.

[22]For more discussion of authentication technologies, see Computer Science and Telecommunications Board, National Research Council, *Computers at Risk*, 1991; *Cryptography's Role in Securing the Information Society*, Kenneth W. Dam and Herbert S. Lin, eds., 1996; *Trust in Cyberspace*, 1999; and *Realizing the Potential of C4I: Fundamental Challenges*, 1999, all published by National Academy Press, Washington, D.C. CSTB's forthcoming study on authentication will address these technologies comprehensively (see footnote 21).

Box 2.7
Appropriate and Inappropriate Blocking

A given filter claims to work over a class of content. Examples of a class include "all Web content," "all content in a particular set of chat rooms," and "all e-mail headed for a particular set of inboxes." Classes for a filter can also be combinations of these things.

At a certain moment in time, let T be the total number of "content items" to which the particular filter could be applied. Break the number T into 4 parts, such that $A + B + C + D = T$, where A, B, C, and D are defined in the table below.

	Inappropriate	Appropriate
Blocked	A	B
Not blocked	C	D

The success of a filter in blocking inappropriate sites is measured by the ratio of A to $A + C$, and the success of a filter in not blocking appropriate sites is the ratio of D to $B + D$. Thus, a completely successful filter would have values of 1 for each of these ratios; that is, only inappropriate sites would be blocked, and all appropriate sites would not be blocked. A value of zero for each of these ratios indicates complete failure of the filter to block inappropriate sites and to not block appropriate sites, respectively. Put another way, the rate of underblocking is $C/(A + C)$, and the rate of overblocking is $B/(B + D)$, and a value of 1 for each indicates the complete failure of the filter with respect to each measure, and a value of zero indicates complete success.

Most filters are assessed against static content. In these cases, it is possible in principle to know the values of A, B, and C for any given filter, since inappropriate and appropriate sites that are blocked (A and B) can be identified, as can inappropriate sites that are not blocked (C). However, the value of D must always be only an estimate, since we cannot know exactly all of the appropriate sites that exist on the Internet. Thus, although the rate of underblocking can be empirically determined, the rate of overblocking can only be estimated.

(Note that filters whose parameters or rules are updated in real time (e.g., parameters or rules that are based on data gathered continuously by software watching the behavior of network users) can result in the numbers T, A, B, C, and D varying with time. In principle, filters can also use additional computing power to more precisely discriminate when traffic is modest, but fall back to less precise algorithms during periods of heavy traffic: T, A, B, C, and D would vary with time in this case as well.)

How should D, the number of not blocked appropriate pages, be estimated? A controversy over methodology was the subject of testimony to the committee. One approach is that the number of appropriate pages should be estimated on the basis of a random sampling of Web pages. A second approach is that the number should be estimated on the basis of actual usage, which weights certain popular Web pages more heavily than those not accessed as frequently. Note that computing the overblock rate in the first way increases it relative to the overblock rate computed in the second way.

For the purpose of determining the accessibility of information in general, the first approach is arguably better. For the purpose of determining the accessibility of information in practice, the second approach is arguably better. The reason that these two approaches are different is that the information needs of people—aggregated as a group—are not uniformly spread over the spectrum of information that the Internet provides. For this reason, someone looking at information needs of large groups in practice might well choose the second approach. However, the information needs of any given individual may not fall within "typical" search parameters—for those with non-typical information needs, the first approach may be more relevant.

Box 2.8
Specific Identification of Hardware and Software

In the earliest days of information technology, any given version of a chip or a software program was released to users in absolutely identical form—every circuit in User A's chip was identical to that in User B's chip, and every bit in User A's software program was identical to User B's software program.

For a variety of technical and business reasons, there is an increasing trend toward individual identification of chips and software. Thus, User A may purchase a computer using a processor with a serial number embedded in it, and readable electronically, and User B purchases an identical computer with an identical processor, but with a different serial number embedded in it.[1] Another example, which will become relevant below, is that every individual network interface card has associated with it a unique Media Access Control (MAC) address (a unique 48-bit number assigned by its manufacturer) that identifies the card in TCP/IP networks. Today's software often requires entering a serial number or authorization key (in the name of preventing piracy) in order for installation to proceed, and there is no particular reason that such a key cannot be embedded in documents or objects processed with that software.[2]

---

[1]For example, according to the Intel Corporation, a processor chip newer than the Pentium II processor (i.e., Pentium III and above) electronically embeds a processor serial number, which serves as an identifier for the processor, and, by association, the system of which it is a part. Though the default setting for the processor serial number is "off," it can be turned on through the use of software. Intel believes that system identification can enable certain benefits, such as authenticating participants in a secure chat room or ensuring security in e-commerce situations. For business users, processor serial number identification will allow information technology departments to provide better information management or improved management of corporate PC assets. See <http://support.intel.com/support/processors/pentiumiii/psu.htm> and <http://support.intel.com/support/processors/pentiumiii/psqa.htm#2>.

[2]See, for example, Greg Lefevre, 1999, "Microsoft's GUID Sparks Fears of Privacy Invasion," *CNN,* March 8. Available online at <http://www.cnn.com/TECH/computing/9903/08/microsoft.privacy.02/>.

In the physical world, the authentication process is conceptually straightforward because of face-to-face interactions. When an individual buying beer presents a driver's license to a liquor store clerk, the clerk can compare the picture on the license to the individual in front of him. Of course, the license could be phony, but the face-to-face nature of the interaction helps to ensure that the subject being compared to the credential is real.[23]

Such assurance is not available when a face-to-face interaction is not possible, as in the automated authentication of a user to a computer system.[24] Automated authentication depends on the prospective system user sharing with the authentication device something the person knows, has, or includes as a feature, such as a "smart card" belonging to the appropriate individual, a secret password, the individual's voice, or a biometric signature such as a fingerprint or retinal pattern.

Authentication is only one dimension of keeping children away from age-inappropriate materials. The second key element is that of ensuring that a user is older than some specified age (e.g., older than 17). While authentication involves assessing the validity of an assertion about the identity of a user, it does not speak directly to the issue of age verification. Assurance about age must, in general, be provided by reference to a document that provides information about it, and today's infrastructures needed to support online authentication of identity generally do not include such documents.

In the physical world, age verification can be provided as a part of the credential being presented—a driver's license generally has a date of birth

---

[23]Indeed, in the physical world, someone who presents a fake ID that is recognized as such by the clerk is subject to arrest.

[24]In principle, age verification could occur through the use of streaming video and audio. In this scenario, a Web camera and microphone located on the user's access point would be used to transmit a high-fidelity voice and video image to a human being working on behalf of the adult content provider. The human being (who might be called a cyberspace "bouncer") would ascertain the adult status from viewing the image and listening to the voice, and if there were any doubt, the bouncer would demand to see a driver's license that the alleged adult could hold up to the camera. Even through voice alone, a trained human verifier can often determine whether the person on the other end is in fact an adult, though this may not always work for very young adults. The human verifier asks questions, and then listens for tone of voice, composure, presence, stuttering, and other things that are not reflected in a typed textual interaction. Because adults tend to have more confidence and self-assurance than children, such voice interactions provide valuable distinguishing information. These scenarios are technically feasible even today, but are likely not to be economically attractive. The reason is that one of the major advantages of Internet commerce is the ability to drastically reduce the extent to which human beings are involved. Given that many adult-oriented Web sites operate on very thin margins, the cost of using such a mechanism would likely be prohibitive.

recorded on it. However, a driver's license would be just as good an authenticator of identity if it did not have the date of birth on it.

In an online environment, age verification is much more difficult because a pervasive nationally available infrastructure for this purpose is not available. One method is based on the fact that many adults (but not very many children) have credit cards—presentation of a valid credit card number is presumed to be an indicator that the presenter is an adult. Taken in the large, this is not a bad assumption—the vast majority of credit cards are in fact owned by adults, and the vast majority of minors do not own or have legitimate access to credit cards. Thus, an adult-oriented Web site that uses credit cards as its medium of exchange presumes that the presentation of a valid credit card also verifies that the card user is of legal age. Entering a valid credit card number grants access to the inside of the site.[25]

Many online adult verification services (AVSs), which provide a verification of adult status to other adult Web sites, also use credit cards.[26] Because the credit card is generally the user's method of payment for the service, the AVS relies on the credit card to verify the adult status of the user.[27]

Another approach to age verification is to rely upon databases of public records (i.e., government-issued documents such as voter registrations and/or drivers' licenses). For example, an individual wishing to gain access to an adults-only service sends an online request to an age verification service (along with a credit-card number to effect payment) for a certification of age for a given individual. He or she also provides appropriate personal information, and the adult verification service checks that information against public records such as state drivers' licenses and voting registration that contain or imply age information.

Even higher confidence in age verification can be obtained by coupling the use of public record databases to an authentication process that

---

[25]Determining with certainty whether a submitted credit card number corresponds to an account in good standing requires an online transaction between the site operator and the credit card company. That is, the site operator transmits the number to the credit card company and the company checks to see if the number refers to an account in good standing. There are other methods that allow the offline identification of some invalid credit card numbers, but they can be defeated with a little effort and sophistication.

[26]Such services also accept applications via 1-900 phone numbers (which children are not supposed to use without parental permission) that charge phone bills automatically and via U.S. mail. Mail applications are supposed to include proof of age.

[27]The "typical" adult verification service provides the user with a special code number. Adult Web sites contract with the service (of which many exist). A user wishing access to one of these adult Web sites enters the code number. The adult Web site then contacts the AVS to confirm that the number is valid, and if it is, grants the user access. (The adult Web site usually pays the AVS a commission for users who are verified in this manner.)

provides assurance of identity. In this case, when adult status is confirmed, a credential certifying one's adult status is mailed (via postal service) to the address of record on those public records. In this context, the postal service serves as an authenticating process that ensures the adult credential is sent to the right person. The individual can then use this special key to obtain access to adults-only services that recognize this special key.

A third approach is to use age verification scripts. An online script can guide a user through a questionnaire that asks, among other things, the user's age, and it can reject users who are underage. To help deal with the problem of lying about one's age, some scripts are written to accept only one attempt at entering age, and so a user who enters "15" at first, is rejected for being underage, and then tries to enter "20" is unsuccessful. In such cases, he or she may have to try again from another computer.

Note that each of these methods imposes a cost in convenience of use, and the magnitude of this cost rises as the confidence in age verification increases. Age verification scripts are very convenient for the legitimate adult user, who must simply tell the truth about his or her age. But they are also susceptible to being fooled by a savvy adolescent who knows that the correct age must be entered. A credit card is less convenient for the legitimate adult user, because he or she must be willing to incur the expense of a subscription (or the hassle of canceling one). However, since most credit cards are owned by adults, the use of a credit card provides additional confidence that it is truly an adult who is seeking to use it. At the same time, some minors do own credit cards or prepaid cards that function as credit cards, while other minors are willing to use credit cards borrowed with or without permission from their parents. (Even when parents review credit card statements, either their own or those of their children, they may not be able to identify transactions made with adult-oriented sexually explicit Web sites, as the adult nature of such transactions is often not readily identifiable from information provided on the statement.) Using public record databases to verify adult status provides additional confidence in age, but increases the amount of personal information that the user must provide to gain access. Mailing the certifying credential to the user provides the greatest confidence of all that the alleged adult is truly an adult, but because the user must wait for the processing and mailing of the adult credential, it is also the least convenient.

Claims have been made that certain "biometric" signatures can differentiate between adults and children. While human physiology does indeed dictate that certain changes in one's body occur as one grows from child to adult, the precise trajectory of these changes varies from individual to individual. However, one's legal status—as being entitled to privileges as an adult that are not enjoyed as a child—is fixed by laws that specify, for example, that individuals even one day over 18 are considered adults and one day under 18 are considered unemancipated minors. No technology today or on the horizon can hope to make such fine distinctions in the case of individuals.[28] For this reason, biometric technologies as a method for age verification are not considered here.

Age verification technologies as integrated into functional systems are discussed in greater detail in Chapter 13.

2.3.3 Encryption (and End-to-End Opacity)

Encryption is used to hide information from all but specific authorized parties. In the most general encryption process, an originator (the first party) creates a message intended for a recipient (the second party), protects (encrypts) it by a cryptographic process, and transmits it as ciphertext. The receiving party decrypts the received ciphertext message to reveal its true content, the plaintext. Anyone else (a third party) who wishes undetected and unauthorized access to the message must penetrate (by cryptanalysis) the protection afforded by the cryptographic process or obtain the relevant decryption key (or use another approach to obtain the key, such as bribing someone to reveal it).

Encryption also has relevance to the protection of digitized intellectual property, such as proprietary images. Because encryption restricts the access of unauthorized parties, encryption can be used to help prevent the dissemination of unauthorized reproductions of digital objects. Encryption is thus the fundamental technology underlying digital rights management systems (discussed in greater detail in Chapter 13). The use of encryption may increase dramatically in the coming years.

In the context of this study, the significance of encryption is that if content, whether acceptable or inappropriate, is encrypted properly, it cannot be identified by third parties. Thus, while it is possible to interdict *all* information flows that are encrypted, it is impossible to interdict specific transmissions on the basis of content—a point with obvious relevance to filtering systems intended to block specific content. Thus, encryption allows transmission and reception of information to occur with essentially no outside scrutiny possible.

---

[28]See, for example, testimony of John Woodward, senior policy analyst, RAND, to the COPA Commission on June 9, 2000. Available online at <http://www.copacommission.org/meetings/hearing1/woodward.test.pdf>.

2.3.4 Anonymizers

As noted in Section 2.1.2, the technology of the Internet itself does not generally require any party to authenticate its identity. Thus, users and online identities (e.g., a screen name or an e-mail address) are bound together through administrative procedures, usually those of an ISP, that are associated with gaining access to the Internet. Through such bindings, any interaction of an individual with an Internet-related service— whether visiting a Web page, sending an e-mail, posting a message, setting up a Web page, or participating in a chat room—is tied to a specific identity that can, in principle, be traced administratively back to that specific individual.

Anonymizers break this binding and decouple an individual from a specific online identity. The anonymizer provides what amounts to an identity that is randomly generated. This identity is then used for posting messages, sending e-mail, participating in chats, and accessing Web pages. (Some anonymizers enable return paths when necessary; for example, the recipient of an anonymous e-mail may wish to reply to the (anonymous) sender.) However, anyone seeking to trace the anonymized identity back to the original user will find a number of barriers that make it very difficult to recover the identity of the original user. One example of an anonymizer useful to publishing information on the Web is described in Box 2.9.

Anonymizers are significant because they enable individuals to undertake activities for which they need not suffer retribution. For an individual living in a totalitarian state, an anonymizer enables him or her to post an anti-government message in safety or to browse forbidden Web sites. In the United States, it enables someone to freely post a message expressing unpopular political views or to browse Web sites in privacy. Commercial enterprises—which need to have a way to accept money—do not have much use for anonymizers, even if they are posting materials that may be controversial. But those with non-commercial interests can use the same technology to anonymously post child pornography or harass or stalk an individual online. When anonymizers are used, tracing the identity of online criminal perpetrators becomes difficult.

2.3.5 Location Verification

The legal regimes of today are ones in which jurisdiction is based largely on geographical borders. For example, as noted in Chapter 4, "community standards" are an important factor in determining whether a given image is obscene. However, the Internet is designed and structured in such a way that geographical borders and the physical location of

---

Box 2.9
Publius: A System for Publishing Anonymously
on the World Wide Web

Publius is a Web publishing system that provides publishers with a high degree of anonymity. Publius encrypts digital content (say, a document) and then fragments this encrypted content for distribution among a number of Web servers (e.g., 100 servers) in such a way that the content can be reconstructed with a certain number of fragments (e.g., 35 fragments). Furthermore, any 35 fragments will do. However, someone possessing 34 or fewer fragments cannot reconstruct the original to *any* degree of fidelity. (In other words, having 34 fragments tells the owner nothing about the contents of the original document.) And, because of this encryption, the cooperating Web servers have no way of knowing what is being stored. Because the cooperation of multiple servers is needed to recreate the document, Publius thus breaks the one-to-one correspondence between a Web document that one might wish to protect and a server. Because any electronic payment today to a specific creator identifies the creator, Publius is difficult to use for pay-per-view sites. But for those who wish to distribute their work broadly and do not care about financial compensation, Publius has major advantages.

---

a user have no significance for the functionality he or she expects from the Internet or any resources to which he or she is connected. This fact raises the question of the extent to which a user's location can in fact be established.

One way to establish location is simply to ask the user where he or she is located upon logging in. Thus, the first screen seen by the user might ask for his or her present zip code (or state, or country). But in the event that the user chooses to be deceptive (e.g., to avoid restrictions on Internet service based on his or her location), the problem shifts to one of determining location through technological means.

Under some circumstances, it can be virtually impossible to determine the precise physical location of an Internet user. Consider, for example, the case of an individual connecting to the Internet through a dial-up modem. It is not an unreasonable assumption that the user is most likely in the region in which calls to the dial-up number are local, simply because it would be unnecessary for most people to incur long-distance calling costs for such connections. However, nothing prevents a user from using a long-distance telephone call (e.g., from Tennessee) to access a modem in California.

In practice, recovering location information is a complex and time-consuming process.[29] As a rule, the information needed to ascertain the geographic location of an IP address associated with a fixed (wired) Internet access point at a given time is known collectively by a number of administrative entities, and could be aggregated automatically. But there is no protocol in place to pass this information to relevant parties, and thus such aggregation is not done today.

The bottom line is that determining the physical location of most Internet users is a challenging task today, though this task is likely to be easier in the future. Appendix C provides additional discussion.

2.4 WHAT THE FUTURE MAY BRING

The hardest part of this report to calibrate is how the future will change the technologies that today scope both the problem and any putative solutions. As of this writing (May 2002), the World Wide Web is not even a decade old, while the creation and adoption rates for new technologies show generally accelerating deployments of these technologies.

The rapid changes of capability in the hardware underlying information technologies will lead to computing that is 100 times more cost-effective, storage 1,000 times more cost-effective, and bandwidth 10,000 times more cost-effective 10 years hence, and it is highly likely that many applications will emerge to take advantage of such increased capability, as has occurred in the past. What follows below is admittedly speculative, but even if any given speculation is far from the mark, taken together these notions paint a portrait of a very different technological milieu in which the age-old problem of "protecting children on the Internet" will play out in the future.

• Mechanisms for financial transactions will change significantly over the course of a decade. Financial transactions are likely to become increasingly less private, as the various forms of payment embody different features to enable traceability. Even cash may become more traceable in the future. This development will favor parents who wish to monitor the expenditures of their children, but will have no impact on those chil-

---

[29]While location information is not provided automatically from the IP addresses that an administrative entity allocates, some location information can be inferred. For example, if the administrative entity is an ISP, and the ISP is, for example, a French ISP, it is likely—though not certain—that most of the subscribers to a French ISP are located in France. Of course, a large French company using this ISP might well have branch offices in London, so the geographical correspondence between French ISP and Internet user will not always be valid for this case, though as a rule of thumb, it is not a bad working assumption.

dren who borrow electronic wallets at home or who access those sources of sexually explicit material that do not charge.

• Voice interaction with computers will become increasingly common, and the capability of computer-generated voices to sound like real people, or even parties known to an individual, will increase. Today, a 55-year-old man can pretend to be a 13-year-old girl using e-mail and instant messages; tomorrow, a 55-year-old man may be able to sound just like a 13-year-old girl over the telephone. It may even be possible for the same 55-year-old man to sound like the girl's mother. In short, technology will offer greater deceptive capabilities, and those that are most at risk from the existence of such capabilities are likely to be children who lack the experience to identify deception.

• Voice interaction will allow younger children, who would find typing difficult, to speak a Web site address to their computer.

• Peer-to-peer interactions will be increasingly common, as the technology will largely eliminate the need for large-scale servers, thus eliminating them as principal points of leverage for any control strategy. It already grows ever more expensive to selectively delete content than to keep it all, and this economic fact will dominate the future with implications for privacy, digital rights management, and the steady accumulation of data that is best described as digital detritus.

• Virtual reality advances will soon defeat the ability of even experts to distinguish pictures that are real from those that are synthetic. Haptic devices (i.e., touch-, motion-, and pressure-sensitive devices) may become more common as a way to interface with computers. Whether then a person, an action, or an event is real or not may soon be irrelevant to many consumers. Action, especially "action" in the sexual and violent sub-meanings of those words, will be as realistic as the audience is willing to pay for, and the prices of such offerings will inevitably drop.

• Locations from which access to the Internet is possible will proliferate wildly. And, with an expansion in the types of information resources that are accessible (e.g., new virtual reality resources), policies that give permission to view, access, modify, or delete any information resource will present an enormously complex problem simply as a result of scale. Even today, fine-grained access control driven by policy is, or soon will be, beyond the scope of human management and may be beyond the scope of mechanistic alternatives. If access control policies are impossible to formulate, the only alternative is an approach that depends on users to exercise self-control. Monitoring of user actions in order to ensure appropriately self-controlled users then becomes the only technical alternative to access control. This is not a statement about the desirability of this outcome, only that it is a possible one if access control policies become impractical.

Although the notions described above are not necessarily desirable from a societal or personal standpoint, they are extrapolations of certain phenomena today, and there are at least some paths from today that could result in their coming true. On the other hand, they may not come true, a point that emphasizes a vast range of uncertainty about the technological future.

What has been true over the years is that those who produce and consume sexual content—both for commercial and non-commercial purposes—have stayed on the leading edge of new technologies.[30] Thus, whatever the technological future is like in detail, it seems safe to predict with reasonably high confidence that sexual content will be disproportionately present in the initial stages of adoption of any new technology. Because technology changes rapidly, no final technological solutions are possible. It is for this reason, among others, that the committee in later chapters emphasizes social and educational strategies for protecting children from inappropriate sexually explicit material.

Finally, many of the issues associated with protecting children from inappropriate material and experiences on the Internet relate to the architecture of the Internet as it exists today, a state of existence that reflects policy and engineering decisions made decades ago. These are not immutable, though major changes that might facilitate control of content delivery could be made only at very considerable cost and at the potential expense of other societal interests.

---

[30]For example, the video cassette recorder, inexpensive video cameras, and CD-ROM technologies found some of their first applications in the production and viewing of sexually explicit "adult" movies and interactive sexual games and entertainment. For one perspective on this point, see Jonathan Coopersmith, 2000, "Pornography, Videotape, and the Internet," *IEEE Technology and Society* 19(1): 27-34.

3

The Adult Online
Entertainment Industry

While far from the only source of sexually explicit materials on the Internet, an important driver of public concerns about the access of children to pornography on the Internet is the online component of the adult entertainment industry (hereafter the adult online industry). Indeed, many of the canonical examples of exposure to pornography point to commercial sites as prominent purveyors of such material that minors can reach and see, and to a considerable extent, the fact that children can come across such material (with or without a deliberate choice on their part) results from the existence of an industry that caters to adult demand for such material. Material available online from these sources (and other non-commercial sources as well) includes images of heterosexual and homosexual intercourse (including penetration), fellatio, cunnilingus, masturbation, bestiality, sadomasochism, bondage, rape, incest, and so on.[1] For this reason, it is helpful to describe certain important characteristics of this industry.

---

[1]Legitimate online adult entertainment businesses are not generally providers of child pornography. However, one firm in the adult online industry that provided access to a range of sexually explicit materials was indicted and convicted on child pornography charges. See Lenny Savino, 2001, "Kid Porn Web Sites Lead to 100 Arrests: Investigation Targets Biggest Such Business Found in U.S.," *Detroit Free Press*, August 9, available online at <http://www.freep.com/news/nw/kids9_20010809.htm>. In addition, some adult entertainment Web sites do cater to viewers wishing to see young women in sexual poses (e.g., through advertising and site copy that promises "hot teens" and "young girls"), and because such content by assumption depicts young women in sexual poses, it is unclear from the images alone whether the young women depicted are in fact over 18 as required by law and merely look like they are younger, or if they are in fact underage.

3.1 THE STRUCTURE AND SCALE OF THE ONLINE ADULT ENTERTAINMENT INDUSTRY

The adult online industry in the United States generates approximately $1 billion in revenues annually,[2] and some in the industry expect this figure to grow to $5 billion to $7 billion over the next 5 years, barring unforeseen change. As the rest of this chapter discusses, revenues can come from a number of sources: paid subscriptions to the site, advertisements carried on the site, sending traffic to other sites, sale of sex-related products, and providing auxiliary services such as adult content search engines, content for other adult Web site operators, or age verification services. For purposes of this report, the term "commercial sources" should be understood to mean sites that charge a fee for access and sites that provide access to content for free but are supported by advertising revenues.

According to the best information available to the committee, subscription sites with adult content exceed 100,000 in the United States (with each site having multiple Web pages underneath it), and about 400,000 for-pay adult sites globally. The business entities responsible for these U.S. sites include about 1,000 U.S. firms operating as genuine business enterprises, with perhaps another 9,000 or so operating as (usually small-scale) affiliates of other established online adult entertainment firms.[3]

Compared to the totality of content on the public World Wide Web, adult-oriented sites account for a relatively small fraction (about 1.5 percent).[4] However, these sites account for a significant amount of Web traffic. According to industry statistics, approximately 70 million different individuals per week view at least one adult Web site on a global basis—20 million view adult pages that are apparently hosted on sites in

---

[2]The total size of the adult entertainment industry is not well known, and estimates range from $4 billion to $10 billion. See Frank Rich, 2001, "Naked Capitalists: There's No Business Like Porn Business," *The New York Times Magazine*, May 20; Emmanuelle Richard, 2001, "The Perils of Covering Porn," *Online Journalism Review*, July 10, available online at <http://ojr.usc.edu/content/story.cfm?request=608>; and Dan Ackman, "How Big Is Porn?," *Forbes.com*, available online at <http://forbes.com/2001/05/25/0524porn.html#story>.

[3]Numbers provided by Bill Johnson, director of marketing, Flying Crocodile Inc., interview, January 2001. An "affiliate" can be a separate business entity or can have an employee or consultant relationship to the primary firm.

[4]The first work in this area known to the committee is that of Steve Lawrence and C. Lee Giles, 1999, "Accessibility and Distribution of Information on the Web," *Nature* 400(6740): 107-109, July 8. (In fact, the Lawrence and Giles result of 1.5 percent holds for the number of *servers* found to be "pornographic" in nature. The statement in the text that adult-oriented *sites* are 1.5 percent of all sites is based on an assumption that on average, a server supports the same number of sites regardless of its content. This assumption is likely to be wrong in detail, but probably holds on average.) The results for sexually explicit information were substantially reproduced in Daniel Orr and Josephine Ferrigno-Stack, 2001, "Childproofing on the World Wide Web: A Survey of Adult Webservers," *Jurimetrics* 41(4, Summer): 465-475.

the United States or Canada. The number of paying subscribers is on the order of several million in the United States, and may be as high as 10 million. The majority of these viewers and subscribers are male,[5] though the fraction of female viewers may be growing. On average, a paid subscription generates $20 to $40 per month in revenue. The majority of subscribers cancel within a month, but of those who remain after a month, the typical retention time is approximately 3 to 4 months.

A profitable adult online business is often difficult to sustain over the long run, despite the high demand. The cost of entry into the business is relatively low, and the availability of a range of services from content provision to free Web site hosting and credit card transaction processing makes it easy to set up an adult Web site. However, because the market is highly saturated (i.e., for a Web site with any given sexual theme, there are likely to be a large number of competitors), and subscription prices more or less capped in price, the business is one with low margins.[6] Thus, profitable enterprises depend in large measure on drawing large volumes of traffic (in industry jargon, "eyeballs") in the hope of converting some of this traffic into revenue (i.e., customers paying for subscriptions). (Box 3.1 summarizes the primary methods used to increase traffic to one's Web site.)

For large firms in the adult online industry, the cost of bandwidth is a major element in their cost structure. Because its products are graphics-intensive, the adult online industry consumes enormous amounts of bandwidth—and the two largest individual buyers of bandwidth in the United States are firms in the adult online industry. However, it is also true that most bandwidth is used by viewers of these sites who do not pay for their use of these sites, because non-paying individuals can see large amounts of sexually explicit material simply by looking at the home pages of these sites, their free "teaser" pages, and their free demos.

The structure of the industry involves a relatively small number of large firms and a much larger number of smaller ones. The major firms (numbering 100 to 200) generate revenue from subscriptions and from providing content to other, smaller businesses. To increase traffic flow, these large firms also pay for traffic that is forwarded to them by other, smaller businesses. These other smaller businesses also receive content from these large firms to display on their own sites. The majority of adult Web pages have adult content that draws customers who can then be referred to another site (where they will encounter subscription offers).

---

[5]Alvin Cooper et al. 1999. "Sexuality on the Internet: From Sexual Exploration to Pathological Expression," *Professional Psychology: Research and Practice* 30(2, April): 154-164.

[6]Some in the adult industry have also argued that credit card fraud has forced many adult merchants to pay much higher credit card processing fees, thereby significantly reducing profit margins.

Box 3.1
Methods for Increasing Traffic to One's Adult Web Site

Online Methods

- Sending unsolicited e-mail ("spam") that advertises the site
- Placing advertisements for the site on other Web sites
- Paying search engine companies for more prominent placement in their search engine's results
- Acquiring domain names with sexually oriented words in them
- Acquiring domain names based on common misspellings of non-sexual Web site addresses
- Acquiring expired domain names that have acquired some reputation for generating traffic
- Paying other Web sites to obtain their exit traffic (otherwise known as mouse trapping)
- Mailing list subscriptions (for which a user must make an explicit "opt-in" choice)

Offline Methods

- Advertising in print media (e.g., an adult-oriented magazine)
- Advertising on TV and radio
- Advertising through cooperating partners (e.g., a store associated with adult entertainment)

3.2 THE GENERATION OF REVENUE

Revenue in the online adult entertainment business, as in other businesses both online and offline, results from the sale of products or services (including subscriptions) or advertising. The largest amounts of revenue are obtained from the end-user customer, who typically uses a credit card to subscribe to a site. As a subscriber, he obtains unlimited access, though the average subscriber only uses the subscription 1.5 times per month (one viewing session typically involves seeing around 75 to 100 pages).

The above models for revenue generation distinguish between adults and children on the basis of the ability to produce a credit card—adults, but not children, are presumed to be the legitimate owners of the credit card used. This assumption is not valid under all circumstances, but does not appear to be an unreasonable approach. However, home pages that serve as billboards for the sites' contents and the generation of revenue through the sale of advertising generally make no such attempt to differentiate between adults and children.

A Web site owner can also obtain revenue from advertisers. Advertisers can choose to simply pay for their ad to be displayed or pay each time a person clicks on their ad. When the ad is displayed the typical advertiser might pay the Web site owner (e.g., $3 per 1,000 displays of the ad—a CPM (cost per mille [thousand]) model). When the advertiser pays for the volume of referrals that the Web site sends to the advertiser (e.g., $0.05 for every user who clicks on the ad displayed and is then transferred to the advertiser's site), it is a CPC (cost per click) model. When the advertiser pays only if and when it gains a new subscriber as a result of the Web site's referrals to the advertiser (e.g., half of the first month's revenue for every subscription that results), it is a CPA (cost per acquisition) model. By contrast, the revenue model for traditional media advertising is most similar to the CPM model, because traditional media cannot track results from advertising to the same degree of precision that is possible on the Web.

A related service is providing consumer Internet traffic to another adult Web site in return for a small per-consumer fee. Such "traffic forwarding" is similar to the fees paid through CPC traffic referrals, except that the consumer is forwarded involuntarily (i.e., without an affirmative choice to be forwarded). This practice is known as "mousetrapping" (or "selling exit traffic" in the industry), and a mousetrapped user who tries to leave a sexually explicit site is automatically forwarded to another such site. This other site may be operated by a different operator, but that fact is irrelevant to the user who just wants to get out.[7] (Technically, mousetrapping refers to a process enabled by JavaScript (a scripting language for Internet browsers) in which the closing of one window automatically directs the user to another Web page. The second Web page can do the same, so that attempting to exit the second page spawns a third page, and so on.[8])

---

[7]Mousetrapping is a practice that often results in user panic, especially when the user is a child. Because the computer is for practical purposes to a non-expert disabled, the only solution available to the non-expert is often rebooting or pulling the plug, which can result in a loss of work and always costs time.

[8]Note that the technology underlying mousetrapping can have entirely legitimate purposes. For example, when a user leaves an e-shopping site, a questionnaire may appear that asks the user for feedback about his or her shopping experience. But in this instance, the user can leave the questionnaire with a single click. The problem with mousetrapping arises when many sites are mousetrapped in succession, so that the user is caught in a virtually endless sequence of new but undesired and unrequested pages and is forced to view each of them. Moreover, if all of these sites are operated by different parties, any regulatory action taken must be taken against each of the parties directing them to cease such practices simultaneously.

All of these payment schedules can be (and usually are) adjusted on the basis of the value of the user to the advertiser. For example, if the traffic sent to the advertiser is highly qualified (i.e., has a higher tendency to subscribe), the payment rate per ad-click might be $0.20 instead of $0.05. If the customer who subscribes to the advertiser's Web site stays more than 2 months, the Web site owner might receive a bonus of an additional 25 percent of the first month's revenue.

As a general rule, traffic with a higher proportion of children has less value to the advertiser, because the vast majority of children are unable to pay for subscriptions. So, advertisers have little incentive to attract children to their sites from the standpoint of obtaining paying customers. However, the incentives are different for the Web site owners who display ads. A Web site owner operating on a CPA model indeed has no particular incentive to send children to its advertisers. But a Web site owner operating on a CPM or CPC model is in a different situation. A display of an ad to a child counts in just the same way as its display to an adult, and the click of a child on an ad that transfers him to the advertiser's site counts in just the same way as an adult's click. Thus, a Web site owner operating on CPM or CPC models (which constitute the large majority of adult Web site owners) has few incentives to refrain from differentiating between adults and children.[9]

This is *not* to say that this is the only incentive operating. Because the Web site owner must negotiate a contract with the advertiser, who is very aware of the value of the traffic incoming from that site, the Web site owner must realize that the advertiser will offer lower commissions if the traffic being referred has low value. Thus, the Web site owner has incentives at the margin to refrain from distinguishing between children and adults, but also significant incentives to refrain from too high an overall percentage of children in the referred traffic.

Revenues from selling traffic to advertisers can be significant, especially if one uses some of the questionable means described in Box 3.1. For example, one firm employing some of these means allegedly earned between $800,000 and $1 million annually from selling traffic to advertisers whose ads were included on its Web sites.[10]

Subscriber retention is extremely difficult for these pay sites without a constant supply of fresh content that they must produce themselves or

---

[9]In principle, sponsors of "affiliate" programs bear the responsibility for policing affiliates that behave in an over-aggressive manner and promote their affiliate Web sites through the use of spam or other improper methods. In practice, some sponsors take this responsibility more seriously than others, and sanctions for improper promotion can range from non-existent to revocation of the affiliate relationship and withholding of payments that would otherwise be received for traffic.

[10]See <http://www.ftc.gov/opa/2001/10/cupcake.htm>.

license from providers. Even then, because sites have designs, styles, themes, and tastes that eventually become tiresome to the member, a high percentage of members leave after the first month, and even more leave after the first few months. But these customers don't give up on adult content. Effectively, they simply transfer their membership by canceling with one site and signing up at another until they become bored and move on again. Additionally, given increasing saturation of the market, margins have been shrinking dramatically for adult Internet businesses. For these reasons, the top sites are dependent on new subscribers far more than they are on recurring revenues from short-term existing members.

Five other business models based on providing services to the primary providers of adult-oriented sexually explicit material are worth noting:

- *Counters* are free services that offer businesses performance statistics, click paths and behaviors, browser technology data, and demographics on the visitors to individual sites. In exchange for the service, the site places on its pages an advertisement for the vendor's company, allowing visitors to click and visit the vendor's portal.[11] From there, the visitor may visit any site using the service, by selecting a link from the directory. The vendor makes money by selling advertising on the portal, and also by selling a portion of the incoming traffic to other adult companies.

- *Indexing services* provide end users with a map or index to the adult Web and receive revenue for forwarding traffic to these sites. For example, Flying Crocodile Inc. (FCI) provides both counters and indexing services. FCI generates more than 150 million impressions tracked per day by FCI. Approximately 20 percent of the large firms have advertising contracts with FCI at any one time. FCI's gross annual revenues are between $12 million and $15 million, and 60 million unique people per week visit the 70,000 sites (global) that contract with FCI.

- *Third-party billing processors* offer their services to adult Internet companies that may or may not have merchant accounts. Third-party billing also avoids potential embarrassment for users who wish to subscribe with some degree of privacy (since the name of the billing party rather than the adult Web site operator appears on the credit-card bill). These services manage the secure transaction processes, transfers of funds, debits, charges, telephone billing, and all associated record keeping for a per-transaction fee that is deducted from the revenues credited to the pay site owner.

---

[11]A portal is a "home base" from which a user may access a variety of content and services that the portal provides. Content may include sports scores, financial news, and headlines; services may include search engines, e-mail, and message boards.

• *Adult verification services* (AVSs) provide certification to adult Web site operators that an individual is an adult. As Chapter 4 discusses in greater detail, a user can provide a credit card number to an AVS (possession of a credit card is regarded as proof of adulthood). In return, he or she receives a special access code that can prove adulthood to all Web sites that use that particular AVS. Often AVSs are used by "free" adult Web sites, which receive a portion of the revenue generated by the AVS required for entry to those sites.

• *Content provision services* provide sexually explicit content to Web site operators that cannot produce their own content. Such content includes still images, videos, live sex chats, interactive videocamera sex shows, and so on.

3.3 PRACTICES RELATED TO MINORS

According to Nielsen/NetRatings, nearly 16 percent of the visitors to adult-oriented Web sites in February 2002 were under the age of 18.[12] One source in the adult industry asserted that traffic sent to some adult sites is 20 to 30 percent children.[13] These sites are usually sites that are intended to be broadly appealing to a wide variety of tastes (rather than those serving more specialized tastes). Even using current AVSs, adult sites receive traffic that is 5 percent children. That said, advances in AVSs and better screening may enable the industry to achieve traffic that is no more than 2 percent children.[14] In addition, sites offering highly specialized, niche products tend to have higher rates of traffic that ultimately purchases subscriptions (and hence lower fractions of children).

In a survey of adult-oriented commercial sites, the majority of adult-oriented sites (about 74 percent) were found to display adult content on the first page (accessible to anyone who visits the page), often through the display of sexually explicit banner ads to other sites. Nearly two thirds (66 percent) did not include a notice indicating the adult nature of the site, and only 11 percent included such a notice and also did not have adult content on the first page. About 25 percent employed practices that hin-

---

[12]Nielsen/NetRatings, February 2002. Nielsen/NetRatings provides Internet audience measurement data and analysis by monitoring actual click-by-click Internet user behavior through a real-time meter installed on the computers of more than 225,000 individuals in 29 countries worldwide. The meter is installed with the permission of the homeowner to record the relevant activities of users and includes an automated login to identify who the user is at specific times. Because the family specifies the ages of household users, the Web sites visited need not determine if the visitor is an adult or a child, a task whose difficulty is addressed in Chapter 2.

[13]Bill Johnson, FCI, 2001.

[14]Bill Johnson, FCI, 2001.

dered the user from leaving the site (e.g., mousetrapping), and only 3 percent required a credit card or other "adult check" to proceed past the first page of the site (that is, most sites allow the user to take a "free preview" in which some additional content is provided).[15]

3.4 WHAT THE FUTURE MAY HOLD

3.4.1 The Structural Evolution of the Industry

A commonly occurring development path in many industries is one of innovation, followed by imitation, and then by shakeout.[16]   In the innovation phase, one or a few parties find new ways to profit from innovation—they provide a previously unavailable product or service for which there is demand at prices that are sufficient to earn a profit. In the imitation phase, a host of other parties copy (perhaps with small variants) the ideas that enabled the first innovators to succeed. Imitation and the creation of "copycat" enterprises continue until the market is saturated and cannot support additional entries into the market. Shakeout is the result, in which a large number of firms (which may be the first innovators or the copycats) give up the business and others consolidate, resulting in a much smaller number of firms each with larger shares of the market. These larger firms are seriously in the business and are likely to adapt to new business circumstances (e.g., markets, regulatory environment) rather than to leave the business.

Since perhaps the mid-1990s (when the World Wide Web began to grow at a rapid rate), the proliferation of adult Web sites suggests that the adult online industry has been in an imitation phase. If the industry continues on the trajectory described above, a shakeout in the industry is likely to occur in the future. If so, the remaining firms are likely to demonstrate a higher degree of corporate responsibility—and that responsibility may well include more serious attempts at differentiating children from adults in giving access to their products and services.

3.4.2 Increased Regulation

What might a more "responsible" adult online industry involve? The following sketch is derived from conversations with representatives from businesses that are likely to become the more established responsible

---

[15]Daniel Orr and Josephine Ferrigno-Stack. 2001. "Childproofing on the World Wide Web: A Survey of Adult Webservers," *Jurimetrics* 41(4, Summer): 465-475.

[16]See, for example, F.M. Scherer and David Ross, 1990, *Industrial Market Structure and Economic Performance*, Houghton Mifflin, Boston, Mass.

citizens described above. Enterprises in this more responsible regime will not use stolen or illegal content, will refrain from the use of fraudulent and deceptive trade practices, will have effective means for preventing fraudulent use of credit cards, and will promote widespread use of AVS systems that prevent minors from being able to view sexually explicit "teaser" images. Noting that all schemes for protection of minors involve a trade-off between the need to inform a potential consumer of the content that is being offered against the risk of exposing minors to overly explicit material, home pages (i.e., the page accessible to users without going through an adult verification check) could contain textual descriptions only or some pictorial content that is obscured in the way that the cover of an adult magazine is obscured when displayed on the newsstand. Such magazine covers may contain suggestive images, but opaque plastic masks essentially everything except the head/face of the cover models. Such obscuration is much more complete than the token blurring that occurs on many adult Web sites covering just the genitals, but nevertheless providing a sense of what is inside. Furthermore, while greater regulation may not be desirable from the standpoint of the industry, responsible firms in the adult online industry appear to be willing to shoulder some regulatory burden as part of the cost of doing business to keep minors away from their services.

One potentially important development in the industry occurred in October 2000, when the Federal Trade Commission took action against seven major firms in the industry for unfair and deceptive trade practices (discussed in Chapter 4). A second occurred in October 2001 in which it took action against a party that used misspellings of common Web sites not oriented to adult entertainment to draw traffic and that engaged in "mousetrapping" of users.[17] A third occurred in November 2001, in which a number of adult entertainment firms on the Internet paid $30 million in fines in response to FTC charges that they illegally billed thousands of consumers for services that were advertised as "free" and billed other consumers who never visited the Web sites at all. In addition, the settlement bars the illegal practices in the future and requires that the defendants post a bond before they are allowed to continue to market adult entertainment on the Internet.[18] The long-term meaning of such actions for the industry is as yet unclear, but coupled with a new administration, it may suggest that the adult industry will be feeling increased pressure in the future. Such pressures may also include increased prosecutory efforts under obscenity statutes.

---

[17]See <http://www.ftc.gov/opa/2001/10/cupcake.htm>.
[18]See <http://www.ftc.gov/opa/2001/11/crescentstlmt.htm>.

There are many paths toward a more responsible industry. One involves, of course, law and regulation that prohibit or mandate certain kinds of behavior. However, since explicit regulation is often quite onerous, businesses in an industry that is subject to regulation may have strong incentives to self-regulate—that is, to adopt codes of behavior to ward off the threat of explicit regulation.[19] Whether self-regulation will characterize the path of the adult online industry remains to be seen, but it is likely to depend on the occurrence of a shakeout that leads to substantial consolidation in the industry and trade groups with influence over a sufficiently large number of individual firms in the business.

3.4.3 Future Products and Services

Today, the vast majority of online adult content consists of still images. The future will bring a greater emphasis on movie content and on streaming, live video content as high-speed Internet connections become generally available to consumers outside the workplace. In 2000, interactive content with live "tour guides" (i.e., a live narrator) was a business model that was being investigated in partnership by Live Entertainment Group and Flynt Digital Media. In addition, a greater degree of niche marketing is to be expected (as discussed below in Section 3.5). And, given the increasing popularity of computer-generated imagery of near-photographic quality, a mix of real and synthetic images may become more common in the future.

Content for transmittal to devices other than computers will become more common as well. For example, *Playboy* will soon begin to offer images for display on personal digital assistants (e.g., Palm Pilots).[20] Haptic (touch-sensitive) content is not yet, and may not be, a product pursued by the industry. However, a variety of companies manufacture products that are intended to provide a tactile counterpart to the visual sexual experience. These products are connected to a computer interface that controls the location, relative force, and degree of stimulation. Actions are initiated by a human being at some other location, by the user clicking on certain sections of a Web page, or even a digitally presented movie. The products include devices that are intended to stimulate a user's genitalia, realistic life-size dolls with computer-driven actuators in

---

[19]For a discussion of self-regulation within a broader statutory framework, see Computer Science and Telecommunications Board, National Research Council, 2001, *Global Networks and Local Values*, National Academy Press, Washington, D.C.

[20]See <http://computerworld.com/nlt/1 percent2C3590 percent2CNAV47_STO66802_NLTPM percent2C00.html>.

certain locations, and body suits capable of electronically stimulating a user's erogenous zones.[21]

Whether or not haptic content will become widely available in the near future is unclear, and a number of technological and economic barriers stand in the way; these barriers include technological complexity, lag times in haptic interactions, the difficulty of plausible haptic rendering of even simple sensations, and the daunting economics today of producing large numbers of small actuators.

3.5 INDUSTRY STRUCTURE, PRODUCT DIFFERENTIATION, AND AGGRESSIVE PROMOTION

According to testimony from representatives of the adult online industry, minors are not a focus of their marketing efforts. Indeed, they reported that because minors for the most part cannot purchase subscriptions, targeting minors would make no economic sense for them (and indeed would be a waste of resources).

Nevertheless, in a saturated market with many firms, there are strong incentives for firms to be increasingly aggressive in their marketing efforts (absent any counter-pressures). Thus, while the adult industry may not go out of its way to target minors, an aggressive marketing campaign on the Internet that seeks to exclude minors will be more expensive than one that is fully inclusive, and hence much of the adult industry does not make any particular effort to exclude minors from receiving or accessing its promotional materials, and exposing some children to its materials is an inevitable byproduct of its business practices. A firm that did make special efforts to exclude minors would place itself at a financial disadvantage because of the extra expense involved. It would also limit its adult audience to a greater degree than a firm that did not make such efforts, because any attempt to exclude minors would inevitably exclude some adults as well.

Such considerations are also likely to play a role in the evolution of the content offered by the industry. For example, the committee heard from well-established firms in the industry that noted that adult Web sites were becoming increasingly specialized to accommodate any imaginable sexual preference or taste (including those that might be regarded as more "extreme"), and that predicted that marketing to these various sexual "niches" would be the route to growth in the future. Indeed, it is possible to see intimations of this prediction today. One can find with reasonable ease sites whose sexual content depicts primarily older women, gay and lesbian

---

[21]A short survey of such devices can be found online at <http://www.stanford.edu/~ereyna/pornsite2/main.html>.

sex, women with large breasts, sex with animals, bondage, and anything else one might desire.[22] This phenomenon is explained by the incentives in a crowded market to differentiate one's particular Web site from all of the rest.

These comments should not be taken to imply that no adult Web site operator takes precautions against exposing minors to its products. On the contrary, there are a variety that do—and some of them testified to the committee. But the committee took testimony from and interviewed only individuals who represented well-established firms in the industry, and was unsuccessful in its attempts to hear from smaller "mom and pop" entrepreneurs. Even among these latter firms, there are some that do take such precautions. Nevertheless, the committee believes that a small-time entrepreneur is more likely than a well-established firm to fail to take such precautions.

Note also that the highly fragmented structure of the industry increases significantly the difficulty of successful self-regulation. Successful self-regulation is commonly associated with the existence of a small number of firms that control a very large fraction of the market and whose behavior can be coordinated in a reasonable manner. This condition does not apply to the adult online industry.

Finally, as in defining "inappropriate sexually explicit material," different people will have different definitions of actions that should count as "taking precautions." There are two aspects to the home page that a user sees when visiting a Web site. The first is content: some possibilities for site content include uncensored sexually explicit images; sexually explicit images with strategically placed blurrings or black spots; images that are merely suggestive but not sexually explicit; text that describes the content of the rest of the Web site; and/or text that tells the user to leave if he or she is a minor. The second is navigation: some possibilities include links that allow the user to see other pages on the site only with payment, links that allow the user to see some other pages on the site without payment, and/or links to other Web sites.

A site whose home page included uncensored sexually explicit images and links allowing the user to see other pages on the site without payment is clearly not taking precautions against minors viewing sexually explicit material—and there are many such sites available on the Internet. But there is a range of precautions that can be taken, and no objective standard for "what is enough." Some of these precautions include offering a text-only page describing the contents of the site in general terms and a warning that one must not be a minor to proceed further. However, nothing prevents a site taking such precautions from also providing free entry to sexually explicit imagery.

---

[22]Note that such specialization is not limited to sexual content.

4

Legal and Regulatory Issues

A variety of legal issues come into play in efforts to protect children from inappropriate sexually explicit material on the Internet. The U.S. Constitution, state and federal statutes, and regulations issued by executive branch agencies all play important roles. In addition, the threat of law and regulation can also push the regulated parties into taking un-mandated actions that they would not otherwise take.

4.1 THE FIRST AMENDMENT

4.1.1 First Principles

The First Amendment states that "Congress shall make no law abridging the freedom of speech or of the press." Through a complex process of constitutional amendment and judicial interpretation, over the past 150 years the Constitution has come to mean that "government shall make no law abridging the freedom of speech"—that is, the First Amendment restricts the actions not only of the Congress, but also of the President, the State of Montana, the city of Pittsburgh, the University of Nebraska, and police officers in Decatur.

On the other hand, like other provisions of the Constitution, the First Amendment restricts only the government. It does not restrict private individuals. Thus, a private individual cannot be said to unconstitutionally "abridge" another private individual's "freedom of speech and press." Only the government, or its agents, can be charged with violating the First Amendment.

To give meaning to the First Amendment, scholars have identified three primary reasons for giving constitutional protection to free expression.

First, freedom of speech and press is a necessary corollary of self-governance. In a self-governing society, it is the citizens and not the government who ultimately must decide on issues of public policy. To exercise this responsibility effectively, citizens must have access to the entire spectrum of information, opinions, and ideas, without interference from the government.

Second, in the words of Justice Oliver Wendell Holmes, "The best test of truth is the power of the thought to get itself accepted in the competition of the market." The idea here is that in all areas of decision making, reaching far beyond the political, and including such questions as whether to marry, or whether to have children, or whether to go to college—the best way of reaching the best decisions for both the individual and the community is to allow all ideas and opinions to contest in a free and open encounter, without interference from the government.

Third, freedom of expression is guaranteed as a means of ensuring individual self-fulfillment. The notion here is that, as, human beings, we have a fundamental need to speak our minds, to express our emotions and desires, and to create and to learn from one another. The constitutional protection of free expression is an essential adjunct of ensuring our common humanity and the opportunity for individual development.

These three bases for providing constitutional protection to the freedom of speech and press are not always consistent with one another and sometimes point in different directions. But, in very general terms, they state the primary values that the First Amendment is thought to serve.

Building on these values, the Supreme Court has identified several very basic principles that have shaped its interpretation and application of the First Amendment. Three such principles are most directly relevant to the issues of interest to this committee:

- First, the Supreme Court has held that the government cannot constitutionally restrict speech because the speech advocates ideas, opinions, or values that the government (or perhaps more accurately the majority of citizens) believe to be "wrong" or "improper." Thus, for example, the government cannot constitutionally prohibit speech calling for the legal repeal of the draft on the ground that such expression might persuade the public to vote unwisely to end the draft, even if the government profoundly believes that the draft is a good thing and that it is essential to our national welfare. The explanation here is simple: under the First Amendment, it is for the citizens themselves to make such decisions, after hearing all the arguments; it is not for the government—or for the majority—to prevent such decisions by shutting off debate.

• Second, the Court has generally held that, except in the most extraordinary circumstances, the government cannot constitutionally restrict speech because the ideas expressed might cause readers or listeners to engage in unlawful or otherwise socially undesirable conduct. For example, the government cannot prohibit opposition to the draft on the ground that such expression might cause others to refuse induction or even to blow up induction centers. Indeed, although the Court has often said that such speech can be restricted if it creates a "clear and present danger" of grave harm, in fact the Court has not upheld a governmental effort to restrict speech on this basis for some 50 years.

• Third, the Court has generally held that the second principle is inapplicable to specific categories of speech that the Court has defined as having only "low" First Amendment value. That is, as the Court explained some 60 years ago:[1]

> There are certain well defined and narrowly limited classes of speech, [such as the obscene and the libelous, that] are no essential part of any exposition of ideas and are of such slight social value as a step to truth that any benefit that may be derived from them is clearly outweighed by the social interest in order and morality.

For these categories of expression, which include not only the obscene and the libelous, but also fighting words, commercial advertising, express incitement, and threats, the Court has held that some forms of government regulation are permissible.

These are the three basic principles that most directly informed the committee's work. They are not exhaustive—they do not deal with a host of other First Amendment issues that are largely beyond the bounds of the committee's concern. But they helped frame most of the questions the committee considered concerning the regulation of sexually explicit materials on the Internet.

4.1.2 The First Amendment, Pornography, and Obscenity

How does the concept of "pornography" square with the First Amendment? It is important to note that there is a potentially confusing issue of terminology. Historically, the term "pornography" has been used in at least four different ways. First, the terms "obscenity" and "pornography" traditionally were used interchangeably. Second, beginning about 20 years ago, the term "pornography" began to be used by feminist scholars to refer to a concept quite distinct from the legal concept of "obscenity"; this feminist concept focused specifically on sexually explicit mate-

---

[1]*Chaplinsky v. New Hampshire*, 315 U.S. 568 (1942).

rial harmful to women. Third, there is the concept of child pornography, which deals with a very specific problem involving the abuse of children in order to make certain kinds of sexually explicit material. Fourth, the term "pornography" is often used as a catch-all synonym for the generic idea of "sexually explicit material," especially that intended to create sexual arousal. For the sake of clarity, it is important to note that the term "pornography" does not have a legal meaning under the First Amendment. To avoid confusion, the committee therefore focuses on the three distinct concepts of "obscenity," "child pornography," and "sexually explicit material."

How does the concept of "obscenity" square with the First Amendment? Throughout the first half of the 20th century, it was generally assumed that the First Amendment posed no barrier to the suppression of obscene expression. The assumption was that obscene expression is of only "low" First Amendment value and can therefore be regulated more readily than other forms of expression.

The Supreme Court did not have occasion to rule on the constitutionality of anti-obscenity legislation until its 1957 decision in *Roth v. United States*.[2] The Court reasoned as follows:

> All ideas having even the slightest redeeming social importance—unorthodox ideas, controversial ideas, even ideas hateful to the prevailing climate of opinion—have the full protection of the [First Amendment]. But implicit in the history of the First Amendment is the rejection of obscenity as utterly without redeeming social importance. Indeed, it is apparent that obscenity, like libel, is outside the protection intended for speech and press. Accordingly, obscene material may be suppressed without proof that it will create a clear and present danger of antisocial conduct.

"However, sex and obscenity," the Court continued,

> are not synonymous. Obscene material is material which deals with sex in a manner appealing to prurient interest. The portrayal of sex, for example in art, literature, and scientific works, is not itself sufficient reason to deny material constitutional protection. Sex, a great and mysterious motivating force in human life, has indisputably been a subject of absorbing interest to humankind though the ages; it is one of the vital problems of human interest and public concern. It is therefore essential that the standards for judging obscenity safeguard the protection of freedom of speech and press for material which does not treat sex in a manner appealing to prurient interest. The proper test is whether to the average person, applying contemporary community standards, the dom-

---

[2]354 U.S. 476 (1957).

inant theme of the material taken as a whole appeals to the prurient interest.

Thus, the specific holding of *Roth* was that if material meets the definition of obscenity, it is not protected by the First Amendment and may thus be restricted without any showing that its sale, exhibition, or distribution will cause any particular harm to any particular person.

For the next 17 years, the Court wrestled with the problem of refining the *Roth* definition of obscenity, which proved difficult because of its inherent subjectivity. It was in this era that Justice Potter Stewart offered his famous quip that "I can't define it [obscenity], but I know it when I see it." As Justice Stewart understood, this observation did not bode well for having a clear and consistently applied constitutional standard.

In 1973, the Court revisited the question. In *Miller v. California*,[3] the Court reaffirmed the idea that obscene expression is of such "low" constitutional value that it is outside the protection of the First Amendment. However, the Court redefined the concept as having three components. *Miller* concluded that, to be obscene, a work, taken as a whole, and judged by contemporary community standards, must appeal to the prurient interest in sex, must depict sexual conduct in a patently offensive manner, and must lack serious literary, artistic, political, and scientific value.

This definition has now been in place for the past quarter-century. Under this regime, and as community standards have tended to evolve toward a greater degree of acceptance of sexually oriented expression, it is generally thought today that only the most hard-core forms of sexually explicit material are sufficient to satisfy the constitutional definition of obscenity. As of this writing (May 2002), prosecutions for obscenity are rare though not unheard of at both the federal and local level.

Nonetheless, it remains the case that the government, consistent with the First Amendment as it has been interpreted, may prohibit the sale, exhibition, or distribution of obscene material, and there is no Constitutional obstacle to a more aggressive policy of prosecuting obscenity on the Internet, subject to the caveats below.

One caveat is the narrowness of the definition of obscenity, as described above. Moreover, enforcing an anti-obscenity prohibition on the Internet presents three additional problems. First, because the definition of obscenity turns on contemporary community standards, there is considerable uncertainty about how one defines the relevant "community" for purposes of the Internet. For example, if X creates a sexually explicit Web site in Amsterdam that Y views in St. Louis, what is the relevant

---

[3]413 U.S. 15 (1973).

community—Amsterdam? St. Louis? Is the "Internet" itself a "community" for these purposes?[4]

Second, there is often a tricky problem of assigning legal responsibility. For example, suppose X makes a threat over the telephone. Can AT&T be held responsible for this criminal use of its phone line? Because AT&T is legally a "common carrier," the answer is no. However, the same type of question can be asked about obscenity on the Internet. If X puts obscene material on a Web site that Y views through, say, America Online, can AOL be held legally responsible for X's conduct? For Internet service providers, the law is evolving in this area.[5]

Third, content transmitted through the Internet presents the issue of what counts as "work as a whole." In the physical world, the work as a whole would include a book, film, or magazine. In an online environment, is the "work as a whole" the Web page on which an image resides, or the entire Web site of which it is a part? No court cases have addressed this point to the best of the committee's knowledge.

4.1.3 The First Amendment and Protecting Children from Exposure to Sexually Explicit Material

As already noted, even if obscenity can constitutionally be prohibited on the Internet, this does not solve the broader problem of the exposure of children to sexually explicit material because of the very narrow definition of obscenity required by the Constitution. This raises the question of whether there are other steps the government can take, consistent with the First Amendment, to protect children from non-obscene, sexually explicit material.

In recognition of the special problems posed by the exposure of children to such material, the Supreme Court has recognized the concept of "variable obscenity." Thus, in its 1968 decision in *Ginsberg v. New York*,[6] the Court recognized that the "power of the state to control the conduct of

---

[4]Indeed, one of the primary challenges posed by the Internet is to the traditional association of geographical co location with the definition of community. To date, most constructions of "community" have, in practice, reduced to some kind of geographical delineation to identify the community in question.

[5]Some analysts argue, for example, that cyberspace calls for the creation of new law and legal institutions that apply specifically to it. See, for example, David R. Johnson and David G. Post, 1996, "Law and Borders—The Rise of Law in Cyberspace," *Stanford Law Review* 48: 1367. Others challenge this view, arguing that it underestimates the potential of traditional legal tools and technology to resolve the multijurisdictional regulatory problems implied by cyberspace. See, for example, Jack L. Goldsmith, 1998, "Against Cyberanarchy," *University of Chicago Law Review* 65(Fall): 1199.

[6]390 U.S. 629 (1968).

children reaches beyond the scope of its authority over adults," that the claim of parents "to direct the rearing of their children is basic in the structure of our society," and that the state "has an independent interest in the well-being of its youth." With these factors in mind, the Court held in *Ginsberg* that the government can constitutionally prohibit "the sale to minors . . . of material defined to be obscene on the basis of its appeal to them whether or not it would be obscene to adults." In other words, the government can prohibit children from having access to certain types of sexually explicit material that it cannot constitutionally ban for adults. (Recent legislation (e.g., the COPA, discussed below) defined such speech as "harmful to minors." In this report, the phrase "obscene with respect to minors" or "obscene for minors" is used interchangeably with "harmful to minors.")

Although this distinction compounds still further the problems of vagueness and subjectivity inherent in the very concept of obscenity—by now creating multiple definitions of obscenity—it is also a useful tool, for it is the doctrine of *variable* obscenity that enables the government constitutionally to prohibit minors from buying, renting, or viewing certain sexually explicit movies, magazines, or books that would not be obscene for adults.

The key limitation of this doctrine, however, is that it works best (perhaps only) in those situations in which it is possible to individuate the audience—that is, to separate the children from the adults. Thus, the doctrine of variable obscenity works reasonably well for movie theaters, video rental shops, and book stores, but not for television and radio. For in those latter means of communication, it is not as easy to separate the children from the adults. And as the Supreme Court recognized in its 1957 decision in *Butler v. Michigan*,[7] the government "may not reduce the adult population . . . to reading only what is fit for children."

To understand this precept, it is useful to consider several recent decisions of the Supreme Court. In *Sable Communications v. FCC*,[8] decided in 1989, the Court unanimously held unconstitutional a federal statute prohibiting "indecent" commercial telephone messages—so-called "dial-a-porn" services. The Court said that if the government wants to protect children in this context, it must do so by technical means rather than by a total ban on the transmission of such messages, for although some limited numbers of children might be able to defeat these devices, a prohibition would have the impermissible effect of "limiting the content of adult telephone conversations to that which is suitable for children to hear."

In *Reno v. ACLU*,[9] decided in 1997, the Court unanimously held unconstitutional the Communications Decency Act of 1996, which prohib-

---

[7]352 U.S. 380 (1957).
[8]492 U.S. 115 (1989).
[9]521 U.S. 844 (1997).

ited any person from making any "indecent" communication over the Internet with knowledge that a recipient might be under the age of 18. "Indecent" was defined in the statute as expression that "depicts or describes, in terms patently offensive as measured by contemporary community standards, sexual or excretory activities or organs."

Although acknowledging the importance of the government's interest "in protecting children from harmful materials," the Court reaffirmed that that "interest does not justify an unnecessarily broad suppression of speech addressed to adults," and that the government "may not reduce the adult population to only what is fit for children."

The Court suggested that the government should explore less speech restrictive means of serving this interest, such as requiring indecent material to be "tagged" in a way that facilitates parental control of material entering the home, exempting from regulation indecent messages with artistic or educational value, and perhaps regulating only some portions of the Internet—such as commercial Web sites—while leaving unregulated non-commercial uses of the Internet, such as chat rooms.

The lesson of these decisions[10] is this: outside the realm of speech that is constitutionally obscene, the government may not prohibit "indecent" or "offensive" or "sexually explicit" or "profane" speech on the Internet in order to protect children, unless the speech is obscene with respect to minors and government regulation does not unduly interfere with the rights of adults to have access to such material. The challenge is thus to

---

[10]See also the following Supreme Court cases. In *Cohen v. California*, 403 U.S. 15 (1971), the Court rejected the idea that profanity could be analogized to obscenity as a form of "low-value" speech and dismissed the notion that such language, which can serve a useful role in public debate, can be prohibited merely because it is offensive to others. In *FCC v. Pacifica Foundation*, 438 U.S. 726 (1978), the Court upheld the constitutionality of a Federal Communications Commission order that a radio station had impermissibly broadcast indecent material when it broadcast in the middle of the day a satirical monologue that involved [the] "seven words you cannot say on the public airwaves." In doing so, the Court suggested some latitude for the regulation of offensive but non-obscene speech in order to shield children, even at some intrusion on what otherwise would be the rights of adults. In *Erznoznik v. City of Jacksonville*, 422 U.S. 205 (1975), the Court held that a city could not constitutionally prohibit drive-in movie theaters whose screens were visible to the public from exhibiting movies that contain nudity, even if the goal was to protect children from exposure to such scenes. In *Denver Area v. FCC*, 422 U.S. 205 (1996), the Court held that the FCC could not constitutionally require cable operators to segregate "indecent" programming on a single, blocked channel and to unblock that channel only on a subscriber's written request. In *United States v. Playboy Entertainment*, 529 U.S. 803 (2000), 120 S. Ct. 1878 (2000), the Court held unconstitutional a provision of the 1996 Federal Telecommunications Act that required cable operators who provide channels devoted "primarily to sexually-oriented programming" either to limit their transmission of such channels to between 10:00 p.m. and 6:00 a.m. or to "fully scramble" those channels so that they cannot even inadvertently "bleed through" to those households that do not want them.

devise mechanisms that reconcile these two powerfully competing interests, where the Court has made clear the strong First Amendment presumption that the government's legitimate interests in protecting children will have to yield to the constitutional interests of adults, to the extent that those interests cannot otherwise be reconciled.

4.1.4 The First Amendment Rights of Minors

Because the First Amendment relates only to government action, children have no First Amendment rights against their parents. Thus, if a parent prevents a child from reading a book or watching a movie, the child cannot sue the parent for violating the First Amendment. But minors "are 'persons' under our Constitution. . . . possessed of fundamental rights which the State must respect"[11] and "are entitled to a significant measure of First Amendment protection."[12]

Moreover, a constitutional issue can arise if the government intrudes in the parent-child relationship. For example, if the government passed a law prohibiting any person from permitting a minor to view a movie that includes nudity without the written permission of the minor's parent, a court would likely hold such a law unconstitutional, at least as applied to older minors, and especially if the nudity were not further qualified. (Note, however, that materials deemed to be illegal—that is, to be child pornography or obscenity—do not enjoy First Amendment protection, either for adults or for minors. Thus, even if a minor has permission from his/her parents to obtain child pornography or obscenity, he or she does not have a First Amendment right to do so.)

It is important to note that the constitutionality of any particular regulation of the speech rights of minors may turn on the age of the particular minor in question. Indeed, as this report discusses in Chapter 5, minors range from 0 to 18 years old, and there are large developmental differences between an 8-year-old and a 17-year-old. The Supreme Court has held that "the strength of the Government's interest in protecting minors is not equally strong throughout the [age] coverage."[13] The constitutional rights of minors, including their First Amendment rights, get stronger as they grow older. As the Court has said, "constitutional rights do not

---

[11]*Tinker v. Des Moines Independent Community School District*, 393 U.S. 503, 511 (1969); see *Planned Parenthood v. Casey*, 505 U.S. 833, 899 (1992), parental consent statute must contain method by which minor can obtain abortion without parental consent; see *In re Gault*, 387 U.S. 1, 13 (1967), minors' right to criminal due process.

[12]*Erznoznik v. City of Jacksonville*, 422 U.S. 205, 212-213 (1975) (citation omitted).

[13]*Reno*, 521 U.S. at 878 (using examples of 17-year-olds); *American Booksellers Association v. Webb*, 919 F.2d 1493, 1504-05 (11th Cir. 1990); *American Booksellers Association v. Virginia*, 882 F.2d 125, 127 (4th Cir. 1989).

mature and come into being magically only when one attains the state-defined age of majority,"[14] and these rights ripen at different times and in different contexts.

The precise contours of the First Amendment rights of minors, even acknowledging that they may well vary with age and maturity, are uncertain. The Supreme Court has held that certain minors have constitutional rights in certain circumstances that trump a general deference to parental authority, for example, in the case of a mature minor seeking an abortion[15] or privacy rights about the use of contraception.[16] Further, it is arguable that mature minors have a First Amendment right to receive information relevant to the exercise of these substantive rights. Whether and in what circumstances a minor has a First Amendment right of access to adult-oriented entertainment Web sites remains an open question. But even if minors do not themselves have a constitutional right to access such material, the government cannot unduly burden the rights of adults to such material in order to keep it away from children.

4.1.5 The First Amendment and Child Pornography

Another facet of protecting children concerns the issue of child pornography. Here, the primary concern is not the exposure of children to sexually explicit material, but the use (or, possibly, the apparent use) of children to make such material. In *New York v. Ferber*,[17] the Supreme Court upheld the constitutionality of a state statute that prohibited any person from knowingly producing, promoting, directing, exhibiting, or selling any material depicting a "sexual performance" by a child under the age of 16. The statute defined "sexual performance" as any performance that includes "actual or simulated sexual intercourse, deviate sexual intercourse, sexual bestiality, masturbation, sado-masochistic abuse, or lewd exhibition of the genitals." The Court explained that, like obscenity, child pornography is of only "low" First Amendment value and that the "use of children" in such materials "is harmful to the physi-

---

[14]*Planned Parenthood of Central Missouri v. Danforth*, 428 U.S. 52, 71 (1976), minors' right to abortion.

[15]*Id*. at 640-3; *Planned Parenthood v. Casey*, 505 U.S. 833, 899 (1992); *Lambert v. Wicklund*, 520 U.S. 292 (1997).

[16]See *Carey v. Population Services International*, 431 U.S. 678 (1977) (plurality opinion). Although *Carey* was a plurality opinion, the holding that teenagers have privacy rights regarding procreation commanded five votes. See 431 U.S. at 681 (plurality opinion) (Justice Brennan, joined by Justices Stewart, Marshall, and Blackmun); *Id*. at 693, 702 (Justice White, concurring) (agreeing with plurality in result and including "with respect to Part IV" in which plurality recognized privacy interests of minors in contraception).

[17]458 U.S. 747 (1982).

ological, emotional, and mental health of the child." The Court added that, unlike obscenity, child pornography does not have to meet all of the requirements of *Miller*.

4.1.6 The First Amendment in Public Libraries

The general principles of the First Amendment are designed primarily for those circumstances in which the government attempts to regulate the free speech rights of individuals in the larger society. Those principles may apply differently in special contexts, such as public libraries and schools. In public libraries, for example, the government has limited resources. It cannot buy all books. It must therefore make choices. In making those choices, it inevitably must decide which books are most necessary and most appropriate for the particular collection. This gives the government, in the form of the library board or the librarian, the authority and the responsibility to make decisions based on content that it could not make in more general regulations of public discourse. For example, although the government cannot constitutionally prohibit all books on any subject but art history, it can constitutionally create a library dedicated only to art history. And although the government cannot constitutionally prohibit all books that are not appropriate for children, it can constitutionally create a library dedicated only to children's books.

On the other hand, even a public library is not free to engage in "viewpoint discrimination." For example, in *Board of Education of Island Trees Union Free School District v. Pico*,[18] the members of a public school board of education decided to remove from the school library certain books, including *Soul on Ice* by Eldridge Cleaver and *Slaughterhouse Five* by Kurt Vonnegut, because they were "improper fare for children." The board members described the books as "anti-American, anti-Christian, anti-Semitic, and just plain filthy." The Supreme Court held that this action would violate the First Amendment if the intent of the board members was to deny "access to ideas" with which they "disagreed."[19]

It should be noted that an important reason for granting a public library broad (but not absolute) discretion to decide which books to include in its collection is the fact of limited resources. This fact is not present in the same way in the Internet context. To the contrary, in the Internet context, where filters may be at issue, it will generally cost more

---

[18]457 U.S. 853 (1982).

[19]As a matter of legal precedent, *Pico* has specific relevance to public school libraries; however, the applicability of its logic to other settings such as public libraries has yet to be determined.

to reduce rather than to expand the "collection." It is unclear how this will affect the constitutional calculus.[20]

Another facet of the public library situation concerns the appropriate role of parents. For example, although a public library cannot constitutionally select which books it will make available to students on the basis of whether the library officials agree or disagree with the ideas presented in particular books, it presumably could decline to lend books to minors (at least younger minors) without parental permission, as long as the library acts in a content-neutral manner itself. That is, a library could insist on parental permission for younger minors to borrow any book from the library, but probably could not limit this requirement only to, for example, "racist" books or books about Scientology.

4.1.7 The First Amendment in Public Schools

In the context of public schools, the Supreme Court has expressly recognized, in *Tinker v. Des Moines School District*,[21] that neither "students nor teachers shed their constitutional rights to freedom of speech or expression at the schoolhouse gate." On the other hand, the Court has also recognized that, in light of "the special characteristics of the school environment," public school officials may restrict expression that would "materially and substantially interfere" with the core activities of the school. Thus, in *Bethel School District v. Fraser*,[22] the Court upheld a public high school's decision to discipline a student for using "vulgar and lewd speech" in a public assembly because such expression "would undermine the school's basic educational mission." Similarly, although a public school may not generally deny a student's right to speak or to access information on school grounds or through school facilities, it may restrict

---

[20]For example, in *Mainstream Loudon v. Board of Trustees of Loudon County*, 2 F. Supp. 783 (ED Va. 1998), the Court held invalid a public library's use of filters (for all patrons) as an unconstitutional prior restraint. More generally, opponents of filtering in public libraries have argued that the use of filters constitutes an unconstitutional prior restraint because the government is technologically preventing the censored material from even reaching potential users. They argue that this is prior restraint because the filter relies not on the threat of criminal punishment after the speech takes place, but on an actual blocking of the speech itself. For relevant Supreme Court decisions, see *Freedman v. Maryland*, 380 U.S. 51 (1965), holding that a movie censorship board that makes decisions about what may or may not be shown publicly is constitutionally permissible if the board is screening for obscenity, but only if the board is required immediately to go to court to obtain a prompt judicial determination that the movie is in fact obscene; and *Southeastern Promotions v. Conrad*, 420 U.S. 546 (1975), holding that a city manager would be required to abide by the *Freedman v. Maryland* requirements.

[21]393 U.S. 503 (1969).

[22]478 U.S. 675 (1986).

expression or access to information that "would undermine the school's basic educational mission," so long as school officials do not attempt to deny access to ideas because they disagree with them.

4.1.8 The First Amendment and the Commercial Advertising of Sexually Explicit Material

The Supreme Court has held that commercial advertising may in some circumstances be regulated more readily than other forms of expression. For example, the Court has permitted government to regulate such advertising when it is false or deceptive in circumstances in which similar regulation of political expression would not be permitted. The interesting—and open—question in this context is whether the government can constitutionally regulate or even prohibit the commercial advertising of constitutionally protected sexually explicit material. In general, the Court has suggested that such regulations would not be constitutionally permissible. In *Bolger v. Youngs Drug Products Corp.*,[23] for example, the Court held unconstitutional a federal statute prohibiting the mailing of unsolicited advertisements for contraceptives because the interest in shielding "recipients from materials that they are likely to find offensive" is not sufficiently substantial to justify the suppression of "protected speech."

This does not mean that all restrictions on the e-mailing of unsolicited commercial advertisements for sexually explicit Web sites would necessarily be unconstitutional. For example, such a restriction might arguably be distinguishable from *Bolger* if it focused specifically on material that is obscene for minors under *Ginsberg*. Moreover, a restriction on the e-mailing of *all* unsolicited commercial advertisements might be constitutional on the theory that it is justified not by the offensiveness of any particular material but because this practice has the potential to overwhelm electronic mailboxes and thus to discourage the use of this valuable means of communication.

4.2 RELEVANT STATUTES AND COMMON LAW

4.2.1 Federal Obscenity Statutes

Federal obscenity statutes restrict the use of computers and the Internet to distribute obscene materials.[24] Section 1465 of Title 18 of the U.S. Code prohibits the use of any means of interstate or foreign commerce or

---

[23]463 U.S. 60 (1983).
[24]Chapter 71 of Title 18 (Criminal Code) contains the federal obscenity statutes.

an interactive computer service to sell or distribute obscenity, and this prohibition applies to adults as well as to children. Section 1470 of Title 18 of the U.S. Code prohibits the use of any facility or means of interstate or foreign commerce to transfer obscene materials to someone under the age of 16 if the person knows that the recipient is under the age of 16. Whether material is within the restrictions of either of these statutes depends on whether a reasonable person in the community would interpret the work, taken as a whole, to appeal to the prurient interest; whether the work, as a whole, is patently offensive; and whether the work, as a whole and in context, lacks serious literary, artistic, political, or scientific value.[25]

4.2.2 Child Pornography Statutes

In general, Chapter 110 of Title 18 provides for civil and criminal penalties for the production, possession, distribution, and sale of child pornography. Historically, child pornography has been defined as a visual depiction involving the use of an individual under 18 engaging in sexually explicit conduct (18 U.S.C. 2256, Chapter 110).[26] The Child Pornography Prevention Act of 1996 (CPPA) amended this definition to include three additional elements: a visual depiction "that is or appears to be of a minor engaging in sexually explicit conduct," a visual depiction that "has been created, adapted, or modified to appear that an identifiable minor is engaging in sexually explicit conduct," or a visual depiction that is "advertised, promoted, presented, described, or distributed in such a manner that conveys the impression that the material is or contains a visual depiction of a minor engaging in sexually explicit conduct." The CPPA also expanded the definition of "distribution" or "receipt" of such depictions through interstate or foreign commerce to include computer channels.[27]

On April 16, 2002, the Supreme Court ruled that the provisions of the CPPA regarding the portion of the definition that refers to "appearing to be a minor engaging in sexually explicit conduct" were unconstitutional. Box 4.1 describes the Court's reasoning on this decision.

---

[25]*Eckstein v. Cullen*, 803 F. Supp. 1107 (ED Va. 1992).

[26]"Sexually explicit conduct" is defined as "actual or simulated sexual intercourse, including genital-genital, oral-genital, anal-genital, or oral-anal, whether between persons of the same or opposite sex; bestiality; masturbation; sadistic or masochistic abuse; or lascivious exhibition of the genitals or pubic area of any person."

[27]P.L. 104-208, Title 1, § 121(a), 110 Stat. 3009. The CPPA amends 18 U.S.C. § 2241, 18 U.S.C. § 2243, 18 U.S.C. § 2251, 18 U.S.C. § 2252, 18 U.S.C. § 2256, and 42 U.S.C § 2000(a) and adds 12 U.S.C. § 2252(a). In addition, the Sex Crimes Against Children Prevention Act of 1995 increases the base-level penalty for creating, distributing, or receiving visual depictions that show, or purport to show, minors engaging in sexually explicit conduct (P.L. 104-71, 28 U.S.C. § 994 nt). The act amends 18 U.S.C. § 2251(c)(1)(A) and 18 U.S.C. § 2252(a).

Box 4.1
Computer-Generated Child Pornography
and the Child Pornography Prevention Act

The Child Pornography Prevention Act of 1996 (CPPA) was enacted in part to address the challenges resulting from the technological advances in the computer-aided creation and production of visual images. In particular, the CPPA incorporated into the definition of child pornography "any visual depiction" that "appears to be of a minor engaging in sexually explicit conduct." Increasingly, graphics software packages and computer animation have the capability to create "virtual" images indistinguishable from photographic depictions of actual human beings—including fictitious children engaged in apparently sexual activity.

On April 16, 2002, in *Ashcroft v. Free Speech Coalition*, the Supreme Court held this part of the CPPA unconstitutional. The Court explained that "by prohibiting child pornography that does not depict an actual child, the statute goes beyond *Ferber*, which distinguished child pornography from other sexually explicit speech because of the State's interest in protecting the children exploited by the production process." The Court added that "the sexual abuse of a child is a most serious crime and an act repugnant to the moral instincts of a decent people." Thus, Congress "may pass valid laws to protect children from abuse, and it has." But "the prospect of crime . . . by itself does not justify laws suppressing protected speech."

The Court emphasized that "where the images are themselves the product of child sexual abuse, *Ferber* recognized that the State had an interest in stamping it out" because the "production of the work, not its content, was the target of the statute." "In contrast to the speech in *Ferber*, [the] CPPA prohibits speech that records no crime and creates no victims by its production. Virtual child pornography is not 'intrinsically related' to the sexual abuse of children, as were the materials in *Ferber*. While the Government asserts that the images can lead to actual instances of child abuse, the causal link is contingent and indirect. The harm does not necessarily follow from the speech, but depends upon some unquantified potential for subsequent criminal acts." The Court reaffirmed that "the mere tendency of speech to encourage unlawful acts is not a sufficient reason for banning it."

The Government also defended the CPPA on the ground that the existence of virtual child pornography will make it more difficult "to prosecute those who produce pornography by using real children" and that the "necessary solution" is to prohibit virtual as well as real child pornography. The Court rejected this argument, noting that "this analysis turns the First Amendment upside down. The Government may not suppress lawful speech as the means to suppress unlawful speech. Protected speech does not become unprotected merely because it resembles the latter."

Finally, the Court made clear that the CPPA does not deal with obscenity. As the Court explained, under *Miller v. California*, to establish that a work is obscene, "the Government must prove that the work, taken as a whole, appeals to the prurient interest, is patently offensive in light of community standards, and lacks serious literary, artistic, political, or scientific value." The Court noted that the CPPA contained none of the *Miller* requirements. In the Court's view, this was fatal, for although "the freedom of speech has its limits," the CPPA reached beyond the limits of permissible regulation.

Finally, the Child Protection and Obscenity Enforcement Act of 1988 and amendments of the Child Protection Restoration and Penalties Enhancement Act of 1990 added requirements associated with 18 U.S.C. 2257. These requirements call for certain parties in the adult entertainment industry to create and maintain records that allow law enforcement authorities to verify the names and birth dates of models and performers depicted in sexually explicit activity if such depictions were made after November 1, 1990. These requirements were developed in 1988 in response to the avoidance of prosecution by producers and distributors of child pornography through claims of ignorance regarding a model's true age.[28] The record-keeping requirements of 18 U.S.C. 2257 call for:

- Records to be maintained that indicate the legal name, stage names, and all other names used by a performer, and date of birth of each performer, obtained by the producer's examination of an appropriate identification document. For depictions made after May 26, 1992, a legible copy of the identification document examined (and a photo) are also required, and names must be indexed by the title or the identifying number of the depiction involved.
- Records to be categorized and retrievable by the name(s) of each performer and according to the title, number, or other similar identifier of the depiction in question.
- Records to be available at the producer's place of business, and made available for inspection to the Attorney General or his delegate for inspection at all reasonable times.

4.2.3 The Communications Decency Act

The Congress's first attempt to regulate children's access to sexually explicit materials on the Internet was the Communications Decency Act of 1996 (CDA).[29] The CDA, enacted as part of the Telecommunications Act of 1996, amended 47 U.S.C. § 223 to prohibit the use of an interactive computer service to send or display, in a manner available to those under the age of 18, any communication that describes or depicts sexual or excretory activities or organs in terms that are patently offensive as measured by contemporary community standards.

---

[28]The text of 18 U.S.C. 2257 and associated implementing regulations can be found online at <http://www.execpc.com/~xxxlaw/sec2257.html>.

[29]P.L. 104-104, Title V, 47 U.S.C.S. § 994 nt. The CDA was enacted on October 21, 1998.

The Supreme Court, reviewing the CDA, determined that the provisions of the CDA relating to the dissemination of indecent or patently offensive material to individuals under 18 violated the First Amendment.[30] The Court struck down these sections of the act as overbroad and unconstitutionally vague, reasoning that the restrictions chilled protected speech and unduly restricted adults' access to constitutionally protected materials.[31] The Court severed the provisions concerning obscene material because obscenity receives no protection under the First Amendment; thus, the obscenity provisions were found not to suffer from the same constitutional infirmities as the provisions regulating indecent speech.

Another aspect of the CDA that remains in force is protection for "Good Samaritan" blocking and screening of offensive material. Prior to the CDA, a service provider that filtered certain kinds of material (e.g., adult-oriented, sexually explicit material) might have incurred liability as a publisher if its filtering of such material was not perfect. (So, for example, an ISP that filtered could not be said to be acting in a "common carrier" mode, and thus might have incurred some liability for the content it made available to the end user.) The CDA provided that service providers could not be held liable on account of any action voluntarily taken in good faith to restrict access to or availability of material that the provider considers to be "obscene, lewd, lascivious, filthy, excessively violent, harassing, or otherwise objectionable, whether or not such material is constitutionally protected."[32]

One consequence of this provision in the CDA is that ISPs cannot be held liable for deciding to refrain from carrying Usenet newsgroups that are, in its judgment, obscene, lewd, lascivious, filthy, excessively violent, harassing, or otherwise objectionable.

One analyst further believes that another section of the CDA absolves schools and libraries of civil liability if students or patrons access inappropriate material. This analyst's reasoning is based on the fact that under the CDA, an "interactive computer service" cannot be treated as the publisher of any information provided by another information content provider, and further that libraries and schools are providers of interactive computer services.[33]

---

[30]*Reno v. ACLU*, 521 U.S. 844, 117 S. Ct. 2329, 138 L. Ed. 2d 874 (1997).

[31]*Reno v. ACLU*, 521 U.S. 844, 117 S. Ct. 2329, 138 L. Ed. 2d 874 (1997).

[32]47 U.S.C. 230.

[33]Nancy Willard (University of Oregon), the analyst, cites two cases in support of this view. First, in *Zeran v. America Online, Inc.* (129 F.3d 327 (4th Cir. 1997)), the Fourth Circuit Court of Appeals expressly held that "[b]y its plain language, §230 (a provision of the CDA) creates a federal immunity to any cause of action that would make service providers liable for information originating with a third-party user of the service." Second, in *Kathleen R. v. City of Livermore* (Cal. Ct. App., 1st App. Dist., A086349, 3/6/01), a mother of a teenage boy

4.2.4 The Child Online Protection Act

Congress's next attempt to regulate minors' access to sexually explicit material on the Internet was the Child Online Protection Act (COPA).[34] COPA amended 47 U.S.C. § 231 to prohibit the communication of material that is "harmful to minors" in interstate or foreign commerce by means of the World Wide Web if it is available to minors. Congress included provisions in COPA that were designed to remedy the problems identified by the Supreme Court in the CDA. Specifically:

- COPA defined a minor as one under the age of 17, whereas the CDA defined minors as individuals under the age of 18.
- COPA applied only to the World Wide Web, whereas the CDA applied to all communications over the entire Internet.
- COPA applied only to Web sites that exist for a commercial purpose, whereas the CDA applied to commercial and non-commercial sites alike. Under COPA, a commercial purpose is found if the site's operator or owner is "engaged in the business of making such communications." The phrase "engaged in the business" is defined as applying to "the person who makes a communication, or offers to make a communication, by means of the World Wide Web, that includes any material that is harmful to minors, devotes time, attention, or labor to such activities, as a regular course of such person's trade or business, with the objective of earning a profit as a result of such activities (although it is not necessary that the person make a profit or that the making or offering to make such communication be the person's sole or principal business or source of income)."[35]
- Whereas the CDA provided a vague definition of "indecent material," COPA restricts only material that is "harmful to minors"—that is, material that satisfies all three prongs of the *Miller*[36] test, as applied to minors. Thus, COPA restricts sexually explicit material only if (1) "the average person, applying contemporary community standards, would find, taking the material as a whole and with respect to minors, [that it] is designed to appeal to . . . the prurient interest"; (2) it "depicts, describes or represents, in a manner patently offensive with respect to minors, an

---

sued the library because her son had accessed sexually explicit pictures through the library's Internet service. The case was dismissed, and the dismissal was upheld in appellate court. The appellate court found that under the CDA, the library was an interactive service provider and was entitled to immunity, and noted that although the purpose of the CDA was to prevent minors from obtaining access to pornography, Congress made a deliberate policy choice not to subject those providing Internet access to tort liability.

[34]P.L. 105-227, Div. C, Title XIV, § 231. COPA was enacted on October 21, 1998.

[35]47 U.S.C. § 231(e)(2)(B).

[36]*Miller v. California*, 413 U.S. 15 (1973).

actual or simulated sexual act or sexual contact, an actual or simulated normal or perverted sexual act, or a lewd exhibition of the genitals or post-pubescent female breasts"; and (3) "taken as a whole, lacks serious literary, artistic, political or scientific value for minors."[37]

Both the CDA and COPA provide an affirmative defense to prosecution if the defendant, in good faith, took reasonable measures to restrict access to regulated material, such as requiring a credit card, debit account, adult access code, or adult personal identification number, or accepting a digital certificate that verifies age. (The use of age verification technologies is discussed in Chapter 13.)

As of this writing (May 2002), a preliminary injunction issued by the U.S. District Court of the Eastern District of Pennsylvania (and upheld in the U.S. Court of Appeals for the Third Circuit) currently prohibits the enforcement of COPA because the court found that the standard used to determine whether material is harmful to minors places an impermissible burden on protected speech.[38] The court explained that using community standards to assess the nature of material is inappropriate in the context of material on the Internet because Web publishers do not have the technological ability to restrict access to their sites on the basis of visitors' geographical location. Without this ability to restrict access on a geographical basis, Web publishers must publish only materials that would not be considered obscene for minors under the standards of the most restrictive community that might gain access to the material or subject themselves to potential liability if a viewer in a more restrictive community finds the material obscene. To avoid the liability that would be imposed by COPA, a Web publisher would have to publish only those materials that would not be considered obscene for minors by Internet users in the community with the most restrictive definition of obscenity.

The Supreme Court heard oral arguments on COPA in late November 2001 and is expected to render a decision by the summer of 2002.

Note added in proof: On May 13, 2002, the Supreme Court held that COPA's reliance on "community standards" to identify what material "is harmful to minors" did not by itself render the statute substantially overbroad for First Amendment purposes. However, it expressed no view as to whether COPA suffers from substantial overbreadth for reasons other than its use of community standards, whether the statute is unconstitutionally vague, or whether the statute survives strict scrutiny. It directed the U.S.

---

[37]47 U.S.C. § 231(e)(6).

[38]*ACLU v. Reno,* 31 F. Supp. 2d 473 (ED Pa. 1999). The Third Circuit Court of Appeals upheld this decision. *ACLU v. Reno,* 217 F. 3d 162 (3d Cir. 2000), *cert. granted, Ashcroft v. ACLU,* 121 S. Ct. 1997 (2001).

Court of Appeals for the Third Circuit to examine these issues, and left standing the preliminary injunction against COPA's enforcement absent further action by the lower courts.[39]

4.2.5 The Children's Internet Protection Act

In December 2000, Congress enacted the Children's Internet Protection Act (CIPA).[40] CIPA took effect on April 21, 2001. CIPA requires schools and libraries that receive federal funds for Internet access from the FCC's E-Rate program,[41] the Department of Education, or the Institute of Museum and Library Services to enforce a policy of Internet safety for minors that includes limiting the online activities of those under the age of 17 through the operation of a "technology protection measure" that "blocks or filters Internet access to visual depictions that are obscene, child pornography, or 'harmful to minors.'" Accordingly, public schools and public libraries that wish to receive these federal funds must install on computers that have Internet access a specific technology protection measure that blocks or filters access to child pornography, obscene materials, or material that is harmful to minors.[42] The technology protection measure must be operative with respect to obscenity and child pornography when adults are using those computers, and with respect to obscenity, child pornography, and material that is harmful to minors when minors are using those computers. (The CIPA also allows, but does not require, giving an authorized person the ability to disable the technology protection measure during any use by an adult to enable access for bona fide research or other lawful purpose.)

---

[39]*Ashcroft v. American Civil Liberties Union,* — U.S. — (2002).

[40]P.L. 106-554, § 1(a)(4), 114 Stat. 2763 (2001). A good summary of the provisions of CIPA can be found online at <http://www.cybertelecom.org/cda/cipatext.htm#1712>.

[41]The "E-rate" program was mandated by the Telecommunications Act of 1996. In that program, phone companies contribute to a fund that the FCC administers to help finance the wiring of K-12 public schools. The program has been important in enabling Internet access for many schools. For more information, see <http://www.sl.universalservice.org/>.

[42]One additional requirement placed on schools (but not on libraries) receiving federal funding for Internet access is that their policy of Internet safety must include monitoring the online activities of minors, though the tracking of Internet use by any identifiable minor or adult user is not required. Further, it is not clear whether technologies other than filters as defined in Chapter 12 will qualify as appropriate "technology protection measures"; some parties have advanced the argument that according to the principles of statutory construction, the use of the phrase "block or filter" rather than simply "block" means that a device that "filters" but does not "block" is consistent with the definition of "technology protection measure." Since CIPA does not provide a definition of the term "filter," at least one of these parties has argued that products that rely on the identification of inappropriate sites (filtering) but which also record access to those sites will be compliant (personal communication, Nancy Willard, University of Oregon).

Under CIPA, material is "harmful to minors" if

taken as a whole and with respect to minors, [it] appeals to a prurient
interest in nudity, sex, or excretion; depicts, describes or represents, in a
patently offensive way with respect to what is suitable for minors, an
actual or simulated normal or perverted sexual act, or a lewd exhibition
of the genitals, and taken as a whole, lacks serious literary, artistic, political or scientific value to minors.[43]

The American Civil Liberties Union and the American Library Association have both filed suit to challenge CIPA on First Amendment
grounds as the act is applied to libraries.[44]

Note added in proof: On May 31, 2002, a three-judge panel of the U.S.
District Court for the Eastern District of Pennsylvania entered a final
judgment declaring Sections 1712(a)(2) and 1721(b) of the Children's
Internet Protection Act (i.e., the provisions that required libraries receiving federal funds for Internet access to employ technology protection
measures) to be facially invalid under the First Amendment and perma-
nently enjoining the defendants from enforcing those provisions.[45] As of
June 13, it is unknown if the U.S. government will appeal the decision to
the Supreme Court.

4.2.6 The Children's Online Privacy Protection Act

The Children's Online Privacy Protection Act of 1998 (COPPA) prohibits the collection, maintenance, and use or disclosure[46] of personal
information[47] from children under the age of 13 on commercial Web sites
that are directed at children[48] or if the operator has actual knowledge that

---

[43]47 U.S.C. § 254(h)(7)(G) (2001).

[44]*Multnomah County Library v. United States.* No. 01-CV-1322 (ED Pa. 2001). Available
online at <http://www.aclu.org/court/multnomah.pdf>.

[45]See <http://www.paed.uscourts.gov/documents/opinions/02D0414P.HTM>.

[46]Disclosure of information means the release of personal information collected from a
child in identifiable form for any purpose, except where such information is used for internal purposes only and the operator does not disclose or use that information for any other
purpose, or making personal information collected from a child publicly available in identifiable form.

[47]For purposes of COPPA, personal information is "individually identifiable information
about an individual collected online, including: first and last name, a home or other physical address, an e-mail address, a telephone number, a social security number, anything that
the FTC determines permits the physical or online contacting of a specific individual, and
information concerning the child or the parents of the child that the Web site collects online
from the child and combines with any of the previously mentioned information."

[48]A Web site directed at children is a commercial Web site that is targeted to children or
the portion of a commercial site that is targeted to children.

the child is under 13, if the information is collected without notice and without verifiable parental consent.[49] COPPA provides that the site operator[50] must allow the parent to refuse to permit the operator's further or continued use, maintenance, or collection of information at any time. It further provides that the site operator may not condition participation in a game, a prize offer, or other activity on a disclosure of information where the information requested is more than necessary to participate in the activity. To ensure the effectiveness of these prohibitions, COPPA authorizes the Federal Trade Commission (FTC) to enact regulations concerning the method and content of the notification provisions and its parental consent provisions.

COPPA provides that a site that is directed at children and collects personal information, or any operator that knowingly collects information from a child, must provide notice on the Web site that discloses the type of information collected, how the operator uses the information collected, and the operator's disclosure practices. The FTC regulations adopted pursuant to COPPA require the operator to place the notice on the home page of the site, as well as at each area where personal information is collected.[51]

The FTC regulations further require that the notice be clearly and prominently displayed. A site that uses a link to the notice must ensure that the link is clearly distinguishable from other links. The FTC regulations also prescribe the necessary content of the notice, which must be clearly written and understandable (Box 4.2).

COPPA also requires the operator to obtain verifiable parental consent to the collection, maintenance, and use of personal information. Under COPPA, the operator must use "any reasonable effort" to ensure that a parent of a child receives notice of the operator's collection, maintenance, use, or disclosure of personal information and that a parent authorizes any collection, maintenance, use, or disclosure of his or her child's information before the information is collected from the child.[52]

The FTC has stated that, until April 2002, it will use a sliding scale to

---

[49]P.L. No. 105-277, Division C, Title XIII, 112 Stat. 2681, 15 U.S.C. § 650 nt. The act amends 15 U.S.C. § 41, et seq.

[50]For purposes of COPPA, a site operator is any person who operates a Web site and collects or maintains personal information from or about site visitors, or the person for whom the information is collected, if the site is operated for commercial purposes.

[51]*How to Comply with the Children's Online Privacy Protection Rule*, November 1999, available online at <http://www.ftc.gov/bcp/conline/pubs/buspubs/coppa.htm>.

[52]COPPA provides exceptions to the requirement that the operator obtain verifiable parental consent in certain circumstances.

Box 4.2
FTC Regulations Implementing the
Children's Online Privacy Protection Act

The privacy policy notice that must be displayed at a Web site that collects personal information from a child must include:

- The name and contact information for all operators collecting or maintaining information collected through the site;
- The type of personal information collected from the child, the method of collection, and how the operator uses the information collected;
- Whether the operator discloses the information to third parties; if so, the operator must also disclose the kinds of business that the third parties are engaged in, the general purposes the information is used for, and whether the third parties have agreed to maintain the confidentiality and security of the information;
- The parent's option to agree to the collection and use of the information without consenting to disclosure to third parties;
- A notice that the operator may not require the child to disclose more information than is reasonably necessary to participate in an activity as a condition of participation; and
- A notice that the parent can review the information provided by the child, can ask to have it deleted, and can refuse to allow any further collection or use of the child's information, as well as the procedures for the parent to do so.

The regulations make clear that the notice may not include unrelated or confusing materials.

SOURCE: Adapted from information available online at <http://www.ftc.gov/bcp/conline/pubs/buspubs/coppa.htm>.

---

assess the measures used to obtain verifiable parental consent.[53] Under the sliding-scale approach the required effectiveness of the method used depends upon the use that the operator makes of the information collected. If the information is only used internally for purposes such as marketing back to the child, the operator may use e-mail to obtain parental consent, as long as the operator also takes additional steps to increase the likelihood that the parent has, in fact, provided consent. However, if the information is disclosed to third parties or made publicly available, a more reliable method must be used to obtain parental consent. A more reliable method includes such measures as getting a signed form from the parent via facsimile or mail, accepting and verifying a credit card num-

---

[53]*How to Comply with the Children's Online Privacy Protection Rule*, November 1999, available online at <http://www.ftc.gov/bcp/conline/pubs/buspubs/coppa.htm>.

ber, taking calls from parents through a toll-free number, or accepting e-mails accompanied by a digital signature. COPPA also provides a safe harbor for Web site operators: an operator will be found to have satisfied the notice and the consent requirements if it is shown that the site implemented a set of self-regulatory guidelines issued by representatives of the marketing or online industries.

4.2.7 State Statutes

All states prohibit the production, sale, or exhibition of obscenity. A typical state law on this subject would incorporate the *Miller* definition, as applied to the community standards of the state. To regulate the distribution specifically to minors of sexually explicit material that does *not* meet the *Miller* test for obscenity, states have often used the phrase "harmful to minors," which derives from *Ginsberg*. For example, the California penal code Section 313 defines "harmful matter" as matter that, "taken as a whole, which to the average person, applying contemporary statewide standards, appeals to the prurient interest, and is matter which, taken as a whole, depicts or describes in a patently offensive way sexual conduct and which, taken as a whole, lacks serious literary, artistic, political, or scientific value for minors." For the remainder of this report, the term "harmful to minors" should be understood as meaning "obscene with respect to minors" (or equivalently, "obscene for minors"), as defined by the Supreme Court in *Ginsberg*.

4.2.8 Regulatory Efforts

The Federal Trade Commission

The Federal Trade Commission enforces the Federal Trade Commission Act (15 U.S.C. §§ 41-58) (the FTC Act), which prohibits deceptive or unfair acts or practices in commerce. A representation or practice is deceptive under the FTC Act if it is likely to mislead consumers acting reasonably under the circumstances and it is material, meaning that the representation or practice is likely to affect consumers' conduct or decisions with respect to the product or service at issue. An act or practice is unfair under the FTC Act if it causes or is likely to cause injury to consumers that is substantial, not outweighed by countervailing benefits to consumers or to competition, and not reasonably avoidable by consumers themselves. Practices within the adult entertainment industry may violate the FTC Act if they utilize deceptive or unfair methods that facilitate minors' access to adult content. In recent years, the FTC has brought eight law enforcement actions focusing on the deceptive or unfair use of new technology that has the effect of luring minors to sexually explicit material on the Internet.[54]

In one action, the FTC filed suit in September 1999 in the U.S. District Court for the Eastern District of Virginia against a number of companies for "page-jacking" and "mousetrapping" in a way that exposed users not seeking it to sexually explicit material.[55]

Page-jacking refers to a practice in which almost-exact copies are made of innocuous Web pages, including all the metadata that informs search engines about the subject matter of the site. These new pages differ from the original pages only in that they redirect a user coming to the new page to another Web site containing sexually explicit, adult-oriented material. Using the metadata, the sham copy of a legitimate Web site would be registered in the databases of search engines along with the legitimate Web site itself, but any user clicking on a search-engine-generated link to the sham copy would be directed to the adult Web site. In this case, the defendants located overseas produced look-alike versions of U.S.-based Web sites that were indexed by search engines. This process diverted unsuspecting consumers, including minors, to a sequence of pornography sites from which they could not easily exit, essentially "trapping" them at the site. The defendants cloned as many as 25 million Web pages, including kids' game sites and movie review sites.

The United States District Court for the Eastern District of Virginia granted a temporary injunction against these practices. Subsequently, one of the defendants settled out of court and agreed to refrain from undertaking such practices, and another was never located (though its actions have ceased).

In a second case, the FTC also took action against the use of executable dialer programs that hijack consumers' modems and connect them to adult sites. Companies advertising "free" adult images disconnected consumers from their local Internet service without their knowledge and reconnected them to long-distance lines, resulting in enormous telephone bills. Consumers victimized by this scheme included a substantial number of minors. The FTC obtained orders halting these schemes and providing redress for financial injury.[56]

In a third case, the FTC has targeted the deceptive use of unsolicited

---

[54]The FTC has a broad program of enforcement in the area of e-commerce and the Internet; the first FTC actions involving the Internet date to the mid-1990s. See <http://www.ftc.gov/bcp/menu-internet.htm>.

[55]*FTC v. Carlos Pereira d/b/a atariz.com*, No. 99-1367-A (ED Va. filed Sept. 14, 1999); press release available online at <http://www.ftc.gov/opa/1999/9909/atariz.htm>.

[56]*FTC v. RJB Telecom, Inc. et al.*, No. 002017 PHX (D. Az., filed Sept. 26, 2001); *FTC v. Ty Anderson et al.*, No. C 00-1843P (WD Wa., filed Oct. 27, 2000); *FTC v. Verity International, Ltd.*,

commercial e-mail to attract consumers, including minors, to adult enter-tainment. Defendants' e-mail messages advised each consumer contacted that his "order" had been received, that his credit card had been charged $250, and that he should call a specified number to cancel the order. This ploy deceived numerous consumers, including minors, into making ex-pensive international calls that connected to an audiotext entertainment service with sexual content. The FTC obtained a court order stopping the scheme and also obtained monetary redress for consumers.[57]

In addition to law enforcement action, the FTC is sometimes able to obtain modification of potentially deceptive practices through informal action. For example, one company set up an adult Web site with the domain name nasa.com, leading consumers to sexually explicit, adult-oriented sites, not the National Aeronautics and Space Administration (www.nasa.gov). At the request of FTC staff, the domain name registry Network Solutions Inc. immediately deactivated nasa.com. In October 2001, the FTC charged an online firm with the use of thousands of "copy-cat" Web addresses to divert Web users from their intended Internet destinations to one of its sites; in response, the United States District Court for the Eastern District of Pennsylvania in Philadelphia enjoined its activities pending further order of the court.[58] These copycat addresses were based on the use of domain names that are confusingly similar misspellings of domain names or famous marks of interest to children. (For example, the firm registered 15 variations of the popular children's cartoon site, <www.cartoonnetwork.com>, and 41 variations on the name of teen pop star, Britney Spears.) Users who misspelled a Web address were taken to the firm's Web sites, where they received a rapid series of advertisements for goods and services ranging from Internet gambling to pornography. Users seeking to leave one of these sites were also mouse-trapped.

FTC staff currently are investigating additional, potentially decep-tive, adult content industry practices that may target minors. These in-clude the use of domain names that are confusingly similar misspellings of domain names or famous marks of interest to children.

Finally, the FTC has launched what it describes as a crackdown on deceptive unsolicited commercial e-mail (also known as "spam").[59] In February 2002, seven defendants caught in an FTC sting operation agreed

No. 00 Civ. 7422 (LAK) (SDNY, filed Oct. 2, 2000); *FTC v. Sheinkin*, No. 00-CV-03636 (DSC, filed Nov. 11, 2000); *FTC v. Audiotex Connection, Inc.*, CV-97-0726 (EDNY, filed Feb. 13, 1997); Beylen Telecom, Ltd., No. C-3782 (court, final consent Jan. 23, 1998).

[57]*FTC v. Benoit*, No. 3:99 CV 181 (WDNC, filed May 11, 1999).

[58]See <http://www.ftc.gov/opa/2001/10/cupcake.htm>.

[59]See <http://www.ftc.gov/opa/2002/02/eileenspam1.htm>.

to settle charges that they were spamming consumers with deceptive chain letters. In addition, the FTC announced that it would mail warning letters to an additional 2,000+ individuals who were involved in this chain letter scheme. Further, the agency will launch a public/private education effort in conjunction with various Internet service provider associations. Though the spam in these cases did not involve adult-oriented, sexually explicit material, spam that does involve such materials is a source of many complaints regarding the exposure of children to inappropriate sexually explicit material.

The Federal Communications Commission

The Federal Communications Commission (FCC) has promulgated rules requiring all television sets with picture screens 13 inches or larger to be equipped with the V-chip, a technology that enables the blocking of the display of television programming based on its rating. (The rating is encoded in the program broadcast, and the V-chip blocks programs from the set based on the rating selected by the parent.) Ratings identify programming with sexual, violent, or other material parents may deem inappropriate (Box 4.3). However, despite much political support for the V-chip initiative, its use remains relatively uncommon in U.S. households. An Annenberg study, *Media in the Home*,[60] found that while 40 percent of parents have access to the V-chip or similar blocking technologies, only half of them use it. Only 50 percent of parents are aware of the content ratings associated with the V-chip, and only 10 percent can correctly identify the age ratings for programs watched by their children. (This survey also found that although parents are more concerned about children's television use than their use of any other medium, over half of the children surveyed (57 percent) had a television in their bedroom.)

The FCC has issued regulations governing practices in the pay-per-call industry, which includes dial-a-porn services. For example, FCC regulations require use of credit cards, access codes, or scrambling as ways to prevent minors from accessing such services.

The FCC is responsible for the development of guidelines for "indecent material" broadcast on the public airwaves. Such guidelines include definitions of indecency (such as the famous "seven dirty words"[61] or the description or depiction of sexual or excretory organs or activities in a

---

[60]*Media in the Home 2000: The Fifth Annual Survey of Parents and Children*, a national poll conducted for the Annenberg Public Policy Center of the University of Pennsylvania, Philadelphia, and released on June 26, 2000. Available online at <http://www.appcpenn.org/mediainhome/conference/report-39.pdf>.

[61]See footnote 10.

Box 4.3
V-chip Ratings

Rating Categories for Programs Designed Solely for Children

• TV-Y (All Children—This program is designed to be appropriate for all children.) Whether animated or live-action, the themes and elements in this program are specifically designed for a very young audience, including children from ages 2 to 6. This program is not expected to frighten younger children.

• TV-Y7 (Directed to Older Children—This program is designed for children age 7 and above.) It may be more appropriate for children who have acquired the developmental skills needed to distinguish between make-believe and reality. Themes and elements in this program may include mild fantasy or comedic violence, or may frighten children under the age of 7. Therefore, parents may wish to consider the suitability of this program for their very young children. Note: For those programs in which fantasy violence may be more intense or more combative than in other programs in this category, such programs will be designated TV-Y7-FV.

Rating Categories for Programs Designed for the Entire Audience

• TV-G (General Audience—Most parents would find this program suitable for all ages.) Although this rating does not signify a program designed specifically for children, most parents may let younger children watch this program unattended. The program contains little or no violence, no strong language, and little or no sexual dialog or situations.

• TV-PG (Parental Guidance Suggested—This program contains material that parents may find unsuitable for younger children.) Many parents may want to watch it with their younger children. The theme itself may call for parental guidance and/or the program contains one or more of the following: moderate violence (V), some sexual situations (S), infrequent coarse language (L), or some suggestive dialog (D).

• TV-14 (Parents Strongly Cautioned—This program contains some material that many parents would find unsuitable for children under 14 years of age.) Parents are strongly urged to exercise greater care in monitoring this program and are cautioned against letting children under the age of 14 watch unattended. This program contains one or more of the following: intense violence (V), intense sexual situations (S), strong coarse language (L), or intensely suggestive dialog (D).

• TV-MA (Mature Audience Only—This program is specifically designed to be viewed by adults and therefore may be unsuitable for children under the age of 17.) This program contains one or more of the following: graphic violence (V), explicit sexual activity (S), or crude indecent language (L).

SOURCE: Adapted from information available online at <http://www.vchipeducation.org/pages/under.html>.

manner that is patently offensive to an average viewer or listener) and regulations that prohibit broadcast of such material during times that children are likely to be listening or watching.

Finally, under the Children's Internet Protection Act, the FCC is responsible for promulgating and enforcing regulations to implement the CIPA.[62]

4.2.9 International Dimensions

Today, the Internet is a global medium that presents challenges to traditional systems of national governance that are based on the existence of geographical borders.[63] Because different nations have different sensitivities toward various types of material (e.g., hate, politics, sexually explicit materials), international consensus on an appropriate regulatory environment for materials on the Internet is hard (if not impossible) to obtain, and few attempts have been made to do so beyond the outlawing of child pornography.

Given this state of affairs, the behavior of foreign parties (e.g., content providers, ISPs, foreign citizens) is difficult to affect directly through the application of U.S. law. Nevertheless, foreign institutional parties (i.e., non-individual foreign players) often operate through the use of facilities and equipment subject to U.S. jurisdiction, and how the United States will be able to use this jurisdiction has yet to be seen.

4.3 LAW ENFORCEMENT, TRAINING, AND EDUCATION

The effectiveness of a statutory framework for regulating the access of minors to sexually explicit material depends on a number of factors. One factor, of course, is the extent to which it can withstand constitutional challenge. But assuming that it is constitutional, factors such as enforcement, training, and education are also relevant.

For example, testimony to the committee from the Department of Justice in October 2000 indicated that it was department policy to prosecute obscenity cases where major producers and major distribution of obscenity are involved, rather than local cases in which community standards are at issue. Moreover, the department's priorities at the time were to prosecute matters related to the production and online distribution of

---

[62]See <http://hraunfoss.fcc.gov/edocs_public/attachmatch/FCC-01-120A1.pdf>.

[63]For more discussion, see Computer Science and Telecommunications Board, National Research Council, 2001, *Global Networks and Local Values*, National Academy Press, Washington, D.C.

child pornography and the luring of minors into illegal sexual activity, with the consequence that federal obscenity prosecutions had declined significantly. This policy emphasis, as described, indicated a significant difference from the emphasis of the previous administration, which had prosecuted obscenity cases with greater vigor.

This is an important point. In the 1980s, the Department of Justice undertook an aggressive approach to the prosecution of obscenity. As noted in Chapter 3, many of the most graphic forms of sexually explicit material that can now readily be found on the Internet (including graphic depictions of sexual intercourse both heterosexual and homosexual, fellatio, cunnilingus, anal intercourse, incest, and bestiality) would have fallen within the prosecutorial policies of the Department of Justice in the 1980s.

By the mid-1990s, however, prosecutorial attention began to shift to concerns about child pornography and sexual predators of children. Because resource limitations inevitably constrain what investigators and prosecutors can do,[64] this shift of attention led to a substantial reduction at both the national and local levels in the number of prosecutions for the sale, production, or exhibition of traditional obscenity.

Today, the conventional wisdom seems to be that community standards about sexually explicit material may well have changed to the point that only the most hard-core depictions could any longer be classified as legally "obscene." But this is speculative. Because of the relative dearth of obscenity prosecutions in recent years, it is in fact impossible to say for certain that a more aggressive prosecutorial strategy directed at online "obscenity," as legally defined by the Supreme Court in *Miller*, could not have a significant impact on the availability of such material on the Internet. Whether the current state of affairs with respect to obscenity prosecutions is due to changes in community standards or a mere lack of prosecutions is an open question. (This point is discussed further in Section 9.1.)

Moreover, the concept of material that is "obscene for minors" has not been fully developed. Although this concept was recognized by the Supreme Court in *Ginsberg*, it has rarely been applied since. In *ACLU v. Reno*, the Court made clear that any effort to regulate such material must be careful not to interfere with the right of adults to gain access to material that is constitutionally protected for them. But with a more creative

---

[64]For example, pursuing an online sexual predator of children through a sting operation is a personnel-intensive enterprise. Because a sexual predator works slowly to build up a relationship of trust with his victims, law enforcement officials must operate in a similar fashion. Participating in such an enterprise is time-consuming. In any event, the number of potentially law-breaking interactions far outstrips any plausible enforcement efforts that could be made.

use of technology to develop effective and simple age verification processes, this concept could take on a more significant role in the future, at least with respect to commercial Web sites.

Another key implementation issue in law enforcement is interagency cooperation and citizen involvement. Jurisdiction for anti-obscenity and anti-child-pornography efforts is shared among the FBI, the U.S. Customs Service, and the U.S. Postal Service, as well as state and local law enforcement authorities. In addition, the National Center for Missing and Exploited Children (NCMEC) has responsibility for providing technical assistance and training to federal, state, and local law enforcement in identifying and investigating cases of child exploitation.

An example of bureaucratic impediments to coordination can be seen in the relationship of the NCMEC to law enforcement agencies. One of the NCMEC's functions is to take reports from the field on child pornography, provide analysis on these cases, and then relay those reports to law enforcement agencies of jurisdiction. To expedite law enforcement action in cases involving ongoing exploitation of a child (and hence calling for immediate intervention by law enforcement to prevent further exploitation), it is desirable that the NCMEC analysis forwarded to law enforcement agencies contain as much information as possible on the alleged perpetrator. Thus, the NCMEC, as a congressionally mandated quasi-law enforcement agency, would benefit from access to information in the FBI's CRS records systems, FBI investigative files, the National Crime Information Center (NCIC), the Interstate Identification Index system within the NCIC, the FBI's Sex Offender Data Base, state motor vehicle registration and drivers' license systems, the wanted-persons index within NCIC, and the National Law Enforcement Telecommunications System (NLETS). However, it does not currently have such access.

Finally, training is an issue. No case is brought unless a prosecutor is willing and able to bring such a case, and prosecutors and investigators vary in the knowledge and ability they bring to the enforcement of laws related to sexually explicit material. For example, a prosecutor must be familiar with the concept of "community standards" relevant and essential to a successful prosecution. In the United States, the NCMEC provides training to law enforcement agencies in all aspects of missing- and exploited-child cases. Training topics include child sexual exploitation investigations, responding to missing and exploited children cases, response planning, and policy development.

5

Children, Media, and Exposure to Sexually Explicit Material

5.1 CHILDREN AND HOW THEY USE MEDIA

The term "minors" spans an enormous developmental range. Specialists in child development distinguish between infancy, early childhood, childhood, preadolescence, early adolescence, and late adolescence. Table 5.1 summarizes some important characteristics of different age ranges.

As a general rule, young children do not have the cognitive skills needed to navigate the Internet independently. Knowledge of search strategies is limited if not nonexistent, and typing skills are undeveloped. These factors tend to limit young children's potential exposure to sexually explicit material on the Internet until about age 10, the transition from childhood to the preadolescent years.

The years between preadolescence and late adolescence can be turbulent times in which youth struggle to develop their own identities. They are eager to be heard, seen, and taken seriously but often lack the experience and maturity to make responsible choices consistently. They test boundaries in developing their emerging adult personalities, and they take risks that adults would deem unwise. They are often socially uncertain, and they value peer approval highly. And, in pre- and early adolescence, hormonal changes generally stimulate their interest in sexual matters. Because of the intensely personal nature of such matters (both sexual and social), the "at-a-distance" nature of Internet communication and the anonymity with which one can seek out a great variety

TABLE 5.1 Some Important Dimensions of Child Development

Age	Characteristics
Infancy (0-2)	• Preverbal and early language skills emerging • Lacks framework for assimilating and understanding sexual concepts • Information needs can generally be met by primary care givers and others in child's immediate environment
Early Childhood (3-5)	• Finds it difficult to distinguish between fantasy and reality; is more easily frightened by "scary things" • Continues to lack cognitive framework for assimilating and understanding sexual concepts, though sexual behavior such as masturbation may occur • Information needs can generally be met by those in child's environment and easily accessible resources such as children's books • Begins to have empathy for others
Childhood (6-9)	• Increasing ability to distinguish between fantasy and reality • Typing and writing skills emerging, but poor at younger ages (e.g., misspellings common) • Decision-making skills on the Internet (as in many areas of life) not well developed • Some emerging information needs require reference books and other materials to support research
Preadolescence (10-12)	• Much better ability to distinguish between fantasy and reality • Better able to use inferential reasoning skills • Decision-making skills developing in more abstract way due to metamemory skills (knowing about knowing, knowing how to know, i.e., strategy) • Typing and spelling skills still problematic • Sexual development beginning for many or at least for their peers; sexuality becoming more interesting; likely a sensitive period for exposure to sexual content • Information needs expanding and increasingly require materials that are not in the immediate physical environment
Early adolescence (13-15)	• Abstract cognitive skills in place that are the same ones that adults have, though skill set not fully developed • Decision-making skills and reasoning skills better developed than in preadolescence, but often impulsive; faith in own decision-making skills (especially in the face of parental positions) may well exceed actual skill • Age of puberty, growing awareness of sexual development and highly curious about his or her own sexuality; some become sexually active with intercourse; most will have some kind of sexual experience (e.g., kissing) • Information needs are broader and relate to the world at large, and the availability of some external sources is important

(continues)

TABLE 5.1 continued

Age	Characteristics
Late adolescence (16-18)	• Highly aware personally of sexual issues and may well be sexually active (80 percent have intercourse by age 20; the mean age of first intercourse is approximately 17 ½ years today) • Decision-making skills and reasoning ability improved over early adolescence • Physically and cognitively mature • Legal rights approaching those of adults, though rights may vary by state • Historically, many were married and having children at this age • Information needs extensive in scope and depth and commonly require access to a wide range of resources beyond the individuals in their immediate environment

of information on the Internet are highly appealing to very social but also sensitive individuals.

Note also that adolescence is a cultural invention—in earlier times, people aged 13 and 14 were regarded as small adults. Children and teenagers had jobs. Many older minors (minors by today's standards) were getting married, having sex, and raising their families. Put another way, these older minors had the rights and the responsibilities of adulthood. Also, there is some debate in the scientific literature about how rebellious adolescents are. For example, even in later adolescence, youth often agree with their parents on very important decisions such as where to go to college. The storm-and-stress view of adolescents is tied to particular theoretical views, namely Erikson's psychoanalytic theory, but not so much to social learning theory, which argues for more continuity in development.

American youth from preadolescence to late adolescence are also intense consumers of various media. As do other individuals, youth use media—including the Internet—for a variety of purposes, for example, news, education, entertainment, information, stimulation, relief from boredom, and emotional arousal. Media use is heavy among adolescents, with television, music, teen magazines, and movies as well as the Internet and video games being important elements.

Television use tends to peak at about age 12 and decreases during middle and late adolescence, and use of other media—music, music videos, magazines, and the Internet—increases during this period. Further, there are some gender differences and differences of socioeconomic status

(SES). Adolescent girls read teen magazines and watch soap operas more than boys do, while boys play video games and watch television more than girls do. Lower SES tends to correlate with more watching of entertainment television,[1] and African Americans watch more television than other Americans, even when SES is controlled for.[2] Children and adolescents also prefer watching programs with characters from their own ethnic group.[3]

American adolescents use various forms of media primarily because of their entertainment value. But media use also helps to socialize adolescents into various adult roles and relationships, contributes to the formation of their individual identities as adolescents, provides assistance in coping with their problems and emotional mood states, and helps to assimilate them into various youth subcultures. For example, private, solitary use of both music and television by adolescents is important in providing them an opportunity to deal with the stress and intense emotions of this stage of development. Teen girls use their bedrooms to read magazines, watch television, listen to music, do their homework, and talk on the phone. For such girls, the bedroom is a place where they use media to help them make sense of themselves and their lives. Preference for certain kinds of music and films helps to connect youth from across the country and the world into a common youth subculture. In short, media are part of the process by which adolescents acquire, or resist acquiring, the behaviors and beliefs of the social world and the adult culture in which they live.

Most children's media use—including time on the computer and online—does not involve parental supervision. Many children have radios, CD players, a television, and even a computer in their rooms. As a result, many parents are not in a position to monitor their children's media activity, nor can they readily provide any feedback or support for children's online activities.

The Kaiser Family Foundation's report *Kids and Media at the New Millennium: A Comprehensive National Analysis of Children's Media Use* (1999) described the children's media landscape, identifying how much time

---

[1]A.C. Huston and J.C. Wright. 1997. "Mass Media and Children's Development." Pp. 999-1058 in *Handbook of Child Psychology*, 5th Ed., Vol. 4, W. Damon, I. Sigel, and K. Renniger, eds. Wiley, New York.

[2]G. Comstock, 1991, *Television and the American Child*, Academic Press, Orlando, Fla.; J. Condry, 1989, *The Psychology of Television*, Erlbaum, Hillsdale, N.J.; and Huston and Wright, 1997, "Mass Media and Children's Development."

[3]J.E. Brand and B.S. Greenberg. 1994. "Minorities and the Mass Media: 1970's to 1990's." Pp. 273-314 in *Media Effects: Advances in Theory and Research*, J. Bryant and D. Zillmann, eds. Erlbaum, Hillsdale, N.J.

young people spend with media and what types of media draw their attention. The average child spends about 5.5 hours daily using media, including television, radio, CDs, or the computer. Young people often use more than one type of media at the same time (e.g., listening to a CD while surfing the Internet) which means that children do a lot of parallel processing in their media use. Children aged 8 to 14 tend to spend more hours using media than do teens aged 14 to 18. This is likely because of the busier and more diverse schedules of older teens.[4]

Perhaps surprisingly, time using the computer in all venues averaged only 31 minutes per day for children aged 8 to 18, with only a portion of that time devoted to online and Internet activities. Television, by far, was still the most commonly used form of media, and this age group had the television on an average of 3.25 hours per day. In this study 62 percent of children had a computer at home. Of families living in affluent communities in which the community income averaged above $40,000, 81 percent had computers compared to 49 percent of families in communities with an average income under $25,000. Schools seemed to mitigate some of these differences, often providing access for children who did not have a personal computer in their homes.[5]

Of the 31 minutes spent on the computer in recreation, children used the computer primarily for games but did spend some time in chat rooms, sending e-mail, and surfing Web sites. Of the group of children who reported using the computer the previous day, games occupied the majority of their recreational time online. The 8- to 13-year-olds using a computer in the previous day logged the longest average recreation times on the computer (over 1 hour), spending 32 minutes playing games, 14 minutes looking at Web sites, 11 minutes in chat rooms, and 8 minutes sending e-mails.[6] Note also that time spent online may increase in the future as the result of two factors: a greater dependence on Web-based information sources and more interaction with online electronic devices (e.g., Nintendo games) that are not online today.

The amount of time children spend using computers and going online is likely to increase as computer use continues to penetrate homes and schools. For example, a 2002 survey by the National Telecommunications and Information Administration found that 89.5 percent of all children aged 5 to 17 use computers, and 58.5 percent of all those children use the

---

[4]Donald F. Roberts, Ulla G. Foehr, Victoria J. Rideout, and Mollyann Brodie. 1999. *Kids and Media at the New Millennium: A Comprehensive National Analysis of Children's Media Use.* The Henry J. Kaiser Family Foundation, Menlo Park, Calif.

[5]Roberts et al., 1999, *Kids and Media at the New Millennium.*

[6]Roberts et al., 1999, *Kids and Media at the New Millennium.*

Internet.[7] The report also found that Internet use is particularly high for teens and preteens (75.6 percent of 14- to 17-year-olds and 65.4 percent of 10- to 13-year-olds, up from 51.2 and 39.2 percent, respectively, in 1998). Furthermore, computer usage (and possibly Internet usage as well) varies by age: in one national survey, 26 percent of 2- to 7-year-olds reported using a computer out of school the day before compared to 44 percent of 14- to 18-year-olds.[8]

According to a survey by Grunwald Associates, family decisions to purchase computers and to obtain Internet access were based on parental perceptions of their children's educational needs.[9] While children and youth are most likely to use the Internet for schoolwork, an important (and large) percentage of their online time is spent for other purposes, including e-mail, chat, and entertainment.[10] A report by the Pew Internet and American Life Project found that about half of regular Internet users of any age (an estimated 52 million) use the Internet for information on health issues such as diseases, clinical trials, treatment, and nutrition, as well as for assistance in making health-related decisions.[11] According to the Kaiser Family Foundation, about two out of three young people (aged 15-24) have used the Internet to search for health information, and 25 percent say they get "a lot" of health information online.[12] These data suggest that the Internet is of great use to adolescents seeking health-related information (including information related to sexual health).

5.2 SEXUALITY IN CULTURE

This report is concerned with the protection of children from inappropriate sexually explicit material on the Internet. But children share a cultural space with adults, and so it is helpful to understand a contempo-

---

[7]National Telecommunications and Information Administration. 2002. *A Nation Online: How Americans Are Expanding Their Use of the Internet.* U.S. Department of Commerce, Washington, D.C. Available online at <http://www.ntia.doc.gov/ntiahome/dn/html/anationonline2.htm>.

[8]Roberts et al., 1999, *Kids and Media at the New Millennium.*

[9]See <http://cyberatlas.internet.com/big_picture/demographics/article/0,,5901_390941, 00.html> for a summary of the Grunwald study. The full study is available online at <http://www.grunwald.com/survey/index.htm>.

[10]National Telecommunications and Information Administration, 2002, *A Nation Online.*

[11]Susannah Fox and Lee Rainie. 2000. *The Online Health Care Revolution: How the Web Helps Americans Take Better Care of Themselves.* Pew Internet and American Life Project, November. Available online at <http://www.pewinternet.org/reports/pdfs/PIP_Health_Report.pdf>.

[12]Victoria Rideout. 2001. *Generation Rx.com: How Young People Use the Internet for Health Information.* The Henry J. Kaiser Family Foundation, Menlo Park, Calif. Available online at <http://www.kff.org/content/2001/20011211a/GenerationRx.pdf>.

rary society in which sexual images and references are common. Media images of sexuality abound, and the children of today are exposed to a wide range of images through many media, including entertainment television (especially sitcom and dramatic programming in prime-time broadcasts, soap operas, music videos, and talk shows), magazines, advertising, film and movies, and news.[13]

• In prime-time broadcast television, references to heterosexual intercourse have increased and have become much more explicit in the last 20 years. The dominant messages of these references suggest that sexual behavior typically takes place between two adults who are not married to each other and that sexual intercourse does not have the consequences with which intercourse may be associated in real life (e.g., pregnancy, sexually transmitted diseases). Talk about sex is more common than the depiction of sex, and sexual intercourse is often implied by context and partial nudity rather than being portrayed explicitly (that is, with full nudity) on the screen. Some programs on cable networks—especially programs carried late at night—often push the envelope further.

• Movies (many of them R-rated, and usually available in theaters, on pay-TV channels, and in video rentals) contain more frequent and more explicit portrayals of sexual behavior than broadcast TV. As in TV, the most frequent sexual activity shown is unmarried sexual intercourse. Sex is often depicted in the context of profanity, alcohol and drug use, and nudity. And sex is often mixed with violence in an attempt to seek further commercial success.

• Newsstands routinely carry adult magazines whose imagery ranges from that depicting simple frontal nudity to very graphic, sexually explicit acts.

• Soap operas have a long history in broadcast entertainment. The sexual behavior portrayed usually involves unmarried sexual intercourse and extended and passionate kissing, with prostitution, rape, petting, and homosexuality occurring less often. Discussions and portrayals of safe sex and contraception are infrequent, though recent soap operas appear to refer increasingly to "taking sexual precautions" and have focused more on pregnancy, both wanted and unwanted, than in previous years.

• Music videos are increasingly common, and many of the visual elements are implicitly or explicitly sexual. These videos often combine sexuality with violence or aggression, and with objectification and sex-

---

[13]Material in the list below has been adapted from Aletha C. Huston, Ellen Wartella, and Edward Donnerstein, 1998, *Measuring the Effects of Sexual Content in the Media: A Report to the Kaiser Family Foundation*, The Henry J. Kaiser Family Foundation, Menlo Park, Calif. Available online at <http://www.kff.org/content/archive/1389/>.

role stereotyping. Visual presentations of sexual activity are common, and a majority of music videos containing violence also contain sexual imagery. Rap music is particularly explicit about both sex and violence; MTV frequently shows combinations of aggression, sex-role stereotypes, and sexual imagery; country music videos also use sexual images, but common themes include breakups and divorce, dating, and romantic love.

• Informational magazines are an important source of information about sex, birth control, and sexually transmitted diseases for many teens, especially teen girls. A significant fraction of the sexual content in teen magazines is devoted to sexual health, with other topics including a focus on decision making about becoming sexually active. Magazines incorporate a substantial amount of information about sexual issues into their articles and serve as an important source of information for young readers.

Although sexual images and behavior are common in the media described above, most of those media generally do not portray sexually explicit material involving full frontal nudity. Rather, they are important elements of a culture at large that seems to accept such portrayals of sexuality.

On the other hand, media portrayals of easy and loose sexuality are not generally reflected in the actual sexual behavior of Americans, and in fact the statistics on actual sexual behavior have changed far less over the last 30 years than media portrayals of sexual behavior. For example, Americans do have more sexual partners in their personal histories than they had two decades ago; nevertheless, most Americans report that in the past year they had zero or one sexual partner. The reason for this phenomenon seems to be that on average, Americans are marrying later but are nevertheless engaging in monogamous sexual activity prior to marriage.[14]

Although 80 percent of individuals have intercourse by age 20, the mean age of first intercourse has dropped only from age 18 for those born in the period from 1933 to 1942 to age 17 1/2 years for those born two and three decades later. Furthermore, teenagers have intercourse only sporadically during the teen years. For example, 19-year-old men surveyed in 1978 had sex on average four times in the past 4 weeks, while a comparable group surveyed in 1988 had sex three times in the past 4 weeks.[15]

---

[14]Robert T. Michael et al. 1995. *Sex in America: A Definitive Survey.* Warner Books, pp. 88-91. *Sex in America: A Definitive Survey* is based on a scholarly volume by Edward O. Laumann et al., 1995, *The Social Organization of Sexuality: Sexual Practices in the United States,* University of Chicago Press.

[15]Michael et al., 1995, *Sex in America,* p. 94.

5.3   THE ROLE OF MEDIA IN PROVIDING INFORMATION ON SEXUALITY TO YOUTH[16]

It is hardly news that adolescents are very interested in matters of a sexual nature and, beginning in early adolescence, go through a developmental process in which they begin to look for information on sex and their bodies as they begin to develop a sense of themselves as sexual beings.

Most people would agree that in an ideal world, young people would seek out their parents for information on sexuality. Parents and children would be able to talk about sex, sexuality, and relationships in a mutually respectful manner in an atmosphere of shared values. In this world, children could raise questions without fear and parents could answer them without embarrassment, anger, or apprehension.

However, in practice, parents are often reluctant to talk to their children about sex. When they do, the information they provide is often more about physiological changes than about the emotional terrain that accompanies sexuality or about managing one's own sexuality appropriately and healthfully. Adolescents are trying to find out if their bodies are developing normally, and they also begin to have questions about relationships and how to manage sexual interactions. They want answers to personal and even embarrassing questions such as, Am I normal? Is my body normal? Am I developing appropriately at the right speed? What is a tampon and how do I use it? How do you date? How do you kiss? How do you say no without hurting someone's feelings? What is a sexually transmitted disease? How do you use contraception? In addition, because it is often difficult for parents to talk about passion and desire and other such matters with their children, young people sometimes find it difficult to "buy into" a clinical discussion.[17] Considering that young people are often surrounded by media images of sexuality that are com-

---

[16]The discussion in Section 5.3 is based largely on Aletha C. Huston, Ellen Wartella, and Edward Donnerstein, 1998, *Measuring the Effects of Sexual Content in the Media: A Report to the Kaiser Family Foundation*, The Henry J. Kaiser Family Foundation, Menlo Park, Calif. Available online at <http://www.kff.org/content/archive/1389/content.html>.

[17]J.D. Brown, K.W. Childers, and C.S. Waszak, 1990, "Television and Adolescent Sexuality," *Journal of Adolescent Health Care* 11: 62-70; V. Strasburger, 1989, "Adolescent Sexuality and the Media," *Adolescent Gynecology* 36: 747-773; J. Strouse and R.A. Fabes, 1985, "Formal Versus Informal Informational Sources of Sex Education: Competing Forces in the Sexual Socialization of Adolescents," *Adolescence* 20: 251-263; and B.M. King and J. LoRusso, 1997, "Discussions in the Home About Sex: Different Recollections by Parents and Children," *Journal of Sex and Marital Therapy* 33: 52-60.

pletely centered around desire, it is not hard to understand why parents and children often do not communicate effectively about sex.[18]

Sex education provided in schools also does not provide a comprehensive picture. Indeed, sex education in schools is sufficiently controversial that its content is very tightly prescribed in terms that will generate the least amount of political argument and heat. For example, 14 states have required that sex education (if it is taught) must teach abstinence or abstinence until marriage. These states do not, however, also require that schools teach information about other forms of contraception, though abstinence-based curricula do emphasize contraceptive failure rates.[19]

In practice, if parents and schools are not providing young people with answers to the questions that they actually have, many will turn elsewhere to get additional information about sexuality. These other sources include their friends—who often have much *mis*information to share—as well as the media.[20] The media may be a particularly appealing source of information for adolescents because it can be accessed anonymously.[21] One can imagine (or perhaps even recall) the types of reactions and resulting feelings of embarrassment that might accompany questioning a peer or parent about sexuality (e.g., from a peer, "You mean you don't *know* that," or from a parent, "Why are you asking that?"). The anonymity of the media, and of the Internet especially, offers a way to obtain information about very sensitive matters about sexuality and sexual health and allows the adolescent to avoid embarrassing face-to-

---

[18]For example, one survey indicated that 72 percent of mothers believed that they had talked with their teenagers about sex, while only 45 percent of those teens agreed. See J. Jaccard and P. Dittus, 1993, "Parent-Adolescent Communication About Premarital Pregnancy," *Families in Society* 74(6): 329-343.

[19]M. Sutton, J.D. Brown, K. Wilson, and J. Klein, 2001, "Shaking the Tree of Knowledge for Forbidden Fruit: Where Adolescents Learn About Sexuality and Contraception," *Sexual Teens, Sexual Media*, J.D. Brown, J.R. Steele, and K.W. Childers, eds., Erlbaum, Hillsdale, N.J.; J.D. Brown and S. Stern, "Sex and the Media," *Encyclopedia of Communication and Information*, Macmillan, New York, in press; and Kaiser Family Foundation, 2000, *Sex Education in the U.S.: Policy and Practice*, Report No. 3049, available online at <www.kff.org/content/2000/3048/Issue percent20Update.PDF> (October 3, 2001).

[20]Sutton et al., 2001, "Shaking the Tree of Knowledge for Forbidden Fruit;" Brown and Stern, "Sex and the Media," in press.

[21]As one data point, consider that sexual health information is rated by online youth as "very important for people their age" in larger percentages (84 percent) than any other type of online information. (Information about drugs and alcohol are regarded as very important by 75 percent of online youth.) See Rideout, 2001, *Generation Rx.com: How Young People Use the Internet for Health Information*.

face encounters.[22] (A major disadvantage of media—especially Internet media—as a source of sexual information is that its accuracy is often not verified. School-age children may be far less cognizant of this fact than would be appropriate, and they are likely to search out information, aware of the advantages of anonymity but unaware of the disadvantages of potential inaccuracy.)

In the absence of other comfortable venues for seeking information, media sources help to fill information gaps for young people, providing information about topics that parents and schools are not discussing. As early as 1980, studies documented the strong influence of the media on an individual's sexual self-evaluation and the lack of influence exerted by family variables.[23] Given the increasing role of the Internet as a source of reliable information for young people as they conduct research for school papers and seek homework help, one can imagine that the media's influence will only increase. In fact, more recent studies have documented that the mass media is a particularly significant resource for sexual information for adolescents.[24]

Research on print media suggests that turning to the media for information on sexuality is also a normative behavior among teens. The majority of adolescent boys have seen at least one issue of *Playboy*, while girls tend to turn to women's magazines—for example, *Seventeen Magazine* for young teens, and for girls older than 14 *Glamour* and *Cosmopolitan*. Magazines like *Glamour* provide very explicit information on topics such as relationships with boys and content devoted to sex, flirting, and various romantic aspects of relationships.

The fact that young people often turn to the media to help deal with some of the issues associated with their changing selves has both positive and negative dimensions. On the one hand, many young people may find

---

[22]On the flip side, the anonymity of the Internet is highly attractive for children actively seeking sexually explicit materials for fantasy purposes. This anonymity provides a freedom to explore a wide range of material without having to reveal one's identity or to engage an adult to assist in the search. Consequently, the embarrassment or shame that he or she might feel is absent (though some of those to whom the committee spoke expressed concerns about "getting caught"), and with it many of the social inhibitions against seeking such content.

[23]J.A. Courtright and S.J. Baran. 1980. "The Acquisition of Sexual Information by Young People," *Journalism Quarterly* 1: 107-114.

[24]Brown et al., 1990, "Television and Adolescent Sexuality"; Strasburger, 1989, "Adolescent Sexuality and the Media"; Strouse and Fabes, 1985, "Formal Versus Informal Informational Sources of Sex Education: Competing Forces in the Sexual Socialization of Adolescents"; King and LoRusso, 1997, "Discussions in the Home About Sex: Different Recollections by Parents and Children."

reassurance that their curiosity about sexuality, and the changes in their bodies, are normal and they need not feel ashamed of their changing physiques. Television and movies in particular, and to some extent print media, may provide information about "scripts" for romantic interaction by depicting scenes in which these activities take place.[25] Teens can watch to see how other people resolve these situations and make judgments as to whether they feel this is an appropriate path to resolution for their situations.[26] In searching the Internet, young people also have a very good chance of finding valid and responsibly presented information on sexual health from reliable sources such as the Surgeon General,[27] Planned Parenthood,[28] or the American Social Health Association,[29] all of which can be reassuring and also may help young people to be more responsible in the choices they make with regard to their sexuality.

On the other hand, using the media as a primary source for information about sexuality has a variety of risks. It can create unrealistic expectations for oneself. For example, bodies portrayed in the media as sexually attractive are often unattainable (e.g., very thin physiques for girls and well-defined, sizable muscles for boys), and a young person who perceives his or her body as not fitting into these norms may be troubled rather than reassured.[30] Another study found that virgin adolescents who believed that media characters experienced high levels of sexual satisfaction were less satisfied with their own state of virginity.[31] Still another

---

[25]L.J. Heinberg and J.K. Thompson. 1995. "Body Image and Televised Images of Thinness and Attractiveness: A Controlled Laboratory Investigation," *Journal of Social and Clinical Psychology* 14: 325-338. A script is a set of expectations about how certain kinds of interaction will unfold and about how one will act in those interactions. More discussion can be found in Chapter 6.

[26]National Research Council and Institute of Medicine. 2001. *Nontechnical Strategies to Reduce Children's Exposure to Inappropriate Material on the Internet: Summary of a Workshop.* Board on Children, Youth, and Families and Computer Science and Telecommunications Board. Joah G. Iannotta, ed. National Academy Press, Washington, D.C. See also the discussion by Jane Brown on pp. 21-26, C. Pardun, 2001, "Romancing the Script: Identifying the Romantic Agenda in Top-grossing Movies," *Sexual Teens, Sexual Media*, J.D. Brown, J.R. Steele, and K.W. Childers, eds., Erlbaum, Hillsdale, N.J.

[27]See <http://www.sexualhealth.com/>.

[28]See <http://www.plannedparenthood.org/health/>.

[29]See <http://www.plannedparenthood.org/health/>.

[30]Heinberg and Thompson, 1995, "Body Image and Televised Images of Thinness and Attractiveness: A Controlled Laboratory Investigation," L. Hofschire and B. Greenberg, 2001, "Media's Impact on Adolescents' Body Dissatisfaction," *Sexual Teens, Sexual Media*.

[31]S.J Baran. 1976. "Sex on TV and Adolescent Self-Image," *Journal of Broadcasting* 20: 61-68.

study found that adolescents were most likely to be dissatisfied with their first sexual experience (intercourse) if they relied on media messages about sexuality.[32] Perhaps more important, media sources often depict in a positive light behavior that is inconsistent with the stated values of many parents and other adults. The messages about sexuality contained in the traditional media romantic script tend to be irresponsible and potentially emotionally and physically unhealthy. These sources answer adolescents' questions about sexuality with messages that do not always represent safe or healthy choices. Adult-oriented sexually explicit material may "up the ante" in that the messages are very explicit and overt, and certainly this type of material can be found easily online.

5.4 DIMENSIONS OF EXPOSURE AND ACCESS TO THE INTERNET

5.4.1 Venues of Access

As noted in Chapter 2, individuals obtain access to the Internet through an Internet service provider (ISP). However, it is quite common for many individuals to have more than one. For many youth, multiple venues for access to the Internet are likely, with home, school, and library access as perhaps the most common channels but with many others as well, all of which have (potentially) different ISPs and thus may offer different terms of service. For example, youth are likely to have access to the Internet at the homes of a friend, in which the operative rules of supervision and/or access are most likely to be those governing the friend. Internet cafes are open to anyone willing to pay access fees by the hour. Museums (especially those with after-school or weekend programs) often provide Internet access and operate under less stringent rules than do libraries or schools. Many youth after-school programs and other community-based programs are providing Internet access and courses on how to use the Internet. Even commercial establishments are beginning to provide terminals for Internet access.[33]

The most frequent venues for youth Internet use are home (74 percent) and school (73 percent). Almost as many youth use the Internet from someone else's household (68 percent). Public libraries account for a

---

[32]Huston et al., 1998, *Measuring the Effects of Sexual Content in the Media: A Report to the Kaiser Family Foundation.*

[33]See, for example, <http://www.eetimes.com/story/OEG20010412S0040> and <http://siliconvalley.com/docs/opinion/techtest/ml071201.htm>.

much smaller fraction of Internet use—only 32 percent of youth used a library for Internet access in the last year. Internet usage is frequent, with 76 percent using the Internet in the week prior to being interviewed, and with an average frequency of 3 to 4 times per week. On the other hand, 61 percent reported that their typical Internet usage is an hour or less on a typical day—26 percent reported spending 1 to 2 hours on a typical day.[34]

One important distinction to make about different venues is the degree to which any given venue is private (or can be made so). A person wishing to view material that may be subject to social sanction is highly unlikely to do so where he or she can be seen doing so. For example, an Internet access terminal in a mall that faces a walkway with many passers-by is unlikely to be the venue of choice for viewers interested in becoming sexually aroused (though it might well be the preferred venue for someone intending to shock those passers-by). By contrast, someone with unsupervised access at home (e.g., in a bedroom with a lockable door) is not subject to social sanctions, and thus can view material free of such constraints.

Note also that the availability of multiple venues of private and/or unsupervised access means that venue-specific approaches are easily circumvented. A child denied access to various types of content at school, for example, is likely to seek it in another venue where it is more easily available. For this reason, approaches to protecting children from exposure to inappropriate material that are venue-specific are not likely to be effective in serving their stated purpose.

5.4.2 Sources and Channels of Exposure

Sexually explicit material can be made available to youth from a variety of different sources and in a variety of ways. One major distinction that often drives the means by which sexually explicit material is made available is whether the source carrying such material is doing so for commercial purposes or has no financial motivations. The commercial online adult entertainment industry that makes sexually explicit material available for profit is generally thought of as the most significant source of sexually explicit material that may be regarded as inappropriate for minors. As described in Chapters 1 and 3, the type of content on such Web sites includes images equivalent to those viewed in music videos

---

[34]Joseph Turow with Lilach Nir. 2000. "The Internet and the Family: The View of U.S. Parents," in *Children in the New Media Landscape: Games, Pornography, Perceptions,* Cecilia von Feilitzen and Ulla Carlsson, eds. UNESCO International Clearinghouse on Children and Violence on the Screen, Sweden.

and those seen in R-rated movies, as well as other images that are extraordinarily graphic, are sexually explicit, and cater to specialized sexual tastes. In most cases, the images that are available for free serve as "teasers" for subscription Web sites that contain much more of the same. Less graphic but still sexually suggestive images may sometimes be found on Web sites associated with firms with a significant "bricks-and-mortar" presence that are using the Web essentially as an advertising medium to draw attention to their products and services (for example, Frederick's of Hollywood and Victoria's Secret).

Noncommercial carriers of sexually explicit content are much more varied—as varied as the motivations for carrying such content. For example:

- Child pornography is often carried by individuals who are not motivated by the prospect of financial reward. Rather, these individuals are often part of a community in which the ethos is that "to get pictures, you must contribute pictures."

- Friends sharing pictures online—the online equivalent of showing a friend a purloined centerfold prior to the Internet—are not motivated by financial reward or even by a community ethos.

- Electronically sending a sexually explicit picture to someone anonymously for purposes of harassment is generally not motivated by the prospect of financial reward.

- Newsgroups containing sexually explicit material do not exist as the result of any financial reward inherent in their existence. Instead, they provide a convenient method for exchanging material according to a much less rigid ethos than that which governs those who exchange child pornography.

- People engage interactively in "cybersex"—online real-time dialog with someone (usually text-based) that interactively describes sexual behavior and actions with one's online partner for erotic purposes and expression. The intent can vary: sometimes, such interactive chat provides fodder for a masturbatory fantasy. In other cases, it is simply a "hack"— making fun of someone else for taking cybersex seriously. In still other cases, it is a prelude to face-to-face meetings and a possible sexual connection. (Interactive chat of a non-sexual sort is also a key element of predatory connections that entice young people to meet face-to-face with other users, an action that may put them in potential physical danger.)

- Individuals often have personal profiles or Web pages on the Internet, which in general are intended to be found by others. For those seeking sexual contact, either in person or online, these profiles may be sexually provocative and explicit, so as to draw attention from those similarly interested.

- Individuals with exhibitionist tendencies find the Internet an easy way to satisfy such desires without the expectation of making money in the enterprise.

The channels through which individuals can be exposed to such content are also diverse. Because the Internet is not merely a repository of Web sites to be passively browsed, but rather a dynamic and interactive system, the opportunity for users to be exposed to inappropriate content is not limited to viewing commercial Web sites alone. For example:

- Bulletin boards or newsgroups may contain explicit imagery or graphic language and may center on inappropriate themes.
- "Spam"—e-mail that is unsolicited—can contain links to inappropriate sexually explicit images. Spam is often associated with operators of adult Web sites seeking to increase traffic to their sites. As noted in Chapter 2, participants in chat room conversations and users of IM software often receive links to such sites.
- Publicly accessible user "profiles" associated with a screen name or a login name are used to provide information about the owner of that name, and often contain links to Web sites. Sometimes, the operator of an adult-oriented Web site will use a sexually provocative screen name to draw attention to the profile, and include a link to that site. Someone who reads the profile will often click on the link, thinking that the profile's owner is an individual and with the expectation of receiving personal information. Because such links often do take the user to a Web site with personal information about the owner, this expectation is not unreasonable. But when the profile owner is the operator of an adult Web site, the link takes the user—unexpectedly—to one containing sexually explicit material.
- Open chat rooms in which Internet users can communicate via text messages in real time are a participatory public forum in which the norms of behavior and communication are often outside of societal norms of decency regarding the representation and discussion of sexuality, aggression, and intergroup relations.[35]
- Instant messages (IMs) are another kind of interactive form that relies on text-based, real-time interaction. However, they are based on a

---

[35]Note also that there can be private chat rooms, in which those who participate do so by invitation or because they know of the chat rooms' existence. For the most part, such chat rooms are not generally subject to intrusions from uninvited guests. Some high school students to whom the committee spoke commented that "when they were younger" they participated in public chat rooms, but as they had become older, they found private chat rooms more congenial and better matched to their interests and needs.

one-to-one interaction (and hence are more private, unlike a chat room), and as a general rule, IMs require at least one party to have some prior knowledge of the other—namely the other party's screen name. (As noted in Chapter 2, screen names or e-mail addresses, which are sometimes the same thing, can be found in public chat rooms, searches for profiles with particular characteristics, and harvesting e-mail addresses from public postings.) Note that depending on the technology, IMs can also allow transmission and receipt of images and sounds, enabling both real-time voice interaction, videoconferencing, and image exchange on a peer-to-peer basis, without the need for sending e-mail or going to a Web site.

• Peer-to-peer networks enable file sharing between individuals. In such networks, the files themselves—the information content of interest to end users—always remain on client systems and never pass through a centralized server (such as one that would host a Web page). Instead, the peer-to-peer network gives end users the ability to search for particular files of interest and to initiate a direct transfer between the users willing to share (and receive) files without the payment of a fee.[36] In addition, peer-to-peer file transfers (as with file transfers effected through e-mail) bypass content filtering, although the function itself can be blocked by certain filters. Box 5.1 highlights one recent report on the use of peer-to-peer networks for obtaining sexually explicit material.

The role of Usenet is important as well. As a broad generalization, the frequency with which minors access sexually explicit content through Usenet is low, especially if these individuals are younger than high school age. The reasons are that Usenet often requires some technical sophistication to use (and is generally text-based), and that the sexually explicit content on the World Wide Web is much easier to obtain and more interesting in addition. (To the extent that minors do use Usenet, it tends to be for the downloading of information objects such as popular music, blockbuster movies, and pirated software.) This should not be taken as an assertion that young people never make use of Usenet, but the committee believes that the primary use of Usenet with respect to sexually explicit

---

[36]In Napster-like peer-to-peer file-sharing networks, a central server holds a publicly accessible index to the files available from end users (but not the files themselves). (Napster was originally designed to handle sharing of digital music files, but there is no particular reason that the files in question must be music files—and indeed, extensions of the Napster protocol can handle other file types.) Other peer-to-peer file-sharing networks, such as Gnutella, eliminate even the centralized server index function. Users of Gnutella-like systems are connected in a Web (rather than to a centralized index), and a query from one user goes to an immediate circle of possible respondents. If not satisfied, the query then goes from those respondents to other respondents. Furthermore, such queries are highly anonymous, though file transfers between end users are not.

Box 5.1
The Use of Peer-to-Peer Networks for
Obtaining Sexually Explicit Material

A report issued in July 2001 by the Minority Staff of the Special Investigations Division of the House Committee on Government Reform drew several conclusions about the use of peer-to-peer networks. Using the terminology "Internet file-sharing programs," the report found that Internet file-sharing programs are rapidly gaining users and that these programs provide free access to thousands of pornographic videos and images. Some peer-to-peer networks are established for the purpose of exchanging such content, while others are created for purposes such as music exchange but nevertheless contain some of these videos and images. Further, it found that the number of children using file-sharing programs is unknown, but is believed to be high.

The inference drawn from the report by the public media was that a large number of children are gaining access to pornography through Internet file-sharing programs, but the report never states such a conclusion explicitly. Based on data regarding popular search terms in Internet file-sharing systems,[1] the report did conclude that one of the major uses of Internet file-sharing programs is to exchange pornographic materials, such as adult videos.

The report further concluded that children in search of music on Internet file-sharing programs are directed to pornographic files. This conclusion was based on the fact that a search for "Britney Spears" videos on one file-sharing service resulted in "hits" more than 70 percent of which were videos with pornographic titles. Searches for other popular musicians, such as Christina Aguilera and Madonna, also produced significant numbers of pornographic files.

SOURCE: *Children's Access to Pornography Through Internet File-Sharing Programs,* prepared for Rep. Henry A. Waxman and Rep. Steve Largent, Minority Staff, Special Investigations Division, Committee on Government Reform, U.S. House of Representatives, July 27, 2001.

[1] For example, the report noted that on one day sampled by the Special Investigations Division, 6 of the top 10 searches were for "porn," "sex," "xxx," and other terms intended to elicit pornography. One search for the term "porn" on a particular file-sharing system yielded over 25,000 entries, more than 10,000 of which were video files.

material tends to be among adults—and it is a prime channel for the exchange of child pornography and other highly "extreme" material.

5.4.3 Extent of Exposure

In 2000, the Crimes Against Children Research Center (CACRC) conducted a nationally representative, interview-based survey with 1,501 youths aged 10 to 17 who use the Internet regularly (Box 5.2). This survey measured the extent to which young people came in contact with sexually explicit material, received sexual solicitations from other users, and were distressed by the incident.[37] Twenty-five percent of youth reported having had at least one unwanted exposure to sexual pictures in the year before the survey was taken. These figures are approximately consistent with findings of a Kaiser Family Foundation/NPR survey taken in 2001.[38] In this survey, 31 percent of children aged 10 to 17 with computers at home reported seeing a "pornographic" Web site, even if by accident. Breaking down by age, 45 percent of those aged 14 to 17 had seen such a site, compared with 15 percent of those aged 10 to 13. Another study by the Kaiser Family Foundation found that among teens (aged 15 to 17) online, 70 percent say they have accidentally come across "pornography" on the Web, though 77 percent said they have never come across it or come across it "not too often."[39]

One in 5 young people reported receiving a sexual solicitation or approach in the last year, and 1 in 30 received an aggressive sexual solicitation.[40] (In the lexicon of the CACRC study, a solicitation is defined as a

---

[37]David Finkelhor, Kimberly Mitchell, and Janis Wolak. 2001. *Youth Internet Safety Survey.* Crimes Against Children Research Center, University of New Hampshire. See <http://www.ncjrs.org/txtfiles1/ojjdp/fs200104.txt>.

[38]See <http://www.npr.org/programs/specials/poll/technology/>.

[39]Victoria Rideout. 2001. *Generation Rx.com: How Young People Use the Internet for Health Information.* The Henry J. Kaiser Family Foundation, Menlo Park, Calif. Available online at <http://www.kff.org/content/2001/20011211a/GenerationRx.pdf>. Note that the use of the term "pornography" in a survey questionnaire is subject to all of the problems discussed in Chapter 1 regarding the definition of "pornography." As that discussion indicates, different people have different understandings of what counts as "pornographic," so one party (but not another) might regard a Victoria's Secret advertisement, the swimsuit issue of *Sports Illustrated,* or a site devoted to gay and lesbian rights as "pornographic." The author of *Generation Rx.com* (personal communication, March 2002) spoke with a 14-year-old girl who reported that a lot of kids her age had seen "porn" movies. When asked to provide an example, she said, "You wouldn't believe how many of them have seen American Pie." ("American Pie" and "American Pie 2" carry movie-industry ratings of R, which indicate admission forbidden for minors without a parent or guardian. The enforcement of such ratings varies across communities and even across theaters within an individual community, and even if enforcement were uniform, the rating—by assumption—indicates that minors can obtain access to such movies with parental permission and consent verified by the parent's presence.) Perhaps the most that can be said from a survey based on an undefined term such as "pornography" is that those who reported coming across "pornography" on the Internet have some sexually oriented concept in mind, even if that concept (and hence the material in question) may vary definitionally (and substantially so) from person to person.

[40]Note also that these figures may well underrepresent the actual incidence of solicitations, because many youth who know that adults are concerned about such solicitations may worry that reporting such incidents could lead to greater parental restrictions on them. Since many older teens think they can deal with such situations, they may not think they are worth reporting.

Box 5.2
The Youth Internet Safety Survey

In the period from August 1999 to February 2000, the Crimes Against Children Research Center at the University of New Hampshire conducted the Youth Internet Safety Survey, a telephone survey of a representative national sample of 1,501 young people, ages 10 through 17, who use the Internet regularly (defined as using the Internet at least once a month for the past 6 months at home, school, a library, or some other place). Parents or guardians were interviewed first for about 10 minutes, and if they consented, young people were interviewed for about 15 to 30 minutes, with the interviewer taking care to preserve privacy and confidentiality during the youth interview.

Youth survey participants were 53 percent male and 47 percent female. Ethnically, they were 73 percent non-Hispanic white, 10 percent African American, 3 percent American Indian or Alaskan native, 3 percent Asian, and 2 percent Hispanic white; 7 percent were in other ethnic categories, and 2 percent did not answer.

Seventy-five percent of the households approached completed the screening necessary to determine their eligibility for participation in the survey. The completion rate among households with eligible respondents was 82 percent. Five percent of parents in eligible households refused the adult interview. Another 11 percent of parents completed the adult interview but refused permission for their child to participate in the youth interview. In 2 percent of eligible households, parents consented to the youth interview, but youth refused to participate. An additional 1 percent of eligible households were in "call-back" status when 1,501 interviews were completed.

The final sample consisted of 796 boys and 705 girls. This is not a representative sample of all youth within the United States because Internet use is not evenly distributed among the population. Internet users tend to have higher incomes and more education than non-Internet users, and, among lower income groups, Internet users are more likely to be white, although this racial difference disappears at higher income levels. While boys are somewhat more likely than girls to use the Internet, the difference is small and is attributable to boys' propensity to play computer games. The sample for the Youth Internet Safety Survey generally matches other representative samples of youth Internet users.

SOURCE: David Finkelhor, Kimberly Mitchell, and Janis Wolak. 2001. *Youth Internet Safety Survey*. Crimes Against Children Research Center, University of New Hampshire. See <http://www.ncjrs.org/txtfiles1/ojjdp/fs200104.txt>.

---

request to engage in sexual activities or sexual talk or to give personal sexual information that was either unwanted or made by an adult whether wanted or not. An aggressive sexual solicitation is a sexual solicitation involving offline contact with the perpetrator through regular mail, by telephone, or in person or attempts or requests for offline contact—all of which constitute a potential risk of physical safety for young people.) Girls in the survey were targeted for sexual solicitations and approaches at almost twice the rate of boys (66 percent compared with 34 percent, respectively).

In general, the young people participating in this study were not very distressed by these experiences. Notably, only 6 percent of youth reported that accidentally viewing a sexually explicit image was distressing to them, and 75 percent of youth who had experienced an online solicitation were not very upset or afraid. (Another survey by the Kaiser Family Foundation found that of online youth aged 15 to 17 who have been exposed to pornography, 45 percent reported being upset by the experience, with 55 percent saying that they were not at all upset or "not too upset."[41]) More young people were very or extremely upset by aggressive solicitations (36 percent), and 25 percent were very or extremely afraid. Younger users (aged 10 to 13) were more distressed by solicitations than were older users—although 22 percent of youth surveyed were 10 to 13 years old, they reported 37 percent of the distressing episodes. This may suggest that younger users have not learned coping strategies for such incidents and have a more difficult time shrugging off such solicitations and that preadolescents are the age group most emotionally vulnerable to sexual solicitations.

The CACRC and Kaiser reports are generally consistent with what the committee heard during its site visits. For example, the children to whom the committee spoke during site visits (mostly older adolescents) were in general not particularly concerned by exposure to sexually explicit material. Some were upset by what they saw, but the large majority brushed it off. (In general, there was a correlation with age—those in the 16 to 17 age bracket tended to be much less bothered by sexually explicit material than those aged 14 to 16.)

Of course, self-reporting can be questioned on the grounds that these teenagers would not have been likely to tell a group of adults about an abiding interest in sexually explicit material or about being upset by such exposure (it would be too "uncool" to do so). On the other hand, what today's adults remember about their own searches of sexually explicit material in their own youths does not necessarily apply to the youth of today. Today's social environment, compared to that of 30 to 40 years ago, is a more sexual one, and much of the material that today's adults sought as teenagers is much more freely available and is thus arguably much less of a "big problem" than in the past.

---

[41]Rideout, 2001, *Generation Rx.com: How Young People Use the Internet for Health Information.*

5.5 INTERNET EXPOSURE TO SEXUALLY EXPLICIT MATERIAL, SOLICITATIONS, AND HARASSMENT

The impact on children of Internet exposure to sexually explicit content must be seen in the context of a much greater availability and wider range of sexual content than in the past. Although it has long been normative behavior for adolescents to seek out images that are sexually explicit (e.g., viewing one's first *National Geographic* and *Playboy* were once rites of passage for many boys), adolescents are bombarded with sexual content in everyday media sources that are to some extent difficult to escape. Images meant to tantalize are embedded in most advertising in television, billboards, and print media, and programming such as music videos, soap operas, and movies contains highly sexualized images and content. Carrying original material and content from many forms of media, the Internet also has a broad range of sexual content.

For many it would appear that the range of content—including nudity, romance, and depictions of sex and intercourse, as well as a variety of sexual proclivities (rape, bondage, bestiality, and so on)—seems to be larger and more accessible than what was easily available in the past. Such changes lead some to speculate that there may be a wider range of social mores and a greater permissiveness about sexuality today.[42]

Given both a broad range of sexually explicit material on the Internet and the numerous ways in which this content can be viewed and accessed, it is worth considering two broad categories of how young people come into contact with this content. Exposure to sexually explicit material on the Internet can occur inadvertently or intrusively (as when one user deliberately seeks to expose another user to this content), or it can occur as a result of a young person's deliberate choice to seek and view sexually explicit material.

Table 5.2 summarizes the various types of inappropriate sexually explicit materials and experiences discussed in this report.

---

[42]One suggestion of such a wider range comes from the case of a Utah video-store-chain owner who was indicted in 2000 for selling obscene material. At trial, his attorney sought and obtained records demonstrating a large consumption of erotic video through the pay-per-view channels of a local hotel chain and through cable and satellite television providers. According to these records, residents of Utah County—by all accounts a highly conservative area of the nation—are larger per capita consumers of such material than the rest of the nation. Thus, his attorney argued, the community standards of Utah County in fact were not breached by the sales of erotic video, which could not be held to be obscene under those standards. The chain owner was acquitted on all counts. See Timothy Egan, 2000, "EROTICA INC.—A Special Report: Technology Sent Wall Street into Market for Pornography," *New York Times*, October 23.

TABLE 5.2 Types of Inappropriate Internet Material or Experience

Types of Material or Experience	Characterization
Inappropriate sexually explicit material	With a few exceptions, such materials are generally delivered to a user for passive non-interactive viewing (e.g., through a Web site or via e-mail).
Child pornography	A category of speech unprotected by the First Amendment, involving material visually depicting minors engaging in sexually explicit conduct, including actual or simulated sexual intercourse, bestiality, masturbation, sadistic or masochistic abuse, or the lascivious exhibition of the genitals or pubic area of the minor.
Obscenity	A category of speech unprotected by the First Amendment, involving sexually explicit material that the average person, applying contemporary community standards, would find, taken as a whole, appeals to the prurient interest, depicts or describes, in a patently offensive way, sexual conduct specifically defined by the applicable state law, and lacks, when taken as a whole, serious literary, artistic, political, or scientific value.
Material obscene with respect to minors	A category of speech involving material that meets the legal test of obscenity as applied in the context of exposing minors to such material. Under the First Amendment, material in this category is protected for adults, though distribution to minors can be regulated.
"Offensive" material	A broad category of speech involving material that some party or another finds offensive to his or her sensibilities (e.g., so called "indecent" material). If offensive material does not fall into one of the above categories, it is protected for both adults and minors under the First Amendment.
Inappropriate interaction with others	Interaction is by definition interactive—the user is an active participant in a dialog with another human being.
Sexual solicitations from strangers	Solicitations in the absence of physical meetings can be bothersome or frightening to young people. However, if such solicitations lead to face-to-face encounters with predators, the consequences can be catastrophic.
Harassment (victim thereof)	A young person can suffer as the victim of online harassment. Such harassment can take the form of threats, taunts, insults, or the public posting of disparagingly altered images (e.g., a composite of a head shot grafted onto a picture of an animal) and may be delivered anonymously or with an identity associated with it.
Other inappropriate material	A broad category, generally protected under the First Amendment, into which various parties have placed materials promoting hate and racism, violence (e.g., bomb making), religious cults, and so on.

5.5.1 Deliberate Search for Sexually Explicit Material

Deliberate access results from a child's conscious choice. For example, a child learns of a Web site providing sexually explicit materials that does not require a password, and uses an Internet browser to view that Web site. Or he or she may search for sexually explicit material using a search engine, typing in terms likely to return links to such material (such as "sex pics"). Or a minor in a chat room might broadcast a message to other chat room participants asking for pictures with explicit sexual content. Or he or she may visit a chat room named so as to attract visitors interested in sexual dialog. Or he or she may sign up to be on a mailing list known to send sexually explicit images to its members via e-mail.

Eight percent of those surveyed in the CACRC survey acknowledged choosing to seek out X-rated Internet sites.[43] Less than 1 percent said they had used a credit card without permission. Of youth who said they talked online with people they did not know in person, 12 percent had sent a picture to someone they met online, and 7 percent had willingly talked about sex online with someone they had never met in person. Five percent had posted a picture of themselves for general viewing; eleven percent had posted some personal information in a public Internet space, mostly their last name. Twenty-seven percent of e-mail users knew that they had posted their e-mail address in a public place on the Internet.

Some of the paths for deliberate and inadvertent exposure to sexually explicit material on the Internet are described in Box 5.3.

5.5.2 Inadvertent Exposure to or Intrusion of Sexually Explicit Material

Inadvertent exposure occurs through no deliberate action on the child's part. In the reference scenario described in Chapter 2, the student intends to search for information on a particular (innocuous) topic, but because the term he uses to search is ambiguous, information on more than one topic is returned to the user. A poor search strategy or misspellings in the terms used for a search can also result in the inadvertent receipt of sexually explicit material: links to sexually explicit material may be returned even if they were not desired by the child. A child may

---

[43]Even though the survey was anonymous and privacy was guaranteed to the survey respondents, such figures are likely to understate the true incidence of such behavior, because of concerns that promises of anonymity might not be kept and reluctance to admit this activity to anyone (anonymous researcher or not).

Box 5.3
Some Paths for Deliberate and Inadvertent Exposure to Sexually Explicit Material on the Internet

Deliberate Exposure

- Searching for sexually explicit terms in a search engine and clicking on the links returned
- Receiving e-mail with sexually oriented content after subscribing to a mailing list known to provide such content
- Going deliberately to a Web site that the user is told contains sexually explicit material
- Trading sexually explicit stories and images among friends and acquaintances through e-mail and other forms of online interaction

Inadvertent Exposure

- Receiving unsolicited e-mail containing sexually explicit material or links to such material (as the result of having been in a chat room—thereby displaying e-mail addresses—or subject to some other technique of "harvesting" e-mail addresses)
- Improperly guessing the address of a Web site and receiving inappropriate material as a result
- Searching for terms with both sexual and non-sexual meaning in a search engine and clicking on the links returned (some of which may contain sexually oriented material)
- Mistyping a request for information or the address of a Web site
- Clicking on a link without really knowing what is to be expected at the site to which the link refers

---

misspell the address of a Web site, and the mistakenly spelled Web address points to an adult-oriented Web site that has obtained the misspelling.[44] Or domain names that are most likely innocuous may have been appropriated by owners of adult Web sites.[45] Confusion between .com and .gov or .edu suffixes can also be exploited to the advantage of the

---

[44]Note that exploitation of misspellings is a time-honored tradition in marketing. One of the most famous stories in this area involved the AT&T 1-800-OPERATOR advertising campaign for collect calls. By dialing 1-800-O-P-E-R-A-T-O-R, the caller was connected to an AT&T operator. MCI owned the number 1-800-O-P-E-R-A-T-E-R (note the misspelling) and took enough of AT&T's business that AT&T discontinued the ad campaign and switched numbers (*Business Week*, June 13, 1994, p. 78).

[45]For example, the name of an indoor professional football team in Texas with a .com suffix leads to an adult-oriented Web site.

adult Web site owner.[46] A user may also mistype the address of a Web site, or improperly guess the address of a Web site,[47] and receive inappropriate material as a result. From time to time, e-mail containing sexually explicit material can be misaddressed.

Intrusion occurs when another party "pushes" such material on the child even though he or she has not asked to receive it. Spam e-mail with links to Web sites containing inappropriate sexually explicit material is one example. Web sites that have pop-up windows that open as quickly as a user can close them are another way this exposure can occur. As stated earlier, users can also send IMs to each other and attach images or provide a link to a sexually explicit Web site.

Inadvertent exposure is not an uncommon experience. According to the CACRC survey, one minor in four (about 25 percent) had at least one inadvertent exposure to sexually explicit images in 1999, with the majority of these exposures occurring to youth 15 years of age or older. In the vast majority of cases (94 percent), the images involved naked persons; in a substantial minority of the cases (38 percent), they involved people having sex. About 8 percent of the images involved violence, in addition to nudity and/or sex. The children who inadvertently viewed these images saw them while searching or surfing the Internet (71 percent), and while opening e-mail, or clicking on links in e-mail or IMs (29 percent).[48] Most of these exposures (67 percent) happened at home, but 15 percent happened at school, and 3 percent happened in libraries.

For those surfing the Web, the inadvertent exposures happened as the result of searches (47 percent), misspelled addresses (17 percent), and links in Web sites (17 percent). And, in 26 percent of these exposed-while-surfing incidents, youth reported that they were brought to another sex site when they tried to exit the site they were in. For those receiving e-mail that resulted in inadvertent exposure, 63 percent were associated with an e-mail address used solely by the individual; for 93 percent of the inadvertent exposures resulting from e-mail, the sender of the e-mail was unknown to the individual.

---

[46]For example, the New York Times reported on a children's financial Web site—designed to teach children about money—that had been closely associated with a Web site offering adult-oriented sexually explicit material. The original Web site for children, produced by Ernst & Young, was located at <http://www.moneyopolis.com>, while the adult Web site was located at <http://www.moneyopolis.org>. See Susan Stellin, 2001, "Pornography Takes Over Financial Site for Children," New York Times, October 26.

[47]A common method of guessing the address of a Web site is to try "www.search term.com," where "searchterm" is a term of interest to the user.

[48]In 17 percent of all incidents of unwanted exposure, the youth said they did know the site was X-rated before entering, but it is not clear to what extent inadvertent exposure resulted from curiosity or navigational naivete despite prior knowledge of the site's X-rated nature.

Note that the line between deliberate access and inadvertent expo-sure is not always clear. For example, many search engines return links to Web pages that include a few lines of text associated with each page. If the child intends to search for an innocuous topic, but uses a search term with ambiguous meaning (e.g., "beaver"), a number of links to sexually explicit pages may be returned, along with those few lines of text. If that text includes terms such as "hot sex" and "XXX," careful users can avoid such materials.

5.5.3 Sexual Solicitations and Approaches

About 3 percent of youth Internet users surveyed by the CACRC received an aggressive sexual solicitation, a rate of exposure far lower than the rate of exposure to sexually explicit material. In addition, 5 percent of youth Internet users were approached sexually, e.g., by being asked sexual questions in a way that caused them to be very or extremely upset or afraid. Girls were aggressively solicited or approached at almost twice the rate of boys, and most of those individuals solicited (77 percent) were 14 or older.

The CACRC survey found that adults were responsible for 34 percent of the aggressive solicitations, with most of the adult solicitors reported to be aged 18 to 25. About 4 percent of all solicitors were believed to be older than 25, and 67 percent of all solicitors were believed to be male. Children made 48 percent of the aggressive solicitations. However, in almost all of the cases where the surveyed youth gave an age or gender for a perpetra-tor, the youth had never met the perpetrator in person, thus leaving the accuracy of the identifying information in question. (For perspective, a report of the University of Pennsylvania Center for the Study of Youth Policy found that 47 percent of confirmed sexual assaults on children (defined as those under the age of 18) were committed by relatives and 49 percent were committed by acquaintances, such as a teacher, coach, or neighbor, while only 4 percent of sexual assaults were committed by strangers.[49])

The concern with solicitations is based on a troubling pattern of be-havior that often characterizes a child's online conversation with a solici-tor in a chat room or via instant messaging. In a typical interaction be-tween predator and victim, the predator begins with dialog that is entirely innocuous.[50] Over time (perhaps weeks or even months), the predator

---

[49]Richard J. Estes and Neil Alan Weiner. 2001. *The Commercial Sexual Exploitation of Children in the U.S., Canada, and Mexico,* University of Pennsylvania, School of Social Work, Center for the Study of Youth Policy, Philadelphia, September 18.

[50]See, for example, Kenneth V. Lanning, 2001, *Child Molesters: A Behavioral Analysis,* 5th Edition, National Center for Missing and Exploited Children, Alexandria, Va.

grooms his target, seeking to build rapport and trust. No single piece of dialog is necessarily sexual or even suggestive, but as the victim begins to trust the (anonymous) predator, conversations become increasingly personal. A young adolescent is strongly motivated by the need to separate from parental authority and to gain acceptance for his or her growing adulthood. Further, he or she is usually inexperienced in dialog with adults (especially adults with cunning and guile) and is likely to be relatively honest in sharing his or her emotional state or feelings. The predator plays on this need for acceptance and a child's naivete. Sexually explicit dialog and/or material is unlikely to be a part of this dialog in its early stages, and may never emerge. When it does, it is introduced gradually and slowly in order to reduce the inhibitions of the victim and make him or her more likely to be willing to meet.

5.5.4 Harassment

In addition to encountering sexual solicitations and inadvertent exposure to sexually explicit material, youth on the Internet are subject to other threatening or offensive behavior directed toward them, including threats of assault aimed at them, their friends, family, or property, as well as efforts to embarrass or humiliate them. Six percent of regular youth Internet users experienced feeling either worried or threatened because someone was bothering or harassing them online, or because someone used the Internet to threaten or embarrass them by posting or sending messages about them for other people to see. Boys and girls were targeted about equally, while about 70 percent of the episodes involved youth 14 and older. Nearly two-thirds (63 percent) of those harassing youth were other juveniles, and almost a quarter of harassment perpetrators lived within a 1-hour drive of the youth. The primary forms of harassment were IMs (33 percent), chat-room exchanges (32 percent), and e-mails (19 percent). About 12 percent included an actual or attempted contact by telephone or regular mail, or in person. According to the CACRC, an important feature of harassment is that, more than sexual solicitation, it involves people known to the youth and people known to live nearby. Some of the threatening character of these episodes stems from the fact that the targets do not feel completely protected by distance and anonymity, and that the harasser could actually carry out his or her threats.[51]

---

[51]D. Finkelhor, K.J. Mitchell, and J. Wolak. 2000. *Online Victimization: A Report on the Nation's Youth.* Crimes Against Children Research Center and the National Center for Missing and Exploited Children, Alexandria, Va.

6

The Research Base on the Impact of Exposure to Sexually Explicit Material: What Theory and Empirical Studies Offer

The empirical research base for understanding the impact of sexually explicit material on children (discussed in Section 6.2) is not extensive, for reasons described in Box 6.1. Thus, reliable information in this domain is hard to obtain, and in the absence of reliable information, controversy abounds (as discussed in Chapter 7). Material in this chapter is derived largely from the Kaiser Family Foundation report, *Measuring the Effects of Sexual Content in the Media: A Report to the Kaiser Family Foundation*, 1998.[1]

6.1 THEORETICAL CONSIDERATIONS

A number of psychological theories suggest some of the impact that media exposure might have on young people. These theories sometimes conflict, and so theoretical predictions regarding the developmental impact of exposure to sexually explicit material are not always consistent with one another. It is also possible that more than one theory may be valid or useful in understanding psychological phenomena. Furthermore, the impact of such exposure will depend on the individual, the context in which the exposure occurs, and the social structure in which the young person is engaged, as well as other factors.

---

[1]Aletha C. Huston, Ellen Wartella, and Edward Donnerstein. 1998. *Measuring the Effects of Sexual Content in the Media: A Report to the Kaiser Family Foundation*. The Henry J. Kaiser Family Foundation, Menlo Park, Calif. Available online at <http://www.kff.org/content/archive/1389/content.html>.

Box 6.1
Reasons for a Sparse Research Base on the Impact
of Sexually Explicit Material on Children

Ethical and Legal Considerations

Ethical and legal considerations limit experiments that would demonstrate the impact that exposure to sexually explicit material has or does not have on young people. For example, consider a study design that called for children to be shown sexually explicit material in order to identify short- and long-term effects of exposure:

• A researcher might run afoul of legal restrictions that limit the showing of sexually explicit material to minors.
• It is generally regarded as unethical to conduct studies that might place participants at risk, even if there is no evidence that it would do so. In general, all that is required is a well-articulated concern about risk, a condition that is clearly met for exposing children to sexually explicit material (e.g., the behavior might be imitated).
• Research involving children without parental consent is regarded as unethical. Furthermore, a high rate of parental refusal of consent—likely in the case of research involving exposing children to sexually explicit materials—undermines the extent to which such research can be generalized, and limits its value.

For these reasons, such a study would be unlikely to be initiated. However, it should be noted that such studies are routinely performed when images of violence rather than images of sexual activity are at issue.

Increasing Conservatism of Institutional Review Boards

Researchers have been able to skirt this issue by measuring the impact of media content of which society is more tolerant. For example, it might be possible for a researcher to study the impact of sexually oriented material or violent material on

It is important to note that young people are not passive recipients of media content.[2] They select what they watch and interpret material using their own experiences and frames of reference. Thus, while some theories may focus on how content may affect young people in general and can suggest ways in which certain content can lead to positive or negative outcomes, all theories acknowledge that this is an interactive process that can yield many different outcomes depending on the person and the

---

[2]See, for example, Henry Jenkins, "Congressional Testimony on Media Violence," testimony presented before the U.S. Senate Commerce Committee, Washington, D.C., May 4, 1999. Available online at <http://media-in-transition.mit.edu/articles/index_dc.html>.

young people if the researcher uses media content that the participants would likely watch as a part their normal viewing patterns (e.g., shows on prime-time television or programs on during after-school hours that are targeted to young people).

This approach, however, can be foreclosed as Human Subjects Review Boards become increasingly more conservative and universities grow more cautious about the possibility of a future lawsuit. For example, Dorothy Singer, co-director of the Yale University Family Television Research and Consultation Center, was not permitted by her Institutional Review Board to conduct a study that would have measured the impact and short-term behavioral responses of children watching the Power Rangers. Ironically, shortly after Singer was prevented from doing this study, a local television station videotaped children's activities on the playground after watching a Power Rangers episode.

Lack of Research Funding

Private foundations such as the Henry J. Kaiser Family Foundation have supported several recent reports on the media.[1] Support from foundations is extremely important and provides the possibility of stimulating new and creative research. However, private funding is rarely stable enough to support longitudinal research, and a foundation's direction often changes in focus every few years. Federal funding is therefore a pre condition for developing a field of knowledge in a systematic and cumulative manner; such support would contribute to longitudinal, developmental studies and nationally representative tracking surveys to stay abreast of changing patterns in children's media use and media impact. However, federal funding in this area—especially with respect to sexual behavior—has been essentially absent.

---

[1] Huston et al., 1998, *Measuring the Effects of Sexual Content in the Media: A Report to the Kaiser Family Foundation*; D.F. Roberts, U.G. Foehr, V.J. Rideout, and M. Brodie, 1999, *Kids and Media at the New Millennium*, The Henry J. Kaiser Family Foundation, Menlo Park, Calif., available online at <http://www.kff.org/content/1999/1535/>.

---

situation.[3] The following list describes several prominent theories that conceptualize the underlying mechanisms through which media exposure may affect young people. None of these theories suggest that viewing sexually explicit material will always have a particular outcome. Rather, they imply that multiple factors, such as children's media use and interpretation of material, affect (and greatly complicate the analysis of) outcomes. These theories are considered in light of sexually explicit material, though they are by no means limited to this type of content alone.

---

[3] Huston et al., 1998, *Measuring the Effects of Sexual Content in the Media: A Report to the Kaiser Family Foundation*.

• *Psychoanalytic theory.* Psychoanalytic theory[4] predicts potentially positive effects from exposure to sexually explicit material presented in media. In psychoanalytic theory, two major drives are sex and aggression. These drives must be released in some way, and one path that psychoanalytic theory develops for drive reduction is fantasy in the form of catharsis. More specifically, in catharsis, sexual drives can be released through fantasy experiences with sexual material, thereby reducing the drive state.

• *Arousal theory.* Zillmann's arousal theory focuses primarily on the immediate effects that sexually explicit material may have on behavior.[5] Television content, for example, can produce emotional and physiological arousal (i.e., activation of the nervous system as opposed to sexual arousal), and increased levels of arousal are likely to produce some type of behavior. However, Zillmann's theory does not imply what these behavioral outcomes will be. Rather, arousal theory states that the personality of the viewer, the environmental circumstances, and one's frame of reference for interpretation will determine the ensuing behavior.[6] In the context of Zillmann's theory, arousal is non-specific. Thus, other factors will determine whether sexually explicit material will result in behavior that is sexual, aggressive, or altruistic. In media research, autonomic arousal, which is related to emotional experiences, is often the focus of inquiries.

An adaptation of arousal theory has been used to understand the possible implications of repeated exposure to sexually explicit material. One possibility is that, in a similar fashion to desensitization to violent material, a viewer continually exposed to sexually explicit material will habituate to that type of content and become desensitized to it as well. Becoming physiologically or emotionally aroused in the near future would then require different material, perhaps more explicit depictions. An alternative outcome is that a viewer who has habituated to material will simply grow uninterested in it, an outcome mentioned by a number of male students interviewed by the committee during site visits who asserted that they initially used the Internet to view adult-oriented Web sites a great deal but that they soon became bored with such material. Habituation does wear off, so a viewer might return to similar material

---

[4]Freudian theory is historically the foundation of psychoanalytic thought. See, for example, Calvin S. Hall, 1954, *A Primer of Freudian Psychology*, The World Publishing Company, New York and Scarborough, Ontario.

[5]D. Zillmann. 1982. "Transfer of Excitation in Emotional Behavior," in *Social Psychophysiology*, J.T. Cacioppo and R.E. Petty, eds., Guilford, New York.

[6]Huston et al., 1998, *Measuring the Effects of Sexual Content in the Media: A Report to the Kaiser Family Foundation*.

once this has occurred, or the viewer might not return to regularly viewing material because the viewer has lost interest.[7]

• *Social learning theory.* In Bandura's social learning theory,[8] young people can learn about sexuality from observing others depicted in the media. Specifically, they may observe the mechanics of sexual behavior, but they will also learn about the contexts in which behaviors occur, the motives and intentions behind the interactions represented, and the consequences for those participating in those behaviors. The messages implicit in media portrayals of sexuality may be particularly powerful when the participants are attractive, are shown as powerful, are rewarded in some way for their actions, or represent characters with whom the young person identifies. In this theory, the behavioral implications are not short-term reactions; rather, this information is used when the young person becomes engaged in a similar real-world sexual situation.

Social learning theory implies three major impacts on an observer: (1) imitation, in which the observer copies a novel behavior that has been seen before; (2) disinhibition, in which a behavior that was previously inhibited is now acted on because there are no negative consequences for the action; and (3) response facilitation, in which a socially desirable behavior increases in frequency as one observes another perform it. [9] Social learning theory separates learning a behavior from performing it. That is, knowledge about how to act in a certain way does not mean that one will do so. Performance requires some form of reinforcement for action to take place. Therefore, in contrast to cognitive approaches, social learning theory is based on reinforcement and traditional learning theory approaches. For example, for a person to imitate a sexual behavior or to have a sexual behavior disinhibited, there must be situational contingencies and reinforcements to support the behavior that has been observed.

Over time, Bandura increasingly incorporated cognitive mechanisms into his theory. Attention to information, retention of that knowledge, production of the learned behavior, and the motivation to do so were always key elements of his theory, but he added to it the concept of self-efficacy, the belief that a person can control the events around him or her. He reframed his theory as social cognitive theory to emphasize cognitive elements, but the mechanistic element of reinforcement remained a key facet of his approach.[10]

---

[7]Sandra L. Calvert. 1999. *Children's Journeys Through the Information Age.* McGraw-Hill, Boston.

[8]A. Bandura. 1971. *Social Learning Theory.* General Learning Press, New York.

[9]Calvert, 1999, *Children's Journeys Through the Information Age.*

[10]Calvert, 1999, *Children's Journeys Through the Information Age.*

• *Cognitive approaches: information processing theory.* Information processing theories are focused on cognitive constructs that develop as a function of experiences. Media provide one such venue for these experiences. Based on experiences, children construct scripts (also known as schemas), which are learned expectations that guide perception, memory, and inferences. These scripts are used to predict how one is to act and how others will act.[11] Stereotypes about sexual behavior are one type of sexual script.

Young children have very few sexual schemas, but as a growing repertoire of expectations develops, these schemas shape future perceptions, memories, and interpretations. Both sexual content in the media and real life experiences shape an individual's schema. As a result, sexual content in the media may have a greater impact on individuals who do not have real sexual experiences. Media that depict sexuality that is safe and positive may help to develop healthy sexual schemas, while content that is permissive of sexual violence or other negative sexual encounters could help to construct sexual schemas that are not beneficial for—or may even be harmful to—the young person.[12]

Theories on schemas and scripts for sexual interactions suggest that any understanding of how the media shape this type of development must include a careful analysis of the messages conveyed by the circumstances of sexual activity, as well as of the types of communication, negotiation, and decision making that occur before, during, and after depictions of sexuality. It also involves a close examination of the preexisting schemas that the individual brings to the media situation.

• *Cultivation theory.* In the field of communications, Gerbner describes cultivation theory, a paradigm based on how media content interfaces with the person who is experiencing it.[13] Media messages that are often depicted can shape the beliefs of viewers, a process that is not unlike the development of schemas. For Gerbner, there are two main effects of media exposure: (1) mainstreaming, in which dominant cultural messages come to be taken as true, even if they are not; and (2) resonance, in which media messages that resonate with one's own experiences have a very strong impact on the viewer. In this approach, heavy exposure to sexual material in the media leads to a view of sexuality based on the predominant media message. If that media message rings true with an individual's own life, that message will be further enhanced.[14]

---

[11]Huston et al., 1998, *Measuring the Effects of Sexual Content in the Media: A Report to the Kaiser Family Foundation.*

[12]Calvert, 1999, *Children's Journeys Through the Information Age.*

[13]G. Gerbner, 1966, "On Defining Communication: Still Another View," *Journal of Communication* 16(2): 99-103; G. Gerbner, 1972, "Communication and Social Environment," *Scientific American* 227(3): 152-160.

[14]Calvert, 1999, *Children's Journeys Through the Information Age.*

- *Uses and gratification theory.* In the field of communications, uses and gratification theory emphasizes the reasons people have for viewing and interacting with various media content. Essentially, individuals use the media for various needs, including information, entertainment, companionship, escapism, and exploration of various aspects of their own sexuality.[15] From this perspective, knowing why a young person chooses a particular type of media content is essential to understanding what the impact of that content will be.

6.2 EMPIRICAL WORK

As noted above, there are few empirical studies on the impact of sexually explicit media on young people. However, researchers have been able to conduct empirical studies using media content other than sexually explicit material—research on violent material is one such example. This is because our society has more permissive attitudes about allowing young people to view violent material than about allowing them to see sexually explicit material. For research purposes, a few studies of sexually explicit material have used college-age viewers as a way of understanding the impact this material may have on children.[16] Note, however, that a college student differs considerably in cognitive, physical, and social maturity compared with a primary- or middle-school student.

6.2.1 Violence

Several correlations have been observed in studies of violent media content and children: exposure to such content is correlated with desensitization, increases in hostility, imitation and disinhibition, and fear and anxiety responses. Desensitization (described in arousal theory) occurs when an emotional response to a stimulus is diminished after repeated exposure to that stimulus. This can be adaptive—a doctor who becomes accustomed to seeing blood and does not have the strong emotional response he or she experienced in medical school can more effectively help patients. The media, however, create fantasy exposures to content that

---

[15]Huston et al., 1998, *Measuring the Effects of Sexual Content in the Media: A Report to the Kaiser Family Foundation.*

[16]E.I. Donnerstein and D.G. Linz, 1986, "Mass Media Sexual Violence and Male Viewers: Current Theory and Research," *American Behavioral Scientist* 29(5): 601-618; D. Zillmann and J. Bryant, 1982, "Pornography, Sexual Callousness, and the Trivialization of Rape," *Journal of Communication* 32(4): 10-21; D. Zillman and J.B. Weaver, 1999, "Effects of Prolonged Exposure to Gratuitous Media Violence on Provoked and Unprovoked Hostile Behavior," *Journal of Applied Social Psychology* 29(1): 145-165.

can cause arousal and, over time, desensitization that is not necessarily (and often not) adaptive. For example, a child who sees a graphic, violent image might become angry or frightened. If this image is a representation and not an actual event, then the typical reactions of "fight or flight" are not appropriate or functional. With repeated exposure, the child may cease to have these emotional responses.[17] Research has shown that desensitization to media violence can result in reduced arousal and emotional disturbance while witnessing actual violence, greater hesitancy to call an adult to intervene in a witnessed physical altercation, and less sympathy for victims of abuse and assault.[18]

Emotional expressions of hostility, fear, and anxiety are also measured within arousal theory. Increases in hostility can correlate with watching violent content in the media. In one study, college students who watched violent films for 4 days were more likely to interfere with another individual's future employment chances (an anti-social act).[19] Repeated viewing of violent material seemed to create an enduring hostile mental framework that discouraged viewers from interacting positively with others, even those who had not provoked them.

Young people of a wide range of ages sometimes experience fear and anxiety as a result of exposure to television.[20] Results can range from nightmares and temporary sleep disturbances to more lasting effects, such as a fear of swimming in the ocean, after watching the movie *Jaws*.[21] The

---

[17]Calvert, 1999, *Children's Journeys Through the Information Age*; J. Cantor, "Media Violence and Children's Emotions: Beyond the 'Smoking Gun'," paper presented at the annual convention of the American Psychological Association, Washington, D.C., October 5, 2001, available online at <http://joannecantor.com/EMOTIONS2_sgl.htm>.

[18]V.B. Cline, R.G. Croft, and S. Courrier, 1973, "Desensitization of Children to Television Violence," *Journal of Personality and Social Psychology* 27(3): 516-546; F. Molitor and K.W. Hirsch, 1994, "Children's Toleration of Real-Life Aggression After Exposure to Media Violence: A Replication of the Drabman and Thomas Studies," *Child Study Journal* 24(3): 191-207; and C.R. Mullin and D. Linz, 1995, "Desensitization and Resensitization to Violence Against Women: Effects of Exposure to Sexually Violent Films on Judgments of Domestic Violence Victims," *Journal of Personality and Social Psychology* 69(3): 449-459.

[19]D. Zillman and J.B. Weaver, 1999, "Effects of Prolonged Exposure to Gratuitous Media Violence on Provoked and Unprovoked Hostile Behavior," *Journal of Applied Social Psychology* 29(1): 145-165.

[20]J. Owens, R. Maxim, M. McGuinn, C. Nobile, M. Msall, and A. Alario, 1999, "Television-Viewing Habits and Sleep Disturbance in School Children," *Pediatrics* 104(3): 552 (Abstract), available online at <http://www.pediatrics.org/cgi/content/full/104/3/c27> (May 25, 2001); M.I. Singer, K. Slovak, T. Frierson, and P. York, 1998, "Viewing Preferences, Symptoms of Psychological Trauma, and Violent Behaviors Among Children Who Watch Television," *Journal of the American Academy of Child and Adolescent Psychiatry* 37(10): 1041-1048.

[21]K. Harrison and J. Cantor, 1999, "Tales from the Screen: Enduring Fright Reactions to Scary Media," *Media Psychology* 1:117-140.

specific types of content that lead to fear will depend on the child's developmental level. For example, preschool-age children are most disturbed by grotesque, visual images, such as monsters, whereas children in elementary school are more likely to be frightened by realistic images in which the danger they perceive could actually happen. Teenagers tend to be more frightened by abstract components of a story. Data from studies during the Persian Gulf conflict showed that elementary school children became frightened by images of exploding missiles, whereas teen viewers were more afraid of the idea that the conflict could spread. Material frightening to a teenager may not even be processed by a younger child, who may not understand the abstract concepts that are less readily visualized.[22]

Social learning theory suggests that children learn through observation and modeling of behaviors and actions, and it is often used to explain the phenomenon of children imitating what they see on television or in films. There are numerous studies documenting a correlation between media exposure to violence and children's aggressive behaviors. For instance, a study in Israeli middle schools after the introduction of the World Wrestling Federation to Israeli television documented the widespread imitation of acts demonstrated on this show that resulted in numerous playground injuries,[23] and a juvenile was recently tried and convicted for homicide against a small girl in what the juvenile claimed was an imitation of professional wrestling moves.[24]

It is unknown if responses to media violence are cumulative (e.g., attitudinal changes resulting from repeat exposure) or instantaneous (e.g., fear responses due to seeing the "wrong" movie at the "wrong" developmental moment), if they are temporary or lasting (e.g., a few nightmares or a lasting fear of specific animals or situations), how the impact of exposure to media violence varies with the kinds of violence being seen, and how the context of viewing violence (e.g., news reports vs. "slasher" movies) may have differential effects on children. Furthermore, additional research is needed before extrapolating results from this research

[22]J. Cantor, 1998, *"Mommy, I'm Scared": How TV and Movies Frighten Children and What We Can Do to Protect Them,* Harcourt Brace, San Diego, Calif.; J. Cantor, M.L. Mares, and M.B. Oliver, 1993, "Parents' and Children's Emotional Reactions to Televised Coverage of the Gulf War," pp. 325-340 in *Desert Storm and the Mass Media,* B. Greenberg and W. Gantz, eds., Hampton Press, Cresskill, N.J.

[23]Donnerstein and Linz, 1986, "Mass Media Sexual Violence and Male Viewers: Current Theory and Research"; Zillman, 1982, "Transfer of Excitation in Emotional Behavior"; D. Lemish, 1997, "The School as a Wrestling Arena: The Modeling of a Television Series," *Communication* 22(4): 395-418.

[24]"Boy Gets Life for 'Wrestle' Killing," *St. Petersburg Times,* March 10, 2001. Available online at <http://www.sptimes.com/News/031001/State/Boy_gets_life_for__wr.shtml>.

on violent material to sexually explicit material, although research on violence may be relevant to sexually violent content.

6.2.2 Sexually Violent Material

Research on the effects of viewing sexually violent images has focused on college-age viewers. Effects observed in these studies were similar to effects seen in studies on violence without sexual content. Studies of young adults (aged 18 to 20) watching an hour of the equivalent of an R-rated film containing sexual violence have demonstrated desensitization effects immediately after viewing. Levels of physiological arousal decreased with additional viewing after the first hour. Furthermore, viewers shown a documentary on battered women after an hour of watching a sexually violent film demonstrated less empathy toward the victims, and gave lower evaluations of how injured the woman was and how painful the experience may have been. Attitudinal changes have also been observed, with both men and women more likely to display callous attitudes toward female victims, such as stating that a rape was the fault of the victim or that she brought it on herself.[25] Women viewers do have slightly different responses from men, and although both show desensitization, women also tend to experience an increase in fear after watching sexually violent content,[26] in large part because they are likely to be the victims of rape.

Although changes in attitude and arousal levels were measured in these studies, it is not clear to what extent these changes may be lasting. For example, normal arousal responses tend to return after 24 hours, and the "long-term" changes in attitudes are based on studies that follow subjects for only a few weeks after viewing the material.[27]

Zillmann's arousal theory suggests that sexually explicit content does not lead to any specific or consistent behavioral outcome in viewers. Although sexually explicit content may produce emotional or physiological arousal, behavioral outcomes—which might include sexual expression, aggressive behavior, or altruism—depend on the personality of the viewer, the environment, and context in which the material was viewed.[28]

---

[25]E.I. Donnerstein and D.G. Linz. 1986. "Mass Media Sexual Violence and Male Viewers: Current Theory and Research," *American Behavioral Scientist* 29(1):601-618.

[26]C. Krafka, D. Linz, E. Donnerstein, and S. Penrod. 1997. "Women's Reactions to Sexually Aggressive Mass Media Depictions," *Violence Against Women* 3(2):149.

[27]See, for example, D.G. Linz, E.I. Donnerstein, and S.M. Adams, 1989, "Physiological Desensitization and Judgements About Female Victims of Violence," *Human Communication Research* 15(4):509-522; D.G. Linz, E.I. Donnerstein, and S. Penrod, 1988, "Effects of Long-Term Exposure to Violent and Sexually Degrading Depictions of Women," *Journal of Personality and Social Psychology* 55(5): 758-768.

[28]Huston et al., 1998, *Measuring the Effects of Sexual Content in the Media: A Report to the Kaiser Family Foundation.*

From the perspective of social learning theory, one can argue that behaviors that are learned are not necessarily performed.

6.2.3 Exposure to Non-violent Sexual Material

Most studies of the impact of sexually explicit material in the media on adolescents' sexual attitudes and practices have been limited to the sexual content in mainstream media. Youth exposed to content involving sexual relations outside of marriage rated such behavior as significantly less objectionable than did their peers who viewed either sexual relations between married partners or non-sexual relations between adults,[29] a finding consistent with social learning theory (i.e., disinhibition) or arousal theory (i.e., desensitization). Viewing music videos increased the acceptability of premarital sex for teenagers as compared to teenagers who were not similarly exposed.[30] In some studies, youth exposed to explicit sexual content that did not involve violence did not become desensitized,[31] while in others, large amounts of experimental exposure to such material led men (and to some extent women) to be more callous toward gender relationships, more likely to overestimate the prevalence of certain kinds of non-mainstream sexual behavior such as sadomasochism and bestiality, less likely to be offended by sexually explicit material, less likely to support restrictions on the distribution of sexually explicit materials, and more likely to support lighter sentences for convicted rapists.[32]

Many media messages suggest to adolescents that they should be thinking about sexual activity, and engaging in it early. Frequent televi-

---

[29]J. Bryant and S.C. Rockwell. 1994. "Effects of Massive Exposure to Sexually Oriented Primetime Television Programming on Adolescents Moral Judgment," pp. 183-195 in *Media, Children, and the Family: Social Scientific, Psychodynamic, and Clinical Perspectives*, D. Zillmann, J. Bryant, and A.C. Huston, eds., Erlbaum, Hillsdale, N.J.

[30]L.E. Greeson and R.A. Williams, 1987, "Social Implications of Music Videos for Youth: An Analysis of the Content and Effects of MTV," *Youth & Society* 18(2): 177-189; J.S. Strouse, N. Buerkel-Rothfuss, and E.C. Long, 1995, "Gender and Family as Moderators of the Relationship Between Music Video Exposure and Adolescent Sexual Permissiveness," *Adolescence* 30(119): 505-521.

[31]D.G. Linz, E.I. Donnerstein, and S. Penrod, 1988, "Effects of Long-Term Exposure to Violent and Sexually Degrading Depictions of Women," *Journal of Personality and Social Psychology* 55(5): 758-768; D.G. Linz, E.I. Donnerstein, and S.M. Adams, 1989, "Physiological Desensitization and Judgments About Female Victims of Violence," *Human Communication Research* 15(4): 509-522.

[32]Regarding callousness toward gender relationships, they were more likely to agree that "pickups should expect to put out" and "a woman doesn't mean 'no' unless she slaps you." Regarding lighter sentences, those with large amounts of experimental exposure recommended incarceration times that were 53 percent as long as those with no exposure at all. See D. Zillmann and J. Bryant, 1982, "Pornography, Sexual Callousness, and the Trivialization of Rape," *Journal of Communication* 32(4): 10-21.

sion viewers are less likely to believe that marriages are happy or lasting, prompted perhaps by the depiction of married couples who are not happy, not having sex, or having sex with a person other than their spouse.[33] Compared to non-viewers, soap opera viewers appear to believe that single mothers have relatively easy lives, with good jobs, high levels of education, significant leisure time, and freedom from poverty. They were also more likely to believe that the male friends of a single mother will be important in her children's lives.[34]

In one study, teenagers frequently viewing television with a high degree of sexual content were more likely to engage in sexual intercourse than those who viewed television with a smaller proportion of sexual content, though it is unclear whether viewing such content contributes to a teen's decision to engage in intercourse, or instead, whether those who are already engaging in sexual activity are more likely to seek out such programs.[35] A longitudinal study found no strong or consistent evidence for links between the amount or sexual content of television viewing by children and the initiation of sexual activity.[36] Other studies have suggested that frequent viewers of mainstream television programs tend to have more negative attitudes toward remaining a virgin and that becoming a non-virgin is a priority.[37]

Many studies indicate that the media seem to have an effect on attitudes, although it is difficult to assess whether these attitudes are long-lasting, the extent to which attitudes are related to behavior, and the degree to which the media, compared with other sources of experience in a young person's life, are influential in shaping the choices a young person makes. For example, although studies have shown that viewing fashion magazines tends to cause lower self-scoring by girls on body image indices, not all girls become anorexic. In one study in which early adolescent females were asked to keep journals about what they observed in the media about love, sex, and relationships, the participants' experience was extremely important in shaping how they interpreted and reacted to sexuality in the

---

[33]N. Signorielli. 1991. "Adolescents and Ambivalence Toward Marriage: A Cultivation Analysis," *Youth and Society* 23(1): 11-25.

[34]M. Larson. 1996. "Sex Roles and Soap Operas: What Adolescents Learn About Single Motherhood," *Sex Roles: A Journal of Research* 35(1/2): 97-121.

[35]J.D. Brown and S. Newcomer. 1991. "Television Viewing and Adolescents' Sexual Behavior," *Journal of Homosexuality* 21(1/2), 77-91.

[36]J.L. Peterson, K.A. Moore, and F.F. Furstenberg. 1991. "Television Viewing and Early Initiation of Sexual Intercourse: Is There a Link?," *Journal of Homosexuality* 21(1/2): 93-119.

[37]Brown and Newcomer, 1991, "Television Viewing and Adolescents' Sexual Behavior"; Strouse et al., 1995, "Gender and Family as Moderators of the Relationship Between Music Video Exposure and Adolescent Sexual Permissiveness."

media.[38] One prepubertal 12-year-old did not want to see sex in the media, while other girls who were beginning to think about relationships were very interested in the romantic heterosexual script. Girls who had been sexually active were more critical of the media's portrayal of sexual interaction and the roles male and females should take (according to these representations). Experience, development, and age made enormous differences in the types of reactions girls had to media depictions about sex.

6.2.4 Caveats and Cautions

Although some literature exists on traditional forms of media (e.g., television, radio, magazines), the empirical research that examines the impact on children of exposure to non-violent sexual material is extremely limited.[39] Social mores and ethical issues generally prevent U.S. scientists from studying the impact of media on sexual behavior (Box 6.1). Because there are so few studies in this area, the empirical research that does exist must be viewed with caution, and in particular must not be viewed as making statements or supporting conclusions that go beyond the research designs employed.

• Correlational studies do not permit one to make causal inferences. For example, in the studies mentioned in Footnote 37, it is possible that a third factor, such as different values and beliefs about sexual activity, is actually responsible for the trend in attitude described and that television viewing is an extraneous variable.

• Some researchers have attempted to avoid the complications of studying minors by observing the impact of sexually explicit material on college-age viewers. These studies seek to extrapolate the impact this material may have on younger populations. It is not clear to what extent this generalization is appropriate because younger individuals have very different developmental needs and experiences than do college-age students. Some research has suggested that college-age students viewing sexually explicit material may develop more callous attitudes toward women and female sexuality, but it has not been clear to what extent these attitudes are lasting.[40]

---

[38]Sarah Keller, 2000, "How Do Early Adolescent Girls Use Media to Shape Their Romantic Identities?," unpublished doctoral dissertation, University of North Carolina, Chapel Hill.

[39]For instance, a Kaiser Family Foundation report reviewed existing research on the media, finding no more than 15 empirical studies on this topic. See Huston et al., 1998, *Measuring the Effects of Sexual Content in the Media*.

[40]Donnerstein and Linz, 1986, "Mass Media Sexual Violence and Male Viewers: Current Theory and Research"; Zillmann and Bryant, 1982, "Pornography, Sexual Callousness, and the Trivialization of Rape."

• Experimental studies typically examine impact on time scales rang-ing from minutes to days (in a small number of cases, effects are mea-sured 3 to 6 weeks after the experimental treatment). For example, view-ing a television program may change a person's immediate state by inducing arousal, leading to inhibition of impulses, or activating thoughts or associations, and in doing so might have immediate influence on one's behavior. However, such studies do not provide an empirical basis for determining impact over longer time scales (e.g., months to decades), and in particular cannot provide a sound empirical basis for claims of long-term deviant sexual behavior resulting from exposure to sexually explicit material in one's youth.

Societal impact is better assessed using longitudinal data that mea-sures long-term effects. Experimental studies do not address long-term impact, and there is significant debate and disagreement over whether results of such experiments can be extrapolated to the long term. For example, some studies of college-age students suggest that males viewing sexually violent movies displayed more callous attitudes toward female victims.[41] However, these attitudes were tested immediately after view-ing the film and several weeks later with no further follow-up. Longer-term effects have simply not been measured. There also is little informa-tion as to how other experiences might interact with and mitigate some of these negative attitudes.

• It is difficult to generalize clinical research to broader populations because of the sampling issue. Those who seek or obtain clinical treat-ment for criminal sexual behavior, for example, are hardly a representa-tive sample of the population that may or may not have been affected by the viewing of sexually explicit material in their youth.

• Empirical studies examining the impact of exposure to other me-dia content (e.g., studies of the impact of viewing violence) cannot be extrapolated with confidence to the sexual domain. Studies that measure the impact of violent material are sometimes used to speculate about the impact of sexually explicit material on the basis that learning processes that underlie both types of content are similar. Although one can envision similarities between the effects of watching violent and sexually violent material, the impact of content that is sexually explicit but not violent may be very different. No research is available to establish the extent to which it is appropriate to extrapolate from studies of one type of media content to other types.

---

[41]Donnerstein and Linz, 1986, "Mass Media Sexual Violence and Male Viewers: Current Theory and Research"; Zillmann and Bryant, 1982, "Pornography, Sexual Callousness, and the Trivialization of Rape."

- Cross-cultural studies—to which researchers sometimes turn to identify possible connections between exposure to sexually explicit material and behavior, and which are made necessary by ethical and legal constraints in doing research in this area in the United States—have limited applicability. For example, cross-cultural studies of youth being exposed to nudity and explicit material at a relatively young age do not show higher levels of sexual addiction or teen pregnancy in European countries compared with the United States. However, European children also receive early, frequent, and comprehensive sex education in a way that is not typical in the United States. This could suggest that such education offers a useful context for interpreting sexually explicit material. It may also suggest that sexually explicit material does not have the type of impact on behavior that some may fear.

6.3 FACTORS AFFECTING THE IMPACT ON MINORS OF EXPOSURE TO SEXUALLY EXPLICIT MATERIAL

The phrase "impact on minors of exposure to sexually explicit material" used by itself obscures a number of important differentiating factors, because "impact," "minors," "exposure," and "sexually explicit material" all have a wide range of meaning. Without considering these differences, an overly simplistic analysis is inevitable. Consider each of these terms in turn.

6.3.1 Impact

As noted above, impact can be measured in the short term or long term. Its magnitude can be large or small (and people with different values will differ on whether a given change in a certain dimension is large or small). And a particular impact may be desirable or undesirable. (The desensitization of a teenager who has been viewing sexually explicit behavior on an adult Web site can be regarded as undesirable, if one believes that such depictions should be shocking and socially unacceptable, or as desirable, if one believes that a desensitized individual will simply ignore such images in the future.) Moreover, "impact" may not be confined to the direct results of exposure to sexually explicit material (for example, impact may also include the punishment that a teenager might receive for viewing such material).

6.3.2 Minors

Children from birth to 17 or 18 vary widely in maturity and developmental perspective. The broad range of cognitive, social, emotional, and moral reasoning and developmental abilities encompassed by this age range means that a 6-year-old will react differently than a 16-year-old to sexually explicit content. The youngest children may not find such images remarkable or memorable because they do not have the cognitive abilities or understand the social meaning of explicit images. In contrast, because they are becoming curious about sex and are experiencing changing bodies and a changing social landscape, those in the 9 to 12 age range may be more vulnerable to disturbing portrayals of sex and sexual activity. (For perspective, note that the mean age of first intercourse is around 17 ½ years of age, as discussed in Section 5.2.)

Among the adolescents to whom the committee spoke, those in high school (the 11th and 12th grades) were much less concerned about exposure to sexually explicit material on the Internet than were middle-school students. Indeed, the 11th and 12th graders noted that they were exposed to similar material in every other part of their lives, and they now found it more annoying than upsetting. By contrast, the middle-schoolers were less nonchalant and tended to be more concerned about such material.

6.3.3 Gender

Gender is also likely to influence the impact of sexually explicit material on young people in part because it will influence how and with what characters young viewers identify. This is not to suggest that girls will only identify with female characters and boys with male characters, but the gender of the viewer will certainly affect how one interprets the treatment of characters. In addition, some research suggests that girls and boys select different types of media (e.g., *Glamour* has a broad female readership) and use them in different ways. For example, some studies suggest that girls use the media to gain insight about interpersonal relationships—in one study girls who viewed a video about teen pregnancy reflected more about the content than boys.[42]

In the context of viewing sexually explicit material (especially images), the overwhelming majority of such material is oriented toward male consumers, with females being the object of sexual activity, and boys tend to be more interested in visual depictions of sexual images than are girls.[43] Put another way, preadolescent and adolescent males are

---

[42]M. Thompson, K. Walsh-Childers, and J.D. Brown, 1993, "The Influence of Family Communication Patterns and Sexual Experience on Processing of a Movie Video," pp. 248-263 in *Media, Sex and the Adolescent*, B.S. Greenberg, J.D. Brown, and N.L. Buerkel-Rothfuss, eds., Hampton Press, N.J.

[43]For example, men demonstrate greater interest in visual sexual stimuli than do women (J.M. Bailey, S. Gaulin, Y. Agyei, and B.A. Gladue, 1994, "Effects of Gender and Sexual

more likely to view online adult-oriented sexually explicit material than are females of the same ages.[44]

6.3.4 Special Needs

The experiences of minors encompass a very wide range, and certain segments of the population may be more susceptible to influence and impact than others. For example, one site visit of the committee took it to a residential school for young girls who had been sexually abused. Staff at the school expressed to the committee the concern that for these girls, sometimes at the start of a very long recovery process fraught with psychological and emotional pitfalls, even one exposure to a sexually violent or abusive image—especially if they were not prepared for it—could be highly damaging to them and to their recovery.

6.3.5 Exposure

One dimension of exposure is the type of stimulus involved—visual, still or moving, textual, and so on. A second dimension is the intensity and duration of exposure—3 hours per day, every day, for 5 years is obviously different from once for 3 minutes in the last 2 years. Most research in this area, sparse though it is, has focused primarily on the impact of exposure patterns that are quite frequent and deliberate rather than incidental or inadvertent and rare, and have involved primarily visual stimuli.

A third dimension of exposure is the context in which it occurs. In particular, parental involvement in adolescent television viewing and dialog about the meanings conveyed in depictions of sexual activity can influence the relationship between viewing and sexual behavior. For example, one study showed that adolescents who did not talk with their parents about television were more likely to have sexual intercourse than those who did.[45] The style with which families communicate about the

---

Orientation on Evolutionarily Relevant Aspects of Human Mating Psychology," *Journal of Personality and Social Psychology* 66(6): 1081-1093). In the context of sexual fantasy, visual imagery is also more important for men than for women (B.J. Ellis and D. Symons, 1990, "Sex Differences in Sexual Fantasy: An Evolutionary Psychological Approach," *Journal of Sex Research* 27(4): 527-555). One caveat: these studies were conducted using adult subjects rather than minors.

[44]In surveying adults, a Nielsen Media survey found that about two-thirds of the users of sexually explicit Internet sites are male. See CommerceNet/Nielsen Media, 1998, Internet Demographic Study, June.

[45]Peterson et al., 1991, "Television Viewing and Early Initiation of Sexual Intercourse: Is There a Link?"

media also seemed to influence the way adolescents interpret sexual content in the media.[46]

A fourth dimension of exposure is whether exposure has been voluntary or involuntary, as discussed in Sections 5.5.1 and 5.5.2. Most of the research known to the committee regarding exposure to sexually explicit material has involved voluntary—and hence anticipated—exposure. Thus, little is known empirically about the impact of involuntary and unanticipated exposure. Given that inadvertent exposure to sexually explicit material on the Internet generally occurs at some point, an important question is the nature and extent of the impact of a surprise encounter.

6.3.6 The Type of Sexually Explicit Material

There is a very wide range of material that different people regard as sexually explicit, including photos of models in bathing suits, couples having intercourse, group sex scenes, sadomasochism, gay and lesbian sex, and erotic texts of the *Kama Sutra* or *The Joy of Sex*, as well as scholarly works such as those of Masters and Johnson.[47] As noted above, the impact of images depicting sexual violence is likely to be different from the impact of images depicting non-violent and consensual sex; presentation of the material is also likely to affect the nature of the impact (e.g., the difference in portrayal of sexuality in *Playboy* compared to that in *Our Bodies, Ourselves*).

Along the lines of presentation, realism in the media (or at least that which young people perceive as being believable portrayals of sexuality) may be more influential than depictions that seem less realistic. Depictions of sexuality that are realistic but romanticized or idealistic may encourage young people to have unrealistic expectations of sexuality and may induce or influence young people to adopt these portrayals as guides to sexual behavior and romantic relationships.[48]

---

[46]Thompson et al., 1993, "The Influence of Family Communication Patterns and Sexual Experience on Processing of a Movie Video."

[47]See, for example, William Masters and Virginia Johnson, 1966, *Human Sexual Response*, Little, Brown and Company, Boston; William Masters and Virginia Johnson, 1970, *Human Sexual Inadequacy*, Little, Brown and Company, Boston.

[48]Huston et al., 1998, *Measuring the Effects of Sexual Content in the Media: A Report to the Kaiser Family Foundation*.

7

Beyond the Science: Perspectives on Impact and the Public Debate

7.1 CHALLENGES TO PARENTS

One of the strongest challenges that many parents face with respect to their children's exposure to sexually explicit material is their own ambivalence toward it. Such parents assert that they object to their children viewing sexually explicit material, but in the conduct of their own lives tolerate it and may even seek it out. This is not to say that all parents who assert such objections behave inconsistently with their stated positions, but the fact that the adult entertainment business is as profitable as it is suggests that at least some parents say one thing and do another. And, even if they do not seek it out, many parents are active and by and large willing participants in a culture that glorifies the particular style of sexual engagement and interaction that is illustrated in the media. Thus, it is important to consider what messages parents are delivering to their children.

A second point to be considered is that traditional nuclear families are increasingly less common. According to the U.S. Census, the number of women living with their own child but without a husband grew by 25 percent from 1990 to 2000. The number of unmarried-partner homes increased by 60 percent in this period. Furthermore, even in nuclear families, stay-at-home parents—who might provide supervision—are in the minority. Of married women with children aged 6 to 17, 39 percent worked outside the home in 1960, 49.2 percent in 1970, and 77.1 percent in 1999.[1] Also, there are same-sex couples living together openly in virtually

---

[1]For the 1960 figure, see "Employment Status of Women, by Marital Status and Presence and Age of Children: 1960 to 1998," Statistical Abstract of the United States: 1999, Table No. 659, p. 417, available online at <http://www.census.gov/prod/99pubs/99statab/sec13.pdf>. For the 1970 and 1999 figures, see "Employment Status of Women, by Marital Status and Presence and Age of Children: 1970 to 1999," Statistical Abstract of the United States: 2000, Table No. 653, p. 409, available online at <http://www.census.gov/prod/2001pubs/statab/sec13.pdf>.

every county in the United States, suggesting that social attitudes about homosexuality may be becoming more tolerant.

Overall, while parents enjoy broad discretion to raise their children as they see fit, it is likely that non-parental influences on children have increased over the past several decades. For example, the extent to which children are engaged with various media has increased considerably. Schools have been asked to take over responsibilities for many activities for which parents have been traditionally responsible, ranging from serving breakfast to providing sex education.

The Internet itself presents particular challenges for parents that are not posed by other media. The generation gap with respect to the Internet is large and profound. Perhaps for the first time, children—as a group—are more knowledgeable than their parents about an increasingly pervasive technology.[2] These "digital children"[3] have never known a world without personal computers, and many have been exposed to the Internet for a very large fraction of their lives (Box 7.1). They also have the time and the inclination to explore the limits of the technology. The result is that, compared to their parents, they are more knowledgeable about how to do things on the Internet and with other forms of information technology, and more knowledgeable about what things can be done and what experiences can be had on the Internet. In practice, such expertise makes the teenager rather than the parents the in-house expert on computers, and such reliance on the teenagers whom one is trying to guide and parent presents interesting challenges not generally faced by parents in the past.

Testimony to the committee provided one very clear example of this phenomenon. A teenager, knowing that her mother would "freak out" at the online solicitations and invitations to view commercial sexually explicit material that she was receiving,[4] simply set up an AOL account for her mother with parental controls set to "young teen," thereby blocking her mother from receiving such material. Her mother, not knowing what was being blocked, expressed surprise that her online experience was much less intrusive than she had been led to believe.

---

[2]The Children's Partnership. 1999. *The Parents' Guide to the Information Superhighway: Rules and Tools for Families Online*, Second Ed. Available online at <http://www.childrens partnership.org/> (October, 5, 2001).

[3]Don Tapscott. 1998. *Growing Up Digital: The Rise of the Net Generation*. McGraw-Hill.

[4]This testimony is consistent with a study undertaken by the Girl Scout Research Institute finding that "30 percent of girls (responding to the study) had been sexually harassed in a chat room, but only 7 percent told their mothers or fathers about the harassment, most fearing their parents would overreact and ban computer usage altogether." See Whitney Roban. 2002. *The Net Effect: Girls and New Media*. Girl Scout Research Institute, New York. Available online at <http://www.girlscouts.org/about/PDFs/NetEffects.pdf>.

Box 7.1
Experiences on the Internet and with Computers

The following information was obtained in a survey of 500 teenagers aged 12 to 17 that was conducted by *Family PC* magazine in the fall of 2000.

Usage

- 80 percent spend 1 to 5 hours a week on e-mail.
- 75 percent spend 1 to 5 hours a week online doing homework and research.
- 66 percent spend 1 to 5 hours a week Web surfing.
- 31 percent have a computer in their room.

The teenagers surveyed had been online for an average of 3.7 years.

Life with a Computer at Home

- 63 percent said they had to compete with parents or siblings for computer time.
- 75 percent said families had a computer before they turned 12.
- 9 percent said the computer came home before they were born.

Interacting with People Online

- 38 percent preferred telephone contact to stay in touch with friends, while 33 percent preferred online mechanisms.
- 83 percent used e-mail to stay in touch with distant friends and relatives.
- 84 percent used instant messaging and e-mail to communicate with other people for any purpose.
- 44 percent used chat rooms, but only 10 percent used chat rooms regularly.
- 32 percent thought it was easier to say personal things online versus face-to-face.

Online Friendships

- 33 percent met someone online with whom they still keep in touch.
- 21 percent arranged to meet their e friend in person.
- Girls were more likely than boys to arrange a face-to-face meeting (26 percent versus 14 percent).

Computer Education

Of the teens surveyed, 55 percent had taken a computer class, including

- 62 percent of boys and
- 51 percent of girls.

SOURCE: *A Field Guide to Wired Teens*. 2000. Digital Research Inc., Kennebunkport, Maine.

Making parenting in the age of the Internet even more challenging is the fact that some real-world lessons do not carry over well to cyberspace. For example, most parents have told their children to "never talk to strangers." As evidenced by many new pen-pal relationships between young people in remote parts of the world, this kind of "communication with strangers" can be an invaluable learning experience that allows young people to develop awareness of global issues and even a global sense of community. However, a sense of online community can also be extremely misleading—especially to neophyte Internet users—in creating a sense of safety and trust that is in fact unwarranted.

Rules of behavior in cyberspace are sometimes different than in real life, and new behaviors and traditions are created. These online social mores are often a mystery to parents, though their children may be quite comfortable with them. For example, technology enables multitasking to a much greater degree than has been possible in the past (e.g., conducting a number of conversations via instant messages and telephone simultaneously),[5] whereas a rule that governs many, though not all, adult interactions with other people is one of paying full attention.

Issues with a long history in the real world play out differently in cyberspace. Parents who once fought with kids about messy rooms and telephone time must now deal with conflicts over computer usage as well. Children—who always resisted the notion of sharing diaries with their parents—must contend with the possibility that their e-mail might be monitored or the history of their Web visits viewed. Academic plagiarism is much easier in an Internet environment and thus is arguably more tempting. Sorting out truth from fiction—a task that has always been important—is more important than ever before given the near-infinite diversity of content on the Web. Bullying—always a problem in some contexts in real life—has its online analogs in harassment, and is sometimes protected by the anonymity provided by the Internet.

Finally, there is often a large gap in what parents perceive their children are doing on the Internet and what these children report they are actually doing (Table 7.1). This, too, reflects an all-too-common and more general disconnect between parental perceptions of their children's behavior and what they actually do.[6]

---

[5]Katie Hafner. 2001. "Teenage Overload, or Digital Dexterity?," *New York Times*, April 12.

[6]For example, in April 1998, the Partnership for a Drug-Free America released a study indicating that many baby-boomer parents "are seriously underestimating the reality of drugs in their children's lives." In support of that claim, the study noted that

• 38 percent of parents said their teenagers might have been offered drugs; 59 percent of teenagers reported having been offered an illicit substance.

• 21 percent of parents acknowledged the possibility that their teenager might have tried marijuana; 44 percent of teens said they'd done so.

TABLE 7.1 Parents' Lack of Knowledge About the Internet Activities of Their Teenage Children

Activity	Parents Who Believe Child Is Doing This Activity	Children Who Report Doing This Activity
Posting personal online profiles[a]	17 percent	45 percent
Having private e-mail accounts[a]	68 percent	81 percent
Corresponding with strangers[a]	30 percent	More than 50 percent
While using the Internet, someone else is regularly in the room[b]	67 percent of parents report that someone else is in the room while their children are online	78 percent say they use the Internet when they are alone
Using the Internet at home for schoolwork at least once a week[b]	76 percent	63 percent

[a]Peter, Schoen, and Berland Associates. 2000. *Web Savvy and Safety: How Kids and Parent Differ in What They Know, Whom They Trust,* September. Available online at <http://www.microsoft.com/presspass/press/2000/nov00/safetywebsitespr.asp>.

[b]National School Boards Association (no date available). *Safe and Smart: Overview of Research and Guidelines for Children's Use of the Internet."* Available online at <http://www.nsbf.org/safe-smart/full-report.htm>.

None of these challenges obviate a parental role, or even a role for other adults, in ensuring a safe and appropriate Internet experience. While some children may know the technology better than their parents, parents and other adults still have important roles to play in shaping the values of their children and in teaching critical thinking and moral skills that allow children to make informed and ethical choices according to the values that are important to them. In short, the parental role is still central in teaching children to protect themselves on the Internet.

- 33 percent of parents said they believed their teenagers viewed marijuana as harmful; 18 percent of teens viewed trying marijuana as risky.
- 45 percent of parents believed their child might have friends who smoked marijuana; 71 percent of teens said they had friends who used it.

Source: Partnership for a Drug-Free America. 1998. *The Boomer-Rang: Baby Boomers Seriously Underestimating Presence of Drugs in Their Children's Lives.* Available online at <http://www.drugfreeamerica.org/NewsCenter/pats/pats1.asp?ws=PDFA&vol=1&grp=NewsCenter&cat=National+Surveys&top=Articles&Pyear=1997&Pname=pats199x.asp&pNum=9>. More recent data from the Partnership for a Drug-Free America, as yet unpublished, indicate similar trends.

7.2 SPECULATIONS AND OTHER PERSPECTIVES
ON POSSIBLE IMPACT

As the discussion in Chapter 6 indicates, the research literature on the impact of sexually explicit material on young people is sparse and inconclusive. Nevertheless, there are a variety of views on the potential negative impact that exposure to sexually explicit material might have on children, some of which are illustrated in Box 7.2. Further, there is no reason to suppose that all negative impacts are necessarily manifested in science-based research studies.

One issue of concern—mentioned by many parents in the committee's site visits as being far more troublesome to them than the issue of exposure to inappropriate sexually explicit material—is the fear that children will be physically victimized by someone whom they met through the Internet. Among many of the students with whom the committee spoke, meeting someone face-to-face whom they had initially encountered online was a common and accepted part of life, more common among girls than boys. Some of these face-to-face encounters occurred at parties, others one-on-one at malls, and in one case at a person's home. Most students knew that they should not give out personal information, such as real names and addresses, but they were generally overconfident in their ability to make judgments in potentially dangerous situations. For example, the committee spoke to one teenage girl who appeared to understand that people often lie online, that meeting Internet acquaintances face-to-face can be dangerous, and that things are not always what they seem. However, when asked if she would meet someone from the Internet, she said, "Sure—if I had any doubts about him, I would never do so—and I only do it with people I know are okay."

Another type of negative impact that has not yet been studied is the damage that results from online attacks on the character of an individual youth. For example, from time to time, the facial image (a head shot) of a student may be grafted onto a sexually explicit image using a software package such as Photoshop. Distribution of such a doctored image can be quite harmful to the student whose face is on the image, perhaps in part because in many cases, it is someone in the young person's physical community who has spread the rumor or image and the receiving audience are other students or friends also in the young person's physical community. On the committee's site visits, a number of students reported problems with online (and anonymous) harassment in the form of spreading rumors about one's character and sexual behavior or threatening someone with bodily harm.[7]

---

[7]Such behavior is similar in some ways to the use of the bathroom wall at school as a platform for someone writing nasty comments about a classmate, but electronic communi-

---

**Box 7.2
Views of the Advocates**

Sexually Explicit Materials Are Bad for Society

Anti-pornography advocates believe that pornography is linked to a variety of socially destructive behavior, such as rape, child molestation, and sexual dysfunction.[1] Furthermore, pornography is seen as disseminating dangerous misinformation about sexual relations and as promoting medically risky sexual practices, especially among adolescent boys, who are large consumers of sexually explicit material. One individual often quoted by those in the anti-pornography camp is Park Elliot Dietz, who has written:

> Pornography is a medical and public health problem because so much of it teaches false, misleading, and even dangerous information about human sexuality. . . . A person who learned about human sexuality in the "adults only" outlets of America would be a person who had never conceived of a man and a women marrying or even falling in love before having intercourse, who had never conceived of tender foreplay, and who had never conceived of procreation as a purpose of sexual union. Instead such a person would be one who had learned that sex at most meant sex with one's children, stepchildren, parents, siblings, pets, and with neighbors, plumbers, salesmen, burglars, and peepers.[2]

Anti-pornography advocates argue further that exposure to pornography that combines erotic images with violent images normalizes sexual assault and desensitizes men to rape. For example, they point to correlations between states in which large amounts of pornography are sold and high rates of rape, and between greater inclinations toward sexual coercion and being raised in home in which fathers read pornographic magazines and talked about watching X-rated movies. They also draw on clinical studies of sex offenders and self-described pornography addicts. For example, they note that a large fraction of sex offenders, child molesters, and those convicted of sexual assault are avid consumers of pornography. As for children, anti-pornography advocates argue that child pornography normalizes and promotes the sexual abuse of children. Graphic imagery is used to persuade children that sexual activity is normal and that other children willingly participate in such activities.

Many of these advocates believe that viewing pornography, even for a moment, can have dire consequences. For example, American Family Online believes that

---

[1]Views of the "anti-pornography" advocates can be found online at <http://www.cwfa.org/library/pornography/1998-06_pp_poison.shtml> and <http://www.chuckiii.com/Reports/Social_Issues/pornography.shtml>. The material in this section is derived from content found online at <http://www.cwfa.org/library/pornography/1998-06_pp_poison.shtml> and <http://www.chuckiii.com/Reports/Social_Issues/pornography.shtml>.

[2]Closing statements of the Meese Commission's Final Report. See Attorney General's Commission on Pornography. 1986. *Final Report.* U.S. Government Printing Office, Washington, D.C., July.

(continues)

---

cation allows such rumors to be forwarded and disseminated much more rapidly—with all of the attendant negative consequences.

Box 7.2 (continued)

"pornography is dangerous, and viewing it (even for a moment) can set off a terrible chain of events."[3] The American Family Association stated that "Ted Bundy started on his road to perversion and murder by innocently looking at 'nudie' magazines as a boy. It only took one time for him to become hooked."[4]

In addition, some commentators argue that even short-term exposure to certain sexually explicit materials has long-lasting physiological effects. For example, Jodi Hoffman, founder of Restore America's Moral Pride, wrote, "Someone on this list . . . has made numerous attempts at convincing us that pornography 'does no harm' to children. . . . Studies have shown that an event which lasts even so much as three-tenths of a second, within five to ten minutes has produced a structural change in the brain. Exposure to porn causes actual brain damage, especially in a child."[5]

Feminist anti-pornography advocates believe that pornography degrades women by portraying them as sexually insatiable objects of male pleasure in a world of sexual inequality, and that pornography contributes to male contempt for women that can ultimately lead to sexual violence and rape.

Finally, anti-pornography advocates argue that pornography eliminates from sexual acts the emotional intimacy needed to promote healthy relationships by reducing women and children to sex objects to be used on demand. Consumption of pornography is seen as the first step toward sexual addiction. Drawing on arousal theory, they argue that consumers of pornography are compelled to partake of more frequent "doses" of more varied and more extreme pornography in order to obtain the same sexual high. Eventually, they argue, the individual must act out the scenes being depicted to obtain the sexual highs—and that the scenes depicted are obviously bad. Such individuals thus become incapable of natural sexual relationships.

Sexually Explicit Materials Have Benefits for Society

A different set of views is expressed by those who believe that the widespread availability of sexually explicit materials has benefits for society.

One writer argues that the insistence on limiting such availability demonstrates restrictive attitudes toward sexual expression, and that "societies which hold restric-

---

[3]See <http://www.afo.net/help/block/Default.htm>.
[4]See <http://www.afajournal.org/archives/24060000438.asp>.
[5]See <http://www.inet-one.com/cypherpunks/dir.1997.10.30-1997.11.05/msg00377.html>.

Still a different kind of negative impact of children's exposure to graphic, adult-oriented, sexually explicit material is attributable not so much to the material per se as to the fact that exposure to such material may occur in a setting when a parent is not available to place the material into context, to explain why viewing such material is inappropriate, or to impart parental values with respect to viewing such material. In this view, children exposed to such material lose the opportunity to hear from a responsible adult making a critical point about the social assumptions underlying such images and portrayals and about values in society.

tive attitudes towards sexual issues tend to breed child abuse."[6] She asserts that such legislated limitations add to "the cultural squeamishness towards sex, which already appears to play a major role in child sex abuse," and that when "children think that sex is taboo, they will remain silent about being abused. If they think that they are doing something dirty because they are being abused, they will feel guilty, responsible for the abuse, they won't speak up and they'll continue to be abused." She further claims that restricting the availability of such materials is potentially hazardous for all women and children, citing the Danish experience in which "pornography was made freely available in Denmark in the late 60's," resulting "in the incidence of sex crimes [and] sexual violence towards women and children, [dropping] markedly." "Far from causing harm," she continues, "pornography appears to have a cathartic effect on people's sexuality. The Denmark experience of the 1960's teaches us that the incidence of sex crimes appears to lower dramatically when pornography is made freely available."

Another writer concluded that "after thorough review of the existing research on effects of pornography and violent material on the viewer, we can answer this question simply: there is no known harm caused by the actual viewing of pornographic materials, and results of aggression studies in relation to violent material have been unable to demonstrate any changes in behavior in children after viewing such materials."[7] She adds, "As of yet, no research has indicated a causal relationship between these materials and anti-social behavior that is said to justify censorship."

Finally, according to another view, "Research attempting to demonstrate a causal link between images and violence has not been able to show such a link. Research on offenders demonstrates that poverty, actual violence, and abuse in the personal lives of offenders—and NOT media images—are the crucial factors in creating a tendency toward violence and criminal behavior."[8] In addition, "Research on serious sex offenders demonstrates that rapists and abusers have been taught repressive messages about sex, masturbation, and pornography, and that anti-pornography activism actually exacerbates the problems that lead to sexual assault and abuse."

---

[6]Patricia Petersen, speech given on May 28, 1999, available online at <http://www.efa.org.au/Campaigns/may28/bris/pp.html>.

[7]Carol Avedon, 1994, Censorship Won't Reduce Crime, Libertarian Alliance Pamphlet No. 24, available online at <http://www.capital.demon.co.uk/LA/pamphlets/censcrim.txt>.

[8]Frequently Asked Questions About "Feminists Against Censorship," available online at <http://www.mit.edu/activities/safe/data/feminists-against-cen>.

A related point was made by a mother who voiced concern because her preadolescent son was worried that something was wrong with him because he was interested in sexual pictures. She felt that his interest was a normal part of growing up but didn't know how to talk to him about it.

Finally, some parents at the committee's site visits said that they saw no problem at all regarding their children's exposure to sexually explicit material, even though they recognized in general terms that there are always some bumps in the path of any child who is growing up. One mother (of two daughters and no sons) told the committee that she didn't know she might have a problem with her daughters until she spoke with the committee and realized the issues the committee was investigating. However, it was not clear from what these parents said whether they did not know what kinds of material were available on the Internet, or if they did know about the nature and extent of that material and were not bothered by it.

As for other potential negative impacts on children, the lack of a substantial base of science-based research allows only speculation. One possibility is that the sexual behavior depicted on adult Web sites and in other adult-oriented material may be emotionally disturbing to the minor himself or herself. To the extent that the dynamic range of sexual activity found on the Internet is broader than the range found in mainstream society, one might suppose that an inexperienced or naïve minor could be disturbed by images drawn from the more extreme end of the spectrum. Someone disturbed by such images might report, for example, that he or she is unable to get such images out of mind, or that he or she had night-mares involving such images.

Several youth who spoke to the committee reported that they were highly upset when they inadvertently encountered sexually explicit ma-terial on the Internet, but not because of its content per se. Rather, they were most concerned and worried about the reaction of their parents to such an event—"My mom would freak out if she thought I was looking at this stuff!" In a couple of cases, such material had a negative impact on the individual because his parent reacted vehemently with punishment and censure.

A related issue was the concern of these youth that their parents or teachers would not believe that they had encountered sexually explicit material by accident. A number of parents who testified at committee site visits echoed this concern, noting that they had not believed their children when they (the children) had said that they had happened upon such material accidentally—and that the reason for their disbelief was that they had never encountered it personally themselves.

Active participation in a certain kind of online culture may affect the participants because they are participating in it, as opposed to viewing it. For example, to protect themselves online, many youth obey the rules laid down by responsible adults about not giving out their real names and addresses online—they lie about such information rather than withhold it. To the extent that they participate in cybersex, which for the most part relates to only the physical aspects of sexual interaction, they are involved in an interaction (often with strangers) that arguably facilitates detached sexual activity without an emotional or personal context. In such a context, sex talk in chat rooms and in instant messaging (often known as "cybersex") is constructed in public (in chat rooms) and in private (in instant messages), is linked to strangers, has little to do with relationships, is explicit, and is often associated with the degradation of women. To the extent that responsible adults believe that it is inappropriate to promote lying and emotionally detached sexual expression, these connections to such online cultures may be regarded as damaging and destructive.

A second common type of conversation in a chat room is "trash talk" that insults and demeans others. Public chat rooms provide a means through which individuals with no prior association (i.e., strangers) can interact with one another and provide no means for independently ascertaining the identity of any given participant. When chat rooms are unmonitored (and most are unmonitored[8]), it is common to see explicit sexual exchanges, joking about physical violence and assaults, degradation of others, aggression, and exchanges involving racial stereotypes and prejudice. Online propositions to engage in cybersex are common, especially for those with identifiably female screen names.

The young people to whom the committee spoke had experienced such online behavior. Consequently, many had stopped participating in chat rooms. Others just ignored obnoxious or offensive IMs, or blocked the senders to prevent them from further contact. It is a further problem that many parents have never been in a chat room and are entirely uninformed about the types of communication that occurs in many of them.

The research regarding chat room behavior is sparse. For example, there are as yet no studies that compare the impact of sexually explicit Web sites to participation in a chat room, or that examine the impact of chat rooms oriented toward sexually explicit interaction and dialog. Because such channels are interactive, participants have greater control over what happens in the course of dialog, and other research on the media has suggested that interactive forms of media in which participants have greater control over the activity have greater influence and impact on the participants than those that are less participatory in nature.[9]

Finally, it is worth mentioning impacts on society as a whole. To the committee's knowledge, such impact has never been the subject of scientific research, and indeed may not be amenable to measurement. It is

---

[8]Some chat rooms are monitored. For example, a number of online services provide monitoring services for chat rooms specifically intended for young users. Monitors have the ability to send warnings, suspend users for certain amounts of time, terminate accounts, and send e-mail to master accounts (presumably seen by parents), and these abilities are in fact used to sanction misbehavior. Monitors specifically watch for inappropriate conduct in the chat room, though effectiveness depends on the attentiveness with which the monitor watches the conversation.

[9]S.L. Calvert and S. Tan. 1994. "Impact of Virtual Reality on Young Adults' Physiological Arousal and Aggressive Thoughts: Interaction versus Observation," *Journal of Applied Developmental Psychology* 15(1): 125-139.

nonetheless important to acknowledge that interactions and behavior that result in reduced respect for human life and human dignity can damage the common good and be negative for society. If Internet exposure to exploitative sex and violence helps to desensitize youth to assaults on human life and human dignity, then society, whose future is these children, will be correspondingly weakened. Objectionable speech and images on the Internet, from which children should be protected or able to protect themselves, do not represent values that strengthen society. The point of protecting children—before, during, or after the Age of the Internet—is to give them time to internalize principles and convictions consistent with those of their parents and the other responsible adults around them, and to participate in a patient process that leads to the building of a stronger society.

7.3 RHETORICAL CONCERNS AND ISSUES OF PUBLIC DEBATE

The research base described in Chapter 6 contrasts with many of the rhetorical points made in public debates over the issue of children's viewing of sexually explicit material. For example, some individuals who believe that exposure to "pornography" is harmful to children regularly cite the most extreme examples of sexual behavior to which most people would object (e.g., sadomasochism, bestiality), but ignore the fact that some of what they would want to make inaccessible to children has been routinely available in *National Geographic* and *Playboy* magazine for decades. Their opposite numbers in the political debate point to the desirability of disseminating information about preventing sexually transmitted diseases, but ignore the fact that such information is widely available in other forums and that much of the sexually explicit material on the Internet has nothing to do with such issues.

It is likely that both sides could reach agreement on the undesirability of exposing children to depictions of the most extreme and most graphic examples of sexual behavior, in the sense that most of those on each side, acting as individual parents, would prefer to keep their children away from such material, regardless of their age. However, they would part company on whether government should play a role; and, as importantly, they would be unlikely to agree on whether material that is less extreme in nature is inappropriate or harmful.

A great deal of sexually explicit material falls into the category over which consensus among diverse groups is not easily forthcoming. For example:

• Sex education is highly contentious, and some public schools avoid teaching anything about this topic because parents have such different perspectives on what information is appropriate to provide to young people. Some parents feel that providing young people with information on birth control is unacceptable because it conveys a permissive attitude about premarital sexual activity, and some believe that it increases the frequency of sexual activity in minors. Others feel that providing information related to sexual health and even access to birth control in schools is socially responsible because it may help to reduce the rates of transmission of sexually transmitted diseases and teen pregnancy by providing a place for young people to obtain information that they would not get from their parents, and cite studies suggesting that sex education does not lead to increased sexual activity.[10]

• Some materials address sexuality in a manner that is meant to explore various dimensions of sexual desire, and these materials inevitably lead to differences of opinion about what behavior should be regarded as "normal," "healthy," or appropriate even for fantasy. The depiction of non-traditional scripts about how people interact romantically and sexually can help to broaden the choices that people make. (The traditional script depicts romantic heterosexuality in which the male character is active and powerful both in pursuit of a female partner and in sexual activity itself. The female character is portrayed as passive and coy and her power derives from luring a male partner.) Instead of turning to such a traditional scene from a movie for perspective on how couples handle intimacy, a young person could go to the American Social Health Association's teen sexual health Web site <www.iwannaknow.org> and join a monitored chat room with other teens to talk anonymously about sexuality. The chat room supervised and facilitated by an expert in sexual health could be a more productive learning experience than the messages a young person receives from a highly romanticized scene from a movie, though others might argue that such chats could give them ideas that they might not otherwise have.

• Other materials depict what it means to be lesbian or gay in sexual orientation; what for some people is a description of positive feelings

---

[10]For example, the Surgeon General's *Call to Action to Promote Sexual Health and Responsible Sexual Behavior* noted that "programs that typically emphasize abstinence, but also cover condoms and other methods of contraception, have a larger body of evaluation evidence that indicates either no effect on initiation of sexual activity or, in some cases, a delay in the initiation of sexual activity. This evidence gives strong support to the conclusion that providing information about contraception does not increase adolescent sexual activity, either by hastening the onset of sexual intercourse, increasing the frequency of sexual intercourse, or increasing the number of sexual partners." See David Satcher. 2001. *The Surgeon General's Call to Action to Promote Sexual Health and Responsible Sexual Behavior*. Office of the Surgeon General, Rockville, Md. Available online at <http://www.surgeongeneral.gov/library/sexualhealth/default.htm> (July 9, 2001).

about one's orientation is for others an endorsement of a perverse lifestyle. Having two same-sex people identified as a couple or depicting them as kissing is very offensive to some people, whereas these activities are accepted without a second thought when a couple is heterosexual.

• As mainstream media content grows more sexually suggestive (e.g., lingerie advertisements, the *Sports Illustrated* swimsuit issue), individuals uneasy with such change might well regard such content as inappropriate.[11]

• Content drawn from mainstream art and science has been called pornographic. For example, a plaque carried on Pioneer 10, the first space probe to leave the solar system, was called pornographic because it included engravings of nude human figures.[12] On some of the committee's site visits, various parties objected to Internet images of classical Greek statues of the human body and Leonardo da Vinci's Vitruvian Man.

• Sexually explicit discussions may also be useful for minors who wish to remain celibate—such discussions might occur among such like-minded individuals in dealing with questions such as how to manage one's sexual desires without succumbing to peer and media pressure.

Extreme sexually explicit imagery to create sexual desire on the one hand, and responsible information on sexual health on the other, are arguably unrelated and, many would argue, easily distinguished. But much content is not so easily categorized. While some extreme sexually explicit material meets legal tests for obscenity (and therefore does not enjoy First Amendment protection), less extreme material may not. Material regarding sexual health, mainstream erotica, lingerie advertisements, and models in swimsuits generally do enjoy such protection, at least for adults and

---

[11]For example, according to FCC Commissioner Michael J. Copps, "Hundreds of Americans have registered their displeasure at the Victoria's Secret program, and the promotional advertising that preceded it, that aired on network television [on November 15, 2001]." By Copps's characterization, most of the complainants thought some of the material was indecent, and many were angered because the program and ads were run during a time in the evening when children were likely to be watching and when indecent programming may not be aired in accordance with FCC rules. See <http://www.fcc.gov/Speeches/Copps/Statements/2001/stmjc128.txt>.

[12]For example, one newspaper published the images on the plaque, but erased the nipples, saying that "[a] family newspaper must uphold community standards." Another newspaper affiliated with a religious denomination said that the plaque should have had praying hands rather than nudes. And a major newspaper printed the image in full, but received a letter from a reader that said, "I was shocked by the blatant display of both male and female sex organs. . . . Isn't it enough that we must tolerate the bombardment of pornography through the media of film and smut magazines? Isn't it bad enough that our own space agency officials have found it necessary to spread this filth even beyond our own solar system?" See William Poundstone. 1999. *Carl Sagan: A Life in the Cosmos.* Henry Holt and Company, New York.

often for children. Is it good or bad to know about and to see non-mainstream sexual behavior? Knowledge about such behavior might create an aversion to it, a desire for it, or simply a person better informed about it. Content and information that fall outside the realm of extreme sexually explicit imagery are thus likely to be the source of greatest contention, and different people fear that such content would or would not fall under regulatory efforts aimed at reducing the exposure of minors to material that is or may be sexual in nature.

Describing material as "inappropriate" is value-laden, in that one person's definition of inappropriate will be different from that of another. One parent may feel that exposure of children to violence is much more harmful than exposure to sexually explicit material, while another may feel the reverse. Moreover, some parents believe that exposure to sexually explicit material poses moral danger (distinct from physical or psychological harm and danger) to their children, while others do not.

7.4 JUDGMENTS IN THE ABSENCE OF A RELIABLE RESEARCH BASE

Reliable information—the outcome of rigorous research—could, in principle, indicate how, if at all, exposure to sexually explicit material upsets minors, whether and how it changes their attitudes and/or their behaviors, and so on. But these effects are neither good nor bad absent a consideration of values. It is one's values that provide the basis for a determination of whether these effects are good or bad, desirable or undesirable.

Consider, for the sake of argument, as a hypothetical example that is not demonstrated in the research literature, that there is a reasonably firm consensus that brief exposure to sexually explicit material does not change sexual behavior but that individual attitudes become more accepting of a variety of sexual behaviors. One person might say that this outcome is bad or wrong if children's attitudes toward certain sexual behaviors have become more accepting, even if their behaviors don't change. Another might strongly approve of the same attitude change. A third person might object to such material as tasteless, crude, vulgar, or worse. Each of these judgments would be informed according to his/her value system.[13]

However, the research concerning the impact of exposure to sexually explicit material on children across their entire development span is not

---

[13]Such differences also occur among larger social groups. For a discussion of such differences between nations, see Computer Science and Telecommunications Board, National Research Council, 2001, *Global Networks and Local Values*, National Academy Press, Washington, D.C.

robust. While the charge to the committee, and much of the public debate, has been predicated on the assumption that exposure to "pornography" has negative effects on children, the committee has heard from a variety of analysts and scholars presenting a range of both experimental and clinical work in this area, and it has reviewed the literature as described above. What has been demonstrated is that there is no scientific consensus on the nature or extent of the impact of exposure to sexually explicit material on children. Furthermore, emotions run so high in this area and strongly held values relating to it are so intertwined with assessments of impact that even good empirical evidence is unlikely to change many minds.

In the absence of reliable empirical evidence, some people will say, "Because the scientific evidence is lacking, we must not act precipitously." Others will say, "Even if the scientific evidence is lacking, we must act immediately." In each case, one's values and prior predispositions have a strong influence on one's assessment of a phenomenon. An individual predisposed to believe that there is a significant negative impact or that there is no significant negative impact will thus require very strong evidence to change his or her mind. Individuals and communities will of course include as a part of their decision-making processes their own subjective evaluations and judgments of the impact of inappropriate material on children.

Thus, one sees in the public debate that judgments about the impact of inappropriate sexually explicit material on children are closely tied to the values of those making the judgments. Controversy is inevitable when these values are strongly held (as one would expect for values concerning sexuality and children) and in conflict with those of others.

Even definitions of "pornography," which itself has no legal definition, or inappropriate sexually explicit material, may differ based on one's world view and values (e.g., one community may object to images of scantily clad individuals, whereas another may only be concerned about exposure to images that are more explicitly sexual, such as those depicting intercourse).

The increasing cultural and social heterogeneity of the United States implies the co-existence of different sets of values. A range of different value sets was demonstrated to the committee, and the committee heard from individuals representing a wide spectrum of views on the impact of sexually explicit material on children. These views range from the belief that such exposure is "very negative, wrong, and harmful" to minors to "not particularly negative, wrong, or harmful." This diversity of values is reflected within the committee itself, but it depends strongly on what type of sexually explicit material is being considered.

As the discussion in Section 7.3 suggests, there is some set of explicit material involving depictions of "extreme" sexual behavior that the committee does believe would be highly inappropriate for viewing by children—this judgment would not be made so much on scientific grounds (as the committee knows of no reliable scientific studies that address this point) as on a sense that such exposure would offend the committee's collective moral and ethical sensibilities.

However, for other, less extreme sexually explicitly material, the general public—and the committee itself—would reflect a range of beliefs about its propriety for children and the extent and nature of its impact on children. Thus, if the committee's task were to come to consensus on the nature and extent of the impact on children of this type of less extreme but still sexually explicit material, the committee would be deliberating for a long time indeed. In short, even with the best of intentions, intelligent individuals with different values working with highly uncertain knowledge are likely to disagree on both likely outcomes and the desirability or undesirability of those outcomes.

But coming to a consensus on the impact of exposure to such sexually explicit material on children is not the task of the committee. As noted in Chapter 1 and in the preface, the committee's task is to provide a clear explication of factors that enter into choices about appropriate approaches to protecting children from inappropriate sexually explicit material on the Internet. To the extent possible, this explication strives to provide reliable information about these different approaches, and it is intended to address that charge with analysis that is as value-neutral as possible.[14]

In the end, however, values must enter into the process of selecting appropriate approaches to the issue of children and inappropriate sexually explicit material on the Internet. In particular, the weights that a decision maker assigns to various characteristics of a given approach are determined by his or her values. One who believes that the impact of such material on children is "very negative" will put different weights on the various factors related to approaches to protection that are articulated in Chapters 8 through 13 and come to very different conclusions than someone who believes the impact is "not very negative." To illustrate with a

---

[14]The committee recognizes that value-neutral analysis, especially in controversial areas, is in practice not possible. For example, values are implicit in the choice of dimensions along which approaches may be analyzed. Indeed, they are implicit in the use of the word "protect" in the committee's legislative charge, which assumes that harm and danger necessarily flow from children's exposure to "pornographic" material. Nevertheless, along the continuum ranging from more value-neutral to more value-laden, the committee sees its task as more aligned with the former than the latter.

small but important example: one who believes that the impact of sexually explicit material on minors is very negative is likely to weight the partial protection offered by filters heavily, and to give much less weight to the fact that filters also screen out some appropriate and useful information. One who concludes that the impact of sexually explicit material is not very negative is likely to place the opposite weights on these factors.

It is with this discussion in mind that this report includes the material presented in Chapter 6, though it is sparse and inconclusive. For matters that concern parents and communities, an inadequate knowledge base cannot be used as a rationale for doing nothing. But the knowledge available, sparse and inconclusive though it is, helps to provide context that frames the choices of parents, teachers, librarians, administrators, and makers of public policy.

7.5 CONCLUDING OBSERVATIONS

The distinction between voluntary or involuntary exposure to sexually explicit material is important. The research base described in Chapter 6 focuses mostly on the impact of voluntary exposure to sexually explicit material—it is in the nature of most psychological research that the subjects of research consent to being exposed to various stimuli. And, as noted above, there is little reliable evidence on the impact on children of exposure to sexually explicit material. However, it is true that some such material has the potential to shock or surprise some people not expecting to be exposed to it, even if many children who accidentally encounter sexually explicit material report that they are not particularly bothered by the experience (Section 5.4.3).

The committee believes that there is a reasonably strong social consensus—one reflected in its own deliberations—that involuntary exposure to sexually explicit material is clearly inappropriate and undesirable and should not be occurring, regardless of one's views on the impact of voluntary exposure, and it is particularly inappropriate and undesirable in the context of minors being exposed to such material or when involuntary exposure is the result of intentionally misleading or deceiving a minor.

To the extent that risk does exist (as indicated by reactions of children to such experiences), it is likely that it is largest for children in an age group who are old enough (namely preadolescents) to engage in unsupervised Internet activity but young enough that they have not been exposed to very much sexual stimuli. Very young children are unlikely to have the technical sophistication needed to explore the Internet in a way that exposes them to sexually explicit material (e.g., they are less likely to use search engines than to stick with a set of prescreened age-appropriate sites) and even if exposed to sexually explicit material are unlikely to have the worldly knowledge that labels such material as inappropriate. Adolescents—especially the older ones—are sexually mature, have been exposed to a great deal of culture and media that are suffused with sexual messages, and are often engaged in sexual activity (including intercourse). Such individuals are as likely to close a screen containing sexually explicit images as to explore it further.

On balance, there is no scientific research consensus supporting a claim that exposure to sexually explicit material does—or does not—have a negative physical, emotional, or psychological impact on children, nor a consensus regarding the existence of a causal relationship between exposure to sexually explicit material and long-term behavioral outcomes in general. (Of course, what happens in the case of any specific individual is outside the scope of such research in any event.) Further, the committee has not established specific definitions of what constitutes inappropriate sexually explicit material, though it remains confident that there is some significant set of sexually explicit material on which it could reach consensus regarding inappropriateness.

The inconclusive results from the sparse scientific literature regarding the impact of exposure to sexually explicit material on children are reflected in a wide spread of committee member views on this subject as well. Although Chapter 6 includes a review of empirical research that explores this topic and a discussion of developmental theories that point to how one might incorporate a scientific framework into making decisions about the strategies to use to guide children's Internet use, there is not a consensus either in the science or in the committee on which to base definitive and authoritative conclusions on the impact of sexually explicit material on children or on the appropriate parental, school, library, or societal response for all children. What this report can offer is data on and careful analyses on a number of factors (e.g., how children use the Internet, means by which children come in contact with Internet content, developmental theory about a child's cognitive and emotional growth) that individuals and communities can consider in formulating a careful approach to this issue.

It is important to keep in mind the difference between a scientific assessment that exposure to certain kinds of sexually explicit material is harmful and a stance that exposure to such material is morally wrong. A moral stance and a scientific consensus are entirely different concepts. Each is important to discourse and action, but they have entirely different epistemological underpinnings, and even if there were a scientific consensus that exposure to such material had no negative impact, one could still make a moral and ethical judgment that such exposure should be avoided simply because it was wrong. A good illustration is found in the committee's views on this subject—despite a wide range of views on the underlying science regarding the impact of exposure to sexually explicit material on children, there is nevertheless some significant set of sexually explicit material that the committee would unanimously regard as inappropriate and objectionable for children.

A nation of communities with very different moral beliefs may never be able to come to a stable consensus on public policy if moral knowledge and values are the primary determinants of policy-making outcomes. Because science incorporates at its core techniques intended to safeguard the process against the influence of personal beliefs, it offers a more value-neutral form of knowledge, and as such offers a form of knowledge around which public consensus can be built. In the case of inappropriate sexually explicit material on the Internet, there is no scientific consensus on the impact of exposure to such material, and so informed decisions about practices and policies cannot be based on empirical evidence. What science can offer in this case is a careful analysis of how, when, and where young people come into contact with various types of inappropriate material. This knowledge can significantly improve local and perhaps even national dialogs on what approaches could be employed to safeguard children on the Internet.

The committee's task is to explicate the factors that should be taken into consideration in determining a course of action, as well as to offer examples of existing approaches that some communities have used to address the issue. Thus, its findings and conclusions about the factors that communities should consider as they formulate policy and practices do not require either a scientific or committee consensus on the impact of exposure to inappropriate sexually explicit material on children. Judgments about impact necessarily affect one's calculus in weighing different factors (and hence on deciding upon recommended courses of action), but they do not necessarily affect what the relevant factors are. Research (existing or future) that helps to say when, where, and in what circumstances exposure may put children at risk can help people to make decisions about what types of approaches may be the most beneficial and cost-effective, and the committee's review of current research is outlined in Chapter 6.

PART II

8

Approaches to Protection from Inappropriate Material

This chapter provides a general framework for understanding what it means to protect youth from inappropriate material. Part of the complexity of the task is seen in the observation that "protect" and "inappropriate material" are terms without clear and unambiguous definition.

8.1 THE IDENTIFICATION OF INAPPROPRIATE MATERIAL

8.1.1 In Principle

The determination that particular material is inappropriate for children begins with a human judgment. The judging party can be a parent, a teacher, a librarian, the child himself or herself, the creator of the material, the carrier (distributor) of that material, a third-party rating service, or a government agency.

Given a particular universe of material (e.g., a set of images), it is likely that any group of judges will agree on some material as "appropriate" and some as "inappropriate," and that there will be some material about which the judges will disagree. Of course, depending on the particular judges involved, the term "inappropriate" could include a very large variety of material, including some or all sexually explicit material, bomb-making recipes, extremist material, birth control information, hate sites, and the platforms of particular political or social groups. Indeed, judgments about inappropriateness are closely tied to the values of those making the judgments.

The general pattern would not change even when judgments are confined to a specific area such as sexually explicit material. Some material would be unanimously classified as inappropriate, some would be unanimously classified as not inappropriate, and some would be indeterminate. Judges drawn from different segments of the U.S. public would disagree strongly about whether certain materials were inappropriate for children, and what is obscene or obscene with respect to minors, in California may well be different from what is obscene or obscene with respect to minors in Tennessee because the community standards of California may be different from those of Tennessee. In other words, as the Supreme Court has made clear, the determination that material is obscene, or obscene with respect to minors, depends on criteria that are extrinsic to the material itself.

In the absence of universal criteria, the most relevant standard for validity or accuracy is the standard of the individual(s) responsible for making decisions about inappropriateness on behalf of the child. Thus, it is often said that the best protection against children being exposed to inappropriate material on the Internet is the presence and guidance of a responsible parent or guardian while the child is using the Internet—the reason is that when such an adult is involved, his or her standards can be trusted as the basis for good judgments for the child's welfare.

When the presence and guidance of a responsible parent or guardian during Internet use are not possible, protection depends on the judgment of a proxy. The proxy's judgments must then be evaluated against the standard of the responsible adult who would otherwise make such decisions for the child. The proxy may be another adult such as a teacher acting in loco parentis, the board of a public library system, another trusted adult, an Internet service provider, a developer of filtering software,[1] a local jury deciding an obscenity case, the U.S. Congress, or a state legislature. But whatever the proxy, the validity of the proxy's assessments about inappropriate material is indicated by its consistency with the judgments of the party responsible for deciding on behalf of the child.

Different proxies have different methodologies for determining inappropriateness. A proxy that uses one reviewer is likely to have a different set of consistencies than an agency that has a hundred reviewers. The former is likely to have a higher reliability than the latter, while the latter is more likely than the former to establish a standard for accuracy or validity that reflects the larger population from which those reviewers are drawn.

---

[1]The developer of software builds into a tool assumptions about what content is appropriate (and for whom) and also establishes the standard of accurate performance that the tool will meet.

Moreover, even if agreement can be obtained on particular content (e.g., that a given image is inappropriate), it is hard to define clear rules about how to identify "similar" material in a consistent manner. Put differently, it is difficult to articulate a set of rules that clearly defines a specific class of "inappropriate" material that is both sufficiently inclusive (includes most or all material that is inappropriate) and sufficiently exclusive (excludes most or all material that is appropriate).

Given a need for proxies, how does a proxy make reasonable judgments about what sexually explicit material may be inappropriate for viewing by children at any age? To answer this question, it is important to distinguish conceptually between reliability (or consistency) and validity.

The most common example to illustrate the distinction between reliability and validity is that of a shooter aiming at a target and firing multiple rounds. Reliability is a measure of the repeatability of the shooter's aim. A tight cluster of shots indicates high repeatability (reliability). However, reliability says nothing about how close that cluster of shots is to the actual target. For that, validity indicates the accuracy of those shots: a small distance between the center of the cluster and the center of the target indicates high accuracy (validity). Validity means that one is measuring what one claims to be measuring. A highly reliable measure may not be valid, and a highly valid result may not be reliable.[2]

In determining whether certain material is inappropriate, reliability refers to the reproducibility of an assessment that a given piece of material is inappropriate. To test for reliability, one might ask an individual to evaluate a collection of materials several times under different circumstances. If this individual's judgments were generally consistent, he or she would be said to be a reliable judge. Because the same person may classify a given piece of material differently depending on his or her mood or from one day to another or what else he or she might have seen or read during that period of time, an individual's reliability as a judge cannot be taken for granted.

Reliability is even more difficult when multiple people are involved in judging content. Different people may classify a given piece of material differently even if they are ostensibly using the same rules for classification. Thus, to determine the reliability of a group of judges, one might ask them to evaluate a collection of materials; if their judgments were generally consistent with each other, this group would be said to make reliable judgments. Key to this process is an agreed-upon operational specification of how to make a judgment.

---

[2]For practical purposes, a variable with low reliability (i.e., with a wide spread) is hard to use for empirical work. However, it can still be highly valid in the formal sense of the term, even if it is not useful.

This definition of reliability implies that machine assessment (a given version of software running on a given computer) is inevitably more reliable (or consistent) than human assessment—given the strictly algorithmic process, the reliability of machine assessment is 100 percent.[3] The reliability of human assessment is likely to be considerably lower, even when the same rules of classification apply to all assessments, simply because people interpret the same rules differently.

Validity is a more problematic concept because there is no universally accepted standard (no "gold standard") for what counts as inappropriate. In other words, there are no universally accepted criteria that define whether something is obscene or inappropriate for viewing by children.

These comments do not exclude the possibility of broad agreement over many possible decision-making parties in a particular instance characterized, for example, by child pornography, just as even the worst-made rifle can make bull's eyes for a particular target with a very large bull's eye. Rather, the accuracy of a rifle is best tested against a target with a very small bull's eye, so that variations in accuracy can be readily observed. Similarly, the validity of a process for making judgments about inappropriateness is best indicated by examining judgments of "questionable" material about which people do not hold similar views.

Reliability and validity (as measured from the perspective of a responsible adult) are the primary determinants of a "good" proxy for that adult. Because different proxies have different methodologies, an individual faced with the responsibility for deciding inappropriateness for a child can, in principle, choose to adopt the approach used by a trusted proxy. Thus, in principle, an individual (e.g., a parent) might choose to trust the judgments of Disney, the American Civil Liberties Union, the Christian Coalition, or another organization that has a well-known reputation for espousing a particular set of views or values.

8.1.2 In Practice

Given the general principles described above, three methods can be used in practice to identify inappropriate material. The decision-making party, whether machine or human, can

• *Make a real-time assessment of the material in question based on the content of the incoming information.* This approach would require the decision-

---

[3]This statement must be qualified if the assessment software relies on elements that change over time. For example, the assessment software may rely on a database that is updated from time to time—with new or additional data, the results of the assessment of, say, a given image may well vary.

making party to screen each item of information immediately prior to the child's viewing of it. Items judged to be appropriate are immediately passed to the child, while items judged to be inappropriate are not.

• *Rely on a tag or label associated with the material in question.* Labels can contain either a description of the material or a judgment about the material. (In principle, a label can be created by the content creator or by another party.) If the label contains a description, the description is a highly condensed description of the material with respect to dimensions of content likely to involve judgments of inappropriateness. Thus, the label might indicate "image contains frontal nudity" because decision makers are likely to want to make decisions based on the presence or absence of frontal nudity. By contrast, the label would not indicate "image contains people," because that fact is not likely to be the basis on which judgments about inappropriateness are likely to be made. Alternatively, the label may contain a judgment about the material (e.g., inappropriate for those 14 and under). In this case, the label represents a time-delayed judgment of content that has been made by a third party.

• *Examine the source of the material.* Some sources can be trusted to provide only appropriate material; others provide a large volume of inappropriate material.[4] Rather than assessing the material itself (an effort that may be unduly time-consuming), the evaluation is based on the source. Note that relying on an evaluation of the source is, in essence, reliance on a label—the name of the source *is* the label, and material from that source is rejected or accepted depending on the particulars of the source's identity.

A second dimension of identifying inappropriate material in practice is a consequence of the size of the Internet. The volume of information on the Internet is so large—and changes so rapidly—that it is simply impractical for human beings to evaluate every discrete piece of information for inappropriateness. Moreover, the content of some existing Web pages changes very rapidly, and new Web pages appear at a very rapid rate.[5]

This fact leads to one of two approaches. One is based on an automated, machine-executable process for identifying inappropriate content

---

[4]Sources of adult-oriented, sexually explicit material are generally consistent in their offerings—such content is available on their Web sites today, and will be available tomorrow (if they are still in business). Yet the content on one such site is often generically similar to that on another site, so "brand loyalties" that keep viewers coming back are hard for any one business entity to establish. The most successful commercial entities are those that have been able to establish such loyalties.

[5]No data was available to the committee on the first point, but on the second point, the number of publicly accessible Web pages increased by 300 million in the period from July to October 2001 (according to the Google statistics on the number of pages indexed).

(generally used for evaluating content "on the fly"); such processes are less expensive than manual processes for screening content, but as a rule, they result in judgments that are less valid than those of human evaluators. Automated approaches must be based on machine-executable rules that are abstracted from human judgments—such abstraction inevitably misses nuances in those human judgments and reduces their validity compared to that of humans. Reliance on labels depends on the label's accuracy, and only a human's action binds a particular label to a given piece of material. And, the identity of a source may not be an adequate indicator of material coming from it.

The second approach is the human-performed explicit identification of specifically appropriate material and the exclusion of everything else (or its reverse—the explicit identification of specifically inappropriate material for exclusion and the inclusion of everything else). This approach is expensive. The first variant runs the risk that large volumes of appropriate material will be excluded, but is likely to result in a very low fraction of inappropriate material being displayed. The second variant captures only some (perhaps a large fraction) of the inappropriate material on the Internet, but allows a large volume of appropriate material to pass.

In practice, a combination of approaches can be used as well—a combination would rely on an automated search for material that *might* be inappropriate, but would rely on a human judgment for the final determination. In this case, inappropriate material not identified in the automated search does not reach a human decision maker and so it mistakenly identified as appropriate. To the extent that the threshold of identification is set so that a greater volume of possibly inappropriate material is identified (so as to reduce the likelihood that inappropriate material is not mistakenly identified), the volume of material that is subject to actual human judgment is increased—in which case the issues regarding human review discussed in the previous paragraph obtain.

8.2   DIMENSIONS OF "PROTECTION"

In the context of "protecting youth from inappropriate material or experiences," the term "protect" has a number of plausible definitions. "Protection" can mean:

• Preventing children from deliberately finding inappropriate material or experiences (e.g., searching out an adult-oriented Web site);
• Preventing children from being inadvertently exposed to such material or experiences (e.g., receiving an unsolicited e-mail containing an inappropriate image or text); and/or
• Developing in the child skills that enable him or her to cope con-

structively with such exposure should it occur and making available a support infrastructure that reduces the harm or injury that might result from being exposed to such material or experiences.

The approaches needed to implement these definitions of protection differ but are not mutually exclusive. Protecting children from deliberate exposure is a very different enterprise—and entails very different costs—compared with protecting children only from inadvertent exposure, though approaches to each may have common elements. Further, teaching a child to cope constructively is likely to be helpful in the event that other protection measures fail.

The primary difficulty of protecting children and youth against deliberate exposure is the fact that many adolescents, especially boys, are highly motivated to seek out sexually explicit materials, including material that is ostensibly limited to adults. Absent a significant change in their desire for such materials, their motivation often enables them to overcome many obstacles in their path, whatever the nature of those obstacles.

"Protection" has other important dimensions. The extent to which a child can be protected is an important element of the debate. It is easy to say that 100 percent protection is impossible—but such a statement begs the question of what "80 percent protection" might mean. Does it mean that the child is exposed to inappropriate material 20 percent as much as another child who does not have such protection? Should the evaluator rely primarily on the number of incidents of exposure? Or are other aspects of the exposure, such as its nature or duration, important as well? An important challenge—as yet unresolved—is to articulate appropriate metrics of protection.

A key dimension of protection is the issue of false positives and false negatives. In deciding whether a given piece of material is appropriate or inappropriate, it is inevitable that some material will be designated as inappropriate when it should have been designated as appropriate—errors of this type are false positives. On the other hand, some material will be designated as appropriate even when it should have been designated as inappropriate—errors of this type are false negatives.

Perfect protection ("100 percent") is possible only at the cost of many false positives—and is in fact simple to provide. A cable with an air gap in it (or, equivalently, disconnecting from the Internet) will provide 100 percent protection in the sense that it will screen out all inappropriate material. But it will also block all appropriate content as well. In the real world, those wishing to provide protection (e.g., parents, school administrators, and so on) must balance the rate of false positives against the rate of false negatives.

A third dimension of "protect" might refer to measures taken to ensure that the child suffers no ill effects from being exposed to inappropriate material. This approach recognizes that absolute protection from inappropriate material is impossible to achieve (except at the cost of total disconnection) and that nurturing a child who is able to place inappropriate material into context, to evaluate and make good judgments about it, and to deal with it appropriately is an important element of the overall goal of keeping children from harm.

The relevance of these different definitions and dimensions of "protect" depends on the developmental maturity of a child. The range from birth to 18 spans a very broad developmental range in a psychological sense. What may be developmentally inappropriate for a very young child may not be inappropriate for a teenager. It can be taken as a given that teenagers will be more interested in sexual matters than will young children, and a site providing a detailed scientific description of human reproduction, for example, may be more appropriate for the former than the latter. Parents and other responsible adults may thus wish to consider developmental factors in weighing the costs and benefits of different approaches to protection.

For example, at very young ages, one might be inclined to shield children from any Internet exposure at all (e.g., confining a very young child's computer experience to CD-ROMs). As he or she matured, a next step might be to allow online experiences only in environments that were specially created for children. Then, at a further stage of maturity, one might seek to educate one's child in safe Internet use and use technology to screen out objectionable material. Finally, one might simply allow unconstrained Internet access but keep an eye on the child's Internet activities. The assumption underlying such a progression is that as the child matures, his or her judgment and capability for responsible action grows, and different kinds of "protection" are necessary. (All of these options are discussed in subsequent chapters.)

In the context of protecting children from pornography and perhaps other types of material as well, it is also important to distinguish between protecting children from being exposed to pornography (the subject of the discussion above) and protecting children from participating in pornography (which is the ultimate and primary rationale for laws that strictly proscribe child pornography). The discussion below and in Chapters 9 through 13 focuses primarily on protection from exposure, but addresses protection from participation as appropriate.

8.3 THE TIME LINE OF PROTECTIVE ACTIONS

Actions can be taken at a variety of times. Actions can be taken to protect a child before potential exposure to inappropriate material, at the moment of that exposure, and after that exposure. For example, as Chapter 10 discusses, various education and media literacy strategies may help the child to decide not to be exposed to inappropriate material. Such strategies must obviously be implemented before exposure—that is, the child must begin to learn (internalize) norms of appropriate conduct and behavior. At the moment of potential exposure, tools such as filters (described in Chapter 12) are relevant, because they can help to block exposure to such material. And, after exposure, a variety of measures (e.g., getting help, reporting to a responsible adult) can help to mitigate any negative effects that may result from such exposure.

8.4 DIFFERING INSTITUTIONAL MISSIONS OF SCHOOLS AND LIBRARIES

Even the same community, libraries, and schools often have very different policies regarding the need for filtering. In some communities visited by the committee, schools had implemented filtering for all school-based Internet connections, whereas the public libraries in that same community did not have filters.

To understand why such differences might arise, consider the different purposes served by public schools and libraries. A public school serves the primary purpose of providing academic instruction for individuals who have not attained the age of majority. Parents send their children to school in the legally enforceable expectation that school personnel will take responsible care to protect them from harm and to provide adequate instruction (i.e., that they will act *in loco parentis*).

By contrast, a public library serves the primary purpose of providing a broad range of information to the entire community in which it is based. This community includes children, but also includes adults, and the information needs of the community—taken as a whole—are generally much more diverse than those of children and youth in school.[6] Thus, given these differing purposes, it is not at all unexpected that school and libraries have different needs and might take different approaches in seeking

---

[6]For example, the position of the American Library Association is that "librarians believe in supporting a wide variety of information needs," and emphasis should be placed "on the patron's right to choose," an emphasis that is "consistent with [the library] profession's commitment to intellectual freedom." Further, "libraries rarely limit what can be read in a library. Librarians do not search patrons' book-bags for titles the library would not purchase, or police reading tables to see if patrons are reading materials consistent with local collection-development policies. In a similar vein, many libraries offer open access to the Internet, so that the patron may choose what to read." See <http://www.pla.org/publications/technotes/technotes_filtering.html>.

to protect children and youth from inappropriate Internet material and experiences.

Approaches of schools and of libraries for protecting children and youth from inappropriate Internet materials and experiences must be assessed against this backdrop. Some elements of these approaches will be similar, but it is also to be expected that other elements will be different because of differences in fundamental purpose.

8.5 THE POLITICS OF PROTECTION AND INAPPROPRIATE MATERIAL—WHO AND WHEN?

Within this framework of different dimensions of "protection" and "inappropriate material," a range of approaches to the definitional process can be identified. One approach, rarely stated but often implicit as the motivating force behind certain policy positions, is the idea that a particular definition of "inappropriate" is appropriate for all communities. Underpinning this approach is the view described in Box 7.2 in Chapter 7 that inappropriate material—and in particular, sexually explicit material—can be so dangerous that even a single exposure of a child can result in very harmful consequences. Examples to support this point of view tend to be drawn from the more extreme sexually explicit material found on the Internet—and not coincidentally material that tends to arouse revulsion in a large segment of the population. Thus, "protection" of children must be as airtight as possible, and false positives that improperly classify appropriate material as inappropriate are preferable to false negatives that improperly classify inappropriate material as appropriate.[7] Note also that if one believes that even one exposure of a child to such material is likely to have long-lasting and profoundly negative effects on his or her development, then nothing less than perfection suffices. For such individuals, technologies that seek to isolate and wall off a child from untoward influences are likely to have considerable appeal.

A second approach asserts that individual communities have the right (and obligation) to define for themselves what is inappropriate. Believers in this philosophy reject the notion that there are, or that there should be, universal standards of inappropriateness. To buttress their view, they tend to draw on examples of material that many people would not find inappropriate or offensive—information that can be characterized as more "mainline" than "extreme." They tend to doubt that exposure to sexually

---

[7]Child pornography is an area where a similar philosophy has led to strong legal protections against the harms of child sexual abuse that typically define the material.

explicit material will have a damaging impact on most children, and thus are willing to accept false negatives as the cost of avoiding false positives. For those who believe in the resilience of children when given appropriate guidance, social and educational strategies that teach a child how to make good decisions about such material and how to cope with it should exposure occur are likely to have more appeal than approaches that rely primarily on technology.

These two approaches represent polar opposites. In practice, most people fall somewhere in between. That is, they might well say that some types of material should indeed be universally prohibited, regardless of community standards (e.g., child pornography), but conclude that for other types of sexually explicit material, communities should be free to decide for themselves.

A third approach, in general independent of those described above, focuses on empowering children to protect themselves. This approach calls for adult definition of inappropriate material (and could be defined either universally or on a community-by-community basis, but in any event would ideally account for developmental maturity) but focuses on the child rather than the adult as the primary decision maker. This does not mean that adults have no role, or that protective mechanisms are inappropriate, but rather that reliance on externally driven protective mechanisms can be reduced as the child's judgment increases. (The appropriate analogy would be that externally driven protective mechanisms for a child whose judgment is developing and maturing serve the same role as "training wheels" serve for someone learning to ride a bicycle.) Under this approach, the goal is not to protect the child from exposure as an end in itself, but rather to educate the child to cope well with offensive or inappropriate materials. This approach is based on the idea that in a free and pluralistic society, one will inevitably be exposed to material that he or she may find disturbing, offensive, or distasteful, and that the best way to deal with such situations is to develop coping mechanisms through experience.

It is also important to consider the time scale over which politics is conducted. In one site visit to a state generally regarded as politically and socially conservative, discussion with those familiar with the local community revealed a difference in the politics associated with schools (which did have filtering for all its schools) and libraries (which did not). The membership of the school board had changed relatively suddenly, on the time scale of a year (one election), whereas the membership of the library board changed very slowly. Thus, filtering could be driven by new members of the school board, whereas library board membership was more stable—and thus changes to policy took longer to implement in the absence of sustained and demonstrable public concern.

8.6 TECHNIQUES OF PROTECTION

Chapters 9 through 13 address the challenges of protecting children against exposure from inappropriate sexually explicit material. This section introduces some general concepts for protection that underpin more specific approaches:

• *Blocking inappropriate material* refers to techniques that *prevent* a child from being exposed to material that has been judged to be inappropriate. Blocking protects against both deliberate and inadvertent exposure. However, all material that is not explicitly identified as inappropriate ("black-listed" material) is treated as appropriate. Blocking can be circumvented by defeating the blocking mechanism, by gaining access to material that is generically equivalent to the blocked material, or by accessing that material in a venue that is not blocked.[8]

• *Restricting a child to appropriate material* refers to techniques that give a child access only to material that is explicitly judged to be appropriate for him or her. Children cannot reach inappropriate material because the only material they can reach has been judged as appropriate. All material that is not explicitly identified as appropriate ("white-listed" material) is treated as inappropriate. Restrictions can be circumvented by defeating the restriction mechanism or by accessing non-white-listed material in a venue that does not restrict the user. The key difference between blocking and restricting is that blocking allows access to everything that has not been blocked, whereas restricting gives access only to what has been approved.

• *Warning a child of impending exposure to inappropriate material* leaves him or her with an explicit choice to accept or decline a viewing. Warning protects against inadvertent exposure to inappropriate material, but not against deliberate exposure. As with blocking, all material that is not explicitly identified as inappropriate is treated as appropriate. However, circumvention is unnecessary, because the ultimate decision about whether to access the material is made by the child.

• *Suggesting appropriate material* to a child provides direction but does not foreclose the exercise of choice. The child may disregard such suggestions, but such suggestions can influence him or her to proceed in "appro-

---

[8]Note the existence of "gray." "Gray" may be material that, while not exactly inappropriate for children, is regarded as not particularly helpful to them—"waste-of-time" material. For example, one could imagine some schools putting Web sites that relate to games, sports, entertainment, and celebrities on a "black list" because spending time on such sites and with such material would not be regarded as having educational value. On the other hand, creative teachers may well be able to extract educational value from such sites—and blocking such material might reduce the educational opportunities available.

priate" directions. Suggestions are, of necessity, more limited than the entire universe of material that might be regarded as appropriate, and thus tend to focus on material that is regarded as being of particularly high value.

- *Deterring the access of children to inappropriate material* depends on two factors: detection of access and subsequent penalty. Detection can be overt or covert, and penalties can vary across a very broad range, from social sanction to incarceration. Deterrence relies on a choice of the individual involved to refrain from accessing inappropriate material, a choice motivated by concern over being detected and of the subsequent penalty. Thus, deterrence is directly relevant to preventing or reducing deliberate access to such material. (However, if the threat of punishment makes the individual more careful, inadvertent access may be reduced as well.) The threat of a penalty being imposed for an inappropriate use detected through monitoring a child's Internet access is an example of an approach that relies on deterrence.

- *Educating a child about accessing inappropriate material* has two components. One is much like deterrence, except that the motivation is different. Whereas deterrence depends on the possibility of detection and punishment, education is an integral part of helping a child choose to refrain from accessing inappropriate material by inculcating an internal sense of personal responsibility. The second component is education about the Internet and the development of critical thinking that can help the child to conduct searches that are less likely to turn up inappropriate material and to recognize inappropriate material more effectively.

- *Helping a child to cope with exposure to inappropriate material* recognizes that some exposure to such material is likely for most Internet users. Coping strategies are especially useful for children inadvertently exposed to inappropriate material and may involve ways of putting such material into context, understanding the difference between fantasy and reality, and so on.

- *Keeping a child "on task."* In an environment in which time limits on Internet access can be enforced, children can be given specific tasks to accomplish. If they are held responsible for these tasks (as they might be in, for example, a school setting), they will simply have less time to seek out activities that are inappropriate.

- *Reducing the accessibility of inappropriate material to children* can result from a variety of actions, including making inappropriate material harder to find and reducing the amount of inappropriate material on the Internet. Supply-side actions have a different structure and are discussed further in Chapter 9.

- *Reducing the appeal of deliberate contact with inappropriate material.* This approach leaves the essential content of such material untouched but makes the user's engagement with the material (and only such material) more difficult, cumbersome, and inconvenient.

It is important to note that the techniques discussed above are not mutually exclusive. For example, a message indicating that access to material has been blocked can also be accompanied by suggestions for alternative but appropriate material instead. Indeed, combining some techniques may enhance effectiveness; such instances must be determined on a case-by-case basis.

8.7 APPROACHES TO PROTECTION

Society has responded to concerns about the possibility that children and youth might be exposed to inappropriate material in a number of ways. For example, consider the following:

• By legislative mandate, a "V-chip" is contained in every new television sold in the United States. The purpose of the V-chip is to give parents greater control over the television content to which their children are exposed.

• In many communities, parents have the explicit right to "opt out" of school-provided sex education for their own children.[9]

• Members of a community often complain to schools or public libraries about materials (usually books) that the complainants feel should not be available to the public, and especially to children. The content of such materials covers a wide range—homosexuality, drugs, religious cults, bomb making, human sexuality, and race relations, to name a few. In some cases, schools and libraries do remove material found to be offensive by members of the local community.

However, these examples do not illustrate a social consensus on their appropriateness or desirability. For example, most parents do not use V-chips in controlling their children's television usage (Box 8.1) and do not

---

[9]For example, Section 51550 of the California Education Code states,

> No governing board of a public elementary or secondary school may require pupils to attend any class in which human reproductive organs and their functions and processes are described, illustrated or discussed, whether such class be part of a course designated "sex education" or "family life education" or by some similar term, or part of any other course which pupils are required to attend. . . . Opportunity shall be provided to each parent or guardian to request in writing that his child not attend the class, [and] no child may attend a class if a request that he not attend the class has been received by the school.

Available online at <http://www.leginfo.ca.gov/cgi-bin/waisgate?WAISdocID=07839714985+0+0+0&WAISaction=retrieve>.

Box 8.1
The V-chip

According to a study of the Kaiser Family Foundation, parents are deeply concerned about sex and violence on TV. More than 80 percent of parents are concerned that their children are being exposed to too much sex and violence on TV. Sixty-three percent are "a great deal" concerned and 18 percent are "somewhat" concerned about too much sexual content; 59 percent are "a great deal" and 23 percent "somewhat" concerned about violent content. Nearly half of parents believe that exposure to sexual content on TV contributes "a lot" to kids becoming involved in sexual situations before they're ready, and the same proportion believe exposure to violence on TV contributes "a lot" to violent behavior in children.

However, while 40 percent of all parents own a TV equipped with a V-chip, few are using it. Only 7 percent of all parents have used a V-chip to control their children's television viewing. Of those parents with a V-chip, half (53 percent) don't know it, about a third (30 percent) choose not to use it, and one in six (17 percent) have used it to block shows they don't want their children to watch. Of all parents who know they have a V-chip, about a third (36 percent) have chosen to use it.

Of the parents who know they have a V-chip but do not use it, half say the reason they haven't programmed their V-chip is that an adult is usually nearby when their children watch TV; a quarter (25 percent) say it's because they trust their children to make their own decisions. Just 2 percent say it's because they think their children would find a way around it, and just 1 percent say it is because they see the V-chip as a form of censorship.

Far more parents have used the TV ratings system than the V-chip. About half (56 percent) of all parents say they have used the TV ratings to make decisions about what shows their children will watch. This is similar to the percent of parents who have used the advisories on music (50 percent) or video and computer games (59 percent). A much larger proportion of parents (84 percent) have used the movie ratings. About a quarter of all parents (28 percent) say that they use the TV ratings "often." Furthermore, most parents (92 percent) who have used the ratings find them useful. About half of the parents who have used the ratings (48 percent) say they are "very" useful. This is similar to how parents assess the usefulness of the movie ratings (53 percent say "very" useful) and the advisories for CDs (52 percent "very" useful) and video games (52 percent).

However, parents have mixed views as to whether TV ratings accurately reflect the content of shows. Of the parents who have used the TV ratings, half say that from what they've seen, most shows are being rated in a way that accurately reflects their content; however, 40 percent say most shows are not being rated accurately. Furthermore, many parents don't understand what the TV ratings mean. For example, most parents of children aged 2 to 6 cannot say what the ratings for young children mean. Just 43 percent can define the rating TV-Y7, 31 percent can define TV-Y, and only 14 percent can recognize that FV stands for fantasy violence. More parents do understand age-based ratings, with 62 percent knowing what TV-14 means, 63 percent what TV-G means, 74 percent what TV-PG means, and 47 percent what TV-MA means. Nevertheless, more parents say the content-based ratings provide the most useful information.

SOURCE: Adapted from Kaiser Family Foundation, 2001, *Parents and the V-chip 2001*, The Henry J. Kaiser Family Foundation, Menlo Park, Calif., available online at <http://www.kff.org/content/2001/3158/Summary.pdf>.

remove their children from sex education classes in school.[10] In the case of removing materials from libraries, a formal hearing process often guarantees that removal will have a high political profile in the community involved, and constitutional issues arise as well.

Nevertheless, there is one example of action taken in this area that the committee believes provides a helpful analogy. In particular, many communities deal with the issue of preventing minors from reading and viewing adult-oriented magazines available at a newsstand through a number of steps. Children are taught by parents not to seek out such magazines, and parents refrain from leaving such magazines lying around the house (social and educational measures). In the stores, adult magazines are placed on the highest shelves, so that they are harder for shorter people to reach (a social measure). They are sealed in plastic, so that browsing them in the store is more difficult (a technology measure). An opaque "belly band" obscures the picture on the front (another technology measure). The picture itself, while sexually suggestive, does not depict either overt sexual activity or the genitalia of the models (a public policy measure). A purchaser of such magazines must usually make the transaction face-to-face with the operator of the newsstand, who can generally distinguish between a 12-year-old boy and an adult and whose very presence helps to deter some minors from even seeking to make such a purchase (another social measure). And the operator of the newsstand may be subject to prosecution if he knowingly sells an adult magazine to a minor under state and local laws that prohibit such sales to minors (another public policy measure).

All of these measures combine into an approach to the sale of adult magazines that has not absolutely prevented minors from viewing their contents, but there is not much controversy about the approach, imperfect though it is. In other words, there is a rough social consensus that this approach is for the most part not unreasonable, either in its implementation or its philosophy. It provides some protection, though the protection is not absolute, and the burden it places on magazine vendors and adult consumers is not particularly significant. Further, the protection that it does provide is adequate for publishers and vendors of adult magazines to be able to plausibly assert that they are taking reasonable steps to keep such material out of the hands of children.

---

[10]When given a choice, only 1 to 5 percent of parents remove their children from comprehensive sexual education classes. See Kaiser Family Foundation. 2000. *Sex Education in America: A View from Inside America's Classrooms.* The Henry J. Kaiser Family Foundation, Menlo Park, Calif.

How should one view approaches to protecting children from inappropriate sexually explicit material on the Internet? While the discussion of the corner newsstand above is helpful in understanding how to think about this issue, cyberspace is unlike a corner newsstand in many ways, and much of the controversy about inappropriate sexually explicit material on the Internet arises because of the differences between the corner newsstand and cyberspace. Nevertheless, a reasoned approach to protection in cyberspace also relies on the three generic elements mentioned in the corner newsstand issue—social and educational measures, technology, and public policy.

There is a broad consensus that the ideal approach for keeping kids safe on the Internet—in any dimension one wishes to consider—is the presence of a trusted, responsible adult providing guidance, pedagogy, and supervision along with encouragement and understanding. But as a practical matter, many children are likely to have some degree of unsupervised access to the Internet or other online services (e.g., because of the infeasibility of continuous parental monitoring of children's Internet use). While parents with the education, resources, and time to understand and deal with the problem may approach the ideal described above, others who do not have these benefits also seek solutions to what they see as a real problem.

It is thus not unreasonable to consider a combination of protective elements whose use can reinforce one another, though the closer one can get to the ideal described in the preceding discussion, the better. For example, parents can place computers at home in public places so that they can better supervise the Internet use of their children. Schools and libraries can teach children to avoid behavior that can lead to inadvertent exposure to inappropriate sexually explicit materials. Technology can be used to create Internet environments for very young children in which all content is specifically designed to be age-appropriate and educational. Public policy measures may be able to reduce the amount of adult-oriented, sexually explicit material that is accessible without some kind of age verification. (All of these elements, and others, are discussed in the following chapters.)

The possibility of such synergistic effects should not be taken to mean that one particular combination of protective elements is right in all cases. Furthermore, no combination of protective elements will be free of trade-offs, both within the space of protecting children and youth from inappropriate sexually explicit material on the Internet and with respect to how this space interacts with other societal issues. Thus, the appropriate combination of protective elements will vary substantially across different communities and styles of parenting, and it is important that parents and communities retain the ability and authority to determine what is best for their children—and how to make those trade-offs—in accordance with their own values.

Chapters 9 through 13 address a variety of options for public policies, strategies, and tools, and some of the benefits of coordinating their use.

9

Legal and Regulatory Tools

This chapter presents a variety of legal and policy options that the committee considered and discussed during its deliberations regarding how best to protect children from inappropriate sexually explicit material on the Internet. However, it should be kept in mind that the legal and policy environment today (as this report is being written) is highly fluid and rapidly changing. Court cases are being heard, and legislation is pending on areas such as privacy, elimination of spam, and protecting kids on the Internet. Furthermore, even if some of these legal and policy options are helpful for regulating sources of sexually explicit material within the United States, a substantial number of sources outside the direct enforceable jurisdiction of U.S. law will remain. This fact might well limit the success of U.S. legal and policy options for regulating sources of sexually explicit material.

Table 9.1 provides an overview of the public policy options described in this report.

9.1 VIGOROUS PROSECUTIONS OF OBSCENE MATERIAL

With all of the difficulties described in Chapter 4 in defining obscenity, it is still the case that material deemed obscene is not protected by the First Amendment. Federal and state obscenity laws impose criminal and civil penalties on the production, distribution, and sale of obscene matrial. In recent years, however, obscenity prosecutions have been relatively rare. Such prosecutions can be very difficult, especially in the context of the

TABLE 9.1 Examples of Advantages and Disadvantages of Various Public Policy Options for Protecting Children from Inappropriate Sexually Explicit Material on the Internet

	One Illustrative Advantage	One Illustrative Disadvantage
Vigorous prosecution of existing obscenity laws	Would clarify existing uncertainties about the feasibility of obscenity prosecutions	Would require personnel and resources that might be used for other law enforcement activity that may be of higher priority
Imposition of civil liability for dissemination of obscene materials	Would enable private parties to take action through the court system when prosecutorial resources are limited	Would generally require some showing of individualized harm, which may be difficult to demonstrate
Required use of age verification systems by commercial suppliers of adult-oriented sexually explicit material	Currently under judicial review; see discussion in Section 4.2.4	
Required use of "text-only" front page to en-sure that first page of Web site is the "warning" page about material in-side being for adults only	Would reduce inadvertent access to sexually explicit material from adult-oriented commercial Web sites	Would not reduce access for children willing to lie about their ages
Required labeling of material that is obscene for minors	Would place a minimal burden on content providers	Would require positive market response for success (e.g., browsers must be capable of recognizing labels, parents must configure browsers accordingly)
Prohibitions on spam containing material that is obscene for minors	Would reduce unsolicited e-mailed advertisements for adult-oriented material	Content-based restriction would make regulation more problematic on First Amendment grounds
Prohibitions on mouse-trapping to Web sites containing material that is obscene for minors	Would improve navigational experience for Internet users	Regulatory target may be uncertain
Stricter enforcement of record-keeping requirements	Would increase costs of compliance with such requirements; might reduce number of commercial entities unwilling to behave responsibly	Would require personnel and resources that might be used for other law enforcement activity that may be of higher priority

TABLE 9.1 (continued)

	One Illustrative Advantage	One Illustrative Disadvantage
Streamlined process for handling reports of violations	Would facilitate citizen reporting of child pornography; would reduce interagency impediments to cooperation in such prosecutions	Might increase false alarms and screening effort required
Self-regulation (e.g., vigorous enforcement of ISP terms of service)	Would likely lead to faster "take down" of material posted in violation of terms of service (which generally includes material that is obscene or child pornography)	Would require vigorous monitoring effort on part of ISP

Internet, where community standards, jurisdictional, and international issues abound.

Nevertheless, vigorous enforcement may help to persuade operators in the adult online industry to change their behavior to act more responsibly in denying access to children. It may also reduce to some extent the number of operators of Web sites carrying obscene material by putting some of them out of business and changing the cost-benefit calculus for other "marginal" operators who would choose to exit the business in a different regulatory climate.

Note that a reduction in the number of Web site operators providing such materials is not likely to reduce greatly the ease with which one can find such material. The reason is that search engines operate in such a way that a given search is more or less independent of the number of such sites. Thus, if there are 100,000 such sites today, a reduction to 10,000 sites would not significantly increase the difficulty of finding such material (or even reduce the likelihood of coming across it inadvertently).[1] Thus, it is likely that the second effect—persuading operators to behave more responsibly—would be larger in magnitude.

It is also important to note that the problem of defining which com-

---

[1]Strictly speaking, the results of a search do depend on the number of Web pages being searched: the more pages in the index, the less often the search engine re-indexes/re-searches the Net for updates and changes. Thus, Web pages that have recently been added to the Internet are less likely to be found when the number of pages in the index is large. However, this is a relatively small effect.

munity's standards should govern obscenity prosecutions for material on the Internet is at issue in current litigation regarding the Child Online Protection Act of 1998 (COPA). As noted in Chapter 4, the Supreme Court held on May 13, 2002, that COPA's reliance on "community standards" to identify what material is "harmful to minors" did not by itself render the statute substantially overbroad for First Amendment purposes, but was silent on the extent and nature of the community in question.

The Court of Appeals reasoned that in dealing with the Internet, unlike other forms of communication, the material is immediately available in all jurisdictions without regard to conventional geographical boundaries. If local community standards govern the definition of material that is obscene for minors, then providers will be liable to criminal prosecution if the material they make available violates the standards of any jurisdiction in the nation. In such a situation, providers will censor themselves by providing only that sexually oriented material that is not obscene for minors in the most conservative community in the nation. The Court of Appeals concluded that such a situation would violate the First Amendment rights of both providers and of citizens of all of the other communities in the nation. This same issue would arise with respect to traditional obscenity prosecutions for material presented on the Internet.

It should also be noted that even if the Supreme Court upholds the Third Circuit Court of Appeals in this instance, this does not necessarily mean that all legislation intended to serve the same goals as COPA will be unconstitutional. For example, one possible solution to this problem would be to require the government in a prosecution of obscenity on the Internet to prove that the material is obscene (or obscene for minors) under *both* national and local community standards. The use of the national standard would avoid the problem that concerned the Third Circuit Court of Appeals, and the use of the local standard would be necessary to ensure that the material was in fact unprotected in the particular jurisdiction in which the prosecution takes place. In any event, this issue is currently pending.

More vigorous prosecution of federal and state obscenity laws—regardless of the outcome—would help to clarify whether the current state of affairs with respect to obscenity prosecutions is due to a liberalization in "community standards," a lack of willingness to undertake prosecutions, or some other factor or factors. Thus, such prosecution could help to establish more up-to-date benchmarks for the field, a development that would provide much-needed guidance for law enforcement professionals dealing with such issues. Finally, vigorous enforcement of laws against false and deceptive advertising and business practices (an example of which is described in Section 3.4.2) could help to reduce exposure to inappropriate sexually explicit material that results from mousetrapping, takeovers of spam that advertises adult-oriented, sexually explicit sites, and so on.

Finally, note also that despite the Supreme Court ruling overturning the provisions of the Child Pornography Prevention Act relating to computer-generated imagery (discussed in Chapter 4), there is no bar to the prosecution of material that is obscene, whether or not it involves computer-generated images. Thus, if material depicts a child engaged in sexual activity, the full weight of the obscenity laws continues to apply should that material be found—through the *Miller* tests—to be obscene.

9.2 CIVIL LIABILITY FOR PRESENTING OBSCENE MATERIAL ON THE INTERNET

Because prosecutors have not been inclined in recent years (i.e., throughout most of the 1990s) to commit substantial resources to obscenity prosecutions, an alternative is to allow private individuals to bring civil actions for damages against individuals or businesses that purvey obscenity on the Internet. Under such a regime, any person who finds obscenity on the Internet could sue the Web site operator for civil damages. This use of the concept of "private attorneys general" is not unknown in the law. But it is exceptionally rare.

Ordinarily, one cannot bring a civil action for damages without showing some legally cognizable harm to the would-be plaintiff that has not been suffered by other persons generally. For example, if X drives his car in excess of the speed limit, he cannot be sued for damages by people who were not individually damaged by his speeding. Similarly, people cannot sue for damages a murderer, a thief, or a drug dealer, without a showing of particularized, specific harm to them as individuals. Although the idea of essentially creating a "bounty" by authorizing such suits has some appeal, it is generally not consistent with the standards of the U.S. legal system or the basic goals of U.S. system for civil actions. And although civil actions for damages are familiar in the realm of expression (for example, civil actions for defamation), they have always required a showing of individualized harm.

A further difficulty is the potential for abuse—using the court system merely to harass providers of material that one group or another finds objectionable.

9.3 OPTIONS FOR DEALING WITH MATERIAL THAT IS OBSCENE FOR MINORS

In recognition of the special problems posed by the exposure of children to sexually explicit material, the Supreme Court held in *Ginsberg v.*

New York that the government can constitutionally prohibit "the sale to minors . . . of material defined to be obscene on the basis of its appeal to them whether or not it would be obscene to adults." In other words, the government can prohibit children from having access to certain types of sexually explicit material that it cannot constitutionally ban for adults. As noted in Chapter 4, this doctrine works best in those situations in which it is possible to separate children from adults, for as the Supreme Court has also observed, the government "may not reduce the adult population . . . to reading only what is fit for children." Thus, in decisions like *Reno v. ACLU*, the Court has made clear that the government may not prohibit material that is "obscene as to minors" on the Internet unless it can do so in a way that does not unduly interfere with the rights of adults to have access to such material.

Further, there is a very wide developmental range from birth to the age of legal majority. The very concept of speech that is obscene for minors has never been well defined, but presumably its content varies with the age of the minor. This creates a problem for any unitary definition for the term. Furthermore, what is obscene, either for adults or for children, turns in part on community standards. But as noted in Chapter 4, it is difficult to define or identify community standards when one deals with the Internet. This may, or may not, present a constitutional problem depending on the restrictions that are imposed on such material (see below).

Although an outright prohibition of material that is obscene for minors would therefore be unconstitutional, more finely tuned proposals, such as those described below, may pass constitutional muster.

9.3.1 Age Verification

In the Child Online Protection Act of 1998 (COPA), Congress sought to remedy the deficiencies in the Communications Decency Act of 1997 (CDA) that led the Supreme Court unanimously to invalidate the CDA in *Reno v. ACLU*. (See Chapter 4.) COPA declares it unlawful to communicate on a commercial Web site material that is obscene for minors by means of the World Wide Web if the material is available to minors. COPA states that it will be an affirmative defense if the defendant, in good faith, takes reasonable measures to restrict access to the material by minors by requiring a credit card, an adult access code, an adult personal identification number, or other appropriate proof of age. As of April 2002, the constitutionality of COPA is currently pending before the Supreme Court of the United States in *Ashcroft v. ACLU*.

As noted above, one issue in this case is whether the use of local community standards in the context of the Internet is consistent with the First Amendment. Another issue is whether the requirement of age verification passes constitutional muster. For example, in a book store one can require proof of age to purchase a book that is obscene for minors, thus providing access to adults while denying access to children. COPA attempts to establish a similar basis for differentiation between adults and minors on the Internet. Because the implementation of age verification on the Internet requires the use of technology, the objection to COPA is that it imposes significant costs on the Web site operator and/or the adult viewers and that by potentially creating a permanent record it violates legitimate privacy interests and chills the freedom of adult viewers.

If the Supreme Court upholds the constitutionality of COPA in *Ashcroft v. ACLU*, this will appreciably advance the interests of those who seek to prevent minors from gaining access to material that is deemed to be obscene for minors. It will not necessarily meet all of their concerns, however. First, COPA applies only to material that is obscene for minors. The precise definition of this concept remains largely undeveloped, and it is not clear how far it will reach. Second, COPA applies only to material on the World Wide Web. It does not apply to chat rooms or e-mail. Third, COPA applies only to commercial Web sites. It does not apply to noncommercial sites. These three limitations on COPA were necessary to meet the concerns of the Supreme Court in *Reno v. ACLU* in invalidating the CDA. Fourth, COPA will be effective only to the extent government actually prosecutes violations with sufficient vigor to have a significant deterrent effect. The lack of Internet obscenity prosecutions in recent years raises questions about whether such prosecutions will occur. Fifth, COPA applies only to Web sites in the United States. For jurisdictional reasons, federal legislation cannot readily govern Web sites outside the United States, even though they are accessible within the United States. Because a substantial percentage of sexually explicit Web sites exist outside the United States, even the strict enforcement of COPA will likely have only a marginal effect on the availability of such material on the Internet in the United States. Thus, even if the Supreme Court upholds COPA, COPA is not a panacea, illustrating the real limitations of policy and legal approaches to this issue. The committee also notes that, even if COPA is constitutional, this does not necessarily mean it is good public policy. The concerns raised against COPA could at least arguably lead to the conclusion that it is insufficiently effective to justify its costs, whether or not it is consistent with the First Amendment.

If the Supreme Court invalidates COPA because age verification procedures in the context of the Internet are too burdensome on the First Amendment rights of adults, this will make it very difficult to regulate material that is obscene for minors in this environment. In the next few sections, the committee presents several legal and regulatory approaches that might be available even if the Supreme Court invalidates COPA.

9.3.2 Plain Brown Wrappers and Age Verification

Many commercially oriented adult Web sites subject the viewer to an assortment of "teaser" images that are intended to entice a viewer to pay in order to see more such images. In many cases, the teaser images include material that may be obscene. To prevent minors from viewing such materials, it might be possible to grant such Web sites a statutory "safe harbor" immunity from prosecution under obscenity laws if the provider places the Web site behind a "plain brown wrapper."[2] Such a "notice" page would contain an appropriate warning indicating that going past this notice page should be done only if the viewer is older than 18, and that going past this notice page constitutes certification that the user is indeed older than 18.[3] The notice page would contain no images, or perhaps images that are obscured in the same way that the covers of adult-oriented magazines are obscured in the newsstands.

The purpose of the notice page is to ensure that anyone who reaches the sexually explicit Web pages of a site has actually read the notice and agreed to its terms. However, many sites today have notice pages and it is still often possible to reach sexually explicit pages on those sites through search engines that index the pages behind the notice page. Thus, by clicking on a link that may be returned by a search engine, the user circumvents the notice page entirely.

To prevent such circumvention, it is necessary to prevent search engines from indexing the pages behind the notice page, and a standard protocol for accomplishing this task is described in Chapter 2 (Box 2.2). For a site that uses this protocol (the "robots.txt" protocol), a Web indexer for a search engine cannot reach the pages behind the notice page, and so search engines cannot return links to those pages and thus users cannot access them directly. Thus, the only way that a user could reach the contents of the adult Web site would be to go through the notice page.

This approach would reduce inadvertent access to teaser images on adult-oriented sites, and thus provide a greater level of denial of such access than is currently in place. Of course, this approach would not

---

[2]The reason for this approach (of granting immunity from prosecution under obscenity laws rather than obscene-for-minors laws in exchange for using age verification technologies and "plain brown wrappers") is that if it were constitutional to prosecute a Web site operator under obscene-for-minors laws, the government would simply do it. However, if such prosecutions are found to be unconstitutional, then the Web site is immune from such prosecutions regardless of what it does with respect to age verification technologies and "plain brown wrappers," and thus an incentive of a different sort is needed to persuade them to adopt such measures. In this case, the incentive is to grant another, different benefit—namely, immunity from obscenity prosecution.

[3]The age of 18 is an age that denotes legal emancipation for a minor, but there is no particular reason that the age could not be some other number.

prevent access by individuals under 18 who are willing to lie about their age. To deal with such individuals, it may be possible to add to the plain brown wrapper an age verification requirement. That is, in order to get past the notice page, proof of age would be required.[4] (A discussion of age verification technologies is contained in Chapter 13.) Such a provision might be constitutional, even if COPA is declared invalid, because the use of age verification is encouraged by the offer of immunity from prosecution for obscenity, but is not legally required.

9.3.3 Labeling of Material That Is Obscene for Minors

Another possibility would be to require any commercial provider of material that is obscene for minors to label that speech in a machine-readable manner that enables parents and others to technologically block the access of minors to such material (Section 12.1 has further discussion of this approach). Because this approach focuses only on a category of speech that can constitutionally be restricted for minors, and does not prohibit adults (or even minors) from accessing it, it may not be unduly burdensome. And if the market responds appropriately, the proposal provides parents with a reasonable degree of control over what their children see.

If the labeling requirement is found to present constitutional difficulties, a less speech-restrictive approach would be to grant safe-harbor immunity from prosecution under "obscene for minors" and obscenity laws for those who voluntarily label their materials in an appropriate manner.

9.3.4 Prohibiting Spam That Is Obscene for Minors

A third approach would be to prohibit any person from sending on the Internet commercial spam that includes material that is obscene for minors. This is less intrusive on First Amendment interests than COPA because it deals only with commercial advertising and it involves sending information to individuals who have not requested it or sought it out.

---

[4]The use of age verification technologies poses a significant privacy issue. Indeed, in the cases of the CDA and COPA, the courts reviewing these acts found that these requirements were unreasonable given the current state of technology and that age verification measures impose significant burdens on Web sites because the verification measures require site visitors to provide personal information. Because users are reluctant to provide this information and are discouraged from accessing sites that require such disclosures, the imposition of age verification requirements may chill or inhibit adults from accessing non-obscene Web sites, both because they might not wish to give personal information and because they may not be able to prove their age. These measures, the courts found, would diminish access to protected speech and thereby impose significant expense on commercial sites.

However, this approach is potentially more problematic than COPA because it restricts the sending of such material to adults as well as to children. Unlike COPA, it does not attempt to differentiate between them.

In general, the Supreme Court has held that the government cannot prohibit the sending of constitutionally protected material (including commercial advertising) to individuals who have not expressly asked not to receive it. In *Bolger v. Youngs Drugs Products Corp.*,[5] for example, the Court invalidated a federal statute prohibiting the mailing of unsolicited advertisements for contraceptives because the interest in shielding "recipients of mail from materials that they are likely to find offensive" is not sufficiently substantial to justify the restriction of "protected speech." The most plausible distinction between the law invalidated in *Bolger* and a ban on sending through the Internet commercial spam that includes material that is obscene for minors is that material that is obscene for minors is constitutionally protected for adults, but not for children. This may not be a sufficient distinction to make a constitutional difference. More modest versions of this proposal, more likely to withstand constitutional scrutiny, would prohibit any person from sending commercial spam that includes material that is obscene for minors (a) without appropriate labeling (e.g., having a warning on the e-mail subject containing a message like "Not appropriate for children under 16 years of age"), or (b) without prior age verification, or (c) after the recipient has objected to receiving such material in the past.

It is important to note that for speech to be regulated under the commercial speech doctrine, it must consist of advertising. Thus, to the extent that the constitutionality of the alternatives noted above turns on the commercial speech doctrine, non-commercial spam or spam that does not consist of advertising could not be restricted.

It is also worth noting that most spam concerning sexually explicit material does not consist of the sexually explicit material itself, but of links to Web sites that have such material embedded within them. Thus, the recipient of the e-mail must affirmatively take some action actually to reach the Web site (e.g., clicking on the link). From a constitutional perspective, there is a significant difference between "inflicting" sexually explicit material on individuals who do not want to be exposed to it and providing those individuals information about how to find such material. Even if the former can be regulated, the latter may warrant greater constitutional protection.

This observation may be especially important in applying the commercial speech doctrine. From a constitutional perspective, there is a

---

[5]463 U.S. 60 (1983).

difference between giving individuals information about how to obtain an unlawful thing and actually providing them with the thing. Making illegal the mere providing of the link might pass constitutional muster if (a) the material at the link could be determined to be illegal (as it could sometimes be under obscenity laws) and (b) the party providing the link is essentially an accomplice under the criminal law. Requirement (b) would not be met merely because someone provided information about how to find obscene material. However, it would be met if the spammer is also the operator of the Web site containing obscene materials (or if the spammer is hired by the Web site operator), because the spam could be regarded as an advertisement for an illegal product and the provider or sender punished on that basis.

Note that a variety of legislative proposals have appeared with the intent of reducing the problem of spam e-mails. For example, one federal proposal calls for prohibiting senders of unsolicited commercial electronic mail from disguising the source of their messages, and giving consumers the choice to cease receiving a sender's unsolicited commercial electronic mail messages.[6] This proposed legislation prohibited senders from including materially false or misleading header information and deceptive subject headings in commercial e-mail, required the inclusion of a valid return address in commercial electronic mail so that the recipient could indicate a desire not to receive further messages from the sender, and penalized further transmissions of e-mail once such a desire had been indicated. States have also sought to regulate spam, as illustrated in Box 9.1.

Still another possibility for regulating spam is a mechanism similar to that for regulating the telephone calls of telemarketers.[7] Thus, it might be feasible for a central clearinghouse to register and maintain specific e-mail addresses or perhaps even entire domain names as a "do not spam" database. The clearinghouse would also be configured to provide database results automatically. Any party sending spam would be required to check the "do not spam" database and eliminate from its mass mailing all addresses contained in the database. Not doing so (and the proof would be the receipt of a spam by someone contained in the database) would subject the sender to some civil liability and/or class-action suit. (Note

---

[6]HR 718, the Unsolicited Commercial Electronic Mail Act of 2001, passed the House on April 4, 2001.

[7]At present, a customer request to refrain from calling must be honored only by the specific company to which the customer has given notice. As this report goes to press, the Federal Trade Commission is proposing to create a centralized national "Do Not Call" registry that would enable consumers to eliminate most telemarketing calls simply by registering with a central "do-not-call" list maintained by the FTC. See <http://www.ftc.gov/opa/2002/01/donotcall.htm>.

Box 9.1
The Washington State Experience with Anti-spam Laws

In 1998, the Washington state legislature passed the Unsolicited Commercial Electronic Mail Act, RCW 19.190.020, which prohibits unsolicited electronic mail that advertises consumer products with a false or misleading subject line or return address. Such e-mail is more commonly known as "spam."

In June 2001, the Washington Supreme Court unanimously upheld the constitutionality of the state's anti-spam e-mail law. The decision involved a lawsuit filed by the Attorney General's Office on October 22, 1998, against an Oregon man, Jason Heckel, and his company, Natural Instincts, of violating the state's new anti-spam law by sending unsolicited commercial e-mail. While the subject of the e-mails was to promote a for-sale booklet titled "How to Profit from the Internet," the subject header was allegedly "Did I get the right e-mail address?"—a ploy to entice recipients to download and read his entire message. In addition, the e-mail allegedly contained an invalid return e-mail address to which recipients were unable to respond.

In March 2000, King County Superior Court Judge Palmer Robinson dismissed the case against Heckel and his company on grounds that the state law violated the Commerce Clause of the U.S. Constitution. But in its ruling overturning Judge Robinson's dismissal, the Washington Supreme Court found that ". . . the only burden the Act places on spammers is the requirement of truthfulness, a requirement that does not burden commerce at all but actually 'facilitates it by eliminating fraud and deception.' "

The case will be remanded to the Superior Court for trial.

SOURCE: Adapted from <http://www.wa.gov/ago/releases/rel_spam_060701.html>.

---

that a mechanism of this sort that was specifically aimed at senders of sexually explicit spam would be much more suspect under the First Amendment because it would not be content-neutral.)

9.3.5 Prohibiting the Practice of Mousetrapping to Web Sites Containing Material That Is Obscene for Minors

Another approach may be to prohibit the practice of mousetrapping at sites that contain material that is obscene for minors without prior age verification. Even if the Court finds COPA unconstitutional, it may be that the act of directing children to material that is obscene for minors without their consent or any affirmative act on their part would be upheld. The act of mousetrapping involves not only exposing individuals to material they would prefer to avoid, but rather actually taking over their freedom of choice and effectively compelling them to view such material. Whether or not all mousetrapping can or should be restricted, a reasonable case can be made for prohibiting operators of Web sites from sending children without warning or choice to sites that will expose them to material that is obscene for minors. A more modest variation would be to require at least a warning before mousetrapping a viewer to a site containing material that is obscene for minors.

9.4 ENFORCEMENT OF RECORD-KEEPING REQUIREMENTS

One element of the federal obscenity laws (18 U.S.C. 2257, as discussed in Section 4.2.2) involves a record-keeping requirement intended to ensure that performers and models depicted in sexually explicit scenes are older than 18. More active enforcement of this provision may better protect minors from participation in the creation of child pornography.[8]

Assuming that strict enforcement of this provision can withstand constitutional scrutiny, such enforcement might also have the effect of increasing the rate at which the adult online Web industry consolidates. Compliance with the regulation would increase the expenses of such providers, and would be likely to drive out of business the small-scale "quick buck" enterprises, while the established adult content providers would simply absorb those expenses as a cost of doing business. (At the same time, as a matter of constitutional doctrine, the intent behind enforcement is highly relevant. If these laws are enforced with the intent of driving out of business otherwise legal business operations, such enforcement might well raise constitutional questions.)

As described in Chapter 3, representatives from the online adult industry testified to the committee that attracting children was not in their business interest. Taking this testimony at face value, and assuming that the "quick buck" providers are the ones that are not discriminating in their attraction of traffic to their sites (i.e., not distinguishing between adults and minors), then enforcement of 18 U.S.C. 2257 might result in a withering of the irresponsible enterprises, leaving behind businesses that take more seriously their responsibilities to deny access of their wares to minors. Note also that the issue of recognizing "sexually explicit conduct" is far simpler than recognizing obscenity, a fact that would simplify considerably the task of prosecution.[9]

---

[8]This point is likely to be most relevant in the context of Web sites that depict "barely legal" models engaged in sexually explicit behavior. Thus, the child pornography at issue is most likely to be images of an older minor engaged in sexual activity.

[9]18 U.S.C. 2257 defines "sexually explicit conduct" as actual sexual intercourse, including genital-genital, oral-genital, anal-genital, or oral-anal, whether between persons of the same or opposite sex; bestiality; masturbation; sadistic or masochistic abuse; or lascivious exhibition of the genitals or pubic area of any person.

9.5 STREAMLINING THE PROCESS
OF HANDLING VIOLATIONS

Prosecutors seeking to enforce child pornography laws rely to a significant extent on lay person reporting of child pornography. That is, law enforcement officials may come across such material in the course of their everyday work, but citizens filing complaints about such material are a major source of leads and tips.

In an Internet environment, the most natural way to file such complaints is likely to be electronic. For example, a concerned citizen lodging a complaint with law enforcement officials should provide the route to which the material came to the citizen's attention and a description of the image. Because images are hard to describe in words, a copy of the image would be desirable to include in the complaint. Indeed, in the case of child pornography, such a copy so forwarded might be the only tangible evidence that law enforcement officials could obtain, as child pornography sites are generally highly transient (and by the time law enforcement officials are able to act on such complaints, the site may be gone). However, if the citizen files an electronic complaint with a copy of the suspect image, he or she may be in technical violation of statutes that prohibit the electronic transmission or distribution of child pornography, even though it is being transmitted to law enforcement authorities or the National Center for Missing and Exploited Children (NCMEC) and even though such evidence might be crucial for the investigation and prosecution of the offender by law enforcement. Instead, complainants must often go through a cumbersome and inconvenient procedure to file such a report.[10]

A similar problem affects the NCMEC. Despite the NCMEC's role in providing technical assistance to law enforcement in the investigation of child pornography, it does not enjoy the same immunity enjoyed by law enforcement authorities to receive, possess, and store complaints of child pornography, and it does not have the authorization to transfer evidence of child pornography from the NCMEC to other designated law enforcement agencies outside the CyberTipline (CTL) system and sometimes even within the CTL system.[11]

---

[10]For example, to report a suspected violation through the NCMEC, they must provide the relevant URL where the image can be found and a textual description of the image. In an online environment, it would be much simpler and easier for the citizen to simply forward the image.

[11]The CyberTipline, operated by the NCMEC, is a national reporting mechanism for use by citizens to report to law enforcement authorities apparent instances of sexual exploitation of children; possession, manufacture, and distribution of child pornography; online enticement of children for sexual acts; child prostitution; child-sex tourism; and child sexual molestation. See <http://www.cybertipline.com> for more information.

Relief for the first problem—i.e., allowing citizens to report suspected child pornography to the NCMEC without fear of prosecution—could enable and encourage more citizen action in this area, while relief for the second problem would enable the NCMEC to proactively forward such evidence to law enforcement outside the CTL system.

9.6 SELF-REGULATORY APPROACHES

Successful self-regulatory approaches are based on the fact that the firms in an industry are generally willing to abide by a common code of behavior, though as noted in Chapter 4, such a willingness may reflect a desire to stave off legislation or other regulation that these firms would find more onerous. One example of self-regulation with respect to certain media content is the willingness of private producers of TV content to provide ratings of their content that can be processed by the V-chip.

Today, a large number of reported instances of child pornography remain on Internet service provider (ISP) servers because law enforcement lacks the resources to investigate every report. An approach used in Europe with some success is employed by the European INHOPE Hotlines. Under the INHOPE approach, European ISPs support a non-governmental organization, staffed by trained specialists to identify child pornography and funded by the ISPs, whose role is to advise Internet service providers of possible postings of child pornography.[12] (Through Internet "Hotlines," this organization takes tips from the public, but screens them for credibility.) Such advisories do not have any binding effect on ISPs, but in fact many ISPs cooperate with such advisories by taking down the offending material because these advisories provide more authoritative advice than that provided by members of the public.[13] In a U.S. context, such a function could be provided by the NCMEC, which currently lacks the authority to provide such advisories.

A second facet of possible self-regulatory efforts might include prominent placement of the CTL reporting icon on adult-oriented Web sites. Today, many such Web sites provide links to information on filtering products, and some even have a banner that says "fight child pornography." It would be simple for these sites to add the CTL icon, which has proven quite useful in reporting online child pornography.

---

[12]Note also that the fact of private support by the ISPs is the key component of the "self-regulatory" dimension of this approach as viewed by the Council of Europe.

[13]Note that the private terms of service to which users must conform as a condition of an ISP's service agreement with the user grant ISPs considerably more latitude in the exercise of such "take-down" authority than would be possible if they were agents of government and hence constrained by legal and constitutional barriers.

Another dimension of self-regulation is the willingness of ISPs to enforce the terms of service to which users must agree. To the extent that these terms of service prohibit posting or sending of inappropriate material, harassment, or other inappropriate behavior (and most terms of service do contain some restrictions along these lines), ISPs have the authority to take quick action against offending users without waiting for legal action.

A third example of self-regulation could be set by the commercial sources of adult-oriented, sexually explicit imagery that provide much of the content for smaller "affiliates." In particular, they could build into their contracts with affiliates conditions that require those affiliates to engage in responsible behavior. Thus, as one possibility, affiliates could be required contractually to put their content behind the Internet equivalent of "plain brown wrappers" with age verification. The firms that supply them with content would be in a position to check on them and penalize them if they did not (by cutting off a content source).

9.7 GENERAL OBSERVATIONS

In its consideration of various public policy options to help shield children and youth from inappropriate sexually explicit material on the Internet, the committee realizes that the viability of many proposals depends on how makers of public policy make certain trade-offs. Proposals that depend on regulating a certain type of content (namely, sexually explicit speech) are inherently more suspect on First Amendment grounds than proposals that regulate speech independent of content.

For example, the committee believes that spam containing material that is obscene for minors should not be sent to children. But laws banning such e-mail to minors are potentially problematic in an online environment in which it is very difficult to differentiate between adults and minors. At the same time, a ban of all spam regardless of content may be seen as too broad because it affects many other interests.

The committee also believes that it would be desirable for adult Web site operators who exhibit material that is obscene for minors to use age verification systems so that children would not be able to access such material. However, in an online environment in which it is very difficult to differentiate between adults and minors, it is not clear whether this can be achieved in a way that does not unduly constrain the viewing rights of adults. Thus, as one illustrative example, the government might offer a grant of immunity from prosecution under obscenity laws to Web site operators who use age verification systems to prevent minors from accessing such material. In this instance, the trade-off is helping to protect children from exposure to certain kinds of inappropriate sexually explicit material in return for limitations on possible obscenity prosecutions.

Enforcement of obscenity laws also presents trade-offs. Increased prosecution of obscenity would likely require increased resources, and those resources must be taken from some other activity. If, as is likely, the other activity represents prosecutions of other crimes, policy makers must make the judgment that it would be wise to pursue more obscenity prosecutions rather than other criminal prosecutions, or that more prosecutions for obscenity would necessarily be the best use of additional resources—if such resources are available. Such judgments are complex and require a careful weighing of many competing factors well beyond the scope of this report.

Several other general observations follow below:

• While the foundation of protecting children from inappropriate Internet materials and experiences continues to be social and educational strategies to instill ethics of responsible choice and coping strategies for inadvertent exposure, public policy has a role in shaping the environment in which children exercise their choices.

• Actions to remove illegal material from the Internet can occur much more quickly if the authority to do so is based on the terms of private contracts (such as terms of service) rather than the requirements of public law.

• Obscenity prosecutions are often difficult to undertake, because community standards are often not knowable in advance of an actual trial. By contrast, child pornography is based on standards that are often easier to identify (e.g., is this material sexually explicit? versus does this material violate community standards?) and as such is easier to prosecute, all else being equal. Nevertheless, more aggressive prosecution of allegedly obscene materials, even if not always successful, would help to clarify the status of this instrumentality.

10

Social and Educational Strategies to Develop Personal and Community Responsibility

A preadolescent boy using an Internet-enabled computer in class is surfing the Internet. On his search engine, he comes across a link to a Web site. He raises his hand and tells his teacher, "I think I am about to go somewhere that I shouldn't go." The teacher stops the class and asks the student to explain to the class why he thought his surfing might have been about to take him to a place that he should not have gone.

10.1 FOUNDATIONS OF RESPONSIBLE CHOICE

Linda Roberts, then at the Department of Education, told the committee the story described above. The boy involved is arguably less vulnerable to being exposed to inappropriate material on the Internet than if he used any technological blocking mechanism for protection. The reason is that his "filtering mechanism" has been internalized—and he has internal criteria for deciding what might constitute inappropriate material.

In other words, a child who faces a free choice—and chooses responsible and ethical options over others—is protecting himself. Thus, the issue at hand is one that relates to the sense of ethics and responsibility and the character underlying a free (and often unaided) choice. Indeed, it has been frequently mentioned to the committee that those who really want to obtain inappropriate sexually explicit material on the Internet will generally find ways of doing so, circumventing all technological measures to curtail access to such material. For determined individuals with the technical skills to do so, only a conscious choice to refrain from such seeking will reduce his or her access to these materials.

Almost by definition, a child is not yet fully mature, even if, as in the case of adolescents, their physiology may be fully capable of sexual engagement. No maturing child is immune to temptation. No curious child is safe from the cyberspace equivalents of touching the hot stove, tumbling into the unprotected swimming pool, and getting into any "nice man's" car.

Children need supervision. They also need love. Parents and teachers provide both. Children need significant adult reference points—significant adults who, in fact, function as reference works. They are there to answer questions and point inquiring minds in the direction of "right" (in the sense of sensible, ethical, correct, and age-appropriate) answers. Experimentation is part of the discovery process; reckless endangerment is not.

As children develop morally and ethically, they internalize principles and values that work from within to prompt external actions. Once internalized, they support "habits" and facilitate habitual behavior. Thus the role of ethical and moral education is to articulate guiding principles for the child that can be freely chosen and, once internalized, serve to prompt appropriate behavior. A person of character is a principled person. Significant adults—parents, teachers, coaches, counselors, clergy—articulate and explain principles to the young, and the learning role of the latter is to assimilate them.

The problem of developing character is compounded by the important role of community. In real life, the presence of a supportive community is generally regarded as a major positive factor in the development of an individual's sense of social responsibility and responsible behavior. But in an online environment (especially an anonymous one), a shared sense of community—with all of the attendant rights and responsibilities—is hard to develop among individuals who see the Internet in purely instrumental terms.[1] Anonymity in particular (as would be true in an environment that does not require individual logins, and as is true for much Web surfing) enables individuals to escape responsibility and to avoid negative consequences for inappropriate behavior.[2]

In any event, encouraging youngsters to become principled persons is no easy task. One path to a principled life focuses on the internalization

---

[1]See, for example, Robert Putnam, 2000, *Bowling Alone*, Simon & Schuster, New York.

[2]True anonymous Web surfing is possible only if one takes special measures to be anonymous. Nevertheless, the perception that one is anonymous on the Internet even without taking special measures is strong, and in any case, a perception of anonymity (or at least privacy) can result simply from having a screen that no one else can see.

of family values, family traditions, and shared meanings within the family that can help to shape the developing character of a child, and help "explain" why a given youngster chooses to do this or avoid that. For those who are religious, this can include faith-based values in this internalization process. These principles and values can serve to help a child judge what is or is not reasonable in a context broader than the immediacy of pleasure and pain, of "getting caught" or "getting away with it."

Indeed, an approach based primarily on punishment presupposes that children engaging in inappropriate behavior will be caught misbehaving. As a practical matter, detection of such behavior will often not occur, especially if those children seek to remain undetected. While the fear of punishment will deter some children, others often do things for which they might be caught and punished in spite of that possibility— fear of punishment is not enough to deter these children from things they really want to do. Moreover, the research literature indicates that the threat of punishment per se is not an effective approach to helping individuals internalize codes of behavior.[3] While such a threat is sometimes effective in deterring undesirable behavior, individuals who find themselves free of the threat often revert to the undesired behavior.

These comments do not detract from the positive role that punishment or discipline may play as *one element* of an approach to education. It is entirely appropriate to impose sanctions for the deliberate violation of rules if such rules have been explained clearly and discussion with children about their rationale and purpose has been entertained. But explanation and discussion are essential for putting these rules into context as appropriate reflections of parental values.

Every parent has the difficult task of determining where trust ends and neglect begins. They want to trust their children, and their children— particularly in the teen years—want to be trusted. But parents don't want to be negligent, and their offspring often find it difficult to appreciate the tug-of-war within a parent's heart between the desire to trust and the fear of neglect. Though parents might wish otherwise, there is no clear and simple line of demarcation.

For example, as noted in Section 10.4, parents can insist that children not have access to a computer in the privacy of their bedrooms. Better to have it outside in the hall, or downstairs in the family room—to have it, in other words, in a place where casual passersby can appear at any time. It is not that the children aren't trusted; it is simply an acknowledgment that

---

[3]See, for example, M.L. Hoffman, 1988, "Moral Development," in *Developmental Psychology: An Advanced Textbook*, 2nd Ed., M.H. Bornstein and M.E. Lamb, eds., Erlbaum, Hillsdale, N.J.; and G.H. Brody and D.R. Shaffer, 1982, "Contributions of Parents and Peers to Children's Moral Socialization," *Developmental Review* 2: 31-75.

children are children and are more likely to do the right thing when they know they might be observed.

By extension, the character issue touches what is commonly referred to as "socially responsible business." This is an area of practical, applied business ethics. As in any other industry, those in the adult entertainment industry have a social responsibility not only to provide return to shareholders but also to behave in ways that promote the good of society. Because society's best hope for a better future lies with its children, all businesses have responsibilities for helping and not hindering the young along a safe path to mature character development.

One dimension of that responsibility is to engage in business lines and practices that uphold human dignity and refrain from exploitation. But a perhaps more important dimension is to help create an environment in which children can play, learn, and explore without fear of coming across material that is inappropriate for them. Thus, for example, entirely apart from legal requirements to do so, those in the adult online industry have important ethical and moral responsibilities to keep their material away from children, even if that has some negative financial implications.

10.2 DEFINITION OF A SOCIAL OR EDUCATIONAL STRATEGY

For purposes of this report, social or educational strategies are coordinated plans of action that seek to develop in young people the ability to make responsible and safe choices about Internet use, to make good decisions about content to be viewed, to reduce their exposure to inappropriate material, and to mitigate the consequences, if any, of viewing inappropriate material. These strategies include activities that educate parents and young people on Internet use and address a variety of issues arising from online use, such as how to reduce exposure to inappropriate material and how to give young people skills to mitigate any possible effects they might experience from encountering sexually explicit or inappropriate material online.

Through its deliberations and on the basis of testimony and other information received, the committee has found that social and educational strategies are foundational for children's safe, effective, and appropriate use of the Internet. This is not to say that technology plays no role—indeed, many technological tools can support the development and teaching of skills, attitudes, and ethical codes of behavior that will enable young people to use the Internet appropriately. Rather, exclusive—or even primary—reliance on technological measures for protection would be an abdication of parental and community responsibility and is likely to be ineffective as well.

Table 10.1 provides an overview of the social and educational strategies described in this report.

TABLE 10.1 Social and Educational Strategies for Protecting Children on the Internet

	Description
Parental supervision	Active, in-person supervision of child's Internet use
Peer assistance	Help provided by sibling or peer mentor acting as guide to child's use of the Internet
Acceptable use policies (AUPs)	Statement explicating in detail what constitutes acceptable and unacceptable use of the Internet and what consequences flow from the latter
Internet safety education (ISE)	Explicit instruction on what constitutes safe Internet behavior and how to recognize dangerous, inappropriate situations
Information and media (I/M) literacy	Facility in using critical reasoning skills to obtain information sought and to evaluate the content of information that is received
Compelling content	Content specifically designed to appeal to children that is non-commercial and educational and/or positive in orientation
Media campaigns	Initiatives featuring media spots and public service announcements about the nature of the Internet, the potential dangers of Internet activity for children, and parental options for exerting influence

10.3 CONTEXTUAL ISSUES FOR SOCIAL AND EDUCATIONAL STRATEGIES

New technology often does not live up to its promises. One reason is that because technology changes rapidly for everyone, technology tools developed to solve problems exposed by other technological developments may be quickly rendered obsolete. But a more important reason is that the underlying issues are social. It is true that the Internet may have

One Illustrative Advantage	One Illustrative Disadvantage
Provides closest connection to the values that the parent wishes to impart to child	Probably not feasible to provide constant active supervision of child's Internet access, especially as child gets older
Provides guidance and influence to which children may be more responsive (compared to parental advice or assistance)	Older sibling may lead younger one into trouble; non-family peer mentors may spend little time with child
Provides clear behavioral guidelines for child about what should and should not be done	Infractions of AUP may not be discovered; without concerted attention, may become just one more form to be filled out
Provides clear guidance for child about how to conduct himself or herself on the Internet	No obvious forum in most existing curricula to include ISE
Emphasizes critical reasoning skills that are valuable in many contexts other than Internet use	No obvious forum in most existing curricula to include I/M literacy
Availability of such material would help to divert children's attention from inappropriate materials and experiences	Child market not preferred by most businesses because adult market is more lucrative
Can contribute a basic awareness of the issues in a broad segment of the population	Absent follow-through in other non-media channels, significant constructive behavioral changes in parents are unlikely

exacerbated public concerns about the access of young people to inappropriate sexually explicit material, but the Internet is more a symptom than the basic issue. Furthermore, those who really want to disseminate inappropriate materials or find inappropriate materials on the Internet have proven adept at circumventing technology-based solutions. As the technology improves, so also do its circumventers, in a never-ending game of action and reaction. This pattern is repeated in almost every instance where technology is used to thwart undesirable behavior.

The committee believes that the fundamental issue is how to teach a young person to make wise choices, to stay in control of his or her online experiences, to be critical and skeptical about the underlying messages in advertising and romanticized and sexualized images, and to report other users soliciting personal information or harassing them. A young person who has been taught effectively about such matters will bring that training to any device that he or she uses and in any venue that offers online access.

An analogy might be drawn to children and swimming pools. Swimming pools pose some threat to the safety and well-being of children. But swimming pools provide benefits to their owners—and children—in many different ways. Technology—in the form of fences around pools, pool alarms, and locks—can help protect children from drowning in swimming pools. However, teaching a child to swim—and when to avoid pools—is a far safer approach than relying on locks, fences, and alarms to prevent him or her from drowning. Does this mean that parents should not buy fences, alarms, and locks? Of course not—because they do provide some benefit. But parents cannot rely exclusively on these devices to keep their children safe from drowning, and most parents recognize that a child who knows how to swim is less likely to be harmed than one who does not. Furthermore, teaching a child to swim and to exercise good judgment about bodies of water to avoid has applicability and relevance far beyond swimming pools—as any parent who takes a child to the beach can testify.

Note also that social and educational strategies are the only way to deal with young people determined to seek out inappropriate material. Those who are determined are bound to find ways to circumvent any technological measures; to the extent that social and educational strategies can reduce the desire and motivation for seeking out inappropriate material or engaging in inappropriate activities, such behavior can be reduced. When technological protection does not work, or when it is not present, the individual involved must rely on his or her own internal resources to cope with the issue, whether it is in choosing to refrain from "getting into trouble" or knowing how to cope with whatever trouble arises.

In designing social and educational strategies, developmental issues are critical. For example, very young children are generally not capable of handling a full range of unconstrained choices. However, as they gradually mature, it is usually appropriate to give them a wider range of choices and increasing amounts of responsibility. Of course, the nature and scope of increased freedoms to choose are not generally based solely on age, but for most young people, age is a relevant factor in teaching them increasingly mature and responsible behavior.[4]

---

[4]In some ways, the developmental issue is similar to that of learning to drive. Licenses for driving an automobile in all states are graduated to some extent (learner's permit and

For example, one time-honored practice of good parenting is to teach children to make responsible decisions by sharply constraining their choices at first and then broadening the universe of choices as they grow more mature and more capable of making informed and wise decisions. Of course, under these circumstances, children may make some mistakes and injudicious choices. But when the universe of choices is limited to those that are at least minimally acceptable, children have a chance to learn how to make good choices by exercising choice. Further, the decision-making skills they acquire in doing so can be carried over to their later lives—in which the universe of choices is not composed exclusively of safe options.

A major point to be considered about social and educational strategies is that they are not simple to implement. They require forethought, planning, and extensive follow-through. They can be costly, both in terms of dollars and in terms of time. Often, they conflict with other pressing needs. For example, most K-12 curricula are already overloaded, and information and media literacy curricula must compete for time in the schedule with physical education, sex education, consumer literacy, and a variety of other pressures on the curriculum. Pediatricians, who can speak with youth about safety and puberty, and must complete health forms to be submitted to schools, have limited time with each of their young patients. Parental efforts must compete with making sure that children clean their rooms, do their homework, get to the soccer or basketball game on time, avoid unhealthy use of drugs and alcohol, and so on.

On the other hand, if the problem of exposure to inappropriate materials and experiences is as severe and consequential as many parents believe it to be, there is no particular evidence indicating that the cost of such programs is exorbitant. Moreover, the benefits that accrue from effective social and educational strategies go far beyond protecting children and youth from inappropriate sexually explicit material. They have relevance to many situations that individuals are likely to encounter, both online and offline, and will help them to navigate their Internet experiences with confidence and wisdom.

10.4 PARENTAL INVOLVEMENT AND SUPERVISION

There is a broad consensus that the best approach to protecting young people on the Internet from inappropriate material and online predators

---

full driving privileges), and in some cases more finely (e.g., teens with solo driving privileges only during the day). While the notion of government licensing for using the Internet is not particularly appealing or sensible, the idea of age-based expectations for appropriate Internet use makes developmental sense. Parents may wish to consider what skills and knowledge related to the Internet they want their children to have before they give them different degrees of unsupervised Internet access.

is the attentive presence of a responsible parent, teacher, librarian, or mentor who is available to provide help and guidance, and to intervene when necessary. While this image does characterize some family situations, parents in most families are pressed for time. Parents in many families today face long workdays, long commutes, and considerable work-related overnight travel. Single-parent households are common, as are families in which both parents work full time. These facts suggest that continual in-person supervision of a child's Internet usage by a parent is not likely to be achieved by many families.

Notwithstanding limits on the time that parents have available, parents can still take actions in the home setting that can help their children to develop a sense of safe Internet use. No one action is definitive, and nothing effective can be done just once, but no sensible parent has ever imagined that the task of parenting and of teaching one's children the skills in navigating through any aspect of life would be easy.

• *Parents can develop a basic understanding of what is on the Internet and what their children can do with it.* The Internet world that most adults inhabit is far more work-centered than the one inhabited by most children, which focuses on social interaction, entertainment, and spontaneous play to a far greater degree. (This suggestion is not much different from the advice given in a non-Internet context that parents should be aware of the movies and TV shows and music that engage a child's attention.)

Such understanding is useful from two perspectives. Parents who do not know what their children can do and see on the Internet may be overly complacent about the dangers to their children. Also, parents who do not know the routes through which their children can be exposed to such inappropriate material and dangerous experiences may be excessively fearful because they lack perspective on the ease or frequency with which such exposures might occur. It is noteworthy that a Pew Internet and American Life survey found that parents who do not use the Internet themselves generally tend to be more concerned for their children's Internet safety than parents with more online experience.[5]

Parents also learn from more experienced parents, child-care workers, and pediatricians, about age-appropriate "harm prevention" steps to take in homes: remove lead paint; install child-resistant clips on drawers where chemicals, knives, or guns are kept; install child-resistant covers for electric outlets; teach children never to use the stove without an adult

---

[5]Pew Internet Project. 2001. *Teenage Life Online: The Rise of the Instant-message Generation and the Internet's Impact on Friendships and Family Relationships.* Pew Internet and American Life Project, Washington, D.C. Available online at <http://www.pewinternet.org/reports/reports.asp?Report=36&Section=ReportLevel2&Field=Level2ID&ID=217>.

present; obtain and use bicycle helmets; and so on. Inquiries to these more experienced and knowledgeable individuals could result in analogous recommendations to new parents regarding Internet safety.

• *Computers can be located in such a way that private, solitary viewing by children is not possible.* For example, computers located in private bedrooms cannot be supervised as easily as computers in public spaces (e.g., in family rooms or dens). When the potential exists for a responsible adult to happen across a screen displaying possibly inappropriate material while the child is there, the child is likely to be motivated to refrain from deliberate misbehavior. Moreover, if the child encounters something upsetting or inappropriate by mistake, it is more likely that he or she can obtain help more quickly and spontaneously. Also, if a computer is located in a public space, the adult supervisor can more easily wander over to inquire about what the child is doing.

• *Parents and their children can discuss household rules and expectations for a child's use of the Internet.* Issues to discuss may include:[6]

—When and under what circumstances Internet use is permissible,

—The amount of time that a child may spend using the Internet,

—The types of activities and Web sites that are acceptable and unacceptable,

—What information may be given out or disclosed when using the Internet, and

—What should be done if the child becomes uncomfortable in using the Internet.

It may also be helpful for parents and children to discuss expectations for the use of the Internet at school. Depending on a given family's values, a school's acceptable use policy may allow certain Web sites or activities to which a parent might object.

• *Parents can explicitly provide instruction and guidance to their children about inappropriate activities and explain why their viewing of sexually explicit materials may be inappropriate.* Parents at one committee site visit went so far as to argue that the best way to educate children about inappropriate sites was to show them some inappropriate sites and engage in a conversation with them about why they were inappropriate. For these parents (and for a number of those who testified to the committee as well), the problem posed by sexually explicit material was not inherent in the sexual explicitness of the material itself, but rather the lack of a responsibly presented explanatory context. In other words, the concern was not so

---

[6]This list is derived from Nancy Willard, 2001, "Supporting the Safe and Responsible Use of the Internet by Students: A Children's Internet Protection Act Planning Guide," Center for Advanced Technology in Education, College of Education, University of Oregon, available online at <http://netizen.uoregon.edu/documents/cipa.html>.

much that exposure to the material itself would be harmful, as the fact that without good explanations for why the material was inappropriate, children would get the wrong messages from it.

• *Parents can set limits for how much time a child may spend online.* When time is constrained, people are more likely to concentrate on the activities that they value most highly. To the extent that children seek out inappropriate material out of idle curiosity, these are the activities that are most likely to be curtailed in the presence of time limits.

• *Parents can become more aware of tools and programs for Internet safety already available to them.* For example, parents may not know about the resources of GetNetWise (Box 10.1) or about the suggestions on the Children's Partnership Web site on strategies they can use at home to guide their children's Internet use (Box 10.2). Parents may also not know about the educational programs offered by their local libraries or by non-profit groups in their area and as such are missing other opportunities to receive training and assistance in this effort (Box 10.3 provides an example).

• *Parents can learn to deal with the fact that their children may be more adept technologically than they are.* It is accepted wisdom that many children—especially adolescents—know more about technology than do their

---

Box 10.1
GetNetWise

GetNetWise is an industry-sponsored organization whose purpose is to create a safe, rewarding, and enjoyable experience for children online. GetNetWise is a user-friendly, family empowering, online resource that contains aggregated and syndicated content, organized into four themes:

• Internet Safety Guide—Resources based on age-level, risk area, and technology;
• Tools for Families—A comprehensive guide to consumer products that allow families themselves to monitor Internet use, filter unwanted content, or control computer use;
• How to Report Online Trouble—Information on recognizing and resolving Internet crime with links to law enforcement offices and children's advocacy groups;
• Guide to Kids Content—Pointers and information about online content that is educational and helpful for kids.

GetNetWise is intended to be a resource for those seeking to be wise online parents, and seeks to provide help to anyone involved in raising children—parents, grandparents, educators, caregivers—everyone concerned with the routine responsibilities of raising children in the digital age.

SOURCE: For more information, see <http://www.getnetwise.org>.

Box 10.2
Age-Based Tips for Guiding Children's Home
Internet Use from the Children's Partnership

Ages 2 to 3 : Computers need not play much of a role in the youngest child's life. However, it doesn't hurt for very young children to see family members using computers and enjoying themselves online. Tips:

- Put your child in your lap as you "play" on the computer.
- Look for books and children's video programs like Sesame Street that include images of children and family members using a computer.

Ages 4 to 7 : While serious computer use isn't a priority for these youngsters, children at this age can begin to make greater use of computer games and educational products. Tips:

- Spend as much time as you can with your child while he or she uses the computer.
- Show lots of tangible results and achievements. For example, print work your child has done on the computer.
- Share an e-mail address with your child, so you can oversee his or her mail and discuss correspondence.

Ages 8 to 11 : At this age, children can begin to directly experience and appreciate more fully the potential of online experiences. For instance, children can begin to use online encyclopedias, download pictures for school reports, or have e-mail pen pals. Tips:

- Set very clear rules for online use and clear consequences if they are broken.
- Teach children to let you know if they encounter anything scary or unusual online.
- Discuss some of the unique aspects of behavior in cyberspace—like anonymity and what it means for your child and for others.

Ages 12 to 14 : At this age, young people can use the more sophisticated research resources of the information superhighway, accessing everything from the Library of Congress's collection to magazines and newspapers to archives from around the world. Tips:

- Since children of this age are more likely to explore on their own, set up clear parental rules, limits, and periodic check-ins.
- Set clear rules about which chat rooms are acceptable for your teenager, and how much time can be spent there.
- Be sure your children understand the actions that can be taken if people harass them online or do anything inappropriate.
- Pay particular attention to games that your teenager might download or copy as some of these games are extremely violent.

(continues)

Box 10.2 (continued)

Ages 15 to 18   : The Internet provides a rich resource for older teens, including information about job opportunities, internships, and colleges; applications to create multimedia reports; and specialized help with foreign languages and other school subjects. Tips:

• Ask your teenager for help researching topics of interest to the family (follow-up on a family discussion, planning a family vacation, and so on).

• Talk to your teenager about new things online and encourage discussion of new experiences.

• Make sure your teenager knows the legal implications of online behavior.

• Watch time limits to make sure your teenager is still pursuing a well-rounded set of activities.

• If your teenager is especially interested in computers, encourage him or her to help younger children with their online explorations (e.g., at the local Boys or Girls Club).

SOURCE: Wendy Lazarus and Laurie Lipper. 1998. *The Parent's Guide to the Information Super-highway*, The Children's Partnership. May. A complete copy of the guide is available at <www.childrenspartnership.org>.

Box 10.3
An Illustrative Internet Safety Program for Parents

The Internet and Your Child is a comprehensive Internet safety and education program for adults in many states, including Alaska, California, Colorado, Connecticut, Georgia, Idaho, Indiana, Kansas, New Jersey, North Dakota, Oregon, Texas, and Washington. Taught by volunteer law enforcement officers and computer professionals, the program offers 7 hours of instruction covering:

• Computer hardware and software basics,
• Windows basics,
• Getting connected to the Internet,
• Internet addressing,
• Newsgroups,
• E-mail,
• Hacking,
• Protecting your privacy,
• Internet fraud,
• Sex crimes,
• Internet chats,
• Filtering and blocking unwanted sites with software, and
• Searching the Internet for information on you or your child.

SOURCE: See <http://www.theinternetandyourchild.org/>.

parents, and this often makes parents feel inadequate or incapable of pro-viding guidance or setting boundaries about their children's Internet activi-ties. Yet, while many children have superior technical skills, parents are still role models capable of exerting strong influence over the social, moral, and ethical development of their children. Furthermore, a noteworthy body of research indicates that parental involvement in their children's media activities is beneficial for young people's development.[7] To cope with a lack of technical knowledge, parents can learn about the technology, as described above. They can also learn about the technology from their children, and learn to listen non-judgmentally so that the child will feel freer to explore situations in which parental input may be helpful.

• *Parents can be aware that their children are often more confident in their abilities to handle themselves online than their actual abilities warrant.* For example, a study by the Girl Scout Research Institute found that girls sometimes "rely too much on their own judgment in making decisions about how to behave online. When asked how they know what is safe or unsafe behavior on the Internet, 84 percent of online respondents cited their own common sense. By contrast, 51 percent of these girls cited learn-ing from parents, 46 percent said television and the media, 29 percent said teachers, 29 percent said friends, and 4 percent said, 'Nothing is that bad online because it is not really real.'"[8] In one committee site visit, a girl of about 15 said that she would never meet anyone face-to-face if she felt uncomfortable about him (or her). She also said she knew that people lied all the time online. But 30 seconds later she said that she could tell when people were lying and that she trusted her instincts.

• *Parents can set good examples for responsible Internet use.* For ex-ample, a parent who views sexually explicit imagery online may well leave traces of such viewing available for his or her child to find later. This may be quite all right if the parent would not object to his or her child seeing such material. But a parent who would object would not be wise to undertake activities that would raise questions in his or her child's mind. Also, a parent who demonstrates a disregard for the privacy of his or her children may find that they are less than careful with respect to marketers and survey takers about sensitive family information such as income or buying practices. Put another way, if a parent tracks a child's online behavior and the child has no privacy, then the child may not respect

---

[7]National Research Council and Institute of Medicine. 2001. *Nontechnical Strategies to Reduce Children's Exposure to Inappropriate Material on the Internet: Summary of a Workshop.* Board on Children, Youth, and Families and Computer Science and Telecommunications Board, Joah G. Iannotta, ed., National Academy Press, Washington, D.C.

[8]Whitney Roban. 2002. *The Net Effect: Girls and New Media.* Girl Scout Research Institute, New York. Available online at <http://www.girlscouts.org/about/PDFs/NetEffects.pdf>.

family privacy if and when opportunities arise to profit from other family members' private information.

A second example arises with the idea of parental review of the sites visited by youngsters on the Internet. If children know this is happening, will they welcome it as a necessary "governor" of their choices, or resent it as a violation of their privacy and an indication that they are not trusted? At younger ages, they are likely to not object, but as children get older, they often develop a sense of personal space about which they are very protective.

The difficulties of engaging in effective parental communications with children are significant—and parents who think they are talking effectively with their children about Internet use may not in fact be doing so. For example, a survey taken by the Kaiser Family Foundation and National Public Radio in 2001 noted that parents were more likely than their children to think that they have rules in place about what their children can do on the computer—that is, about three-fourths of all parents interviewed said that they have such rules, but only half of all children interviewed agreed.[9] Further, only 38 percent of older children (aged 14 to 17) said that their parents know "a lot" about the things they do on the Internet and the Web sites they visit.

The discussion above regarding things that parents can do to promote and facilitate the safety of their children on the Internet is presented only in outline form, and the committee does not believe that, by themselves, these guidelines and tips provide an actionable agenda. To be a real guide for concrete action, much more in the way of specifics is needed.

However, to the committee's knowledge, there is no comprehensive curriculum for parental education about the Internet. Many of today's workshops emphasize what parents must be afraid of, but they omit affirmative steps that parents can take. As one example, the list above suggests that parents talk to their children about what counts as inappropriate material. But such conversations can be very awkward for parents. What are some sample dialogs or approaches that a parent might use to raise the subject? Providing such dialogs is beyond the scope of this report, but resources must be made available to help parents address such issues.

Box 10.4 provides some speculations on ideas for promoting parental education (and Internet safety education, which is discussed in Section 10.8.1).

---

[9]See <http://www.npr.org/programs/specials/poll/technology/>.

Box 10.4
Speculations on Ideas for Promoting Parental
Education and Internet Safety Education

• Television and other mass-market entertainment programming that provides role models for parents interacting with their children in ways that enhance Internet safety

• Interviews on TV and radio talk shows during which concrete tips on Internet safety can be provided to parents

• Short courses on Internet safety offered by schools, libraries, and community centers

• Links to training in computer ethics and codes of responsible behavior

• Discounts for Internet service provider subscriptions for parents who complete a program of online training in Internet safety

• Awards to youth of various ages for achieving age-appropriate levels of Internet proficiency, to include appropriate safety knowledge and education. Such a program might be modeled on the physical fitness awards given to youth on behalf of the President's Council on Physical Fitness and Sports[1]

• Graduated privileges for Internet use at school as a function of the safety instruction a student has completed

• Government or foundation support for developing Internet safety curricula for parents and youth

---

[1]The program is known as the President's Challenge. More information can be found online at <http://www.fitness.gov/challenge/challenge.html>.

10.5 PEER ASSISTANCE

For certain topic areas, many and perhaps most youth learn as much from peers or near-peers (e.g., siblings) as they do from parents, teachers, and other adult figures. Indeed, a Department of Justice report finds that

[F]or many children, having an older youth to talk to and spend time with—someone who provides encouragement and friendship—can mean the difference between dropping out of school and graduating, or between getting involved with drugs and developing the strength and self-confidence to resist such pressures. Youth involved in mentoring programs, in fact, have been shown to be less likely to experiment with drugs, less likely to be physically aggressive, and less likely to skip school than those not involved in such programs. Peer mentors provide the important extra support that many younger people need to make it through a difficult period in their lives—when peer pressure and the desire to fit in are strong influences. . . . Peer mentoring programs match older youth with young students in one-on-one relationships to provide guidance for the children. Through this special relationship, peer mentors provide advice and support and serve as role models for younger people who need help.[10]

Of course, mentoring is also beneficial for the older youth in that they are put in a position of responsibility and often rise wonderfully to the task. Older youth may be more likely to stay out of trouble and make even better decisions because they know that they have someone watching and potentially imitating their behavior.

Given research supporting the notion that peer or near-peer mentoring of youth may be quite helpful to some young people in avoiding crime and drugs and staying in school, it is not unreasonable to suppose that such relationships may be helpful in promoting appropriate use of the Internet. For example, a program of the Chicago Public Libraries trains college student volunteers to help users with computer technology in the library. They receive a week of training, and then they wander the floors of the library to help young users on the Internet. For example, they provide surfing suggestions that steer users to educational sites. These young users learn about the Internet but also have the opportunity to interact with somewhat older college students who serve as role models. Not incidentally, these volunteers also provide monitoring of usage that helps to keep children away from inappropriate or non-enriching Internet material.

Older siblings can be a particularly rich source of peer assistance. For example, in a number of site visits, older adolescents often expressed concern about the Internet experiences of their younger siblings, and tried to help them stay out of trouble on the Internet by providing advice and guiding them to appropriate sites.

Note also that summer programs (e.g., camps) could also provide Internet safety instruction in an environment where youth are relaxed. Camp counselors are often older youth and may be able to provide semi-structured mentoring and guidance.

Peer assistance works best when there is a broad consensus among the peers that certain behavior is inappropriate or unsafe. Thus, peer assistance is likely to be most effective in steering children away from, say, would-be child molesters or racist or hate sites. However, if the peer assisters themselves do not believe that exposure to adult-oriented, sexually explicit material is a big deal (as may be the case for some individuals), they are less likely to be as vigilant or zealous in their efforts to provide assistance.

---

[10]See Office of Juvenile Justice and Delinquency Prevention, 1999, *Mentoring—A Proven Delinquency Prevention Strategy*, U.S. Department of Justice, Washington, D.C., available online at <http://www.ncjrs.org/html/youthbulletin/9907-4/mentor-*.html> (where "*" ranges from 1 through 8).

10.6 ACCEPTABLE USE POLICIES

An acceptable use policy (AUP) is a set of guidelines and expectations about how individuals will conduct themselves online.[11] AUPs are increasingly common in schools, and they are applicable to home and library use as well (especially when Internet access is conditioned on accepting terms that accompany a library card). AUPs vary, but they almost always contain provisions against viewing sexually explicit Web sites, and perhaps other kinds of material (e.g., instructions for bomb making, hate sites). AUPs can also address outgoing material, such as child-posted e-mail and Web sites—such provisions are generally directed toward the possibility that one child might create and disseminate sexually explicit pictures as well as harass, defame, and stalk other children. Furthermore, AUPs must be acknowledged explicitly by those affected. An example of one school's AUP is provided in Box 10.5.

The theory of the AUP is that by making young people responsible for the content they create and the behavior that they demonstrate, they will learn to be responsible for making good choices about the "paths" they choose in cyberspace, thereby learning skills that are relevant and helpful in any venue of Internet usage. Of course, for an AUP to be effective, deliberate violations cannot go without response or sanction (e.g., loss of Internet privileges, call to parents, detention if violations occur in a school context, grounding if in a home context). Accidental violations should be seen as an opportunity to educate the user about how to avoid such content in the future, how to remove it from the screen, and if necessary how to report it to an Internet service provider.

Furthermore, AUPs must be read, and young people must take them seriously. In a number of site visits, students appeared relatively ignorant of what their school's AUP stated. A number of teachers noted that they believed AUPs were not generally read, because they were simply one of a large number of forms that students had to bring back signed. (This is consistent with recent research suggesting that students often do not recall the content of the AUPs they signed earlier in a school year, and with the finding that some who signed them do not even remember having done so).[12] Thus, some explicit attention in the school, library, or family to the AUP is warranted to underscore its importance.

---

[11]The term "AUP" is sometimes applied by Internet service providers to their rules of use; more generally, such rules are known as terms of service. Terms of service for ISPs are not intended to govern children's use of the Internet, but rather are put into place to protect the ISP from legal liability and conduct (such as sending spam) that reduces network efficiency.

[12]Janet W. Schofield and Ann L. Davidson. 2002. *Bringing the Internet to School: Lessons from an Urban District.* Jossey-Bass, New York, pp. 319-320.

Box 10.5
Acceptable Use Policy of Eau Claire,
Wisconsin, Area School District

The Eau Claire Area School District offers a good example of policies that establish a set of expectations about the manner in which students and staff will use school networks and technologies. This acceptable use policy sets rules about a number of topics and includes guidelines to facilitate safety online, as well as respect for copyrighted material—relevant to preventing students from using the Internet's resources to plagiarize material. It forbids use of the Internet for activities that are not in support of the educational objectives of the school district. What follows is the Eau Claire Area School District's acceptable use policy, the full text of which can be found online at <www.ecasd.k12.wi.us/departments/technology/network/inetpol.html>.

Use of the Internet and Other Computer Networks

The Internet is an electronic network connecting thousands of computer networks and millions of individual subscribers all over the world. Access to the Internet will allow students to explore the rich resources of thousands of university libraries, governmental databases and other online sources while exchanging electronic mail with Internet users throughout the world. Instructional and library materials are routinely evaluated by school district personnel prior to purchase in order to ascertain that such materials are consistent with district goals and guidelines and that they support and enrich the curriculum. However, use of the Internet, because it may lead to any publicly available fileserver in the world, may open classrooms to electronic information resources which have not been screened by educators for use by students. Some items accessible via the Internet may contain material which is inaccurate, defamatory or offensive. Access to the Internet and other computer networks requires that school officials develop guidelines for use. Such guidelines should address the teacher's responsibility for training and guidance, the student's responsibility for appropriate use, and the principal's responsibility for supervising the use.

Internet and Other Computer Networks—Use Guidelines

The following guidelines define "appropriate use" of the Internet.

1. All use of school resources to access the Internet must be in support of and consistent with the educational objectives of the Eau Claire Area School District.

As a rule, AUPs are most effective when they are developed in conjunction with parents, community members, teachers, school library media experts, school administrators, and students. AUPs developed jointly with the school and community are more likely to incorporate the particular sensibilities of parents and can be designed to address specific concerns, resulting in higher degrees of buy-in, acceptance, and legiti-

2. Transmitting any material in violation of any U.S. or state regulation or school board policy is prohibited. This includes, but is not limited to, copyrighted material and material that is threatening or obscene.

3. Hate mail, harassment, discriminatory remarks and other antisocial behaviors are unacceptable in Internet and other network communication.

4. All information accessible via the Internet should be assumed to be private property and subject to copyright protection. Internet sources should be credited appropriately, as with the use of any copyrighted material. Example: The Columbia Guide to Online Style http://www.columbia.edu/cu/cup/cgos/idx_basic.html

5. Users have a responsibility to respect the privacy and property of other users. Users should not intentionally seek information about, obtain copies of, or modify, files, data or passwords of other users.

6. For their own safety, users should not reveal any personal information, such as addresses, phone numbers, or photographs.

7. Employing the Internet for commercial purposes is prohibited.

8. Users should not expect that files stored on district servers will always be private. School and network administrators may review files and communications to maintain system integrity and to ensure that the network is being used responsibly.

Teachers will inform students of what is considered appropriate use of the Internet, describing student privileges, rights and responsibilities. As much as possible, teachers will guide students toward materials which have been reviewed and evaluated prior to use. The use of home pages, bookmarks, lists of Web sites, and cataloging Web sites in the library system will help match Internet resources to the curriculum.

Because computer use is essentially an individual experience, however, primary responsibility for appropriate use of the Internet resides with the student. A user agreement form will be signed by the student and parent prior to their use. Failure to follow appropriate practices may result in disciplinary action including loss of the individual's access to the Internet.

Principals will supervise the use of the Internet and other computer networks in their schools. Procedures will be put in place to ensure that students receive appropriate instruction and supervision in the use of the Internet and other computer networks.

NOTE: The committee makes no representation that this acceptable use policy does or does not comply with the requirements of the Children's Internet Protection Act that schools and libraries receiving E-rate funding must adopt and implement an Internet safety policy.

macy. For example, one community may be more concerned about the exposure of young people to sexually explicit material while another might worry more about the consequences of young people spending time in chat rooms. The development of an AUP through extensive community involvement—including those affected—can sometimes be painful, but the process offers the community a chance to consider the balance it wants to try to strike between entirely unregulated Internet access and more-restricted use. Such discourse can prevent future tensions among community members (e.g., students, teachers, parents, library patrons) by allowing difficult and potentially contentious issues to be resolved. Note also that the contents of an AUP are likely to need updating as the concerns of the community evolve. Thus, some mechanism for periodic review is an essential aspect of AUP formulation.

In addition, how an AUP is presented to the community can affect its success. If it is presented in the absence of explanation or context, neither students nor parents are likely to understand its rationale for being. Thus, context-setting activities—such as parents being given some instruction on using the Internet (e.g., Section 10.4)—might well accompany the introduction of an AUP to the community.

While increasingly common, AUPs do raise a number of issues.

• To what extent, if at all, should an AUP for a young person set the expectations for adult behavior and use? An argument for similarity is that an AUP gains in legitimacy (with all of the desirable consequences for behavioral adherence) when it is seen to be uniformly applied. An argument for difference is that the legitimate needs of adult supervisors (parents, librarians, teachers, and so on) are different in some ways from those of children—while harassment may never be appropriate for anyone to engage in, adults may need access to a different set of information on Web sites than do children.

• AUPs that do not differentiate between the needs of younger and older children are likely to be overconstraining or underconstraining to one group or another. For example, older adolescents may need access to a different set of information on Web sites than primary school children do. An AUP that imposes on these older children restrictions that are designed for younger children does not provide a realistic code of behavior for these older children.

• An AUP states behavioral goals. But after policy statements have been distributed and signatures on AUP forms gathered, a key question remains—to what extent are students and library patrons in fact complying with a given AUP? Some estimate of compliance can be derived from data about violations, a point that suggests that such data must be kept and tabulated if a broad understanding of an AUP's effectiveness is to be achieved. But walk-by monitoring may be of limited effectiveness simply because the personnel are not available in sufficient numbers to check usage regularly, and children themselves may not be entirely forthcoming if they violate the policy deliberately. (In this regard, the problem raised by AUPs is similar to those raised by any honor code.) However, technical tools for monitoring Web usage in the aggregate (without individual tracking of users) can provide important information on conformance to an AUP. This point is discussed further in Chapter 12.

• Many users of AUPs are drawn to them because they provide a broad "catch-all" for behavior that may be objectionable but not explicitly listed as inappropriate. For example, the prohibitions on viewing sexually explicit adult Web sites complement the restrictions imposed by filters that block many but not all such sites. Thus, a student who takes advantage of underblocking in a filter to reach a sexually explicit adult Web site is still subject to sanctions for violating the AUP. Of course, the logical complement to this argument is that a student who gets into trouble for violating an AUP may well argue, "If it was against policy, why wasn't it filtered?" A student who does not understand the limitations of technology may therefore feel that he or she has been treated unjustly for violating an AUP.

• More generally, AUPs must clearly specify what material or behavior counts as inappropriate if they are to be useful as guides to behavior. Actions taken to penalize inappropriate behavior or access to inappropriate materials may well be subject to legal challenge in the absence of clear specifications.

• To what extent, if any, does the existence of an AUP shield a school or library from liability? To the committee's knowledge, there is not a body of case law that establishes the existence and use of AUPs as part of a defense against liability for improper use of school or library computer facilities. However, in the case law of discrimination and harassment, the courts have established[13] that the existence of internal policies or practices is an important element of an affirmative defense against such allegations,[14] and the logic of this case law might carry over to the use of AUPs.

• AUPs define responsibilities that users have. A complementary issue is the nature and scope of rights that users have. In particular, a question arises regarding the extent to which an individual has rights to obtain information that go beyond what a parent might be willing to grant. What kinds of information, if any, would be in this category? Many librarians and others acting in a supervisory but non-parental role would argue that it is important for a children (especially older adolescents) to have access to some such information. Some examples offered by these individuals include information about other races and cultures,

---

[13]*Faragher v. City of Boca Raton*, 524 U.S. 775 (1998).

[14]Lauren B. Edelman, Christopher Uggen, and Howard S. Erlanger. 1999. "The Endogeneity of Legal Regulation: Grievance Procedures as Rational Myth," *American Journal of Sociology* 105(2): 406-454.

other religions, evolution, contraception, homosexuality, guns, and prevention of sexually transmitted diseases.[15]

The Children's Internet Protection Act (discussed in Chapter 4) requires that many schools and libraries develop an "Internet Safety Plan" that addresses "access by minors to inappropriate matter on the Internet and World Wide Web; safety and security of minors when using electronic mail, chat rooms, and other forms of direct electronic communications; unauthorized online access by minors, including 'hacking' and other unlawful activities; unauthorized disclosure, use, and dissemination of personal information regarding minors; and measures designed to restrict minors' access to materials harmful to minors."[16] Note the strong similarity between the mandated Internet Safety Plan and what is covered in most AUPs.

10.7 AFTER-THE-FACT STRATEGIES

It is highly likely that children will, from time to time, encounter inappropriate sexually explicit material. Thus, it is reasonable to consider what a child might do after such exposure in order to minimize whatever deleterious effects, if any, might occur.

Perhaps the most important point for adults to keep in mind is that many children may be better able to handle exposure to inappropriate material than adults give them credit for. As noted in Chapter 5, most of the older teenagers with whom the committee spoke reported that today much of the sexually explicit material they encountered online was not a big deal to them. Even younger teenagers—in particular the teen Cyberangels[17] who testified to the committee—seem to have been exposed to such material without apparent harm.

Nevertheless, parents and other adults do have a responsibility to help children cope with inadvertent exposure to inappropriate Internet material or experiences. One obvious strategy is for a child so exposed, if

---

[15]In practice, it would be quite difficult for a parent to make an individual decision about every accessible Web page of information or every book in a library to which a child has access. But the notion does underlie an important thought question: assuming that this array of decisions could be encoded on a smart library card, so that the child could *never* have access to information to which a parent objected, how would parents, librarians, and teachers wish to proceed?

[16]P.L. 106-554, § 1(a)(4), 114 Stat. 2763 (2001). A good summary of the provisions of the CIPA can be found online at <http://www.cybertelecom.org/cda/cipatext.htm#1712>.

[17]These teenagers were members of Teenangels, a group of specially trained 13- to 17-year-old volunteers for the Cyberangels online safety organization (see <http://www.cyberangels.com>).

he or she is upset, to seek assistance from an adult—parent, teacher, and so on. However, for the child to be willing to seek assistance, the adult must not penalize him or her for doing so. Recall that many teens reported to the committee that they had been upset in their first accidental encounters with sexually explicit material on the Internet not because of the scenes depicted, but because of their concerns about parental (over-) reactions. Schools, too, have been known to overreact, and it should be noted that children talk to parents and other adults more freely if conversation can occur in an open and accepting rather than in a punitive or judgmental environment. Thus, such encounters should be regarded as teachable moments in which the child can learn from the adults around him or her.

A second strategy is to seek help independently, though knowing how to obtain help is sometimes difficult. For example, some ISPs provide methods for reporting of spam e-mail, whether they involve inappropriate sexually explicit material or other kinds of material, harassing instant messages (IMs), e-mail, or offensive chat room dialog. However, one would be well advised to understand the mechanics of how to get help before one encounters a problem.

A third empowering strategy is to provide the child with instruction on how to report the offensive material to an appropriate party. For example, if offensive material is passed by a filter, it might reduce the child's feeling of being victimized if he or she could report it to the parties determining the filtering policy. In the context of schools, a student who is inadvertently exposed must have a clear and safe path for reporting such an incident. By doing so, he or she can avoid allegations of intentional access as well as help the school better understand how such accidental access occurred and how it might be better prevented in the future.

Another dimension of after-the-fact strategies involves the possibility that a young person is being "groomed" by a predator. Parents should be aware that such engagements can happen in spite of their admonitions to their children to avoid strangers. Thus, it is particularly important to maintain open channels of communication in which a child can share experiences and feelings about being online. Note also that a young person may feel guilty about turning on an online friend.[18] Also, in some cases, a teenager may well tell a peer about intentions to meet with someone that he or she has met online. Thus, peers and older teens can often play a role in helping their friends and siblings—by trying to talk them out of going to a meeting or alerting an adult.

---

[18]In this context, the term "turning on Joe" means reporting to responsible authority that Joe wants to meet, even if Joe has told the child not to tell anyone.

Note that after-the-fact strategies are consistent with the discussion in Section 12.4 about instant help.

10.8 EDUCATION

10.8.1 Internet Safety Education

In the physical world, safety education for children involves things such as teaching children how to cross the street safely, how to deal with strangers approaching them, and how to react when there is a fire in the house. Such strategies are taught to children so that they will be better able to avoid situations in which they might be harmed, and to deal with these situations better if they should find themselves in one.

Safety education for children on the Internet has similar goals. While many students to whom the committee spoke said that they learned to be safe on the Internet through experience, explicit Internet safety education (ISE) provides children with dos and don'ts that decrease the likelihood that they will have an unsafe experience online. It also provides strategies for children who do happen to encounter unsafe situations.[19] ISE is an application and extension of the critical thinking and judgment skills that parents and teachers and communities hope to instill in children to cope with other dangers in life. Further, it requires awareness of the dangers so that they will not be surprised when they encounter them. Three examples of ISE include the following:

• For young people who might encounter a stranger online, it is helpful for them to know about how sexual predators and hate group recruiters typically operate. In particular, they obtain as much personal information as possible and then, armed with such information, provide compliments, positive statements, and other flattery in order to build an emotional bond with their target. An example might be that if the young person says that he does not have many friends, the stranger might say "that is hard to believe," or "your peers are really missing out, but you are probably too mature for them," and so on. Young people, often taught to be polite to others, should understand explicitly how such a "seduction" process works, what to expect, how to recognize it, and how to deal with the situation, and may need to be taught how to be assertive online in ending contact with another user or declining and/or blocking instant messages from users who harass them.

---

[19]For purposes of this discussion, "unsafe" is construed broadly. That is, an unsafe Internet experience is defined here as one that makes the child feel uncomfortable, or one that an adult would feel was inappropriate and potentially harmful for the child.

- Recognizing an impending access to inappropriate material—especially material of an adult nature—is a helpful skill as well. For example, while most experienced Web surfers know how to use the few lines of text accompanying a link that is returned by a search engine, novice surfers do not. For these individuals, identifying some of the keywords that flag sexually explicit adult-oriented material and how they are displayed in a search engine's "returned links" may be helpful. Similar strategies are likely to be useful when processing unsolicited e-mail that seeks to draw attention to adult-oriented Web sites.
- Knowledge of when it is appropriate to provide personal information online is increasingly important. Imparting such knowledge involves teaching children about what information is private as well as their right and responsibility to protect that kind of private information from others. For example, if one is doing registration online for classes at one's school, it is perfectly appropriate to provide personal information such as name, address, and the like. But for a teenager to provide such information to a stranger in a chat room is far less wise, and children of all ages would be well advised to refrain from giving out such information without explicit parental permission.
- Knowledge of how one might recognize unsolicited commercial e-mail (spam) without opening it would enable children and youth to delete much of it and thereby reduce their potential exposure to inappropriate material.[20] Knowledge of how to behave on the Internet so as to reduce vulnerability to spam would reduce the volume entering their mailboxes.

Note that the introduction of any particular lesson in ISE should be tied to a sense of the child's developmental level. For example, being able to identify impending access to inappropriate material is a helpful skill when a child starts to use the Internet without active and continuous adult parental supervision. But whether this skill is helpful or should be introduced prior to this point is less clear.

---

[20]For example, one can often identify spam on the basis of the subject line and the purported sender of the mail. (An e-mail from hotsexybabe@example.com with the subject line "best porn on the Net" is highly likely to be spam containing links to adult-oriented, sexually explicit material.) Such e-mail can be easily deleted without being read, and an informed user who chooses to read the e-mail is reading sexually explicit material more or less voluntarily. On the other hand, some spam senders anticipate such behavior on the part of the user by forging sender addresses (the mail appears to be from support@example.com and use misleading subject lines (e.g., "about your e-mail program"). Spam from such parties cannot be identified as sexually explicit in nature, and a user who reads such mail will be exposed to its content involuntarily.

Box 10.6
An Example of a Library Offering for Internet Safety Education

The Chicago Public Library's home page for kids and teens is designed to be a safe portal to the Web. In addition to child-appropriate resources such as the Teen Edition, Homework Help, Good Reads and Great Books, and resources for parents, teachers, and youth librarians, it also contains an interactive quiz that poses one question at a time that can be answered with a yes or no button that calls up the correct response as well as feedback about the question. For example, the second question in the quiz is, If I see stuff on the Internet that makes me uncomfortable should I keep it a secret? Depending on your answer you get either a bouncing star graphic if you answer correctly or a "Danger" sign if you answer incorrectly. Both answers are accompanied by the following text: "If you are at home, tell your parents right away if you come across any information that makes you feel uncomfortable. If you are at the public library, tell a librarian and then leave that page right away."

SOURCE: See <www.chipublib.org/008subject/003cya/sign/sign.html>.

In some ways, non-school programs are well suited for ISE (Box 10.6 provides one example). For example, a number of Girl Scout merit badges related to computers and the Internet could easily and naturally accommodate a requirement for Internet safety. After-school or summer programs, in which computer usage is likely to be less structured (and thus have more potential for students getting into Internet trouble), are a good venue in which to learn and exercise ISE skills in a supervised environment. Religious education programs, which already deal with ethics, can include some Internet safety instruction as well.

As discussed in Section 7.1, parents are often far less knowledgeable about technology than are their children. Similarly, teachers—especially those at the high school level—often know less about the Internet than their students.[21] Because many elements of good ISE depend on some technical knowledge (though framed in an appropriate context), effective ISE depends on these adults obtaining the necessary skills themselves. Workshops for parents, pre-service professional education in teachers' colleges and library schools, and in-service programs for professionally active teachers and students all have a role in imparting such skills to adults.

Finally, a number of interactive games and programs seek to teach

---

[21]Schofield and Davidson, 2002, *Bringing the Internet to School: Lessons from an Urban District.*

children Internet safety and responsible Web use. These include Net-Smartz,[22] SurfSwell Island,[23] and MISSING.[24]

See Box 10.4 for some ideas on promoting Internet safety education.

10.8.2 Information and Media Literacy

Information literacy refers to a set of abilities that enables people to "recognize when information is needed and have the ability to locate, evaluate, and use effectively the needed information."[25] An information-literate individual is able to determine the information needed, find the needed information effectively and efficiently, evaluate the information received, and assess its sources critically; incorporate selected information into his or her knowledge base; use information effectively to accomplish a specific purpose; understand the economic, legal, and social issues surrounding the use of information; and access and use information ethically and legally.[26]

Media literacy, a newer term, expands on information literacy in two primary ways.[27] First, media literacy extends to information presented in all forms of media, not just print. Information literacy was never specifically restricted to print, but in practice it is often understood in that primary context. Second, and more importantly, media literacy includes the ability to produce and communicate information for the benefit of others. Also, some analysts believe that media education is focused on information conveyed by and through the mass media, such as newspapers, tele-

---

[22]See <http://www.netsmartz.org>. NetSmartz was developed by the NCMEC.

[23] See <http://disney.go.com/family/surfswell2001/index.html>. SurfSwell Island was developed by the Disney Corporation.

[24]See <http://www.livewwwires.com/index2.htm>. MISSING was developed by Live-WWWires, a Canadian organization that seeks to promote Internet safety among youth.

[25]American Library Association. 1989. Presidential Committee on Information Literacy. Final Report. American Library Association, Chicago. Available online at <http://www.ala.org/acrl/nili/ilit1st.html>.

[26]This set of abilities is taken with a few modifications from <http://www.ala.org/acrl/ilintro.html#ildef>.

[27]More information on media literacy can be found from the following sources, from which parts of the discussion in this paragraph are derived:
- <http://www.ci.appstate.edu/programs/edmedia/medialit/article.html#What is Media Literacy>.
  - <http://interact.uoregon.edu/MediaLit/FA/MLArticleFolder/defharvard.html>.
  - <http://interact.uoregon.edu/MediaLit/FA/MLArticleFolder/defresponse.html>.
  - David Considine. 1994. *Telemedium: The Journal for Media Literacy* 41(2) (Strategies for Media Literacy Inc. and the National Telemedia Council, Madison, Wisc.).

vision programs, and the like.[28] Others add to the definition an understanding of the role that audiences play in creating meaning from the
information found in media content.[29]

The need for information and media literacy was raised by most of
the teachers and librarians with whom the committee spoke. In general,
they saw young people—their students—as being far too uncritical in
their acceptance of information found on the Internet, and they felt that it
is important for students to develop the skills usually associated with
information and media literacy—especially with respect to skills related
to critical evaluation.[30]

In some cases, they regarded the harm that could come to students
from uncritical acceptance of information on the Internet as much more
detrimental than anything they might see in the way of sexually explicit
images—hate and racist sites (e.g., featuring Holocaust denial) and sites
promoting cults were often mentioned. (Of course, all of these teachers
were working in a filtered Internet environment, and this assessment
might have been different if filters had not been present.) Information
and media literacy offers a set of cognitive skills that can protect against
misleading information or a disturbing image by teaching young people
how to recognize underlying messages, criticize them, and develop productive counternarratives.

Skills related to the critical evaluation of information are not explicitly related to reducing the exposure of youth to inappropriate sexually
explicit material on the Internet. After all, if the concern is that young
people are viewing graphic sexual images, one does not need particularly
sharp skills to determine if a picture is truly sexually explicit. By contrast, it is often necessary to pay close attention to the content of other
kinds of Web sites in order to determine the meaning of the information
contained therein. (Thus, it is often easier to make a determination that
something may be sexually explicit, compared to a determination that it is
inappropriate in some other way—sexual images can be identified at a
glance, whereas racist or hate text must be read.)

---

[28]Barry Duncan et al. 1989. *Media Literacy Resource Guide*. Ontario Ministry of Education,
Toronto, Ontario, Canada.

[29]Rick Shepherd. 1993. "Why Teach Media Literacy," *Teach Magazine*, Oct./Nov. (Quad-
rant Educational Media Services).

[30]Whether these teachers and librarians actually spent the time in class to teach information and media literacy in anything but the most cursory fashion is a different matter.
Indeed, many teachers ignore such matters because they are not seen as part of the discipline they are teaching. Nevertheless, the comments of these teachers and librarians indicated at least an awareness of the need for information and media literacy.

Though the skills of critical evaluation tend to be more useful in helping youth to deal with other types of material that may be inappropriate, once an exposure to sexually explicit images has occurred, critical evaluation is still relevant. For example, the sexually explicit images found on adult-oriented Web sites generally do not provide "safer sex" messages. A good understanding of the role that sexual imagery plays in modern media could provide occasion for useful reflection. Critical evaluation thus provides skills that youth can use to help deal constructively with exposure to inappropriate material.

Skills related to finding information are perhaps more relevant to the task of reducing exposure to sexually explicit material. For example, performing an effective Web search—that is, one that retrieves relevant information and minimizes the amount of undesired information—requires the selection of the right set of keywords, familiarity with Boolean logic, choosing the right search engine for the topic, and knowing how to navigate through a browser so that it is easy to enter and exit Web sites, databases, and other online resource tools. Such skills can help to reduce the likelihood that a searcher might come across inappropriate material inadvertently. For example, if a search engine returned a link to a Web site that the searcher had learned to recognize would likely contain adult-oriented sexually explicit material rather than information on reproduction or sexually transmitted diseases, he or she could simply refrain from accessing that site.

Programs in media literacy generally focus on understanding media messages in context. That is, the "face" content of a media message is only one aspect of it. A media-literate individual understands how to evaluate the truthfulness and reliability of a media message, and also knows to ask about the motivations and intent of the party or parties responsible for distributing that message. (Some such literacy is provided in consumer education programs and materials, such as those provided by *Consumer Reports*.)

The significance of such literacy in the context of evaluating content found on the World Wide Web is obvious, where a good deal of Web content is not reliable or accurate by any standard. But media literacy also has relevance to an adolescent who may be exposed to inappropriate sexually explicit materials, either deliberately or inadvertently. Media literacy can help a young person ask questions such as:

- Why are these pictures being shown to me?
- Is what I am seeing a true and realistic image of what sex is like?
- Why are other people drawn to these images?
- What important things are not being shown in these images?

- What are the circumstances that led the individuals being depicted into their being photographed?
- Could an adult help me better understand what I'm seeing?

In short, media literacy can help to promote a more detached, more evaluative, and more reflective view of media, messages, and one's own self. By doing so, it may well strengthen impulse control and empathy, and help lead one to question one's own behavior—and is likely to reduce the exposure resulting from impulsive behavior.

Information and media literacy also addresses the responsible placement of information on the Internet, for example on Web sites and in e-mail. Thus, the creation of information must be undertaken in a responsible manner that communicates what the creator intends. Responsibility might, for example, include the notion that the posting of composite photographs (e.g., face of a classmate pasted onto a naked body without permission) constitutes unethical and inappropriate behavior. Repeated e-mails to a party (e.g., one person asking another for a date) can be regarded as harassment if the subject of the e-mails has requested a cessation of such e-mails.

The research base for understanding the effectiveness of information and media literacy training and education is thin, but two experimental studies provide evidence that suggests beneficial effects in the short run. One study provided some information and media literacy instruction to elementary school children viewing violent cartoons.[31] This instruction asked them to think about the feelings of the victim of violence throughout the episode—and those who received such instruction did not experience a desensitizing change in attitude toward violence nor did they find the cartoon to be as funny as those not receiving such instruction. Another study focused on girls in their early teens, instructing them in how to think critically about media messages regarding how women should think about romance, love, and sexuality.[32] They responded by criticizing the media because they felt the media encouraged them to focus too much on romance and trying to attract men. If such studies can be generalized, helping youth to understand how and why sexually explicit adult-ori-

---

[31]A.I. Nathanson and J. Cantor. 2000. "Reducing the Aggression-promoting Effect of Violent Cartoons by Increasing Children's Fictional Involvement with the Victim," *Journal of Broadcasting and Electronic Media* 44: 125-142.

[32]Sarah Keller, "How Do Early Adolescent Girls Use Media to Shape Their Romantic Identities?" unpublished doctoral dissertation, University of North Carolina, Chapel Hill, 2000. Some of the results from this dissertation can be found in National Research Council and Institute of Medicine, 2001, *Nontechnical Strategies to Reduce Children's Exposure to Inappropriate Material on the Internet: Summary of a Workshop.*

ented materials are produced and consumed may be of some assistance in helping to "inoculate" these youth to some of the effects of such materials.

As with much education, information and media literacy is likely pursued best in a one-on-one context. By talking to a student searching for information on a particular topic, adults can teach him or her effective search strategies for such information. Once a number of sources are found, talking to the student about how to evaluate those sources can help to develop critical thinking skills. Of course, one-on-one interaction is also labor-intensive, and a one-on-one format is less feasible in situations in which many students must be served. In such situations, group and in-class instruction can also be helpful.

For application in a mass education environment, a variety of schools have adopted educational standards that address certain information and media literacy skills. For example, the state of Wisconsin has adopted learning standards that call for fourth graders to be able to use Web sites that have been preselected and bookmarked by the teacher, eighth graders to know effective search strategies, and twelfth graders to be able to evaluate Internet content for validity and reliability as well as to assess the search engines for effectiveness and the way in which they return information.[33]

10.8.3 Collateral Issues

Internet safety education and information and media literacy can be regarded as elements of a comprehensive approach to education in which the use of technology is fully integrated with pedagogical goals. Although a full discussion of education that is well integrated with technology is beyond the scope of this report, the following points are worth consideration:

• Internet safety is only one dimension of productive and appropriate use of the Internet. It is also a dimension of appropriate use that young people learn not to use the Internet for socially detrimental and/or illegal purposes. For example, harassment conducted online is no less serious than harassment conducted offline. The use of a computer to penetrate another computer, even if that second computer has weak security, is analogous to walking into someone else's house without permission, even if the door is unlocked. In short, responsibility is also an important dimension of one's Internet use.

---

[33]See <http://www.dpi.state.wi.us/dpi/standards/pdf/infotech.pdf>.

• Professional development for educators using the Internet is important and must go beyond the mere mechanics of how to use a search engine and how to send e-mail. That is, educators must learn how the Internet can support pedagogical objectives as well as how to teach Internet safety.[34] Both pre-service and in-service teacher training is thus called for.

• Ethical and legal behavior on the Internet and in using technology is a part of the technology education standards developed by the International Society for Technology in Education for students, teachers, and administrators.[35] To the extent that technology education becomes an important part of K-12 education, issues related to ethical and legal behavior will have to be addressed.

• To integrate technology into schools, an adequate technology infrastructure is necessary. For a variety of reasons, today's information technology is not well adapted to the needs of K-12 education. Developing a generation of information technology adapted for the special needs of schools is the focus of a National Research Council project in progress as this book goes to press.[36]

10.9 COMPELLING AND SAFE CONTENT

In various site visits, teachers reported to the committee that their most effective strategy for dissuading students from engaging in inappropriate activities on the Internet was to keep students "on task"—focused on activities relevant to the educational task at hand. Often, teachers prepared for a class by compiling a list of helpful Web sites appropriate for that class. Such a list, combined with restrictions on the amount of time students were allowed to use school Internet facilities, resulted in "students not having time to get into trouble," according to these teachers.

A generalization of this strategy would call for the creation of Internet content that is compelling and educational for young people, so compelling that they are less inclined to spend their time searching for inappropriate material or engaging in inappropriate or unsafe activities. Material that is productive, stimulating, and developmentally beneficial could include more Web sites devoted to sexual health and education so that

---

[34]For example, the CyberSmart! program is a professionally developed curriculum for K-8 students and supports teachers in educational efforts to introduce responsible and effective Internet use. For more information see <http://www.cybersmartcurriculum.org>.

[35]See <http://www.iste.org>.

[36]See <http://www7.nationalacademies.org/ILIT/> for information on the NRC project on improving learning with information technology.

curious adolescents could obtain reliable information on sexuality rather than, or at least before, finding sexually explicit material that lacks information or that depicts unprotected sex or other unsafe sexual practices.

An analogy can be drawn to the development of high-quality television programming for children. An example of commercially supported programming in this domain is NickJr, a component of the Nickelodeon network's programming. NickJr is supported by advertising revenues and is popular among its target audience,[37] suggesting that high-quality television programs can be of interest and of educational value to some children, that associated Web sites that support these messages may be equally valuable for their development, and that this kind of programming can be viable in the commercial marketplace. Note also that the NickJr Web site also has quality software, derived from its TV programming, that is oriented toward preschool-aged children.

On the other hand, commercial sources of content depend on a financial base that relies almost exclusively on ratings, which implies that their content must be oriented toward mass markets (for example, their content is more commonly "action-oriented" with more violent material that more easily draws an audience, and cannot economically be tailored to niche markets). Further, because the production and airing of commercial material are often subsidized by getting children to buy products, it is generally less expensive to develop child-oriented commercial material; children also like a flow back and forth between television and online content, giving commercial content a further appeal. Major commercial sources have the resources to experiment with different approaches to their online offerings, an important characteristic in a new environment in which successful formulas for engaging children with healthy Web content are largely unknown. From their physical-world presence, they also have brand recognition (e.g., Disney, Nickelodeon, and Sesame Street) that enables many parents to trust the content they provide.

Because non-commercial sources do not rely on mass markets for financial viability, they can execute more readily on their mandate to educate. For example, the content of non-commercial programming can be tailored more finely to smaller age-appropriate ranges, or to topics and approaches that are more highly specialized. While non-commercial programming does not in general have the mass market appeal of much commercial programming, the availability of non-commercial programming would tap into the needs of a number of smaller markets, potentially meeting demand that is not manifested in a commercial environ-

---

[37]Sandra Calvert et al. 2001. "Children's Online Reports About Educational and Informational Television Programs," *Journal of Applied Developmental Psychology* 22(1): 103-117.

ment. The committee also believes that the presence of non-commercial sources such as PBS changes the environment for commercial providers by creating greater incentives for commercial providers to do more interesting and creative programming and raising the standard of quality. (This change in the environment is at least as important as the quality programming for which it is directly responsible.) Box 10.7 describes some possible non-commercial content developers.

In the Internet arena, Yahooligans is a Yahoo-sponsored "kids area" with sections on sports, news, jokes, games, chat, bulletin board postings, and online special-interest clubs. It also provides resources for education (oriented toward school work), sports, computers, and entertainment, as well as information for parents, teachers, and children for Internet safety. The theory is that young people would choose to go to these sites and portals voluntarily, which in turn would keep them away from adult material.

The approach of creating content that specifically appeals to children has a number of benefits. One major appeal is that the evaluation of educational Web sites is more feasible than trying to evaluate online content as a whole. Because the volume of material to be evaluated is so much smaller, considerable effort (hours rather than seconds) can be expended

---

Box 10.7
Potential Non-Commercial Developers of Content for Children and Youth

• Children's museums and science centers: information and content-oriented Web sites are often part of their outreach services.
• Non-profit educationally related groups such as the Jason Foundation and Global School Network.
• Government agencies: a number of agencies have sites or Web pages that are oriented toward children. Examples include the Federal Resources for Educational Excellence (<http://www.ed.gov/free>) and NASA (<http://www.nasa.gov/kids. html>).
• Universities have a mission to disseminate information to the general public.

Finally, corporate support can be non-commercial in nature as well. For example, MCI/Worldcom supports an effort known as the MarcoPolo project (<http://marcopolo.worldcom.com/>). The materials found on the site are not tied to child-oriented products and hence do not seek to entice children to acquire dolls or playing cards or other toys. Blue Web'n (<http://www.kn.pacbell.com/wired/bluewebn/index.html>) is supported as a public service by Pac Bell and consists of a searchable database of about 1,000 outstanding Internet learning sites categorized by subject area, audience, and type (lessons, activities, projects, resources, references, and tools). Other firms, such as Scholastic Inc. and Classroom Connect, offer some free educational content as a lead-in to other products and services available for a fee. Education World, an educational publication, offers a portal with access to educational content; this site is supported by advertising, but the advertising is directed toward adults rather than children.

to produce an evaluation that is thorough, rigorous, feasible, and can grapple with the extent to which a site is developmentally appropriate, relevant to young people's needs and interests, and user-friendly.[38] In addition, the availability of good Web sites that attract the attention and interest of young people relieves to some extent the burden on parents to provide direction. These educational Web sites could also include information on online safety as well as other educational content.

Good content can also draw on a scientific understanding of the developmental needs and milestones of children in cognitive, social, emotional, and moral dimensions. For example, based on such research, schools in Wisconsin have developed Internet-related educational objectives that students must meet by the end of certain years and that teach skills such as effective searching and how to evaluate online content for truthfulness and validity.

It appears to be quite difficult, however, to find business models that can independently support the development of such content for the Internet. One of the ironies of the Internet is that adult entertainment is one of the very few businesses that have been able to make a profit on the Internet, while markets for high-quality Internet content for children languish. Experience in the wake of the dot-com meltdown illustrates that building any Internet-based business is difficult, but it appears to be especially difficult to create good offerings for children. Some of the key challenges include:

- *Limited bandwidth.* Even at broadband speeds, most children find content coming over the Internet frustrating. (Adults do as well.) Video or animation, especially over a dial-up connection, can be quite jerky, making it virtually unwatchable by many children. Furthermore, other media such as TV, video games, and PC-based software offer content that tends to be much more watchable, and the instant response that these other media offer places Internet content at a significant disadvantage. Content can be designed to work well over the Internet. Nevertheless, it is likely that content creators will be making creative sacrifices in order to

---

[38]In the committee's December 2000 workshop, Sarah Keller described the evaluation process of the ASHA Web site, <www.iwannaknow.org>, a project in which she is currently involved. This process began with a content analysis that compares the information available on the site to the recommendations established by the Sexual Information and Education Council, SIECUS, a recognized authority on sex education. The analysis was used to create an online survey to measure the site's impact on teen knowledge, attitudes, and intended behaviors. The site was evaluated using the American Library Association's recommendations on navigability, accuracy, authority, currency, and objectivity (see <www.ala.org/internettoolkit>).

obtain viewability—placing such content at a disadvantage with respect
to content carried in other media.

• *Privacy concerns.* Online businesses that are directed at children
must comply with a variety of regulations emanating from the Children's
Online Privacy Protection Act (COPPA). While such regulations have
benefits, COPPA has also imposed costs on such businesses that they did
not previously incur,[39] and it is likely that the added costs of complying
with COPPA have increased the operating burden felt by some developers of material for younger children and resulted in a smaller volume of
such material.

• *Safety concerns.* The newness of the Internet and the media publicity regarding untoward Internet experiences (e.g., abductions resulting
from Internet-enabled interactions) have made many parents fearful of
allowing their younger children on the Internet.

• *Financing.* Even in the high-flying days of venture capital, it was
hard to develop plausible business models for how an Internet service
oriented toward children would eventually be profitable. Advertisers are
often uninterested in targeting children online, and Web sites that offer
traffic that consists mostly of children are not in high demand.

Finally, creating compelling and safe content de novo is not the only
way to assemble collections of such material. Portals and Web sites that
lead to developmentally appropriate, educational, and enjoyable material
on a broad range of appealing topics (not just sex and sex education)
would help to keep young people away from inappropriate sexually explicit material (as well as other types of inappropriate material) by providing a venue that children preferred. Lists of appropriate Web sites
suitable for classroom or in-home use are a "poor-man's" analog to these
kinds of portal—teachers and/or parents can create lists of interesting
and appropriate Web sites for easy browser access by bookmarking them,
and even a list of such sites on paper would be helpful in many circumstances. Also, school districts and libraries are creating portals to educationally oriented Web sites to help students do their work.

10.10 PUBLIC SERVICE ANNOUNCEMENTS
AND MEDIA CAMPAIGNS

Because many adults do not know much about the need for Internet
safety, or about the nature and extent of dangers on the Internet, they

---

[39]For example, COPPA requires a parent to send a note through the postal service or to
fax a form to document parental permission for answering questions that ask for personal
information, both of which are time-consuming, inefficient, and costly to process.

often do not know what they do not know. Thus, they can be complacent and do nothing about protecting their children on the Internet, or they can exaggerate the dangers, believing from media scare stories that "pornography" and sexual predators on the Internet are as ubiquitous as commercials on television or radio.

By themselves, public service announcements (PSAs) and media campaigns cannot provide comprehensive education about complex topics. However, they are ideal for relatively simple messages. For example, the late 1980s saw a major public awareness campaign offering the message, "It's ten o'clock. Do you know where your kids are?" A similar campaign today for Internet safety might offer a message like, "What did your kids do online today?," or "You, too, can learn about protecting your kids on the Internet!" or "Would you let a stranger in your child's bedroom?" to encourage the placement of computers in public parts of the home.

Since the mid 1990s, a number of concerned companies in the Internet publishing industry have sought to demonstrate their interest in educating the public at large about the dangers that the Internet can present to children. These industry-sponsored self-policing programs include AmericaLinksUp, which ran roughly from December 1997 to October 1998, and GetNetWise, which started in the spring of 1999 and still exists today.

AmericaLinksUp was spawned by the Internet Online Summit: Focus on Children held in Washington, D.C., in December 1997. The conference consisted of a day of Clinton Administration, congressional, and Internet industry leaders speaking to the importance of establishing a public-private partnership to protect the public interest and obviate the need for introducing legislation to regulate the Internet. One of the outcomes was AmericaLinksUp, which was funded primarily by several major media companies, including AOL, Time Warner, and the Walt Disney Company, to demonstrate corporate commitment to raising public awareness about the importance of parents monitoring their children's activities on the Web and of children being aware of the dangers that can be encountered when surfing the Web. AmericaLinksUp created television and radio PSA spots that were designed to target parents and children as separate demographic groups. ABC Television Network, ABC Radio Network, Turner Broadcasting System, and Lifetime Television all provided air time pro bono during August and September of 1998 to broadcast these PSAs. Despite the fact that the PSAs were very emotionally evocative, AmericaLinksUp most likely had minimal impact due to the limited nature of any media campaign that has virtually no media budget.

Operated under the auspices of the non-profit Internet Education Foundation, GetNetWise was in many ways the successor to America-LinksUp, and is supported by a wide range of Internet-related corporations and public service organizations. GetNetWise had a larger agenda than simply promulgating children's safety on the Internet; it extended to promoting how families could enjoy the Internet together, as well. Get-NetWise launched a major Web site designed to be the focal point on the Web for all Internet public interest information. GetNetWise.org still is in operation today, although the initial publicity campaign surrounding its launch in mid-1999 has diminished, as has awareness of the initiative.

Overall, despite the significant amount of energy and resources expended to produce the PSAs for AmericaLinksUp and to launch the Web site and public relations campaign for GetNetWise, there is little evidence that either of these industry initiatives has had a major impact on diminishing the safety problems presented by the Internet for children. If any conclusion can be drawn from the programs, it is that, while they do offer value (although that is difficult to measure) by raising people's awareness, it is difficult to sustain interest among industry participants over any extended period of time. For such campaigns to be most effective, companies must believe it is in their commercial interest to finance them (i.e., there must be a threat of some harm, such as potential governmental regulation or loss of revenues, or some promise of benefit, such as greater public awareness of their concerns for the welfare of children). To truly make a difference, public awareness campaigns must be funded on an ongoing basis and be part of a multifaceted umbrella program that makes Internet safety the responsibility of all key stakeholders in promoting children's safety on the Internet.

Another possibility is that strategies, along the lines of current campaigns to discourage drug and tobacco use among children, could be designed to discourage children from seeking out sexually explicit materials. Such strategies are likely to be controversial, in the sense that they would call public attention to sexually explicit materials. Moreover, most of the literature suggests that health communication campaigns, such as anti-smoking and anti-drug media campaigns, are least effective when they are not conducted in concert and coordination with appropriate community-based supports.[40]

10.11 FINDINGS AND OBSERVATIONS ABOUT SOCIAL AND EDUCATIONAL STRATEGIES

1. Social and educational strategies directly address the nurturing of character and the development of responsible choice. Because such strategies locate control in the hands of the youth targeted, children may make

---

[40]Thomas E. Backer and Everett M. Rogers, eds. 1993. *Organizational Aspects of Health Communication Campaigns: What Works?*, Sage, Newbury Park, Calif.

mistakes as they learn to internalize the object of these lessons. But explaining why certain actions were mistaken will help children to learn the lessons that parents and other adults hope that they will learn.

2. Though education is difficult and time-consuming, many aspects of Internet safety education have been successful in the past several years. While it is true that Internet safety education, acceptable use policies, and even parental guidance and counseling are unlikely to change the desire of many adolescent boys to seek out sexually explicit materials, parents are more aware of some of the other dangers (such as meeting strangers face-to-face) and know more about how to protect their kids then ever before. (This is true even though more needs to be done in this area.) Children are better educated about how to sense whether the person on the other end of an instant message is "for real." Many of them have developed strategies for coping, and children with such strategies increasingly understand the rules of the game better than many parents. Little of this was true 5 years ago.

3. Social and educational strategies are generally not inexpensive, and they require tending and implementation. Adults must be taught to teach children how to make good choices in this area. They must be willing to engage in sometimes-difficult conversations. And, social and educational strategies do not provide a quick fix with a high degree of immediate protection. Nevertheless, they are the only approach through which ethics of responsible behavior can be cultivated and ways of coping with inappropriate material and experiences taught.

4. Social and educational strategies have relevance and applicability far beyond the limited question of "protecting kids from porn on the Internet." For example, social and educational strategies are relevant to teaching children to:

- Think critically about all kinds of media messages, including those associated with hate, racism, senseless violence, and so on;
- Conduct effective Internet searches for information and navigate with confidence;
- Evaluate the credibility and motivation of the sources of the messages that they receive;
- Better recognize dangerous situations on the Internet;
- Make ethical and responsible choices about Internet behavior—and about non-Internet behavior as well; and
- Cope better with exposure to upsetting and disturbing experiences and material found on the Internet.

11

A Perspective on Technology-Based Tools

There are a number of tools for protecting children from inappropriate Internet material and experiences. Most common are filters that attempt to block certain types of content, but tools for monitoring usage, verifying age, and protecting intellectual property fall into this domain as well. While each of these tools offers some degree of protection, there are many factors that enter into choices about what technology, or technologies, should be used, or whether technology is appropriate at all.

11.1 TECHNOLOGY-BASED TOOLS

As in many other areas of life, the Internet is an arena in which many adults (mostly parents) attempt to stay aware of their children's activities and some young people, particularly adolescents, attempt to evade parental oversight. Technology-based tools for protecting children from exposure to inappropriate Internet material and experiences promise "hard" security against unknown threats and offer to compensate for parental lack of knowledge about how to understand and control the Internet usage of their children. Because they appear to promise such security, it is easy to believe that all that must be done is to install the technology and then one can forget about the problem.

To be fair, technology vendors rarely make such claims explicitly. But the rhetoric of public discourse about technology solutions to "the problem" most definitely has such a tone. Indeed, the advocacy of technology-based solutions has much of the same tone as commercials in which cereal is seen to be "part of a balanced breakfast," a qualification of approximately 1 second in a 30-second commercial extolling the virtues and pleasures of the cereal.

Moreover, technology that helps to create a problem and technology that helps to solve it are another instance of the familiar measure/countermeasure game. In banks, better safes inspire bank robbers to develop better methods for cracking safes, which in turn inspire still better safes. When safes become too hard to crack, bank robbers can turn to high-tech fraud as a way of draining money from banks, starting the cycle all over again in a different domain. This implies that no technological solution is durable.

The desire for simple, inexpensive, decisive technology-based solutions is understandable. But as noted in Chapters 8 and 10, a strong infrastructure of social and educational strategies that help children develop an internal sense of appropriate behavior and response is foundational for children's safety on the Internet. Technology-based tools can serve useful roles in much the same way that "training wheels" have a useful role in teaching children to ride bicycles. In addition, technology can strengthen the positive effects of good parenting, and serve as a backup for those instances in which parents are temporarily inattentive (as all parents are from time to time).

For purposes of this report, tools are defined as information technology devices or software that can help to reduce the exposure of children to inappropriate material and experiences on the Internet. These devices or software can be installed in any one of a number of locations. Material on the Internet originates at a "source." It is then transmitted through a variety of intermediate points and is finally displayed on the user's screen. Inappropriate material can be identified at any point before the material appears on the user's screen—allowing some appropriate action to be taken at any of these points. Box 11.1. describes in greater detail some of the points of content identification and control.

It is also worth noting that there are technological and business pressures that are likely to ameliorate the problem. These include the following:

- The development of most industries follows a pattern of innovation, copycat, and then shakeout. The wide proliferation of adult Web sites suggests that the industry is in its copycat phase. If the industry continues on the traditional trajectory, shakeout in the industry is likely to occur in the future. If so, the remaining players are likely to demonstrate more corporate responsibility in differentiating children from adults in giving access to their products and services, although non-commercial sources of sexually explicit material are likely to be unaffected by this trend.

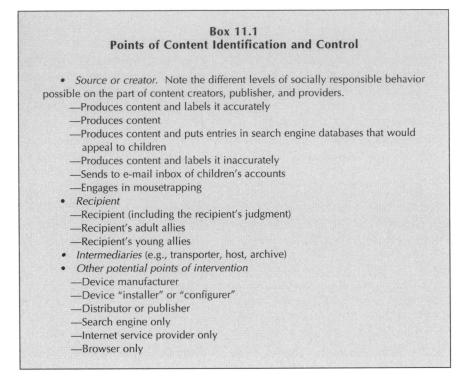

Box 11.1
Points of Content Identification and Control

- *Source or creator.* Note the different levels of socially responsible behavior possible on the part of content creators, publisher, and providers.
    —Produces content and labels it accurately
    —Produces content
    —Produces content and puts entries in search engine databases that would appeal to children
    —Produces content and labels it inaccurately
    —Sends to e-mail inbox of children's accounts
    —Engages in mousetrapping
- *Recipient*
    —Recipient (including the recipient's judgment)
    —Recipient's adult allies
    —Recipient's young allies
- *Intermediaries* (e.g., transporter, host, archive)
- *Other potential points of intervention*
    —Device manufacturer
    —Device "installer" or "configurer"
    —Distributor or publisher
    —Search engine only
    —Internet service provider only
    —Browser only

- Decentralization of the Internet (discussed in Section 2.1.2) is an enabler for a variety of technology-based tools that can be deployed by end users (e.g., individual families, schools, and libraries) to increase the range of options available to help parents and other responsible adults fulfill their responsibilities.
- Some technological developments, such as the trend away from open chat rooms to closed instant message rings, will make it more difficult for spammers and molesters to find individual victims.
- As today's children become parents, the generational divide in technical knowledge and sophistication may begin to close.

These comments should not in any sense be taken to mean that technology-based tools themselves are useless or unnecessary, and the remainder of this chapter, as well as Chapters 12 and 13, describe how such tools might be useful. Nevertheless, the statements immediately above are collectively a message that not all technology or business trends bode ill with respect to the exposure of children and youth to inappropriate sexually explicit material and experiences on the Internet.

11.2 CONTEXTUAL ISSUES FOR TECHNOLOGY-BASED TOOLS

All tools to protect someone from inappropriate content require judgments about what content should be deemed inappropriate. While all decisions about what is inappropriate are derived from human judgments, the decision regarding any given content can be made by a computer program that seeks to mimic these human judgments (and examines the content itself as it is coming into the computer) or by people who examine that specific content, generally in advance (and sometimes far in advance) of an actual attempt to access this content.

Not all tools, or even a given type of tool, are equally adept at identifying all kinds of inappropriate material. For example, for reasons described in Chapter 2, the identification of certain types of inappropriate sexually explicit material—e.g., that which is found on adult Web sites—is considerably easier from a technical standpoint than the identification of other types of sexually explicit material or other types of content that may be judged inappropriate (e.g., material on bomb making, hate speech, religious cults).

Chapters 12 and 13 address several generic categories of tools. But before turning to those tools, it is helpful to make a number of comments that apply across most technological options for protection.

- The party that decides that a given tool is appropriate is almost always the party that must manage its use. Management of a tool includes decisions about setting it up initially, maintaining it, and configuring it so that it does the appropriate things in the particular environment. It also entails decisions about the appropriate users (i.e., the children or youth in question) and when and under what circumstances they are subject to the restrictions imposed by the tool. Further, the decision-making process for considering the use of a given tool must consider a wide variety of factors that may include some emanating from external sources (e.g., government).
- Technology solutions are brittle, in the sense that when they fail, they tend to fail catastrophically. In general, the catastrophe is not that they suddenly allow the child to access all possible kinds of inappropriate material (though this can sometimes happen), but rather in the sudden violation of expectation that the given technology would not fail. A child who has not been educated about what to expect and how to deal with problematic material found on the Internet, but has been "protected" by technology alone, will not have the coping skills needed to deal with such exposure.
- Ease of use is a major factor in implementation of any technical tool. Tools do not provide effective protection if they are so difficult to use that

they go unused, and the complexity of a tool's setup and ongoing maintenance is a major factor in a tool's suitability. As a general rule, the "default" settings of a tool are the ones that are most often used. And, there is a distinct trade-off between simplicity of use and customizability to a user's specific preferences. Customization may, for example, require a user to specify preferences in many different domains—partial frontal nudity is acceptable while full frontal nudity is not (except in images of classical art); violence is acceptable, while religious cults are not, and so on. But a user, faced with such choices, often tends to opt for the simplest solution—which is likely to be "not OK" for all of the specified domains because of the defaults built into the software by the vendor. Further, the wide variety of computing environments often forces vendors into requiring a "setup" procedure to adapt the tool to the user's particular hardware/software configuration. And, because of the constantly changing nature of the Internet, the tools must constantly be updated in order to remain current and valid. This puts the onus on the user to acquire a fair degree of technical know-how. Unless this step can be made easy for the user, only the most skilled or dedicated users will bother to use such a tool.

• As a general rule, most technology-based tools can be circumvented with sufficient effort. Furthermore, the history of information technology suggests that a method of circumvention, once discovered, is often proliferated widely.[1] Not everyone is privy to such information, of course, but those who care about the topic—and about circumvention—can usually find it with a relatively small effort. What technology can do is to pose barriers that are sufficient to keep those who are not strongly motivated from finding their way to inappropriate material or experiences, and the fact that technology can be circumvented does not mean that it will always be circumvented. For many people, circumvention will not be worth the effort. For others, the circumvention techniques will not always be available. Still others may not receive the word on circumvention. Sometimes, circumvention may be illegal even if feasible. For such reasons, technology-based tools have utility even though circumvention techniques exist. Nevertheless, as most parents and teachers noted in their comments to the committee, those who really want to have access to

---

[1]Specifically, when the circumvention is based on a software technique (as it has usually been to date), the circumvention can be easily broadcast at very low cost to many individuals. When changes to hardware are involved (as happens relatively rarely), proliferation of such changes is more difficult. A number of high school students told the committee that once one of them finds a circumvention of some sort, he or she shares it with other interested students almost immediately. For example, a high school student developed a way to bypass his school district's filtering system, and publicized it by sending an e-mail to every teacher and administrator in the district. See <http://www.salon.com/tech/feature/2001/06/14/net_filtering/index1.html>.

inappropriate sexually explicit materials will find a way to get them, and technology is relatively ineffective in the long run against those who are strongly motivated. From this point it follows that the real challenge is to reduce the number of children who are strongly motivated to obtain inappropriate sexually explicit materials. This, of course, is one focus of the social and educational strategies described in Chapter 10.

• Tools can and do improve over time as more effort is put into research and development. Some improvements are possible with better design and implementation of known technologies. Other improvements await advances in the underlying technologies—and may eventually be incorporated into technology-based tools. However, almost by definition, technological improvements are likely to be evolutionary rather than revolutionary, and so it is unwise to base any approach to protecting children and youth from inappropriate Internet materials and experiences on the hope of revolutionary technological breakthroughs.

• Tools such as filters that are implemented on the local client machine (i.e., at the receiver's point of interaction) tend to be easier to circumvent than those elsewhere (e.g., those embedded in the network or in the enterprise that provides service). The reason is that tools co-located with the receiver are more readily accessible to the potential circumventer, and thus more subject to inspection, manipulation, and unauthorized or improper alteration or disabling. Moreover, tools that run on the client machine add an additional layer of complexity that can make a computer less reliable and more prone to lockups and system crashes.

• Because currently deployed technologies do not yet support access policies to be associated with an individual rather than a workstation, a simple change of venue (i.e., a movement of the child or youth to another place where the Web can be accessed) is often all that is necessary to defeat the most effective technological tools for protection. A change of venue may be a deliberate attempt to avoid technologically imposed restrictions, as in the case of students using home computers with Internet access to bypass filtered access at schools. Alternatively, it may be entirely accidental, in the sense that a venue that the minor uses for reasons of convenience on some occasions, for example, may not offer the same technological tools in its computing environment as the ones that he usually uses.

• One of the principles underlying the architecture of the Internet is that to the extent possible, functionality resides at the end points of a communication, rather than in the middle. Thus, to the extent that end-to-end encryption is used, on-the-fly content identification by the content carrier (e.g., the Internet service provider (ISP)) is impossible, and therefore interdiction based on such identification is impossible. (In practice, this fact gives the interdictor of content only two choices: to allow all unknown traffic to pass, or to block all unknown traffic. Allowing all unknown traffic to pass is likely to permit some inappropriate content through, while blocking all unknown traffic is likely to block some appropriate content.)

• As with social and educational strategies, informed decisions about the use of technology-based tools (whether to use them and if so, which one(s)) must take into account the developmental stage of the children for whose benefit they would be deployed. Some tools are most appropriate for younger children, who are presumably more impressionable, less experienced in the ways of the world, and less skilled in the use of information technology, and for whom the consequences of exposure to inappropriate material of any sort might be considerable. Other tools, perhaps allowing more discretion on the part of the user, might be more appropriate for older youth that are more experienced and mature.

• Improvements in technology can be rapidly deployed compared to the time scale on which social and educational strategies change. That is, communities may be involved in the decision to use technology-based tools, but do not generally get involved in the technical design or implementation of those tools, which are usually within the discretionary purview of the tool designer and vendor. By contrast, social and educational strategies for a community (though usually not for individual families) are often extensively debated, and once debated, an extensive training effort is then needed to promulgate a new approach.

• The deployment of technological tools entails some financial cost, both initially and in ongoing costs. Thus, one potential social inequity is that those lacking in resources will be denied the benefits of various tools—a "digital divide" issue.[2] Advocates of using tools might argue

---

[2]For example, in 2000, 54 percent of public schools with access to the Internet reported that computers with access to the Internet were available to students outside of regular school hours, and secondary schools were more likely than elementary schools to make the Internet available to students outside of regular school hours (80 percent compared with 46 percent). Large schools (1,000 or more students) were more likely than medium-sized and small schools to make the Internet accessible to students outside of regular school hours (79 percent compared with 53 and 49 percent, respectively). In addition, schools with the highest minority enrollment reported Internet availability outside of regular school hours more frequently than schools with the lowest minority enrollment (61 percent compared with 46 percent). Such statistics suggest that schools do provide a considerable amount of out-of-class Internet access for many students—and it is likely that many of these students do not have Internet access at home. (Statistics are taken from A. Cattagni and E. Farris, 2001, *Internet Access in U.S. Public Schools and Classrooms: 1994-2000*, NCES 2001-071, Office of Educational Research and Improvement, U.S. Department of Education, Washington, D.C. A Kaiser Family Foundation/NPR poll taken in 2001 found that schools are playing an important role in equalizing access to computers for kids. Specifically, African American children and children from lower-income households are considerably less likely to use a computer at home than are white kids or kids from higher-income families, whereas virtually the same percentage of all kids have used a computer at school. See <http://www.npr.org/programs/specials/poll/technology/>.

that it would be desirable for all people, rich and poor, to enjoy the protection benefits that such tools confer, but if economics make such equity impossible, better for some to enjoy such benefits than for none to do so. On the other hand, detractors of tools, especially of tools whose use is made mandatory, can argue that laws such as CIPA—which make the use of filters mandatory in exchange for e-rate funding—force the problems of filters on the poor.

11.3 THE QUESTIONS TO BE ASKED OF EACH TOOL

Chapters 12 and 13 discuss seven major types of technology that can be used to protect or limit children's exposure to inappropriate sexually explicit material on the Internet. These include filtering, adoption of specialized domain names, surveillance and monitoring, age verification technologies, instant help, tools for controlling spam, and tools for protecting intellectual property. To provide the basis for a systematic understanding of each of these tools, the committee found the following set of questions useful.

- *What is it?* The answer to this question provides a clear description of the tool and a discussion of its variants. While the need for a clear description may be obvious, the public debate has often been hampered by a lack of common understanding about exactly what option is being discussed.
- *How well does it work?* What are the benefits that the product is intended to offer? As noted in Chapter 8, "protection" is a term with multiple possible meanings, and not all options provide the same kind of protection. Only after the nature of the protection offered has been established is it meaningful to ask about the tool's effectiveness. Note that effectiveness is a multidimensional concept, and efforts to reduce a tool's effectiveness to a single metric are generally not useful.
- *Who decides what is inappropriate?* All options presume some definition of inappropriate material, and such definitions reflect the values held by the decision-making party involved. Indeed, as indicated in Chapter 5, there are few universally held and objective standards for defining or recognizing inappropriate material. An understanding of the locus of definitional control is thus important, because who "should" be responsible for decisions about what is inappropriate for a child is at the center of much controversy. Advocates can be heard for the responsible party being the child, the child's parents, the child's teacher, a representative of the school, the city council, the state legislature, the U.S. Congress, the Supreme Court, local juries, and so on.

- *How flexible and usable is it?* It is rare that a given implementation of an option is perfectly matched to the needs of its user, and the details of implementation may make a given product unsuitable for a user, even if, in general, the philosophy underlying the product is consistent with a user's needs. (An example is the ease with which user-enabled "overrides" of product settings is possible.) A product may also have other features that enhance or detract from its usability. Note also that people are usually of two minds about the flexibility of a product. On the one hand, they generally believe that a product with greater flexibility can be customized to their needs to a greater extent. On the other hand, they find the actual exploitation of a product's flexibility to be a chore that they tend to avoid. As a result, the most common use of any technology tool is in its default "out of the box" configuration. (Thus, for practical purposes, it is fair that any assessment of a tool place great weight on what the tool does out of the box.)

- *What are the costs entailed and infrastructure required to use it?* Protection against inappropriate material does not exist in a vacuum, and in general, an infrastructure is necessary to support the long-term use of a tool that provides maximum protection consistent with the user's other functional requirements. Costs should be understood broadly, and they include financial costs, ease of implementation, ease of use, false positives and false negatives, interference with the functions being served in the chosen environment, and lack of transparency about the option in operation.

- *What are the implications of using it?* It is rare that the adoption of an option will have no side effects, and understanding the possible unintended consequences (which may be desirable or undesirable) may affect judgments about a tool's desirability.

- *What is its future?* Some technologies whose effectiveness is limited today may increase in effectiveness tomorrow as research progresses. Or, the technology necessary for a certain type of a tool might exist but not be implemented in any product now on the market. And, different environmental circumstances may lead to different levels of effectiveness—which is especially true of tools or strategies whose effectiveness increases as others make use of them.

12

Technology-Based Tools for Users

This chapter discusses tools for the end user, here the party responsible for making decisions on behalf of the child or youth in question. Thus, the "end user" may be a parent in the case of a home or family, a maker of school policy (e.g., a school principal or a school district), a maker of policy for a public library (or library system), or some other similar individual or body. The focus on tools for end users is important because such tools are intended to empower end users by providing a wide range of options for the children in their care, more or less regardless of what other Internet stakeholders do or do not do. (The only exception concerns instant help, in which the user is the child seeking help.)

Table 12.1 provides a preview of this chapter.

12.1 FILTERING AND CONTENT-LIMITED ACCESS

Filters are at the center of the debate over protecting children and youth from inappropriate sexually explicit material on the Internet. A good filter allows a specific filtering policy to be implemented with accuracy, has enough flexibility, and can be implemented with a minimum of undesirable side effects. Box 12.1 describes the dimensions of choice that GetNetWise identifies for filters.

12.1.1 What Is Filtering and Content-Limited Access?

Today, Internet access is largely unrestricted. That is, a user who does not take some explicit action to limit the content to which he or she is

TABLE 12.1 Technology-Based Tools for the End User

Type of Tool	Function	One Illustrative Advantage
Filter	Block "inappropriate" access to prespecified content; typically blocks specific Web pages, may also block generic access to instant messages, e-mail, and chat rooms	Can be configured to deny access to substantial amounts of adult-oriented sexually explicit material from commercial Web sites
Content-limited access	Allow access only to content and/or services previously determined to be appropriate	Provides high confidence that all accessible material conforms to the acceptability standards of the access provider
Labeling of content	Enable users to make informed decisions about content prior to actual access	Separates content characterization (e.g., sexually explicit or not) from decisions to block; multiple content raters can be used
Monitoring with individual identification	Examine a child's actions by an adult supervisor in real time or after the fact	Rarely prevents child from reaching appropriate material that might have been mistakenly flagged as inappropriate
Monitoring without individual identification	Watch the collective actions of a group (e.g., a school) without identifying individuals	Can provide useful information about whether or not acceptable use policies are being followed
Spam-controlling tools	Inhibit unsolicited e-mail containing sexually explicit material (or links to such material) from entering child's mailbox	Can reduce the volume of inappropriate e-mails significantly
Instant help	Provide immediate help when needed from an adult	Provides guidance for child when it is likely to be most effective, i.e., at time of need

NOTE: The "end user" is generally the adult supervisor who makes decisions on behalf of a child. (This is true in all cases except for instant help, in which the user is the child seeking help.)

One Illustrative Disadvantage	Voluntary versus Involuntary Exposure
In typical (default) configuration, generally denies access to substantial amounts of Web material that is not adult-oriented and sexually explicit	Protects against both deliberate and inadvertent exposure for sites that are explicitly blocked; can be circumvented under some circumstances
May be excessively limiting for those with broader information needs than those served by the access provider	Very low possibility of deliberate or inadvertent exposure, given that all material is explicitly vetted
Effectiveness depends on broad acceptance of a common labeling framework	Likelihood of exposure depends on accuracy of labels given by labeling party
Potential loss of privacy zone for child	Warnings can help to deter deliberate exposure; ineffective against inadvertent exposure
Does not enable individual account-ability for irresponsible actions	Warnings can help to deter deliberate exposure; less effective against inadvertent exposure
Among users concerned about losing personalized e-mail, reduced tolerance for false positives that block genuinely personal e-mails incorrectly identified as spam	Mostly relevant to inadvertent exposure (i.e., unsought commercial e-mail containing sexually explicit material)
Requires responsive infrastructure of helpers	Mostly relevant to inadvertent exposure

Box 12.1
GetNetWise Questions About Filters

Does the product control:

- Access to Web pages?
- Use of e-mail?
- Access to chat rooms?
- Movement of files in and out of your computer (FTP)?
- Access to newsgroups (Usenet)?
- Access to various forms of instant messaging?
- Access to other Internet capabilities?

How are standards of "inappropriateness" managed?

- By the company alone?
- By the user selecting categories to be filtered from a list of preset categories?
- By the user developing his or her own list of material to be filtered, based on the company's list of material to be filtered as a starting point?
- By the user adding to or subtracting from the company's list of material to be filtered?
- By the user developing his or her own list of material to be filtered, starting from scratch?

To what extent can the criteria for determining inappropriateness be reviewed? Can the user review

- The list of keywords?
- The list of filtered URLs (Web page addresses)?
- The company's criteria for filtering a Web page?

On what basis does the company determine what content is inappropriate?

- PICS ratings (an independent rating system)?
- Using the Web page address (URL)?
- Human review of Web sites?
- A list of keywords?
- A list of keywords combined with an analysis of the context in which they appear?

What are the categories of inappropriate material? These might include, for example,

Violence/profanity	Intolerance	Questionable/illegal and
Partial nudity	Satanic/cult	gambling
Full nudity	Drugs/drug culture	Alcohol and tobacco.
Sexual acts	Militant/extremist	
Gross depictions	Sex education	

exposed has access to any content that the Internet provides through Web pages, e-mail, chat rooms, and the like. This report uses the term "filter" to refer to a system or service that limits in some way the content to which users may be exposed. The vast majority of filters block access to content on specific Web sites (though these sites may be specified as a class). Other filters also block access on the basis of keywords appearing either in a user's query to a search engine or contained in the about-to-be-displayed Web site.[1] Some filters provide the capability to block more broadly, so that an individual may be denied access to other common Internet services, such as interactive services (e.g., e-mail, chat rooms), Usenet newsgroups, file downloading, peer-to-peer connections, or even e-commerce with credit card usage.

Users who wish to use a filter have a number of technical options:

• *Client-side filters.* Filters can be installed on the devices (today, desktop and laptop personal computers) that serve as the Internet access point for the end user. Client-side systems are installed as local software, in the same way that any other software is locally installed, except that standard uninstallation (which would disable the filter) can be done only by someone with the appropriate password. The party with the appropriate password is also generally responsible for configuring the profile of the system for those they are seeking to protect from inappropriate materials. A common personal use is a client-side filter installed at home by a parent wishing to protect children from inappropriate material. Client-side filtering is also feasible in an environment in which only some access points in a local area network must be filtered—for example, in a library attempting to segregate "children's areas" from areas for all patrons.

• *Content-limited Internet service providers.* As a feature of their offerings, a number of ISPs provide Internet access only to a certain subset of Internet content. Content-limited ISPs are most likely to be used by organizations and families in which the information needs of the children involved are fairly predictable. Today, such dedicated ISPs are a niche

---

[1]The actual content of a list of such keywords is usually held as proprietary information by the vendor of the filter. However, such lists include a variety of "four letter words" associated with sex, reproduction, and excretory functions, words such as "sex," "naked," and so on. Other words that might be singled out for inclusion include "bomb," "bondage," "fetish," "spunk," "voyeurism," "babe," "erotica," "gay rights," "Nazi," "pot," "white power," "girlz," and "hard-core pornography." (These examples are taken from Lisa Guernsey, 1999, "Sticks and Stones Can Hurt, But Bad Words Pay," *New York Times*, April 9.) Also, a more sophisticated form of filtering is based on the analysis of word combinations and phrases, proximity of certain keywords to certain other keywords, the presence of various URLs, and so on. In some cases, text-based analysis may also be combined with the analysis of images on the Web page in question. As a rule, tools based on this more sophisticated filtering are not broadly marketed today.

market and typically have subscriber bases in the thousands to tens of thousands. All subscribers—which are often families and less often institutions—are subject to the same restrictions. Some content-limited ISPs, intended for use by children, make available only a very narrow range of content that has been explicitly vetted for appropriateness and safety. Thus, all Web pages accessible have been viewed—and assessed—for content that is developmentally appropriate, educational, and entertaining. (This approach is known as "white listing"—all content from sources not on a white list are disallowed,[2] as discussed in Section 2.3.1.) Chat rooms and bulletin boards are monitored for appropriate content, and those violating rules of chatting or message posting are disinvited, forcibly if necessary. E-mail and instant messages (IMs) can be received only from specified parties and/or other users of the system. Other content-limited ISPs, intended for use by both children and adults, allow access to all content that is not explicitly designated by the ISP as inappropriate. Monitoring and limits on e-mail are less strict or non-existent.

Some services allow multiple "login names" or "screen names." A screen name is an online identity, similar to a CB radio "handle." Each online session uses a single screen name, and families can choose not to give the adult or "administrative" screen name password to youth. An online account may have multiple screen names, and a user with appropriate privileges (usually associated with paying for the master account) can create arbitrary screen names at will for himself or someone else on his account as long those names are not already in use. With each name can be associated unrestricted access or more limited access to online content (which may include both Internet and proprietary content). In the case of America Online (AOL), a parent can identify the age of the child for whom he or she is setting up a screen name. AOL then puts into place default limitations based on the age of the child, which the parent can then adjust if necessary. Such limitations might include, for example, Web access only to age-appropriate content or to everything except explicitly mature themes, receipt of e-mail only without file attachments or embedded pictures, and access only to chat rooms intended for children (or no chat room access at all).

• *Server-side filters.* Server-side filtering is useful in institutional settings in which users at all access points within the institution's purview

---

[2]Note that sources on a white list can be specified in advance or identified as appropriate because a source contains one or several "good words" that may be found on a "good-word" list. For an example of the latter, see Gio Wiederhold, Michel Bilello, Vatsala Sarathy, and XioaLei Qian, "A Security Mediator for Health Care Information," pp. 120-124 in *Proceedings of the 1996 American Medical Informatics Association Conference*, Washington, D.C., October.

must conform to the access policy defined by the institution. Server-side filtering might be used by a school district that provides Internet service to all schools in the district or a library system that provides Internet service to all libraries in the system. Server-side filters are located on systems other than the client.[3] An institution may contract with an ISP to implement its filtering policy, or it may install a filter in the server that manages a local area network (e.g., that of a school district or a library system).[4] (Note that there are no fundamental technological impediments to having filtering policies that differentiate between schools within a district, so that a high school might operate under a policy different from that for an elementary school. Such differentiation is simply a matter of cost.)

• *Search engine filters.* In a special class of server-side filters are those that are today part of major search engines such as Google, AltaVista, and so on. Each of these search engines has the capability of enabling an Internet safety filter (hereafter "filtered search engine"). When activated by the user, these filters do not return links to inappropriate content found in a search, but they also do not block access to specifically named Web sites (so that a user knowing the URL of a Web site containing inappropriate sexually explicit material could access it).[5] Other search engines are explicitly designed for use by children. For example, Lycos and Yahoo both offer a special kids-oriented version of their general purpose search engine that restricts the universe of a search to child-appropriate areas. (This is the white-list approach.)

Filters can be used to block certain incoming inappropriate information (an application that is the most common use of filters), to block access to certain Internet services (e.g., file downloads), or to block selected out-

---

[3]The distinction between server-side filtering and content-limited ISPs is not a technical one, because content-limited ISPs use server-side filters. Rather, the point is that server-side filtering provides a degree of institutional customization that is not possible with content-limited ISPs, which tend to offer one-size-fits-all filtering policies.

[4]The use of server-side filters may degrade performance. In particular, a server-based filter may rely on "proxy servers" that are unable to take advantage of the caching techniques that are often used by major Internet providers to speed the retrieval of commonly requested pages. Such a filter would be forced to retrieve information from its host server and take whatever performance hit that might entail. In other cases, performance is improved because without irrelevant material taking up space in the cache, retrieval of relevant material is faster.

[5]In practice, a responsible adult would set the filtering provision to the "on" setting, and save the configuration. Thereafter, other requests on that client to the search engine would encounter the "on" setting. The setting can also be turned "off" through entering a password known only to the individual who initially set it (a possible problem if that person is the teenager in the household who manages the family's information technology).

going information. All technology-enforced methods for blocking access to inappropriate information require a determination that certain pieces of content are inappropriate.[6] Content can be deemed inappropriate on the basis of the methods discussed in Section 2.3.1.

Many filter vendors establish lists of "suspect" Web sites (compiled as a list of specific URLs and/or IP addresses) deemed sources of inappropriate content.[7] The number of such sites may range from several hundred thousand to 2 million. In addition, many vendors establish lists of keywords (typically hundreds of words) that represent inappropriate content. Far fewer employ image analysis or statistical techniques to analyze text.

In addition, techniques for textual and image analysis can be used to identify and block e-mail containing inappropriate content and for blocking outgoing content as well. For example, the technology that identifies inappropriate content by searching for keywords can also prevent those words (or some set of them) from being used in e-mail messages or in chat rooms. (In this case, the adult supervisor can augment the keyword list to include certain phrases that should not appear, such as specific addresses or phone numbers.)

Filters are perhaps the most widely deployed of all technological tools intended to protect children from exposure to inappropriate material. The majority of schools have deployed filters,[8] while around 25 percent of

---

[6]Note that content that is transmitted through certain channels such as attachments to e-mail, videoconferences, instant messages, or peer-to-peer networking (in a Gnutella-like arrangement) is very difficult (arguably impossible) to block selectively, though a filter can block all interaction through these channels. Moreover, to the extent that the content of traffic is determined interactively, neither labeling nor sites are likely to provide a sufficient basis. The reason is that interactive sources, almost by definition, can support a variety of different types of interaction—the best example of which is an online friend with whom one may exchange sports trivia, conversation about school homework, and inappropriate sexually explicit material. Only real-time content recognition has a chance of filtering such content.

[7]Note also that the list of blocked sites often includes sites that could help users circumvent the basic filtering. Thus, sites providing information on how to circumvent filters are often included on the list, and a number of filters block sites that allow language translation (Seth Finkelstein and Lee Tien, 2001, "Blacklisting Bytes," white paper submitted to the committee, available online at <http://www.eff.org/Censorship/Censorware/20010306_eff_nrc_ paper1.html>) or access to Web archives (Seth Finkelstein, 2002, *The Pre-Slipped Slope— Censorware vs. the Wayback Machine Web Archive*, available online at <http://sethf.com/anticensorware/general/slip.php>).

[8]According to the National Center for Education Statistics, nearly three-fourths of all schools use blocking or filtering software. See A. Cattagni and E. Farris. 2001. Internet Access in U.S. Public Schools and Classrooms: 1994-2000. NCES 2001-071. Office of Educational Research and Improvement, U.S. Department of Education, Washington, D.C. Available online at <http://www.nces.ed.gov/pubs2001/internetaccess/>.

libraries filter at least some workstations.[9] Through AOL's parental controls (Box 12.2), a substantial number of Internet-using children enjoy the benefits and endure the costs of filtering. However, as a percentage of all children using the Internet, the fraction whose Internet access is filtered apart from school usage is small.[10]

It is noteworthy that filters are increasingly common in corporate and business settings and thus affect the Internet use of adults.[11] Many companies, driven primarily by concerns about productivity and time wasted on non-business Internet activities and about the possible creation of hostile work environments and the consequent liability, use filters to prevent inappropriate use of company IT facilities.[12]

12.1.2 How Well Does Filtering Work?

Denying access to inappropriate material through technological means, filters are intended to protect against both inadvertent and deliberate access. However, as discussed in Section 2.3.1, all filters are subject to over-blocking (false positives, in which filters block some appropriate material

---

[9]By contrast, around 57 percent of public libraries do not filter Internet access on any workstation, while about 21 percent filter access on some workstations. About 21 percent filter all workstations. See Norman Oder. 2002. "The New Wariness," *The Library Journal*, January 15. Available online at <http://libraryjournal.reviewsnews.com/index.asp?layout= article& articleid=CA188739>.

[10]A survey conducted by *Family PC* magazine in August 2001 found that of 600 families surveyed, 26 percent used parental controls of some kind. About 7 percent of those using parental controls (about 1.8 percent of the total) used off-the-shelf store-bought filtering packages. The rest used filtering offered by an Internet service provider. (This study is not available in print, because it was scheduled for publication in October 2001, and Ziff Davis, the publisher of *Family PC*, terminated the magazine before that issue was printed.)

[11]For example, a survey taken by the American Management Association in 2001 found that 38 percent of the firms responding do use blocking software to prevent Internet connections to unauthorized or inappropriate sites. Seventy eight percent of the responding firms restricted access to "adult" sites with explicit sexual content, though it is not clear how the remaining 40 percent are enforcing such restrictions. (The survey suggests that they are doing it by actively monitoring Internet use.) See American Management Association. 2001. *2001 AMA Survey, Workplace Monitoring and Surveillance: Policies and Practices*. Available online at <http://www.amanet.org/research/pdfs/emsfu_short.pdf>.

[12]Potential overlap between the business market and the school and library filtering market raises the following operational concern: a blocked category may be defined by a vendor so that it is appropriate in a business environment, but that definition may not be appropriate in a school or library context. For example, information about sexually transmitted diseases, safe sex practices, and pregnancy may not be necessary in most business environments (and hence an employer may have a legitimate business reason for blocking such information), but many would argue that older students using school facilities should not be blocked from receiving such information.

Box 12.2
AOL's Parental Controls

AOL's parental controls provide a number of options for restricting in some ways the privileges associated with a given screen name.[1]

- An *online timer* limits the amount of time a user can spend online.
- *Web access* is provided at three levels—unrestricted, unrestricted except for Web sites that are explicitly deemed inappropriate, and limited only to Web sites that are explicitly deemed appropriate for children.
- *IM controls* allow or prevent the user's sending and receiving of instant messages.
- *E-mail controls* allow or prevent the user's sending and receiving of e-mail, and can further be set to allow e-mail only from certain parties.
- *Chat controls* can be set to allow the user to participate in any chat rooms, in only selected monitored chat rooms appropriate for children, or in no chat room at all.
- *Download controls* allow or prevent the user's sending and receiving file attachments (which may include images).
- *Newsgroup controls* allow or prevent the user's gaining access to Usenet newsgroups.

AOL parental controls distinguish between four categories: Kids Only, Young Teen, Mature Teen, and 18+ (General Access) categories.

- *Kids Only* (12 and under) allows access to age-appropriate features and content through AOL's Kids Only Channel and the rest of the Internet (when accessed through AOL). Fee-based services such as shopping, instant message notes, access to member profiles and all chat rooms, home pages based on AOL, and links to Web sites obtained in e-mail are blocked.
- *Young Teen* (13 to 15) allows access to age-appropriate interactive features and information on AOL and the rest of the Internet (when accessed through AOL). Fee-based services such as shopping, instant message notes, access to member profiles as well as private and member chat rooms, home pages based on AOL, and links to Web sites obtained in e-mail are blocked.
- *Mature Teen* (16 to 17) gives the most freedom compared to other children's categories, and allows access to most interactive features and information on AOL and the rest of the Internet (when accessed through AOL). Web sites with explicitly mature content are blocked. Internet newsgroups and fee-based services are blocked.
- *General Access* (18+) allows full access to all features and content on AOL and the rest of the Internet.

SOURCE: America Online.
[1]A screen name is an online identity, similar to a CB radio "handle." An individual may have multiple screen names, and a user with appropriate privileges (usually associated with paying for the master account) can create arbitrary screen names at will for himself or someone else on his account as long those names are not already in use.

from the user) and underblocking (false negatives, in which filters pass some inappropriate material to the user). While the issue of underblocking and overblocking should not, in and of itself, rule out filters as a useful tool, the extent of underblocking and overblocking is a significant factor in understanding and deciding about the use of filters.[13]

There is no agreed-upon methodology for measuring a filter's effectiveness, as might be indicated by an overblocking rate and an underblocking rate (discussed in Section 2.3.1).[14] Filter vendors sometimes provide estimates of overblock and underblock rates, but without knowing the methodology underlying these estimates, the cautious user must be concerned that the methodology is selected to minimize these rates. (The discussion in Box 2.7 illustrates some of the problems in estimating these rates. Note further that the lists of blocked Web pages change constantly, with both additions and subtractions made regularly.)

Underblocking results from several factors:

• New material appears on the Internet constantly, and the contents of given Web pages sometimes change. When content changes, the judging parties must revisit the sources responsible for the content they provide frequently enough to ensure that inappropriate information does not suddenly appear on a previously trusted source or that the inappropriate material remains on the Web pages in question. Technology is available that can indicate if a page has changed (thus flagging it for human assessment), but not to tell if it continues to be developmentally and educationally appropriate. Vendors of filtering systems generally provide updates from time to time, but there is inevitably a lag between the time inappropriate material first appears and the time that item is entered into the list of blocked sites. (Content-based filtering systems are not subject to this particular problem.)

• The algorithms (i.e., the computational techniques) used to identify inappropriate material are imperfect. For example, the emergence of

---

[13]Note also that legal challenges brought against the mandated use of filters in institutional settings have relied significantly on the existence of underblocking and overblocking as inherent flaws in the technology that make filters unsuitable for such use.

[14]For "bake-offs" comparing Internet filters, see Christopher D. Hunter, 2000, "Internet Filter Effectiveness: Testing Over and Underinclusive Blocking Decisions of Four Popular Filters," *Social Science Computer Review* 18 (2, Summer), available online at <http://www.copacommission.org/papers/filter_effect.pdf>; Karen J. Bannan, 2001, "Clean It Up," *PC Magazine*, September 25, available online at <http://www.pcmag.com/article/0,2997,a%253D12392,00.asp>; and "Digital Chaperones for Kids," *Consumer Reports*, March 2001. For a critique of the *Consumer Reports* analysis, see David Burt, 2001, "Filtering Advocate Responds to Consumer Reports Article," February 14, available online at <http://www. politechbot.com/p-01734.html>.

new slang for sexual acts will thwart filters based on keyword recognition until the new slang is incorporated into the filtering criteria. Another possibility is that the use of clothed people having sex may thwart image-recognition algorithms based on the assumption of searching for naked people.

  • Sites with adult-oriented content are often given names that are close in spelling to the names of legitimate sites. For example, <http://www.whitehouse.com> is often reached by people intending to reach <http://www.whitehouse.gov>. While most filtering programs have fixed this specific problem, close-but-not-identical names can pop up for a large number of legitimate general-purpose sites.

Overblocking arises from three factors:

  • Content may be less than clear-cut, especially in the context of machine-assisted understanding. As noted in Chapter 2, both text and images can be ambiguous.[15] Moreover, the precise definition of what should be blocked is inevitably subject to the vagaries of individual judgments. For reasons discussed below, filter vendors generally have more incentives to block ambiguous information than to allow it to pass, a fact that leads to overblocking.

  • Information on the Internet is updated constantly. Thus, a site that may have been blocked for good reason in the past may post new information that does not meet the criteria for blocking. As in the case of underblocking, until records of the site are updated in the filter, that filter will continue to mark such sites as inappropriate even if the information contained therein is perfectly innocuous.

---

[15]Two particularly egregious examples include Beaver College and online biographies of individuals who have graduated magna cum laude. Beaver College in Pennsylvania recently changed its name to Arcadia College because its name was being filtered out ("beaver" has crude sexual connotations in American English slang). Beaver College spokesman Bill Avington was quoted in *Wired* as saying, "We have a lot of evidence that people aren't able to get our information in high schools because of Web filters in the libraries" that block out sites with "Beaver" along with other presumed smut words. He continued, "With so many people using the Net as the initial means to look at colleges, that's a serious disadvantage." In addition, he claimed that filters sometimes block e-mail from Beaver college staffers to prospective students. (See Craig Bicknell, 2000, "Beaver College Not a Filter Fave," *Wired*, March 22, available online at <http://www.wired.com/news/politics/0,1283,35091,00.html>; and CNN story, 2000, "Beaver College Changes Oft-derided Name to Arcadia University," November 20, available online at <http://www.cnn.com/2000/US/11/20/embarrassingbeaver.ap/>. The "magna cum laude" problem was demonstrated when filtering software blocked access to all biographies of COPA Commissioners who had graduated magna cum laude (see <http://www.cdt.org/speech/filtering/001002analysis.shtml>).

- A site (or a given Web page) may contain both appropriate and inappropriate material. If the filter cannot separate appropriate from inappropriate, it will usually block (overblock) the entire site or page.

The above three factors are basic to the fundamental imperfection of the filtering process. A fourth factor that can lead to overblocking results from the ways in which some filtering systems are implemented. If a filter blocks sites on the basis of the IP addresses of adult-oriented, sexually explicit sites, and those sites are hosted on a server that makes use of IP-based virtual hosting (described in Chapter 2), other non-adult sites hosted on that server (and sharing those IP addresses) will be blocked.[16]

Note an important distinction between overblocking and an overly broad scope of blocking (i.e., an overly broad blocking policy). Overblocking is inadvertent and results from the inability of the automated systems for blocking to perfectly track human decision making. The model human decision maker, examining overblocked material, would conclude that the material should in fact have been free to pass. An example would be a search for "beaver dams" that results in pages being blocked because the word "beaver" is present on the page.

An overly broad policy is more subjective, and results from a disagreement between the end user and the human decision maker about what information the end user should be allowed to receive. From the

---

[16]The magnitude of overblocking due to IP-based virtual hosting is unclear. One estimate (Art Wolinksy, 2001, "FilterGate, or Knowing What We're Walling In or Walling Out," *MultiMedia Schools*, May/June, available online from <http://www.infotoday.com/mmschools/may01/wolinsky.htm>) suggests that such overblocking far outstrips overblocking for other causes. However, a number of factors should be considered in assessing the potential impact of IP-based virtual hosting:

- Most large sites are not hosted on virtual hosting services. Furthermore, large sites tend to be more heavily promoted and are often more likely to appear in a prominent position in a search engine's result list. Thus, large sites—which typically account for the Web requests of most users—are much less likely to be improperly blocked than smaller sites.
- Many virtual hosting services ban adult-oriented, sexually explicit material and other material that they regard as offensive as well, and they enforce their acceptable use policies vigorously. Thus, the amount of sexually explicit material hosted overall by such services is likely to be small. (But, if such a service does host even one site containing inappropriate sexually explicit material and that fact is picked up by a filtering vendor that uses IP-based filtering, it will exclude all of the acceptable sites on that host. All of the acceptable sites that are improperly blocked will stay blocked until the hosting service eliminates the inappropriate site and the fact of elimination is communicated to the vendor.)
- Different implementations of filtering (e.g., use of name-based filtering) can lead to the same intended result without the overblocking caused by IP-based filtering. As a rule, the primary reason for wishing to use IP-based filtering is technical—when a hosting service is used primarily for adult-oriented, sexually explicit material, IP-based filtering reduces the amount of storage and processing needed by the filter.

perspective of the end user, a certain piece of material is blocked inappropriately. However, upon examination of that blocked material, the human decision maker concludes that the blocking decision was proper. For example, a student may wish to search for information on marijuana. But Web sites containing the word marijuana may be blocked because of a policy decision to block information about drugs.[17]

The effectiveness of a filter also depends on whether its use is enforced at all sites available to a child. In a specific venue, filters will block some material that some parties deem inappropriate—and there is a reasonable argument to be had over whether the blocking that occurs is worth the cost of overblocking. But it is impossible for a filter deployed in a school to block material sought in a cyber-café or at home, and filtering limited to schools and libraries will not prevent the access of children to inappropriate sexually explicit material if they are determined to search for it and have other venues of access. The most common unfiltered venues are home Internet access or Internet access provided at a friend's home. (Filtering at home is not the norm,[18] even though a significant fraction of U.S. youth do have Internet access at home,[19] a point well represented by the adolescents to whom the committee spoke during its site visits.)

Filters that are not based on real-time content-based identification of inappropriate content can be circumvented by users in a number of ways,[20] both direct and indirect:

---

[17]The distinction between overblocking and an overly broad scope of blocking is further complicated by the fact that from time to time, a given site can be used for multiple purposes. Most filters include adult-oriented Web sites in their "to be blocked" categories. However, a high school student undertaking, for example, a study of the economics of the adult online industry might have an entirely legitimate purpose for seeking access to such sites. More generally, any student wanting to study a controversial issue and needing to consult sources for different sides of an argument may well find that advocates of one point of view or another are blocked because they are regarded as "inappropriate"—where, in practice, "inappropriate" is likely to mean "controversial."

[18] See footnote 10.

[19]According to Grunwald Associates, 17.7 million children aged 2 to 17 had Internet access from home in the last quarter of 1999. (The Web site <http://cyberatlas.internet.com/big_picture/demographics/article/0,,5901_390941,00.html> provides a summary of the Grunwald study. The full study is available online at <http://www.grunwald.com/survey/index.htm>.) The U.S. Census indicates about 65.7 million children in the United States in this age bracket, for a percentage of about 27 percent.

[20]Many filtering products, especially those on the client side, are easily breakable by knowledgeable users. See Michael J. Miller, 2001, "When Does Web Filtering Make Sense?," *PC Magazine*, September 25, available online at <http://www.pcmag.com/article/0,2997,s%253D1499%2526a%253D12632,00.asp>.

- It may be possible to defeat the filter itself. When this occurs, a specific Web page that the filter should block is made accessible to the user. Defeating the filter may sometimes be accomplished by:
— Uninstalling the filter;
— Obtaining the privileges needed to disable the filter. While such privileges are intended for the parental supervisor (and are usually password-enabled), the ability of youth to obtain privileges is not uncommon in households in which the resident teenager serves as the de facto system administrator because of superior technical knowledge);
— Accessing the Web page indirectly through a proxy server,[21] a translation service, an anonymizing service, or some other route;
— Finding a click route to the page other than the one that was directly blocked; and/or
— Manipulating the reload/refresh and back/forward keys.

Note that defeating a filter can be more difficult when the filter is server-based, because the circumventer does not have direct access to the system on which the filter resides. Further, note that because a child-oriented content-limited ISP would most likely be chosen by families interested in filtering for fairly young children (say, 10 and younger), the likelihood that the ISP's restrictions could be circumvented is substantially lower than it would be if users included older youth.

In addition, inappropriate material (sexually explicit and otherwise) can flow to a child through routes other than Web sites—peer-to-peer file transfers such as those available through Gnutella, e-mail attachments, and so on. While some filters can be set to block the use of such routes, such blockage is indiscriminate and insensitive to the content carried on these routes.

- The user can obtain information that is generically similar to the information on the blocked Web page. As a general rule, information not associated with a specific source is resident on many locations on the World Wide Web, and the likelihood of all of those locations being blocked is low. These comments apply particularly to sexually explicit material, especially material containing images. An individual seeking explicit images for the purpose of sexual arousal is not particularly sensitive to which of hundreds or thousands of images on as many Web pages can be retrieved.

---

[21]A proxy server is a server that happens to be accessible from the client machine. The use of a proxy server, which can channel all requests "around" a server-side filter, can enable circumvention. Many local area networks, however, are configured in such a way as to prevent the use of proxy servers.

It is also true that the content provider could provide ways of circumventing filters. For example, misspelled sexual words (e.g., "pormography," "dicck," "0rgy") may be used in a site's metatags to circumvent filters that search for keywords. As a general rule, though, commercial vendors of sexually explicit material argue that they are not economically motivated to expend a lot of effort to get through these filters, because children are unable to pay for such material. Those providing other types of content without commercial intent may be more likely to attempt to circumvent filters.

Many of these methods of circumvention do not apply to filters that are based on real-time content-based identification of inappropriate content. However, filters that are based on real-time content-based identification are not nearly as commonly available as filters based on lists of inappropriate sites and keywords. Furthermore, the technology of content-based identification is relatively sophisticated compared to that required for developing lists of sites and keywords, and hence is more difficult to implement properly.

The effectiveness of label-based filters depends on the ubiquity of labels for Internet content and the willingness of the user to decide which labels indicate content that should be blocked. Label-based filters, such as those that incorporate PICS-compliant labels, are built into the major Web browsers, Internet Explorer (IE) and Netscape. However, PICS-compliant labels are not in wide use as of this writing (May 2002; but see Section 12.1.5). Both IE and Netscape provide the user with the option of allowing or blocking unlabeled material, with the consequence that users of these browsers can either have access only to a very small segment of the Web (if unlabeled material is blocked) or enjoy minimal protection from inappropriate material (if unlabeled material is allowed). For this reason, label-based filters today do not work particularly well in reducing exposure to inappropriate material unless one is willing to tolerate a very high rate of overblocking. Whether they will work more effectively in the future depends on the extent to which Internet content will be labeled.

While filters are designed to reduce children's access to inappropriate material on the Internet, there are some interesting psychological and social phenomena related to their use. In most of the schools and libraries that the committee visited, teachers, librarians, and administrators told the committee that filters played a very small role in protecting students and library users from inappropriate material, largely because most of these students and library users had unfiltered Internet access somewhere else (usually at home). (Of course, for the significant fraction of students without non-school access, such comments did not apply.[22]) Neverthe-

---

[22]U.S. public schools are increasingly providing Internet access to students outside regular school hours. For example, 80 percent of public secondary schools provided such a service in

less, the school or library filter served a useful political purpose in forestalling complaints from the community about "public facilities being used for shameful purposes."[23] In virtually every school the committee visited, avoiding controversy and/or liability for exposing children to inappropriate sexually explicit material was the primary reason offered for the installation of filters.[24]

In a public library setting, filters have also been used to prevent the display of material that would be regarded as offensive to other patrons walking by. For example, one technique used to shock other patrons is to display an adult-oriented Web site on a public Internet terminal and to "hide" it behind the terminal's screen saver (which places some innocuous image on the screen on top of whatever is on the screen). When an unsuspecting user clears the screen saver image, he or she is suddenly surprised by a sexually explicit image.[25]

Teachers and librarians can derive substantial benefit from filters. For example, most schools and libraries have acceptable use policies (AUPs, as discussed in Chapter 10) that forbid use of school or library computer resources for certain purposes, such as viewing sexually explicit sites. In the absence of a filter, a teacher or librarian must confront the user and inform him or her that such use violates the AUP. For many, such confrontations can be unpleasant and can provoke anxiety. To the

---

2000. In addition, schools with high minority enrollments provided Internet availability outside of regular school hours more frequently than schools with lower minority enrollments (61 percent versus 46 percent), a figure consistent with the notion that minority students may rely on schools to provide access more than do non-minority students. See A. Cattagni and E. Farris. 2001. *Internet Access in U.S. Public Schools and Classrooms: 1994-2000.* NCES 2001-071. Office of Educational Research and Improvement, U.S. Department of Education, Washington, D.C. Available online at <http://www.nces.ed.gov/ pubs2001/internetaccess/>.

[23]Indeed, in one community, the public library system provided filters for 10 to 20 percent of its Internet access points but made no special attempt to guide children toward these filtered workstations. Nevertheless, the presence of these filters on 10 to 20 percent of its workstations was sufficient to allow it to assert to the community that "the library provides filtered access," an assertion that seems to have met the concerns of local government.

[24]In the site visits of the committee, committee members explicitly avoided leading questions regarding the motivation for use. So, when teachers said, "Our school has filters" (which was true in all schools visited), committee members asked, "Why do you have them?" "What is the benefit having filters?" It is in this context that teachers said "to reduce exposure to liability." For the most part, the committee believes that given the overall context of all of the comments received in this manner (e.g., the accessibility of the Internet in unfiltered non-school venues for a large number of students), the avoidance of liability was indeed a primary or at least a very important reason for having filters in schools. Nevertheless, the committee recognizes the possibility that responders felt the protection benefits were so obvious so as not to need mentioning.

[25]Of course, a filter is not the only way to solve this particular problem—it would be almost as effective to install software that would clear the browser cache and return to the library's home page after a short period of inactivity.

extent that a filter reduces the possibility of a student or library patron viewing such sites, it also reduces the frequency of such confrontations. In addition, given community pressures for teachers and librarians to supervise or monitor the use of Internet resources by students and library users, filters reduce the burden on teachers and librarians to police usage and free time for other, more productive activities. Finally, many teachers and librarians are themselves uncomfortable in viewing certain types of inappropriate material[26]—and in the committee's informal discussions in its site visits, this was especially true for many sexually explicit images.

Even apart from the claimed benefits of preventing exposure to inappropriate material, filters can offer children other benefits. In the school environment, teachers reported that filters helped them to keep students "on task" while doing school-related Internet work by reducing the distractions that might otherwise be available to them (the students); Box 12.3 provides some data on the extent to which filters may keep students on task. A number of younger students with whom the committee spoke during various site visits thought that the parental use of filters (generally AOL's parental controls) was a positive indication of their parents' concern, independently of whether they felt the filters were effective. (According to the Kaiser Family Foundation, about two-thirds of teenagers and young adults support the Children's Internet Protection Act when provided with a description of it. This view does not vary among those who go online a lot or who have been denied access to Web sites because of filtering.[27])

Because they confine the user only to material explicitly considered appropriate, child-oriented content-limited ISPs provide the greatest degree of protection for children. By design, their approach seeks to minimize underblocking at the expense of overblocking—all questionable exposure is blocked or at least monitored. For example, they evaluate for educational or developmental benefit every Web page that is accessible to a child. Under these circumstances, the likelihood of exposure to inappropriate content is very low, especially with respect to sexual imagery. Interactive dialog in chat rooms and on bulletin boards is monitored, so that the first posting or sending of inappropriate messages can be censured. (Such censure also provides observers with a lesson in the conse-

---

[26]In a preliminary finding issued in May 2001, the Equal Employment Opportunity Commission found that pornography downloaded on library computers was intended to create a sexually hostile work environment for a group of Minneapolis librarians. See Michael Bartlett, 2001. "No Internet Filtering Is Sex Harassment for Librarians—EEOC," *Newsbytes*, May 25. Available online at <http://www.newsbytes.com/news/01/166171.html>.

[27]Victoria Rideout. 2001. *Generation Rx.com: How Young People Use the Internet for Health Information.* The Henry J. Kaiser Family Foundation, Menlo Park, Calif. Available online at <http://www.kff.org/content/2001/20011211a/GenerationRx.pdf>.

Box 12.3
Student Use of Filtered Internet Access at School

How do students actually use filtered Internet access at school? One study examined the usage in schools in which a given filtering system was used. In particular, the 300 most frequently accessed sites were examined, and these 300 sites accounted for "roughly half" of the total page views. For each instance of access to these 300 sites, the per-page viewing time was recorded, with the results shown below in the table below.

	Fraction of Total Page Views	Fraction of Over-all Time Spent on All 300 Sites	Average Time Spent on Site in This Category
Portals and search (sites that attempt to branch out and connect users with content)	56.8 percent	51.7 percent	46 s
Instructional reference and computing (sites that could be used for specific instructional purposes by teachers or students, general research and reference resources, and computer net work resources)	14.2 percent	20.0 percent (41.4 percent)	60 s
Music, games and fun (sites geared to entertainment and leisure)	10.6 percent	9.5 percent (19.7 percent)	48 s
Commerce and e-services (commercial sites offering products or online services)	10.5 percent	10.0 percent (20.7 percent)	51 s
News and sports (online versions of national news, sports magazines, local news)	5.0 percent	6.2 percent (12.8 percent)	50 s
Business and finance (financial news sites and online brokerage firms)	1.5 percent	1.9 percent (3.9 percent)	52 s
Communities (sites providing content targeted to specific demographic groups and typically containing a large amount of user-generated content such as chat and message boards)	1.4 percent	0.7 percent (1.4 percent)	44 s

According to these data, in-school Web access to sites related to e-commerce, chat and message board services, and recreational activities accounted for 20 percent of student activity. If access to portals and search engines is spread out proportionately over all other categories, non-educational Internet accesses accounted for 40 percent of student activity. Noting that these data are derived from schools in which a filtering system was in place, it is likely that the filter inhibited to some extent student use of inappropriate (and hence non-educational) sites, and so in the absence of the filter, the fraction of student Internet accesses spent on non-educational activities might have been higher than 40 percent. These data suggest that the presence of the filter does not keep students "on task" for much of their Internet time, but it is unknown what would have happened if the filter had not been present.

SOURCE: N2H, Inc. Analytic Services. 2000. *K-12 Internet Use*, N2H2 Winter Quarter, Learn-ings Report. Available online at <http://web.archive.org/web/20000930212613/www.n2h2.com/edwhite/edwhite.pdf>.

quences of such behavior.) The identities of e-mail and IM senders is not monitored, but because they are restricted for the most part to users of the service, the universe of those who might engage a child in e-mail or IM dialog is much smaller than on the entire Internet. Perhaps of equal or greater benefit, at least from the perspective of some adults, is that the content accessible to kids has definite educational or developmental value, rather than being simply not inappropriate.

12.1.3 Who Decides What Is Inappropriate?

Filtering is based on the premise that a party or parties other than the child himself or herself decides what content is inappropriate. In general, the first pass at determining potentially inappropriate content is the vendor of the filter or the content-limited ISP. For those who choose to accept without change this determination (as is the case with subscribers to content-limited ISPs or those who do not wish to customize further), this initial determination stands.

For example, a school that installs a filter without additional customization accepts the determination of the vendor about what is or is not appropriate. Even if it does undertake customization, it uses the vendor's determination as its point of departure, and detailed editorial control on a site-by-site basis for all sites in the vendor's database is not possible in practice.

To accommodate those who wish to customize the characterization of inappropriate material for their own individual or institutional needs, filter vendors usually offer two options (which may be combined or implemented by themselves):

• The characterization of inappropriate material can be divided into content categories with labels such as pornography, sex education, hate speech, violence, weapons, cults, and so on. (For example, a list of inappropriate URLs or keywords flagging inappropriate content might be grouped into such categories.) These filters then provide the user with the option of blocking or accepting content by category, so that a user can, for example, block only pornography and hate speech while accepting all other content categories. Category-by-category blocking obviously reduces the list of blocked URLs to a subset of the original list.

• Some filters enable the end user (or, more precisely, the end-user supervisor who knows the appropriate password) to create a local "exceptions" list, which specifies additional URLs to be blocked or URLs that should be allowed even if they are on the blocked list. For example, despite the filter, a child may view a URL that the supervisor deems inappropriate. A filter with this option enables the supervisor to add that

URL to the list of blocked sites. If a child is blocked from viewing a particular site, it may be apparent from the description accompanying the original link (e.g., as displayed by a search engine) or from the site name in the link that the site should not be blocked. In this case, a "user override" can be used to unblock the site. For practical purposes, the number of such sites that are either added to or subtracted from the original list is small compared to the size of the original list.

The vendor's characterization of inappropriate content is quite significant, as it is at the very least the primary point of departure for a user's customization (described below) even when such customization is possible.[28] Filter vendors have many incentives to err on the side of overblocking and few to err on the side of underblocking. Based on its site visits, the committee believes that the reason is that schools and libraries, which are the largest users of filters for purposes of this report, tend to receive many more complaints from parents and the community about sites that are not filtered (i.e., complaints about underblocking) than about sites that are filtered improperly (i.e., complaints about overblocking).[29]

---

[28]One concern raised by analysts such as Nancy Willard is that filter vendors sometimes have strong connections to religious organizations, and that the social and cultural values espoused by these organizations may drive the vendor's characterization of inappropriate content. For example, Willard finds that "most of the companies have filtering categories in which they are blocking web sites . . . known to be of concern to people with conservative religious values—such as [Web sites involving] non-traditional religions and sexual orientation—in the same category as material that no responsible adult would consider appropriate for young people." She also notes that "because filtering software companies protect the actual list of blocked sites, searching and blocking key words, blocking criteria, and blocking processes as confidential, proprietary trade secret information it is not possible to prove or disprove the hypothesis that the companies may be blocking access to material based on religious bias." At the same time, Willard finds that while "information about the religious connections can be found through diligent search, such information is not clearly evident on the corporate web site or in materials that would provide the source of information for local school officials," though she acknowledges openly that "it is entirely appropriate for conservative religious parents or schools to decide to use the services of an ISP that is blocking sites based on conservative religious values. It is equally appropriate for parents to want their children to use the Internet in school in a manner that is in accord with their personal family values." See Nancy Willard, 2002, *Filtering Software: The Religious Connection*, Center for Advanced Technology in Education, College of Education, University of Oregon, available online at <http://netizen.uoregon.edu/documents/religious2.html>.

[29]As with so many other "null" observations, the absence of complaints about overblocking can be interpreted in many ways. One interpretation is, of course, that overblocking simply does not occur very much (and/or that filters do not block a great deal of useful and appropriate information). But information collected through site visits is not consistent with this interpretation, and testimony to the committee suggests other explanations as well. For example, the relative lack of complaints may be partly explained by the

In the various site visits conducted by the committee, only a few students or parents reported making a formal complaint to the school about a site needed for research or schoolwork that was blocked by a school's filter, even though they (mostly high school students) often reported that information on the blocked sites might have been useful for legitimate academic research purposes.[30]   (The same was not true with most teachers, who reported that educationally relevant sites were blocked regularly. Still, in a number of cases, they were able to use their supervisory privileges to obtain access to blocked sites.) And, given that schools and libraries install filters largely to forestall complaints, it is clear that filters that do not generate complaints would be highly preferred.

As for label-based filters, the labeling party can be either the content creator or any third party. However, it is the adult or adults directly responsible for determining what a child should or should not see who make the actual decision about how content labeled in a certain manner should be handled.

Because the vendor's philosophy regarding inappropriate material is the primary determinant of what will and will not be blocked, trust is a fundamental element in the user's selection of a filter. That is, the user places considerable trust in the vendor's judgment about what is and is not appropriate (or in the case of labeling, places trust in the labels determined by various content raters). Thus, a person who wishes his or her religious values to be reflected in the content that is accessible to his or her children might choose a filter or a content-limited ISP that is sold by a firm with similar religious commitments. A person who wishes his or her children's Internet experience to be limited to positive, developmentally

---

fact that filters for institutional use are increasingly flexible (see Section 12.1.4). If blocked pages that are needed for educational purposes, for example, can be obtained quickly (e.g., in a matter of minutes), the issue of overblocking need not be as salient. (One school system told the committee that a filter used previously had not allowed such flexibility and had resulted in a large number of complaints from teachers and students. Other faculty and librarians in other locations told the committee that unblocking sites was cumbersome and difficult.) A second reason for the lack of complaints is likely to be the fact that once a filter is in place, the expectation of users is that access will be filtered. The committee heard stories of a number of complaints regarding filtering when filters were first installed, but in most such instances, the complaints ceased after a few months. Students without home Internet access seemed to accept a school's filtering policy as a given, and simply adapted to it, even if they were prevented from accessing valuable information. One librarian told the committee that a blocked Web page was analogous to a book that was not present in the library, and that the alternative approaches to obtaining the information were similar to using interlibrary loan. Students with Internet access at home have no particular reason or incentive to complain aside from issues of efficiency or convenience.

[30]In general, when students encountered blocked sites at school, they simply went to another venue to reach those sites—most of the students to whom the committee spoke had unfiltered home access.

appropriate, and educational material may choose a filter or a content-limited ISP that explicitly screens content for such criteria, rather than another vendor that might screen content for inappropriateness.

Finally, "viewpoint discrimination" (discussed in Chapter 4) generally cannot be practiced by public institutions, but the law in this area is currently unclear. In particular, it is not clear how a court would decide whether a public institution's use of a particular filter vendor's determinations of inappropriate material constitutes such discrimination—for instance, where the line is drawn between viewpoint discrimination and content discrimination, and what weight should be given to the extent to which the institution relied upon the filter vendor's settings. It is also not clear to what extent public schools, as opposed to public libraries, may engage in certain kinds of viewpoint discrimination.

12.1.4 How Flexible and Usable Is the Product?

Server-side filters can be easier to use than client-side filters, if only because they do not require installation on the client. Nevertheless, almost all filters allow some degree of customization to a parent's (or other adult supervisor's) requirements. Filters can (but do not necessarily) allow flexibility in many dimensions:

• *Changes to the criteria used for blocking.* Sites or keywords to identify inappropriate material can be added or subtracted by the end user: when a filter program erroneously blocks a site, or fails to block something the user deems inappropriate, the parent or other administrator of the program can create an exception list that deletes or adds the site from or to the black list. An important consideration is the extent to which the blocking criteria are known to the user. While nearly all filter vendors provide a list of categories that are blocked, very few provide a public list of all of the sites on their default "to be blocked" list,[31] and to the committee's knowledge, no filter

---

[31]In general, they protect the list by encrypting it and had hoped that the Digital Millennium Copyright Act (DMCA) would outlaw reverse engineering to decrypt such lists. However, on October 27, 2000, the U.S. Copyright Office issued its final rule implementing the anti-circumvention provisions of the DMCA. The statutory provisions of DMCA prohibit the circumvention of technical measures that prevent the unauthorized copying, transmission, or accessing of copyrighted works, subject to this rulemaking of the Copyright Office. The final rule establishes two exceptions to the anti-circumvention provisions, one of which allows users of Internet content filtering programs to view lists of Web sites blocked by such software. The Copyright Office recognized a First Amendment interest in access to this information and stated the need for circumvention in this instance "since persons who wish to criticize and comment on them cannot ascertain which sites are contained in the lists unless they circumvent." This exception to the DMCA rule may have an impact on the ongoing public debate about filters. In March 2000, two programmers who revealed the list of thousands of Web sites blocked by the Internet filtering program CyberPatrol faced charges of copyright violation.

vendor provides a list of the objectionable words sought in keyword searches. Most companies that do not release the list of blocked sites regard such lists as intellectual property and argue that the non-release protects the effort that went into creating them. However, if users of these products do not know the criteria explicitly, they will know that sites are blocked only when access to those sites is blocked and they are told that they have been blocked. Thus, they cannot make an a priori determination of such a filter's fitness for use.

• *Ease of making authorized changes.* A filter to which anyone can make changes would not be very useful. In general, the ability to make changes is restricted to "authorized parties." The effort and time needed to implement a change can vary. Some filtering systems allow individuals (e.g., teachers, librarians) with the appropriate password to add or subtract a site or a keyword essentially instantaneously. Others require the submission of a request to the filter vendor—which then evaluates the request and implements it or not at its discretion, a process that may take days or even longer. For educational purposes, the former is likely to be much better than the latter. On the other hand, increasing the effort needed to implement a change is likely to reduce the number of changes to the original filtering policy, an outcome that may be regarded as a benefit for those who want to enforce a uniform policy, or who have little faith that adult supervisors will act judiciously.

• *Granularity of content categories.* Different vendors divide "inappropriate" material into different categories, using more or fewer categories depending on their intended user base. Categories may be divided into subcategories (e.g., "sex" might be divided into "pornography" and "sex education," or nudity might be differentiated as "full frontal nudity" versus "partial nudity").

• *Age or grade differentiation.* As discussed in Chapter 5, information that is inappropriate for one age or grade level may not be inappropriate for older ages or higher grade levels. (Specifically, the information needs of high school students are typically different from those of students in middle school.) Some filters allow more or less restrictive filtering depending on age or grade.

• *Individually configured filtering policies.* In a home context, a parent might wish to have different filtering policies (or none at all) for children of different ages. (Such differences would reflect the parent's belief that older children with more maturity and a broader scope of information needs might also require broader and less restricted Internet access.) To support different filtering policies, a filter would require the child to log into the system so that the child's individual filtering profile could be used. Individual policies can also support age or grade differentiation—requiring a student to log in with his or her grade (or associating a grade with an individual login). In a library context, an age-appropriate filtering policy might require the system to ask the user if he or she were over 18, and if under 18, ask the user to enter his or her age, thus providing the information necessary to set an age-appropriate policy.

Many filtering products add a variety of features meant to offer parents, teachers, and others even further control. Some of these include:

• *Time windows for blocking.* Under some circumstances, the inappropriateness of a site may depend on the time of day. For example, in a school environment, sites referring to games and media entertainment may be inappropriate during school hours (because they constitute "off-task" material) but appropriate in an after-school program in which Internet usage may be less restricted.

• *Records or logs of attempted access to inappropriate materials.* To understand patterns of usage, records of attempted access may be kept. Note that such records, if individual logins are not used, can reflect attempted usage only from a given access point; further, if individual logins are not used, no records can be matched to individuals.

• *Bi-directional filtering.* Some filters enable the blocking of certain outgoing user-entered information, such as phone numbers, addresses, foul language, and so on. Such blocking can be used to promote the safety of children and to enforce prohibitions against giving out such information. In addition, some filters can block certain types of Internet access entirely: instant messages, e-mail, chat rooms, file transfers, and so on. As noted in Chapters 2 and 5, e-mail, chat rooms, and instant messages allow the child to send as well as to receive, and thus to engage in text-based interaction with other parties. File transfers allow images, video clips, and sound files to be sent and received. Usenet newsgroups—similar to bulletin boards—contain a great deal of content that is un moderated and inappropriate for children by the standards of many adults.

In general, flexibility adds to the complexity of the filter—usually in its initial configuration and sometimes for its use. For example, there is debate about whether consumers prefer less nuanced granularity and simpler choices, or prefer to have detailed control over their filtering. Some products have garnered praise for offering a simple age-by-age default set of parameters on what to block that may then be overridden with more levels of nuance.

In a number of filter-using sites visited by the committee, the flexibility of an installed product (especially the ability to unblock selected Web sites) was not used by administrators and teachers. In some cases, they were simply unaware of the capability; in others, they lacked either the time or the knowledge to do so. In still other cases, the ability to unblock sites was limited to district-level administrators (rather than the local administrators or teachers). During site visits, a number of teachers told the committee that requests sent to district-level administrators to override sites often met with resistance, and were slowly acted on and often refused. Furthermore, to the extent that flexibility is tailored for different individuals (e.g., for middle school students versus high school students), identification of these individuals is required—and the appropriate policy must be mapped to the access points of those individuals.

An additional dimension of functionality is the provision of explanations for blocking. A site that is blocked for no apparent reason has a lower perceived legitimacy than a site that is blocked for a stated reason. For example, many filters tell the user that a site has been blocked because it falls into Category X, where X may be pornography, sex education, weapons, violence, and so on. By contrast, a site that is blocked simply with the message "access denied" does not provide the child with useful feedback, and may increase his or her motivation to go to a nonblocked access device to retrieve the information. Note that filtered search engines provide the lowest level of transparency of all—because a filtered search engine never returns even a link to content that is deemed inappropriate, the user has no way of knowing what has been filtered out or even that anything has been filtered out.

12.1.5 What Are the Costs of and the Infrastructure Required for Filtering?

Financial Costs

As with all technology deployments, the financial costs of using filters can be divided into acquisition costs and maintenance costs. Acquisition costs can be quite low, especially for server-based filters in which an installation of the filter at each access point need not be undertaken. Maintenance costs of server-side filters are usually absorbed into a per-year per-seat charge.

However, payments to the vendor are not the only cost, as some onsite effort must be made to ensure that filters are working properly. Onsite technical support is generally necessary. Management of the environment must be taken into account as well—in particular, teachers, librarians, and parents may be faced with managing requests to unblock sites that are blocked. In an institutional environment, there are costs of teaching the responsible adults what the filter can and cannot do, and providing training that familiarizes them with operating in a filtered environment. When filtering impedes their own legitimate searches for information, they must know how to obtain that information despite the presence of filtering. And, for those institutions that rely on centralized (e.g., district-based) administration of the unblocking function, the staff time needed to manage these decisions can be significant (and hence costly).

Use of content-limited ISPs appears to entail fewer financial costs than the use of server-side or client-side filters. Because the major selling point of using a filtered ISP is that the user gets to delegate to another party all of the responsibilities of deciding upon and enforcing a filtering policy, it is likely that users will be comfortable for the most part with the default policy of the filtered ISP. Thus, the costs of filtered ISPs for this class of users will be relatively small. Also, filtered ISPs makes the cost of updating the filtering algorithm or database invisible to most users.

One trend pushing toward the lowering of filtering costs is that the basic technology of filtering is increasingly available in certain common hardware products. For example, a variety of hardware routers for home or small office use (generally to support a small local area network at a home or office site) have native site-based filtering capabilities (that is, they have the ability to exclude traffic from specified sites). Some also have the ability to search for objectionable keywords embedded into site URLs. If trends toward hardware-based filtering continue, such filtering may well become ubiquitous. If and when vendors of these hardware products provide these routers with lists of sites to be blocked, with updates as a service to purchasers, the cost may well drop significantly.

Restrictions on Information Flow

As noted in Chapter 5, it is likely that in most communities there would be a rough consensus on some kinds of sexually explicit material on the Internet that should be made unavailable to children. But on other kinds of sexually explicit material, such consensus would be unlikely. Moreover, some of such material would undoubtedly constitute protected speech according to established First Amendment interpretations.

The discussion in Section 12.1.2 points out that overblocking is inherent in any process that makes decisions about what to filter (so is underblocking, but underblocking is not a restriction on information). Thus, for inappropriate sexually explicit material that might loosely be classified as "for adults only," some material that should not be placed into this category will be—and will therefore be improperly blocked.

Filter vendors often provide options for blocking entire categories in addition to the category of sexually explicit material: violence, weapons, pro-choice and anti-abortion material, gay and lesbian lifestyles, and so on. Much of the material in these categories does not fit the legal definition of material that is "obscene with respect to minors," but based in the default setting of many filters, would be blocked anyway. While this restriction is not a legal problem in the context of home use, it may present a problem in publicly funded institutions, which are constrained by the requirements and current interpretations of the First Amendment.[32]

In an educational context, the restrictions on information flow associated with filters may lead to substantial problems for teachers and librarians who are trying to develop useful and relevant educational activities, assignments, projects, and so on. Indeed, some teachers reported to the committee during site visits that sometimes their lesson preparations were hampered by the fact that their Internet access was filtered at school. In other cases, when they prepared a lesson plan at home (with unfiltered Internet access), they were unable to present it at school because a site they found at home was inaccessible using school computers.

Restrictions on information flow may also reduce the benefits of the Internet as an information retrieval mechanism. Specifically, one of the advantages of the Internet is that it facilitates the comparison of how different sources treat a given topic. While it is true that there are often many unblocked sources for basic information (and hence blocking any one of these sources may not be critical in this context),[33] advanced work in which the specific source providing information affects its presentation or credibility is more adversely affected by overblocking. Such might also be the case when alternative political points of view or analyses may be blocked as being inappropriate.

Psychological Costs

Another potentially major cost of filters is that their use reduces opportunities for young people to practice responsible behavior on their own. That is, to the extent that filters work as they are intended (i.e., they block rather than discourage access to material that may be inappropriate), children have fewer opportunities to choose—and thus fewer oppor-

---

[32]A study by the Kaiser Family Foundation found that among teenagers aged 15 to 17 who have sought health information online, 46 percent reported that they experienced blocking from sites that they believed were non-pornographic. For example, 15 percent of those who were blocked reported that they were searching for information on sexual health topics. See Rideout, 2001, *Generation Rx.com: How Young People Use the Internet for Health Information*.

[33]Because of keyword filtering, sites containing certain keywords may be blocked. However, synonyms to these keywords may not be filtered, and sites with these synonyms will not be blocked.

tunities to learn how to make responsible decisions. Such children may well have greater difficulty in developing internal standards of appropriateness. In addition, while some youth have reported that the use of filtering by their parents makes them feel loved, others have reported that it makes them feel untrusted by their parents.

Filters also create forbidden fruit—in this context, specific content that is made (more) desirable simply because it is inaccessible. A common response to forbidden fruit is to engage in more active and determined efforts to obtain it. Given the technological sophistication of some teenagers, these efforts often succeed. Even worse, from the standpoint of minimizing exposure of children to such material, the results of technical circumvention efforts are often widely circulated, with the ultimate effect of greater exposure to inappropriate material rather than less, at least within the immediate circle of individuals close to those with the necessary skills.

The introduction of filters may also serve to create resentments and resistance among the children to whom they are targeted. That is, because filters are explicitly intended to limit one's freedom of access, it is entirely possible that introducing filters, especially into an environment in which unrestricted access was the rule, would create tensions and anger in the children against those responsible for the decision. This dynamic is likely to be most significant in a family environment, in which parental rules are generally negotiated to some extent with children.

Finally, unfair treatment of youth can result from the use of filters. A young Internet user, knowing that the Web sites she or he is viewing are filtered, can make the reasonable assumption that what is not filtered conforms to parental or organizational policy (e.g., an acceptable use policy, as discussed in Chapter 10), and thus that access to those unfiltered sites is not restricted. However, because filters inevitably allow some inappropriate material to pass, this may not be a good assumption, and a child who relies on a filter that allows objectionable material to be viewed can get into trouble with parents or organizational authority.

Infrastructure

Because a critical issue in filtering is the extent of underblocking and overblocking, users are well advised to test in advance what may be improperly blocked or passed. Apart from this predeployment testing, source- or content-based filters require minimal infrastructure. However, label-based filters require content providers or third parties to cooperate in labeling content. To develop such an infrastructure, providers and third parties must have incentives to label content. The minimal success of labeling schemes for Internet content to date suggests that the present environment does not provide such incentives.[34]

Note also that labeling by third parties entails essentially the same type of effort that must be undertaken by filter vendors to develop lists or criteria for inappropriate content. For labeling to be useful, a large volume of information must be examined and rated; otherwise, the user is left with the choices described in Section 12.1.3.

Recognizing that the primary impediment to the success of rating schemes is the extent to which Internet content is currently not labeled, the Internet Content Rating Association (ICRA) has undertaken a global effort to promote a voluntary self-labeling system through which content providers identify and label their content using predefined, cross-cultural categories (Box 12.4). ICRA is a global, non-profit organization of Internet industry leaders committed to making the Internet safer for children while respecting the rights of content providers.

According to ICRA's chief executive officer, ICRA hopes that over the next several years the most popular Web sites and portals, those accounting for the most Internet traffic, will have labeled with ICRA. If these efforts are successful, ICRA labels will be associated with sites that account for a large fraction of Web traffic, though not necessarily with a large fraction of existing Web sites. The operators of these sites will encourage their business partners and the sites they host to use ICRA labeling. (However, because these sites do not in general have a business relationship with other Web sites that might turn up through use of their search engines, these other Web sites cannot be expected to be labeled in general.)

Another approach is to mandate—by government fiat—the labeling of all Web content. But such an approach involves a number of significant issues:

- Such compelled speech raises important First Amendment issues.
- The enforcement of label accuracy is complex. Even labels created by the content owner may be inaccurate.
- The volume of Web information is so large that a government mandate requiring labeling would impose an enormous expense on content providers.

---

[34]It is interesting to note that industry labeling initiatives in other media have been more successful and widely accepted and used; these other media include movies (through the MPAA), TV (through a joint effort of the Motion Picture Association of America, the National Association of Broadcasters, and the National Cable Television Association), and software CD-ROMs and games (through the Interactive Games Developers Association). One reason for this success is that the volume of content produced in these media is much smaller than the volume of content produced for the Web.

Box 12.4
The Labeling System of the Internet Content Rating Association

The Internet Content Rating Association (ICRA) labeling system takes the presence or absence of the following factors into account in generating content labels:

Nudity and Sexual Material

Erections or female genitals in detail
Male genitals
Female genitals
Female breasts
Bare buttocks
Explicit sexual acts
Obscured or implied sexual acts
Visible sexual touching
Passionate kissing
None of the above

Context this material . . .
• Appears in a context intended to be artistic and is suitable for young children
• Appears in a context intended to be educational and is suitable for young children
• Appears in a context intended to be medical and is suitable for young children

Other Topics

Promotion of tobacco use
Promotion of alcohol use
Promotion of drug use
Gambling
Promotion of weapon use
Promotion of discrimination or harm against people
Material that might be perceived as setting a bad example for young children
Material that might disturb young children
None of the above

Violence

Sexual violence/rape
Blood and gore, human beings
Blood and gore, animals
Blood and gore, fantasy characters (including animation)
Killing of human beings
Killing of animals
Killing of fantasy characters (including animation)
Deliberate injury to human beings
Deliberate injury to animals
Deliberate injury to fantasy characters (including animations)
Deliberate damage to objects
None of the above

Context—this material . . .
• Appears in a context intended to be artistic and is suitable for young children
• Appears in a context intended to be educational and is suitable for young children
• Appears in a context intended to be medical and is suitable for young children
• Appears only in a sports-related context

Language

Explicit sexual language
Crude words or profanity
Mild expletives
None of the above

Chat

Chat
Moderated chat suitable for children and teens
Neither of the above

SOURCE: See <http://www.icra.org>).

• Web content can be posted in many different national jurisdictions, and it would be easy for content creators and providers to evade such a mandate by moving offshore.

Apart from government-required content labeling, the widespread use of labels will turn on private incentives. Incentives can be positive—by labeling, a content provider or creator could receive some financial benefit, either directly or by attracting more parties to its content. However, the committee did not see a compelling business case for how content providers or creators can benefit commercially from labeling, and testimony to the committee indicated how difficult it is to develop child-friendly Internet businesses. Or, incentives can be negative—by labeling, a content provider or creator might receive immunity from prosecution (for example, for obscenity) for the content being labeled (e.g., as adults-only). Such a safe harbor might be particularly applicable in labeling of sexually explicit material (as discussed in Section 9.3).

To date, child-centered content-limited ISPs are small enterprises, and many efforts to establish a viable business model for providing good, attractive, and educational content for kids have foundered, as noted in Chapter 10.[35] Thus, it is an open question whether children will be able to take advantage of consistent, dependable, long-term service of this nature Note also that because content is explicitly vetted for appropriateness, it is likely that the content offered by such ISPs would be more limited—and hence more suitable for younger children whose information needs are generally less than those of older children.

By contrast, certain Internet portals, such as Yahoo and Lycos, have search engines that search only within the appropriate (and educational) child-oriented universe of content. Available for free, these search engines return only links to appropriate and educational content, and as long as the child does not surf outside these links, a responsible adult can have confidence in his or her child's activity.

12.1.6 What Does the Future Hold for Filtering?

Image-Only Filtering

Visual imagery often results in a highly visceral impact compared to textual descriptions of the same image. As discussed in Section 6.3.3, males tend to respond to visual sexual imagery more than females do.

---

[35]Of course, entrepreneurs in other areas are also struggling to find viable long-term Internet business models.

And, as a general rule, sexually explicit text does not generate nearly the same controversy that sexually explicit imagery generates.[36]

A filter that blocks images on Web pages that have been determined to be inappropriate rather than all of the content of the Web pages themselves is thus well suited to meet this concern. Most of today's filters block specific Web pages, based on criteria established by their filtering policies. But there is no technical reason that the filter could not instead block all images contained on those Web pages, while passing through all text on those pages. (However, icons and text rendered in image format, such as those in banner advertisements and sidebars, would be blocked as well. And, concerns about overbreadth of blocking would remain, so that given images of the Greek gods, Leonardo DaVinci's Vetruvian man, paintings by Rubens, and Michelangelo's David might still be blocked.)

Such a filter addresses many of the concerns raised by students, teachers, and librarians about children who need information that would otherwise be blocked by a page-blocking filter; as a general rule, such information is presented textually and would be passed by an image-blocking filter. Of course, to the extent that the concerns of filter advocates involve text, an image-blocking filter is not helpful.

A more sophisticated approach to filtering of embedded images would involve analyzing them. Very small images are likely to be only icons, and very small images (say 200 x 200 pixels) do not convey much excitement. The content of larger images could be analyzed using technology described in Section 2.3.1 and Appendix C, and if found to be sexually explicit, those images would be blocked (subject to all of the difficulties inherent in image recognition).

Selective Degradation of Service

As discussed in Chapter 8, it is possible to reduce the appeal of deliberate contact with inappropriate material. Such an approach changes the yes/no approach to filtering to one in which the user can still gain access to material that might have been improperly classified as inappropriate, but only at some cost. Two easy technical methods to do so are slowing down the speed with which images of offensive content are displayed or reducing the visual resolution (or the audio fidel-

---

[36]In the future, it may be possible that other kinds of content (e.g., sound files associated with sexually explicit content) will be regarded as being as objectionable as images. (Recall that "dial-a-porn" services had some appeal for adolescent youth, and that the availability of such services to minors created significant controversy in the early 1990s.) If that future comes to pass, the media containing such particularly objectionable content might also be selectively blocked (e.g., by blocking all sound files on sexually explicit Web pages).

ity) of such images. Presuming that such content can be identified, a child who must wait a few minutes for an image to be displayed is likely to lose patience with it. Such a tactic is most relevant if the child knows that the image being sought is inappropriate—it reduces the immediate gratification usually available from Internet downloads, and it increases the risk of being discovered in the act. (It also provides more time for the child to reflect—Do I really want to do this? Am I being responsible?) Similarly, an image of significantly reduced resolution is far less appealing than one with high resolution. Another possible approach depends on penalizing the user after viewing inappropriate content by automatically logging out, freezing the computer so that a reboot is necessary, or simply delaying for several minutes the child's accessing of other Internet content.

Approaches that depend on degradation of service force the child to make decisions about whether the cost and inconvenience of access are worth the appeal of accessing content that adults might deem inappropriate.

Bundling Filters with Other Functionality

Filters are a special-purpose tool. Parents and others who purchase and install filters or filtering services thus can be assumed to feel that the problems raised by unfiltered Internet access are worrisome enough to warrant such efforts. However, other individuals may be concerned but reluctant to foster resistance or resentment that their introduction might generate (as discussed under "Psychological Costs" in Section 12.1.5). For such individuals, associating filters with packages that provide other useful features may make it easier to obtain the benefits of filtering. For example, parents wishing to obtain filtering services might subscribe to a content-limited ISP, and "sell" it to their children on the basis of additional content that the ISP would make available to them.

Warning Rather Than Blocking

Built into any filter is a specification of content that should be blocked. Instead of blocking access, a filter could warn the child of impending access to inappropriate material, but leave it to his or her discretion whether or not to access the material. Because the child does have choices, such a feature would have pedagogical advantages with respect to helping children to make responsible choices, assuming an environment structured in a way to facilitate such assistance. (A feature to warn of impending access to inappropriate material might or might not be combined with logging of such access—a point discussed in Section 12.2 below.)

Opportunities for Internet Safety Education

Because child-oriented content-limited ISPs are oriented toward providing information especially for kids, they provide unique opportunities for Internet safety education. For example, these opportunities might include material that provided context for children and explained concepts about judging the value and or validity of the site being flagged or blocked.

Future Prospects

Over time, filtering is likely to gradually improve, decreasing both underblocking and overblocking. However, these improvements will almost certainly be incremental rather than revolutionary, and users would be well advised to view with some skepticism claims of revolutionary improvement. (For example, the phenomenon of blocking breast cancer sites because a user performed a search for "breast" is now rare. However, the reason this particular error is no longer frequent is that many users complained about it, and breast cancer sites were specifically taken off the black list.[37])

One goal is quite unlikely to be met—the generation of a class of objectionable or inappropriate material from a single example. It would be highly desirable for a user who has received an objectionable image (for example) to be able to tell a filtering program, "I don't want to see any more stuff like this." But what counts as "like this" is virtually impossible to generalize from one example, which is why even the best training systems today require hundreds or thousands of samples of objectionable material to offer any hope of even a minimally adequate categorization of material.

12.1.7 What Are the Implications of Filtering Use?

Today's filters cannot be the sole element of any approach to protecting children from inappropriate sexually explicit material on the Internet

---

[37]The first widespread instance of such blocking occurred in 1995 when a major online service provider blocked all sites containing the word "breast," including those dealing with breast cancer. In the wake of widespread complaints, the service provider in question quickly restored access to breast cancer sites. Since then, this particular problem has occurred only rarely, as a number of techniques described in Section 2.3.1 can be used to avoid problems arising from simple-minded keyword matching. Still, the problem has not been eliminated entirely, and a recent instance of a Web site involving breast cancer being blocked was brought to the committee's attention in January 2002 (personal communication, Bennett Haselton, Peacefire.org). In this instance, the reason for such blocking apparently arises from the use of IP-based virtual hosting.

(or any other inappropriate material), and it is highly unlikely that to-morrow's filters will be able to serve this role either. But they can be a useful element, as long as their limitations are kept in perspective. In particular, with or without filters, Internet-using children will have op-portunities for encountering some non-zero amount of inappropriate material, and thus regardless of the benefits that filters do confer, they will have to internalize codes of conduct and appropriate online behavior if they are to be safe.

Using a child-oriented content-limited ISP is approximately analo-gous to allowing a child to watch only selected videos on television, rather than broadcast or cable television. And, as in that case, the use of such a practice is most likely appropriate for fairly young children. However, as a child's Internet information needs outgrow what a kid-friendly service can provide, he or she will have to turn to other sources. Other sources—by definition—will provide information that is less thoroughly vetted, and will likely involve exposure of the now-older child to some inappro-priate information; however, an older child may well be better able to cope with inadvertent exposures to such material. Furthermore, there is no guarantee that the point at which a child's information needs outgrow a kid-friendly service will coincide with the point at which he or she can cope well with such exposure, and it is likely that the former point occurs earlier than the latter point.

As for server- and client-side filtering, it is helpful to regard such filtering as "training wheels" for children on the Internet as they learn to make good decisions about what materials are and are not appropriate for their consumption. An adult who explains the purpose of the filter to the child (and different explanations are appropriate at different ages), and who can provide some in-person guidance when the child first encoun-ters blocked material, is in a much better position to help the child inter-nalize the rules than an adult or institution that simply installs the filter with no explanation or rationale either before or after the fact. Indeed, the latter situation is what the detractors of filters have in mind when they argue that the use of filters can lead to a false sense of security: a filter user (parent, library, school), knowing that a filter is in place, will then be tempted to assume that all is well, and then fail to exercise appropriate oversight or to take other measures when such oversight or other mea-sures would still be necessary.

Underlying much of the concern about the deployment of filters—even on a voluntary basis—is a fear that the creation of a technical infra-structure that supports filtering will inexorably, over time, lead to even stronger pressures for formal content regulation (a so-called "slippery slope" argument).

Furthermore, even without the pressures for formal content regulation, those advocating the free flow of information are concerned that authorities (parents, schools, libraries, businesses, and others) will find the use of filters irresistible to block any kind of content or information that they find objectionable, and not just for children. (Just such a sequence of events was related to the committee in one of its site visits: a county-wide library system installed filters to block sexually explicit material from all patrons, not just children, though the concerns were first raised in the context of children's access to such material.)

12.1.8 Findings on Filters

1. Filters have some significant utility in denying access to content that may be regarded as inappropriate. However, many of today's youth have access to unfiltered Internet venues (e.g., at home, at a friend's house), and school and library filters do not block content accessed from these other venues.

2. All filters—those of today and for the foreseeable future—suffer (and will suffer) from some degree of overblocking (blocking content that should be allowed through) and some degree of underblocking (passing content that should not be allowed through). While the extent of overblocking and underblocking will vary with the product (and may improve over time), underblocking and overblocking result from numerous sources, including the variability in the perspectives that humans bring to the task of judging content.

3. Filters are capable of blocking inappropriate sexually explicit material at a high level of effectiveness—if a high rate of overblocking is also acceptable. Thus, filters are a reasonable choice for risk-averse parents or custodians (e.g., teachers) who place a very high priority on preventing exposure to such material and who are willing to accept the consequences of such overblocking. (For example, these individuals may be more inclined to take such a stance if the children in question are young.) Such consequences may include the blocking of some material that would be mistakenly classified as inappropriate sexually explicit material, and/or the blocking of entire categories of material that are protected by the First Amendment (a consequence of more concern to publicly funded institutions such as public libraries than to individual families).

4. Automated decision making about access is generally inferior to decision making with a responsible adult involved in the decision-making process. Furthermore, to the extent that the content of concern is in multimedia formats and unaccompanied by textual descriptions, automated decision making is subject to a high degree of overblocking (iden-

tifying content as objectionable when it is benign) and underblocking (identifying content as benign when it is objectionable).

5. To the extent that Internet content is created or produced in real time (e.g., a live videoconference over Webcams), it will be impractical to insert a human reviewer into the decision making process about whether access to that content should or should not be granted—thus weakening the role that filters play.

6. Overblocking must be distinguished from overly broad blocking policies. Overblocking is a mistake—content is blocked that should not have been blocked, even in the judgment of the human being responsible for identifying content that should be blocked (the censor). Overly broad blocking policy represents a disagreement with that human being in which the content seeker asserts that certain content should be accessible and the censor believes that content should be blocked.

7. Based on information gathered in its site visits, the committee believes that filters are deployed by schools and libraries at least as much for political and management reasons as for the protection of children, because the deployment of filters enables staff to pay more attention to teaching and serving library patrons.

8. Because most filters are deployed to forestall complaints, and complaints are more likely to be received about underblocking rather than overblocking, filter vendors have more incentive to block content that may be controversial than to be careful about not blocking content that should not be blocked.

9. Transparency of operation is important, in the sense that filters that inform a user that a site is being blocked—and that provides the reason for blocking—are more likely to be seen as legitimate than those that do not provide such information.

10. The use of blocking filters does not promote the development of responsible choice in children. With removal of the option of making certain choices, children are denied an opportunity to choose—and hence do not learn appropriate decision making skills from the fact of blocking.

11. Filters are a complement to but not a substitute for responsible adult supervision. Using filters without adult supervision and/or instruction for users in what constitutes appropriate behavior is not likely to result in children learning what is or is not appropriate behavior. Furthermore, filters cannot guarantee that inappropriate material will not be accessed.

12.2 MONITORING

Tools that provide monitoring of the Internet activities of children have been proposed by some as an alternative to filters in certain con-

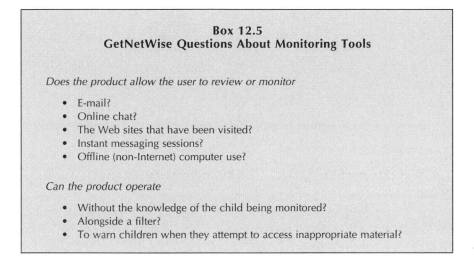

Box 12.5
GetNetWise Questions About Monitoring Tools

Does the product allow the user to review or monitor

- E-mail?
- Online chat?
- The Web sites that have been visited?
- Instant messaging sessions?
- Offline (non-Internet) computer use?

Can the product operate

- Without the knowledge of the child being monitored?
- Alongside a filter?
- To warn children when they attempt to access inappropriate material?

texts.[38] Tools for monitoring have not received nearly the same attention as filters, but are potentially controversial as well. Box 12.5 describes the dimensions of choice that GetNetWise identifies for monitoring tools.

12.2.1 What Is Monitoring?

Monitoring, as a way of protecting youth from inappropriate content, relies on deterrence rather than prevention per se. In some cases, it is the threat of punishment for an inappropriate act that has been caught through monitoring that prevents the minor from behaving in an inappropriate manner. In other cases, "catching someone in the act" can provide an important "teachable moment" in which an adult can guide and explain to the child why the act was inappropriate, and why this content is on the Internet.

Monitoring a child's use of the Internet is a generic approach that can be implemented in both technical and non-technical ways. Adult supervision of Internet use, a non-technical strategy, is discussed in Chapter 10. But the technical methods for monitoring someone's use of the Internet are many.

- The simplest means of monitoring are built into the browser or the operating system. Parents and other monitors do not need to rely on any additional technology to do this simple monitoring.

---

[38]John Schwartz. 2001. "Schools Get Tool to Track Students' Use of Internet," *New York Times*, May 21.

—The major Internet browsers have a "history" file that indicates all of the sites visited most recently. (The time frame for which such histories are kept can be adjusted by the user—a typical default time frame is 20 days.) Such a history file can be easily viewed by an adult supervisor, a step that requires no additional technology and very little computer savvy. On the other hand, older kids may be knowledgeable enough to erase the history file (it takes just one click) or even to forge a history file with enough innocuous entries to allay suspicion.

—Most browsers make use of a temporary "cache" that contains images that have been displayed on a user's screen. Inspection of this cache can show most of the images that have appeared recently on a user's screen.

—Cookie files can indicate the sites with which a child has interacted, as well as who has received information from the child. In Windows, for example, the cookie file is found in the Windows program directory and can be viewed using any text editor.

• Commercially available monitoring systems go a step further:

—Certain devices and programs can capture all of the keystrokes made by a child. Thus, comments or input made by a child can be recorded for future inspection.

—The workstation of a supervising adult can be set up to capture and/or display the contents of a child's monitor in real time. Thus, a supervisor (e.g., a teacher or librarian) could monitor what appears on a child's screen from his or her office.

—E-mail is generally not encrypted in storage, and thus may be readable by an adult who is responsible for a child.

Monitoring tools can provide a variety of functions, enabling a responsible adult to review incoming and outgoing e-mail, instant message and chat room dialogs, Web pages accessed, and so on. Further, such tools may or may not provide notification to the child that monitoring is occurring.

A monitoring tool can also use technology to identify inappropriate material (the same technology that filters incorporate) so that it can provide a warning to the child when he or she is about to be exposed to inappropriate material. The child can then decide whether or not to heed that warning. If the child does not, the monitoring tool may or may not provide a record of that access. Warnings can also be accompanied by making a log of access to such exposures or notifying a responsible adult about such access.

Depending on the tool selected, monitoring tools can be used at home and in libraries or schools. One distinguishing characteristic is that monitoring tools generally require human responses to detections of access to inappropriate information, or at least the threat of such a response. Thus, a parent or librarian or teacher must be involved to talk to the minor engaged in inappropriate behavior—and in institutional contexts the cost of reviewing access logs and following up on these reviews would likely be substantial.

For monitoring to be effective, usage must be tied to specific individuals. Thus, in an institutional setting, individual logins—which tend to be more common in higher grades than in lower ones—are necessary if monitoring information is to be acted on after the fact of inappropriate usage.[39] (If immediate action is taken, individual login information is not needed, since an adult can simply walk over to the Internet access point and talk to the child in question.) The same is true in a home setting, especially with multiple individuals accessing one computer. Indeed, without the ability to associate a given Web access (for example) with a given child, individualized guidance—or punishment—cannot be provided.

As with filters, monitoring is also increasingly common in corporate and business settings.[40]

12.2.2 How Well Does Monitoring Work?

Because monitoring tools do not place physical blocks against inappropriate material, a child who knowingly chooses to engage in inappropriate Internet behavior or to access inappropriate material can do so if he or she is willing to take the consequences of such action. However, the theory of monitoring is that knowledge of monitoring is a deterrent to taking such action.

Note, however, that unless warnings are given repeatedly and in different forms, users are known to habituate rapidly to them—and behave as though they had never been given.[41] Warnings—in and of them-

---

[39]Note also that individual logins are a necessary though far from sufficient aspect of maintaining computer, network, and system security. In the absence of individual logins, it is essentially impossible to hold any specific individual responsible for actions that might compromise security. For more discussion, see, for example, Computer Science and Telecommunications Board, National Research Council, 1997, *For the Record: Protecting Electronic Health Information,* and 1991, *Computers at Risk: Safe Computing in the Information Age* (National Academy Press, Washington, D.C.). Thus, there are advantages for institutions to consider individual logins for reasons entirely apart from protecting their youth from inappropriate material.

[40]See, for example, Associated Press, 2002, "IM Monitoring Grows in Popularity," April 12. Available online at <http://www.msnbc.com/news/737956.asp?0si=-#BODY>.

[41]See Computer Science and Telecommunications Board, National Research Council, 1996, *Cryptography's Role in Securing the Information Society,* Kenneth W. Dam and Herbert S. Lin, eds., National Academy Press, Washington, D.C.

selves—are not likely to deter inappropriate access in the long run. The same habituation may not be true, however, of warnings or monitoring associated with a human presence. An adult supervisor who forces a non-routinized interaction with a child has a far better chance of capturing his or her attention.

Browser histories log Web sites that have been viewed, though to learn the actual content of these sites, the adult supervisor must either examine these Web sites or make inferences about their content on the basis of the site's URL. Keystroke monitors are equally capable in monitoring Web sites, e-mail, and anything else that requires user input. Monitoring of screens being used by children, if done on a large scale (i.e., many screens being supervised by one person), in practice monitors access to inappropriate imagery. Text also can be monitored remotely, but in this case, the adult supervisor cannot tell at a glance if the text contains inappropriate material, and thus must spend more time in reading that text to make a judgment.

Because monitoring leaves the choice of access up to the child, inadvertent access to inappropriate material is possible. (For this reason, monitoring is arguably less appropriate for children whose decision making capabilities have not matured.) But the child also retains the choice to gain access to information that may be relevant to his or her information needs, and thus the problem of overblocking described in Section 12.1.2 does not exist.

Judgments about the effectiveness of monitoring are mixed. Monitoring—coupled with punishment—has deterrence effects at least in the short term and at least for some fraction of youth. But because the decision making party is the youth, rather than an adult (e.g., the filter vendor), denial of access to inappropriate material cannot be assured. Moreover, as with filters, a change of venue will often suffice to eliminate overt monitoring.

A critical dimension of monitoring is the kind of adult response that is coupled to a detection of inappropriate access or behavior. If an adult offers guidance and explanation rather than punishment (as is most appropriate if a violation is accidental), the youth may learn how to differentiate—for himself or herself—appropriate from inappropriate actions. To the extent that this is true, protection from inappropriate material may be extended to non-monitored venues and for much longer periods of time. (On the other hand, once clear explanations for rules have been provided, punishment for intentional infraction of rules is entirely appropriate for demonstrating that infraction carries consequences.)

Another critical dimension is whether monitoring is covert or overt. Covert monitoring, if undiscovered, is more likely to provide information about what the child is doing "when left to his or her own devices." And, if undiscovered, the individual being monitored will not change venues. But covert monitoring—by definition—cannot deter, because the youth in question must be aware that monitoring is happening if it is to have an effect on his or her behavior.

Moreover, undertaking monitoring covertly leaves the question of what the responsible adult should do—if anything—in the event that monitoring reveals that the child is behaving inappropriately. If the adult does nothing except watch, learning that is directly coupled to inappropriate access or behavior cannot occur, and the inappropriate behavior may well continue. Yet, if the adult does respond to such a revelation, he or she may be forced to disclose the fact of monitoring, with all of the attendant consequences (e.g., a child who reacts negatively because the adult is changing the rules from what was expected).

In principle, an adult could act without disclosing the fact of monitoring—for example, the adult may draw the child into a general discussion of appropriate Internet behavior without reference to any specifics that might be associated with the child's behavior. However, many adults are likely to find it difficult to act on such information without revealing the source.

Overt monitoring can deter. But it can also have negative effects, as described below.

If monitoring is coupled to explanations and guidance about appropriate and inappropriate behavior, there is some potential that this application can promote the long-term development and internalization of appropriate behavioral norms. But the explanation and guidance are essential. If, as is much more likely in an institutional setting and in many home situations, the primary or exclusive consequence of detection of inappropriate access is punishment, such learning may well not occur. Even more destructive would be punishment resulting from inadvertent access to inappropriate material, as one can easily imagine might be imposed by an adult supervisor who did not believe an assertion by his or her charge that the inappropriate Web page was viewed by accident.

Finally, as with filtering, monitoring can be circumvented by a change of venue in which monitoring is not present.

12.2.3 Who Decides What Is Inappropriate?

Decision making is shared between adults and youth. It is the responsibility of responsible adults (e.g., parents and school officials) to provide general guidelines about what constitutes inappropriate material or behavior. However, it is the responsibility of the youth to interpret these guidelines. And it is the interaction between adult and youth that can provide guidance in any particular instance.

For those products that identify inappropriate material, the relevant decision makers are the same as those for filtering.

12.2.4 How Flexible and Usable Are Products for Monitoring?

Given the burden imposed on responsible adults when all access is monitored, some monitoring products make a record only when inappropriate material has been accessed. Of course, such a product requires definitions of inappropriate material—and all of the discussion above in Section 12.1 is relevant to such definitions.

Monitoring can also be intermittent. For example, a product may take a "snapshot" of a given computer screen that records its contents at random intervals that average once an hour. In this case, the auditing burden is directly proportional to the frequency of screen capture and the number of screens being monitored. Monitoring software that never records the screen when Web content from an innocuous site is shown further reduces the number of snapshots that need to be reviewed.

Real-time display of a child's screen can be performed at any level of resolution desired. In the instance when the supervisor's monitor displays simultaneously "screen shots" of multiple user screens (e.g., all of the monitors in use by a class), each image appears in a smaller "thumbnail" version that makes reading most text on those screens difficult or impossible while at the same time usually enabling the supervisor to determine if an image is being displayed. Moreover, many inappropriate sexually explicit images are easy for humans to recognize even at low resolution and/or smaller size. The product might then offer the supervisor the chance to "zoom in" on this screen shot for closer examination, and perhaps capture the image for documentation purposes.

Records of access may be kept or not, and if kept, at different levels of detail. For example, recorded screen images can be kept at high resolution, enabling the reading of words on the screen, or at low resolution, enabling only a general identification of pictures that may be on the screen. Keystrokes can be recorded for differing lengths of time, enabling a supervisor to know in detail what the minor has done. And, some monitoring packages allow the tracking of timing and sequencing of access that would help administrators to distinguish between intentional and unintentional access.

Tools for monitoring Web usage in the aggregate (without individual tracking of users) can provide important information on whether usage conforms to acceptable use policies. Such tools would not compromise individual privacy (indeed, individual logins would not even be required), but would provide data on the Web sites children visited and the Internet activities in which children engage. Such data could then be reviewed to determine the extent to which a given audience is in fact conforming to an AUP.

If the system is configured to not monitor Web browser windows where the same page has not been on the screen for at least some period of time, perhaps 15 seconds, and to never monitor e-mail where the same incoming item has not been on the screen for at least that period of time, then the young person may not have the anxiety that "the adults will discover I inadvertently saw this material, but won't believe it was unintentional." Youth will know that as long as they quickly determine that the content is inappropriate, and exit that Web site or that e-mail, no record will be established and no adult will know. To the committee's knowledge, current monitoring software does not have this "do not capture within threshold feature," as it opens a potential loophole: a student clicking through a series of pages of inappropriate Web content, as long as each page is on the screen for less than the threshold time.

12.2.5 What Are the Costs and Infrastructure Required for Monitoring?

Financial Costs

The primary financial cost of monitoring is the human effort and labor needed to monitor usage. Monitoring records can be extensive, and in the absence of automated tools to flag questionable accesses, the examination of extensive audit records is both tedious and time consuming. (Recording screen images frequently for a large number of users also consumes hard disk space at a rapid rate.)

A second cost in the institutional setting is that the effort needed to manage individual logins is significant. Login names and passwords must be managed, and procedures must be set up to deal with children who lose or forget passwords, passwords that become known to other individuals, revocation of passwords and login names, and so on.[42]

Psychological and Emotional Costs

Punishment that is given soon after undesirable acts are initiated is more effective in deterring a repetition of such behavior than is punishment administered long afterward, suggesting that monitoring systems

---

[42]For more discussion, see CSTB, NRC, *Computers at Risk*, 1991, and *For the Record*, 1997.

are unlikely to build positive habits in students unless feedback is received more quickly than may be practical in most situations. (Feedback is needed in minutes or hours, whereas review of access logs may take days or weeks. On the other hand, real-time monitoring can provide opportunities for feedback to the child when the offense occurs.) To be effective in deterring undesirable behavior, punishment must be consistent, which suggests that intermittent monitoring, which saves time and energy, will not be conducive to helping students learn to resist the temptation of seeking out inappropriate materials. To be a component of effective discipline also requires that the basis for punishment (or consequences) not be seen as arbitrary authority but rather an explanation for why certain behavior is unacceptable.

A second point is that monitoring and privacy can be antithetical. While the desirability of privacy as an element of an appropriate developmental environment is a cultural issue, most of Western society places privacy in high regard, especially for adolescents who are at a developmental stage during which they often seek some separation from their parents. A need for privacy is an essential component of separation as adolescents begin to create their own identity, an identity that includes an understanding of himself or herself as a sexual person.[43] There are some personal issues that adults want to keep to themselves because they are embarrassed or have other feelings or behaviors that they do not want to share generally. Many children (especially adolescents) have those same feelings. To deny them that personal freedom by constant electronic monitoring may convey a lack of trust by an adult community that tells them that there is no personal space that belongs to them and them alone.

Monitoring can easily be regarded by youth as a violation of privacy and an unwarranted intrusion that demonstrates a lack of trust, and one common unfortunate consequence is that when mistrusted, an individual often proceeds to act in ways that justify that mistrust. Certainly parents do monitor their children's activities, but the balance of how much children and adolescents are watched varies, depending on characteristics such as age, gender, maturity, and parenting practices. In general, a child's need for personal freedom increases as he or she grows older.

---

[43]According to a survey by the Kaiser Family Foundation in 2001, teenagers place a high value on privacy with respect to their Internet usage: 76 percent of online youth agreed that "looking up information online is good because I can look things up without anybody knowing about it." Where looking for health information is concerned, 82 percent said that confidentiality is very important. A sizable minority of young people are concerned about the privacy of their online searches for information, with 40 percent saying they are worried that the computer might keep track of what they do online. See Rideout, 2001, *Generation Rx.com: How Young People Use the Internet for Health Information.*

Furthermore, children who are constantly watched by parents have less opportunity to develop their own internal controls about their own behavior. They have less opportunity to confront the challenges of life that ultimately develop character, for it is that struggle that makes us who we are. Parents cannot always watch their children. It is then that the effectiveness of socialization is put to the test, for it is what children do in the absence of a parent or an adult that tells of their character. A child who has not internalized parental values may well attempt to break the rules whenever an adult is not watching, for the rules are outside, not inside, the child. By contrast, a child who has internalized those rules generally follows them, regardless of whether they are being watched. Sometimes they will fail, but they can also learn from those mistakes.

At the same time, the level of privacy that students can expect in school—in using a computer as well as in other aspects of school life—is different from what they can expect at home, and school computer systems are not private systems. The expectation of privacy when students use computers in schools is more limited, as demonstrated by a variety of actions that have been supported in court decisions, including searches of student lockers, backpacks, and so on. Thus, provided that students have been given notice that their use is subject to monitoring, the use of monitoring systems raises fewer privacy concerns.

In libraries, privacy expectations have traditionally been fairly high. That is, libraries have traditionally protected the materials used by their patrons, and have even resisted the efforts of law enforcement authorities to investigate such use. Thus, monitoring in a library context—even with explicit notice—may violate such privacy traditions.

Note also that technological monitoring has a different psychological relationship to the one being monitored than does in-person oversight. Consider, for example, a student using an Internet access terminal in the school library. In one scenario, a school librarian walks the floor periodically; if she sees something suspicious on the student's screen, she walks over and asks, "What are you doing?" In a second scenario, the screen on the Internet access terminal is displayed on the school librarian's terminal (in her office) for several seconds at random intervals ranging from once every 5 minutes to once every 20 minutes. Five or ten seconds before the image of the screen is transmitted to the librarian's terminal, an unobtrusive but noticeable warning flashes on the student's terminal to indicate that monitoring is about to take place. In addition, the display on the librarian's terminal is blurred so that words cannot be read, but blurred images can appear, and no records of the screen on the terminal are kept. If the school librarian sees something going on that warrants attention, she can leave her office, walk over to the student, and ask, "What are you doing?"

For most people, the first scenario feels like responsible supervision. However, reactions to the second scenario are decidedly mixed, despite the fact that the monitoring system described does nothing that the librarian does not do. What accounts for this mixed reaction?

One factor is that the person being monitored from the librarian's office would have no particular assurance, beyond the say-so of the librarian, that any of these assertions would be true. However, where the monitoring takes place by walking the library floor, it can be seen that the librarian is not taking photographs of the library patrons or their screens. But more importantly, the fact of technological monitoring is also likely to change the nature of the relationship between school librarian and student. In the first scenario, the interaction between librarian and student is a human one, and the events have unfolded for the reasons that one would expect—a chance encounter that leads to an open question. But in the second scenario, the school librarian approaches the student with apparent foreknowledge of what the student is doing, and the question is more disingenuous than open. An additional point is that the foreknowledge provided by the monitoring system invites the librarian to jump to conclusions about what the student is doing, and she will be less likely to give the student the benefit of the doubt when she does engage him. Under such circumstances, a useful educational experience is less likely to occur than if she approached the user with an open mind.

Infrastructure

While filters can be installed on the client side without the cooperation of any other party, real-time monitoring requires a mechanism for displaying the contents of one monitor on another. When tools for monitoring are used on a large scale, a sufficient number of responsible adults is necessary to provide in-person intervention. (How many adults are required depends on how thorough the monitoring is.)

An alternative is after-the-fact review of behavior or actions, a process that requires storage of logs, screen snapshots, and so on, and automated tools to flag suspect behavior. The administrative burdens can be sharply reduced if the records reflect only potentially suspect accesses and exposures rather than all Internet use.

12.2.6 What Does the Future Hold for Monitoring?

As noted above, one major difficulty with monitoring is the effort needed to review audit trails. Thus, there is a role for automated tools that can review audit trails to identify patterns of behavior that are worth further investigation. For example, tools could be available that:

- Identify problematic viewing, resulting from accessing known problematic sites or by analyzing material on Web sites for inappropriate content;
- Determine how long someone stayed on inappropriate sites or in what sequence sites were accessed; and
- Notify responsible adults in real time of access to inappropriate sites (e.g., in a home context, notification might consist of a light flashing on a monitor carried by the parent when a child using the Web is accessing a potentially inappropriate site, or an e-mail sent to a parent). Alternatively, a request for access to a potentially inappropriate site can be transmitted to a responsible adult for approval within a certain period of time (e.g., 1 minute). If approval arrives, access can be granted and the decision remembered by the system.

Some of the functionality described above is available in some monitoring products today, but it is far from common.

12.2.7 What Are the Implications of Using Monitoring?

In general, our society subjects criminals to a high degree of monitoring because they have proven untrustworthy. For the most part, individuals follow societal rules, not through constant monitoring and the invasion of privacy, but because they have learned to internalize the values underlying those rules. Put another way, if laws were followed only because of police monitoring and enforcement, then we would need as many police as other people to maintain law and order.

Children make mistakes, and criminals make mistakes, but to be a child is not to be a criminal. Nevertheless, active supervision of children is often appropriate—not because they are criminals but because it is the responsibility of adults to teach them how to internalize the appropriate values and to become better at avoiding inappropriate behavior as they mature.

For example, responsible parenting always entails monitoring children in inverse proportion to their capability and maturity, something only a parent can ultimately determine. But as noted in Section 12.2.5, the wise parent couples monitoring with education and discussion in support of helping the child internalize the parents' values, an outcome that will help him or her (or them) to behave appropriately whether parents are watching them or not. Parents have rights to what might be called the "imposition of sanctions," which, like any other part of parenting, fails if used alone.[44] As always, the density of loving wisdom in a parent's

---

[44]Even these rights have limits. Parents, for example, cannot subject their children to abuse in the name of discipline.

actions is everything, and it is the nature of the existing parent-child relationship, the intent of the monitoring process, and how it is carried out that counts in understanding its ultimate implications.

Is the monitoring of children and adolescents a step in the erosion of privacy for all citizens? Many people believe that it is, and point to other measures that they find equally disturbing—employers who track the behavior of their employees, and commercial online sites that track the behavior and clicks of those who pass through them. The monitoring of children raises special concerns because of the fear that a younger generation will grow up never having known a world in which they had rights to privacy, and thus never realizing what rights they might have lost.

Others argue that such fears are overplayed, pointing to social and commercial benefits of increased customization of information delivery and an assumed lack of government interest in the affairs of ordinary people, as well as the fact that schools are expected to act in loco parentis with respect to the students in their care. Indeed, some believe that it would be a positive development in society if adults in all venues felt some responsibility for looking after the welfare of children and for supervising children when they are in a position to do so.[45] Resolving this question is beyond the scope of this study, but noting the question raised by monitoring of children is certainly not.[46]

12.2.8 Findings on Monitoring

1. Monitoring that warns when exposure to inappropriate material may occur is an alternative to filtering and eliminates the problem of overblocking associated with filtering.

2. Overt monitoring in concert with explicit discussion and education may help children develop their own sense of what is or is not appropriate behavior. Monitoring coupled primarily with punishment is much less likely to instill in children such an internal sense. In general, the simple presence of monitoring equipment and capabilities (or even the assertion of such capabilities) may create a change in behavior, though the change in behavior is likely to be restricted to the situation in which monitoring occurs.

3. Because human intervention is required on a continuing basis, monitoring is more resource-intensive than filtering. For the same reason, monitoring is more likely to be construed as a violation of privacy than are other techniques that simply block access.

---

[45]In this instance, there are debates about the role of technology in supervising children vis-à-vis an in-person adult doing so.

[46]A current CSTB study on privacy in the information age will address these issues.

4. Covert monitoring leads to an entirely different psychological dynamic between responsible adult and child than does overt monitoring. (Furthermore, because people habituate to warnings, children may respond to overt monitoring as though it were covert—i.e., more negatively.)

12.3 TOOLS FOR CONTROLLING OR LIMITING "SPAM"

"Spam," e-mail that is similar to the "junk mail" that an individual receives through the post office in the brick and mortar world, is sent—unsolicited and indiscriminately—to anyone with a known e-mail address. E-mail addresses can be purchased in bulk, just as regular mailing lists can be purchased: a typical rate for buying e-mail addresses is 5 million addresses for $50. Alternatively, e-mail addresses can be found by an e-mail address "harvester." (See Box 12.6 for more details.) Spam

---

Box 12.6
Activities That Result in Spam Mail

In an informal test, a CNET study identified a variety of behaviors that were likely to result in spam mail being sent to users. In this test, the researcher opened 12 free e-mail accounts (and monitored some older ones), dedicating each to one typical online activity (including the activity of doing nothing). He also provided an e-mail address on a number of "sign-up" sites, posted messages on message boards around the Web, registered domain names, and visited chat rooms. Over the course of a few months, he checked to see which activities attracted the most unsolicited e-mail to an account, and then he tried to figure out how to remove the spam.

His conclusions were that posting messages on certain message boards run by unscrupulous operators and participating in AOL chat rooms (even those that were not sexually oriented) or in an online lottery were activities that resulted in the greatest volume of spam mail (as much as 10 spam messages per day). Activities such as registering a new domain and placing e-mail links on one's own Web site resulted in intermittent spam e-mail—months with nothing, and then sudden bursts. Some common activities (including shopping online, registering at member sites, subscribing to an e-mail newsletter, signing up for a free e-mail account (and doing nothing with it, not even registering in an online directory), and registering software online) often thought to generate spam in fact resulted in virtually no spam at all.

The researcher also found that while many spam messages offered a way to remove oneself from spam lists ("only the most egregious porn spam" did not), he found that many of the offered opt-out processes did not necessarily work (e.g., opt-out links were invalid). He found that clicking unsubscribe links did result in elimination of spam, but also noted that his experience may not be typical.

SOURCE: Adapted from Matt Lake, 2001, "We Reveal the Riskiest E-Mail Behaviors on the Net," July 26, available online at <http://cnet.com/software/0-3227888-8-6602372-1.html>.

refers to any form of unsolicited e-mail a person might receive, some of which might be sent by publishers of adult-content Web sites. A typical spam message with sexual content would contain some "come-on" words and a link to an adult-oriented Web site, but would in general arrive without images.

Policy issues associated with spam are addressed in Chapter 10.

12.3.1 What Are Technologies for Controlling Spam?

Technologies for controlling spam fall into two categories—tools that seek to conceal the e-mail address (because if an e-mail address is not known, spam cannot be sent to it) and tools that manage spam once it has been received. Whether an individual can implement such tools varies with the ISP and/or e-mail service used.

To conceal e-mail addresses with certain ISPs, one can create different login names. For example, online services such as AOL enable a user to create more than one login name that can serve as an e-mail address. An individual can thus use this special login name for activities that might result in spam (e.g., for participating in a chat room). This special name becomes the attractor for spam, and mail received at that address can be deleted at will or even refused. A number of services (some free, some not) automate this process, enabling users to create special-purpose addresses that can be turned off or discarded at will. In addition, e-mail systems may allow a user to disallow all e-mail except e-mail from a specified list of preferred addresses and/or domain names.

To manage spam that does reach the user's mailbox, a number of tools are available. Most of these tools depend on the ISP or the use of an e-mail program with filtering capabilities (e.g., Eudora, Netscape Messenger, Microsoft Outlook). Spam e-mail can be identified and blocked on the basis of:

- *Content.* Content-based analysis examines the text, images, and attachments to e-mails to determine its character. (The technology for content-based analysis is much like that for content-based filtering, as described in Section 2.3.1.)
- *Source.* E-mail being received from a particular e-mail address or a particular domain name may be defined as spam after a few examples have been received. AOL mail controls are based in part on identifying certain sources as spam sources.
- *Addressees.* For the most part, spam mail is not explicitly addressed to a specific individual. Instead, a spam e-mail is addressed to a large number of people in the "blind copy" field. (On the other hand, "blind

copies" (bcc: foo@example.com) sent to an individual and e-mail sent through mailing lists to which an individual has subscribed also make use of the hidden address technique.) Mail filters (e.g., one based on "procmail," a mail processing system for Unix and some other platforms) can check and file or delete an e-mail if it arrived at the user's location via blind copy addressing. (Steps can be taken to set up exceptions for mailing list messages and bcc: messages from legitimate correspondents.)

Users can also take a number of procedural measures. For example, Web sites often ask for information from the user. By inserting false information (e.g., indicating an income lower than is actually true), it is sometimes possible to avoid marketing attacks based on demographic information consistent with the group being targeted by the marketers.

Internet service providers also take measures to limit spam. For example, AOL limits how fast other users can repeatedly enter and exit chat rooms, because a pattern of repeatedly and rapidly entering and exiting chat rooms can also be an indication that someone is harvesting e-mail addresses. Most ISPs also have lists of known spammers from which they refuse to carry traffic.

12.3.2 How Well Do Spam-Controlling Technologies Work?

Spam-control technologies for dealing with e-mail that has arrived in one's mailbox suffer from the same underblocking and overblocking issues that are discussed in Section 12.1.2. One important issue is that spam often contains links to inappropriate sexually explicit material rather than the actual material itself, and no content-screening spam-controlling tool known to the committee scans the content for links that may be embedded in an e-mail.

That said, some spam-controlling technologies are highly effective against spammers. Those that restrict the e-mail that can be received to a given set of senders are very effective (i.e., do not accept mail unless the sender is on a list of permissible senders or from specific domains). On the other hand, they also sharply restrict the universe of potential contacts, so much so that a user may fail to receive desired e-mail. (For example, a friend who changes his or her sending e-mail address will not be able to reach someone who has identified a white list of preferred senders.)

ISP-based or e-mail-service-based spam filters are partially effective. For example, the researcher mentioned in Box 12.6 found that the spam filter on one popular free e-mail service reduced the volume of spam by about 60 percent, though it still passed more than one message per day. Spam filters that are based on content analysis techniques have all of the problems with false positive and false negatives that Web filters have.

12.3.3 Who Decides What Is Spam?

Some spam filters have preconfigured lists of known spammers. But in general, it is the user who must decide what is spam and what is not. Of course, the difficulty—especially for a child—is to recognize spam without opening the e-mail. In some cases, it is easy to recognize from the header or subject line. But many spam messages reveal themselves only when they are opened. (Note also that one person's spam is another person's service or information. Unsolicited notices for ski vacations or material on a local political candidate may be useful to some individuals and useless to others.)

12.3.4 How Flexible and Usable Are Products for Controlling Spam?

Because many ISPs filter out spam for most users, users of those ISPs need not take any action at all to reject spam. However, when spam leaks through the ISP filters (or if e-mail is not filtered for spam at all), as is typical of most e-mail, the user must take action.

Note that unsolicited e-mail, and the resources and attention it consumes, is not limited to sexually explicit e-mail for youth. It would be reasonable to assume that the number of parties sending unsolicited e-mail, the frequency with which they send it, and the volume that they send will all increase. Therefore, approaches to this problem are likely to be developed, regardless of the concerns about youth and sexually explicit material. However, this can easily turn into another race: as better spam-discriminating technologies are invented, alternative ways of wrapping the unsolicited e-mail are invented, and the cycle continues.

12.3.5 What Are the Costs and Infrastructure Required for Using Spam-Control Products?

Spam can be controlled in a variety of locations. When control is located at the receiver, locally installed software spam filters can help to process and eliminate spam. Conceptually, the cost of local spam filters is similar to that for content filters. However, spam filters must be integrated into software for processing e-mail in general.

Control points based in the network (or an ISP) are both more complex and more comprehensive. Some ISPs have extensive capabilities for detecting the sending of spam mail (e.g., by monitoring the volume of e-mail sent in a given time interval), preventing the "harvesting" of e-mail addresses, and so on, and developing these capabilities entails substantial effort.

Individual organizations often incur cost in configuring software and servers to stop spam from going through their own internal networks. Such efforts are often undertaken to help manage internal bandwidth more effectively.

Finally, there may be costs incurred for infrastructure that may be needed to support legislative efforts to curb spam. For example, one method for dealing with junk mail and phone telemarketers is to establish a clearinghouse where people can register their names, addresses, and phone numbers. But the effectiveness of this approach is based on the fact that it is in the marketer's self-interest to refrain from wasting phone and mail effort and time on people unlikely to buy. Because sending spam is so much cheaper than mail and phone calls, a similar approach is unlikely to work effectively without some kind of legal cause of action that can be taken against those who ignore the clearinghouse. (Policy-based solutions are discussed in Chapter 9.)

12.3.6 What Does the Future Hold for Spam-Controlling Systems?

There has been an acceleration of commercial organizations introducing their messages into schools, although almost always after signing an agreement with the school board (which agreement usually includes new funds flowing to the school to supplement the budget). However, schools may wish to install some mail filtering before the marketing department of some soft-drink manufacturer decides to send e-mail to students just before lunch, promoting its product while also, to prevent uproar, giving "the spelling word of the day," "the math hint of the day," or whatever. It is easier for the school district to add another item to the spam filter than to have its lawyer sue the sender of the e-mails. As in the case of age verification technologies, expanded use of "mail deflection" beyond issues of sexually inappropriate material may warrant the trouble of installing spam-controlling systems.

12.3.7 What Are the Implications of Using Spam-Controlling Systems?

As described in Chapter 9, legislative efforts to curb spam do have societal implications.

12.3.8 Findings on Spam-Controlling Technologies

1. Spam-controlling technologies generally do not allow differentiation between different kinds of spam (e.g., hate speech versus inappropri-

ate sexually explicit material). Rather, they seek to identify spam of any nature.

2. Spam-controlling technologies that filter objectionable e-mail have more or less the same screening properties that filters have. That is, they do block some amount of objectionable content (though they do not generally screen for links, which are often transmitted in lieu of actual explicit content). However, they are likely to be somewhat less effective than filters at preventing such e-mail from being passed to the user because users are likely to be more apprehensive about losing e-mail that is directed toward them than about missing useful Web sites, and thus would be more concerned about false positives.

3. Behavioral and procedural approaches to avoiding spam (rather than filtering it) have at least as much potential as spam-controlling technologies to reduce the effect of spam. However, using such approaches adds somewhat to the inconveniences associated with Internet use.

12.4 INSTANT HELP

The technologies discussed in Sections 12.1 and 12.2 are intended to prevent the exposure of children to inappropriate material. Instant help is a tool to deal with exposure after the fact.

12.4.1 What Is Instant Help?

The philosophy underlying instant help is that from time to time children will inevitably encounter upsetting things online—inappropriate material, spam mail containing links to inappropriate sexually explicit material, sexual solicitations, and so on. When something upsetting happens, it would be helpful for a responsible adult to be able to respond promptly. An "instant help" function would enable the minor to alert such an adult and appropriate action could then ensue, could provide another channel to law enforcement through which threats, and solicitations, and obscene materials or child pornography could be reported.

To the best of the committee's knowledge, there are no commercially available tools that provide instant help. But current technology could easily support an instant help function. For example, a secure one-click call for help[47] could be:

---

[47]Security for this "one-click" button is an important element of help—the functionality of the button must not be disabled, as it is in mousetrapping (when the "back" button sends the user to a new adult-oriented Web site).

- On ISPs, an "always-on-top" button that would connect the user directly to a trained respondent;
- On Internet browsers, a "plug-in" represented by a button on the toolbar;
- On search engines, an icon that would always be displayed on the results page;
- On e-mail readers, an "I object to this e-mail" button on the toolbar;
- On a computer desktop, a button that activates an application that allows a remote helper to take over control of the user's machine and view the screen.

These buttons might be as simple as an icon for the CyberTipline (CTL) that would serve as an easily accessible channel for the public to use in reporting child pornography. The CTL icon has proven to be an effective tool in reporting obscene or child pornography because it is user-friendly and is the most direct method to report such images to the appropriate law enforcement authority. Because the CTL icon was built for the sole purpose of interfacing with the public to facilitate reporting to law enforcement computer-assisted crimes against children, it is more effective than other mechanisms for such reporting.

Depending on the context of the technology through which the user is coming into contact with inappropriate content or interactions, a wide range of functionality is possible once the button is clicked. For example, "instant help" on a browser or an ISP could immediately connect the user to a helper who provides assistance. To provide context, an image of the screen could be transmitted to the helper. Such assistance might be most useful if the user encounters a solicitor or inappropriate conversation in a chat room or an instant message. Or, if a user encounters inappropriate material, the last several Web pages viewed could be shared with the helper, who could assist the user in whatever action he or she wished to take (e.g., sending URLs to the CyberTipline). For Internet access on a LAN, instant help could be configured to summon assistance from a responsible adult within the LAN, such as a teacher or a librarian.

Instant help would be applicable in both home and institutional contexts. Implementing instant help functionality must be undertaken by service providers and technology vendors. But such functionality is not helpful without a human infrastructure to assist those seeking help—the human infrastructure may be provided by the ISP, a parent, a school, a library, or even an expanded National Center for Missing and Exploited Children (NCMEC).

12.4.2 How Well Might Instant Help Work?

By providing assistance to the minor, instant help could potentially reduce the negative impact that may result from exposure to inappropriate material or experiences. Such exposure can come from either deliberate or inadvertent access, but in practice instant help is more likely to be useful in the case of inadvertent access. Instant help obviously does not enable the user to avoid inappropriate material but does provide a means for trying to cope with it. It also provides opportunities to educate children about how to avoid inappropriate material or experiences in the future, and it might lead to the creation of more civil norms online. It provides immediate assistance in the case of aggressive solicitations and harassment. Finally, it might lead to greater law enforcement activity if the materials involved are obscene or constitute child pornography.

Metrics of effectiveness that indicate the extent to which children are not exposed to inappropriate materials do not apply to instant help. Rather, effectiveness is better assessed on the basis of the quality of the assistance that helpers can provide, and the responsiveness of the instant help function. Assistance that arrives 20 minutes after the user has pressed the instant help button is obviously much less helpful than if it arrives in 5 seconds, and of course, human helpers must be trained to handle a wide variety of situations.

A specialist trained to provide this kind of help to youth, or a peer with special training, could potentially be more effective than the child's own parent or teacher or librarian. However, because this approach has never been implemented on a wide scale, staffing needs for instant help centers are difficult to assess. In many urban areas, crisis intervention hotlines (focused on helping people subject to domestic abuse, or feeling suicidal, struggling with substance abuse addictions, and so on) exist, but there are none known to the committee that give training to their volunteer staffs concerning children's exposure to sexually explicit material on the Internet.

12.4.3 Who Decides What Is Inappropriate?

Unlike other tools, the locus of decision making in the context of instant help rests with the minor. The minor decides what is upsetting and determines the situations in which he or she needs help.

12.4.4 How Flexible and Usable Is Instant Help?

The purpose of an instant help function is to ensure that something can be done with very little difficulty. Thus, the flexibility and usability of an instant help function are paramount.

For example, individual parents, libraries, or schools could customize who is contacted when the instant help button is pressed. Thus, a family with strong religious ties could set instant help to alert helpers from a group associated with their religious tradition, while a school district could set the instant help button so that in the elementary school, a message went to a staffer in that building and in the middle school, to a staffer in the middle school building. This is in some sense analogous to the national phone emergency number 911 going to a local 911 dispatch center based on the exchange from which 911 was dialed.

12.4.5 What Are the Costs and Infrastructure Required for Instant Help?

The infrastructure and institutional cooperation needed for instant help to work successfully are considerable. Vendors must be willing to use precious screen space to provide instant help buttons. The infrastructure of helpers must be developed and deployed. For an ISP, such an infrastructure might well be expensive; for the NCMEC or law enforcement agencies, it would be very expensive. But for a school or library (or even for responsible adult guardians), the infrastructure of helpers may already be in place.[48]

The costs are roughly proportional to the size of the helper infrastructure; helpers (who could be volunteers) must be trained in how to respond to a call for help.

Note also that a skilled adult predator or even adolescents bent on mischief could create a flood of diversionary instant help requests so that the responding individuals would become backlogged, during which time the predator could attempt to continue an interaction with a young person. Thus, some mechanism for protection from "flooding attacks" would be needed by any responding center that serves a large number of anonymous end users or devices.

12.4.6 What Does the Future Hold for Instant Help?

To the committee's knowledge, instant help functionality has not been implemented anywhere, and it remains to be seen if children would actually use it if and when they are confronted with inappropriate material or

---

[48]It is true that in schools or libraries a child should be able to request help from these individuals without instant help features. The primary advantage of clicking an instant help icon is that it can be done privately and without drawing attention from other users.

experiences that upset them. Thus, some small-scale piloting of the concept to evaluate how it might work is likely to be very helpful before any major effort to implement instant help is considered.

12.4.7 What Are the Implications of Using Instant Help?

A potential downside of a "low-cost" implementation that would require the child to describe the material and how he or she got there is that the child might be forced to focus more on the inappropriate material, perhaps causing at least discomfort to the child who may be better off if transferred back to appropriate activities as soon as possible. Such a negative outcome could be avoided if the inappropriate material could be automatically transmitted to the helper. (Since the material may well not be present on the child's screen when he or she contacts the helper, the automatic display of material might have to retrieve the last several screens—this may be a difficult technical task under some circumstances.)

In cases where a new type of offensive material or communication begins to occur for the first time on the Internet, the first instant help response center to identify this new material could share that information with schools and parents, other instant help response centers, youth (as warnings), or even filtering vendors. In that sense, instant help might harness all youth who use it to improve the monitoring of the Internet for new offensive material or communication. Dissemination of the insights of the staff of an instant help center should be considered a networked response, as opposed to the response of assisting a child when requested. The Internet technical community has experience with networked response in the CERT system to propagate information about worms, security holes, and the like.

12.4.8 Findings on Instant Help

As the committee is unaware of any implementation of instant help that fits the description above, there are no findings to report.

13

Technology-Based Tools Available to Non-End Users

Complementing the discussion of Chapter 12 on tools for the end user, this chapter focuses on tools for other Internet stakeholders, such as Internet service providers, content providers, or operators of adult-oriented Web sites. As a general rule, these tools are most relevant to entities that have some commercial reason for existing—they have less relevance to non-commercial sources of sexually explicit material (e.g., individuals with exhibitionist preferences, friends sharing sexually explicit images, and so on).

Table 13.1 provides a preview of this chapter.

13.1 A .XXX TOP-LEVEL DOMAIN

13.1.1 What Is a .xxx Top-level Domain?

A .xxx top-level domain (TLD) would be reserved for those entities providing adult-oriented, sexually explicit material.[1] For example, www.foo.xxx would name a site on which such content would be found, and any pages within it (e.g., www.foo.xxx/example1) or any subdomains (e.g., www.fetish.foo.xxx) would be assumed to have similar content as well. A key element of proposals for .xxx is whether the use of .xxx would

---

[1]".xxx" is pronounced as "dot-xxx."

TABLE 13.1 Technology Tools for Use by Non-End Users

Tool	Function	One Illustrative Advantage
.xxx domain (mandatory)	Requires that Web sites with adult-oriented sexually explicit content must have a .xxx suffix	Provides a way of identifying adult-oriented sexually explicit material from these sites with minimal effort
.xxx domain (voluntary)	Gives any content provider the option of selecting a domain name with a .xxx suffix	Enables sites that wish to be known for providing sexually explicit material to self-identify, thus making inadvertent access to such sites less likely
.kids domain	.kids domain names reserved for site with content appropriate for children	Provides high assurance that material from .kids Web sites is appropriate for children
Age verification technologies	Seeks to ensure that someone seeking to access adult-oriented sexually explicit content is actually an adult	Places a major obstacle in the path of minors seeking adult-oriented sexually explicit content from commercial sites
Tools for protecting intellectual property	Provides tools for content owners to help control dissemination of images they own	Reduces dissemination of illegally copied sexually explicit images, which constitute a significant amount of the adult-oriented material available online

be voluntary or mandatory. If use were mandatory, all providers of adult-oriented content would be required to place such content on a Web page with the .xxx TLD, and penalties would be established for not doing so.

Today, assignment of domain names in some TLDs is done on a purely voluntary basis, whereas for other TLDs, an adjudicating body determines eligibility. For .com, .net, and .org, registrars of domain names perform a strictly administrative function; for the .edu, .mil, .gov top-level domains, some institutional entity decides that an organization is or is not eligible. However, regardless of the TLD involved, the content that a domain name owner wishes to place on its Web site is not necessarily related to the assignment of the domain name to that owner, and there is no requirement today for such a relationship.

One Illustrative Disadvantage	Voluntarey versus Involuntary Exposure
Requires difficult-to-obtain clearly specified and international standard for what constitutes material that must be placed in .xxx domains	Similar to filtering; prevents both kinds of exposure to .xxx domains, but is not useful against materials not found in .xxx domains
May lead to stronger political pressures for mandatory inclusion in .xxx domain; also likely to leave many Web pages containing objectionable materials unidentified as such, thus facilitating inadvertent access	Similar to filtering; prevents both kinds of exposure to .xxx domains, but is not useful against materials not found in .xxx domains
Requires difficult-to-obtain clearly specified and international standard for what material is appropriate for children; does not allow for age-based differentiation among children	See discussion in text of content-limited Internet service providers
Little applicability to non-commercial sources of sexually explicit material	When implemented, can prevent both deliberate and inadvertent access for minors, although if user is willing to lie about age, may not be able to protect against deliberate access
Hard to use against non-commercial sources of sexually explicit material that do not depend on Web distribution (e.g., Usenet, peer-to-peer networking)	Not applicable

Proponents of a .xxx domain argue that it would provide an easy way of recognizing material presumed to be inappropriate for children, obviating the need for a laborious inspection of Web pages for such content and simplifying the filtering task by simply blocking access to sites in the .xxx domain.

The institution authorized to establish new top-level domains is the Internet Corporation for Assigned Names and Numbers (ICANN), a nonprofit corporation that was formed in October 1998 to assume responsibility for the IP address space allocation, protocol parameter assignment, domain name system management, and root server system management functions previously performed under U.S. government contract by the Internet Assigned Name Authority (IANA) and other entities.

If and when a .xxx TLD is established, it would remain for product vendors to build software that would provide users with the option of rejecting all domain names ending in .xxx. Parents, schools, teachers, and other concerned adults would then have to be willing to exercise the options enabled in the software.

13.1.2 How Well Would a .xxx Top-Level Domain Work?

In essence, the use of a .xxx TLD amounts to a label to identify content as inappropriate or appropriate for children that is based on the source of that content. Thus, from the standpoint of the end user, all of the pros and cons of label-based filtering described in Chapter 12 apply to the use of a .xxx domain.

A .xxx domain would be intended to facilitate the blocking of access to sexually explicit material. Thus, in principle, it—along with filters—would help to protect against both deliberate and inadvertent access. From a filtering perspective, the effectiveness of such schemes depends on the reliability of the assumption that adult-oriented, sexually explicit material will be confined to a .xxx domain.

By definition, a .xxx domain name is reserved for sexually explicit material—and is thus irrelevant for any other material that is non-sexual in nature. It is likely that certain parties will have some incentives to place their content in such a domain.[2] After all, they wish their content to be found, and segregating it into an adult-oriented TLD helps to make it found. (Indeed, a concentration of adult-oriented Web sites may in fact provide children and adults with a "target-rich" environment in which they could much more easily seek out sexually explicit material.) On the other hand, a .xxx domain does not deal at all with the issue of peer-to-peer transfers, e-mail attachments, and so on. For example, college students may post collected sexually explicit material on various servers run by universities or public Web hosting services—and there is no guarantee that all sexually explicit material will be contained on Web sites in the .xxx domain, even if all commercial adult-oriented providers choose to cooperate.

---

[2]For example, Seth Warshavsky, president of the Internet Entertainment Group, an adult entertainment company, told the U.S. Senate Commerce Committee in 1998 that he would like to see a .adult domain: "We're suggesting the creation of a new top-level domain called '.adult' where all sexually explicit material on the Net would reside." See "Congress Weighs Net Porn Bills," CNET article, February 10, 1998, available online at <http://news.cnet.com/news/0-1005-200-326435.html>.

Two issues related to a .xxx TLD are whether the use of the TLD is mandatory or voluntary, and whether there is an adjudicating body that monitors the content contained in one or another of these TLDs.[3] Today, no Web site owner is forced to use a given TLD, and there is no adjudicating body that determines if the content on a Web site matches its TLD.

For a .xxx domain, these two issues are related. Mandatory use of a .xxx domain for sexually explicit material would imply creating a body whose role was to decide what content must be placed into a .xxx domain, and thus would affect all domain name owners, not just those associated with adult-oriented content. However, because "harmful to minors" laws are community-specific, a single body might be tempted to use a "lowest common denominator" approach to such decisions. Thus, some organizations and firms would be forced to use a .xxx domain even if they did not believe their content was adult-oriented and sexually explicit. (Stigmatization might also result from forced placement into a .xxx domain, with the .xxx TLD becoming a de facto ghetto into which all controversial material is placed.) Coupled with filters that block Web sites with a .xxx suffix, this approach would lead to a bias in favor of overblocking. On the other hand, in the absence of an adjudicating body, or if the use of a .xxx domain is voluntary, adult-oriented, sexually explicit material could easily be found on non-.xxx domains. Filters designed to block sites based solely on the .xxx TLD designation would be ineffective against such content, and so commercial sites uninterested in differentiating between children and adult traffic could take advantage of the lack of the .xxx TLD. A voluntary .xxx domain might also reduce filter overblocking, since operators of sites with sexually explicit material that was not oriented towards adult entertainment (e.g., museums, medical schools) would not choose a .xxx domain name and hence would be less likely to be blocked.

A final—and critical—question for the mandatory use of a .xxx TLD is how it would apply internationally. That is, how would U.S. law be able to compel foreign Web site owners to use a .xxx domain?[4] (Such a question is particularly relevant given the commonness of full frontal nudity in many mainstream foreign publications and Web sites.)

---

[3]An adjudicating body refers only to an entity that could make such a determination. A wide range of entities fit such a characterization—from an organization or agency established with a charge to make such determinations to a court or jury instructed to make such determinations in accordance with applicable law.

[4]A particularly thorny issue in this regard concerns the implications of such efforts for attempts by foreign governments to enforce their laws on Web sites based in the United States. For more discussion, see Computer Science and Telecommunications Board, National Research Council, 2001, *Global Networks and Local Values*, National Academy Press, Washington, D.C.

13.1.3 Who Decides What Material Should Be
Confined to .xxx Web Sites?

For voluntary use (in the absence of adjudicating bodies), only the organization in question makes decisions about what material is adult-oriented and sexually explicit. For non-voluntary use requiring an adjudicating body, the adjudicating body makes decisions about what should and should not be placed in each domain, thus raising the question of what community's standards would be used by the adjudicating body and how they would be determined.

13.1.4 How Flexible and Usable Are Schemes
Based on a .xxx Top-Level Domain?

The usability of schemes based on .xxx would depend in large part on whether or not domain names with these suffixes contain the content implied by the TLD (as described above).

Another issue is whether the .xxx TLD would receive ICANN endorsement. A number of schemes have been proposed to circumvent ICANN in the establishment of other TLD names. Such proposals have been controversial, because they violate principles that have been regarded by many as integral to the smooth operation of the Internet. In particular, a non-endorsed TLD name might not be uniformly accessible from every Internet access point (and today only a very small percentage of Web users could access sites based on non-endorsed TLDs), and under some circumstances, a user seeking to access a site based on a non-endorsed domain name might wind up at different Web sites depending on the location from which it was accessed.[5]

13.1.5 What Are the Costs and Infrastructure
Required for a .xxx Top-Level Domain?

For .xxx domain names, the adjudicating body must make decisions about every Web page that is posted on the Internet, because it must decide if such material belongs in a .xxx domain name. Such a task is daunting, and it is virtually impossible that an adjudicating body could do so. More likely, it would undertake what sampling it could do at reasonable expense and would examine non-.xxx sites that were reported as having sexually explicit content.

---

[5]This point is discussed in more detail in a Computer Science and Telecommunications Board report on domain name systems that is currently in preparation.

In addition, a .xxx domain would pose a number of technical difficulties.[6] An adult Web site may reside on a .xxx domain, and indeed may wish to reside on such a domain. However, consider the example of a university—which hosts a wide variety of content, some of which is deemed to be adult-oriented and sexually explicit by the adjudicating body. Web pages for such content will—by assumption—reside underneath the .edu domain of the university. Under a .xxx domain name, another separate category in the domain name service tree must be maintained by the university. Alternatively, a university could require that projects containing such content set up their own Web servers in the .xxx domain, which does not involve a high cost. Project Web sites under the .edu domain could contain links to the Web sites in the .xxx domain.

A second technical difficulty is the fact that the domain name service of the Internet supports page redirection. That is, the owner of the site www.safe_for_kids.com has the technical capability to force individuals intending to visit the www.safe_for_kids.com site to visit a .xxx Web page instead, whether or not the owner of the .xxx Web page wishes this redirection to happen.[7] Such a scenario raises a question of responsibility if a minor is channeled to the .xxx site. The owner of www.safe_for_kids.com has no sexually explicit content on its site, but is responsible for directing the minor to the .xxx site. The owner of a .xxx domain name may have taken no actions to attract children to the .xxx site. Who bears responsibility for this exposure?

13.1.6 What Does the Future Hold for a .xxx Top-Level Domain?

At least one legislative proposal has been offered to support the establishment of .xxx domains.[8] As this report goes to press in May 2002, the prospects of these proposals are unclear.

---

[6]See ".xxx Considered Dangerous" online at <http://search.ietf.org/internet-drafts/draft-eastlake-xxx-01.txt> for more discussion of these and other technical issues.

[7]In redirection, the request from the user's software (e.g., browser) arrives at the site whose address was entered, but that site does not return content. Instead, the site returns a standard Internet message saying, "The content you seek is located at this address," and the user's software immediately fetches data from that address. Since the first system may send an address without a symbolic host name, but rather with a numeric IP address, such as that in the message "the content you seek is located at http://111.222.333.444/aWebPage.html," client-side filtering has no clues that this is actually a host in the .xxx domain. Redirection exists in the Internet protocols because organizations do change what systems host their content but still want the old well-publicized URLs to work, and because it can be used as part of load balancing: a nearly overloaded server can redirect some percentage of requests elsewhere, potentially based on the geographic location of the requester as inferred from the IP address.

[8]See, for example, <http://www.adlawbyrequest.com/legislation/tldsex.shtml>, which describes a proposal supporting .xxx.

13.1.7 What Are the Implications of Using a .xxx Top-Level Domain?

The establishment of a .xxx domain, even if use is voluntary, would establish a "big fat target" for subsequent regulatory efforts. In other words, even if its use is voluntary, it may not remain that way for long as policy makers take note of its existence.

13.1.8 Findings on a .xxx Top-Level Domain

1. A .xxx domain that is selected voluntarily may have some appeal for enterprises that are involved primarily in providing access to sexually explicit material intended to arouse desire (i.e., what is often known as "pornography") and that use a distribution channel requiring the use of domain names. Such enterprises are likely to use a .xxx domain as a part of their advertising strategies.

2. A .xxx domain would have little effect on (a) sexually explicit material that is not intended to arouse desire but which some parties may regard as inappropriate anyway, (b) a mixed-use domain (e.g., a university with a .edu Web site with a faculty member who does research on human sexuality or studies the evolution of sexuality in art and media and wishes to post research materials on a university Web site), or (c) sources of inappropriate sexually explicit material that are located outside the United States (if these sources do not wish to be identified with a .xxx domain).

3. The use of a TLD to identify inappropriate content would require software (e.g., Web browsers) that can be configured to block content coming from .xxx sites. Conceptually, this arrangement is identical to that of filtering based on content, except that the task of developing black lists and white lists is made much easier.

4. The benefits associated with a .xxx domain would depend on the association of a TLD with specific content. This fact raises the question of an institutional entity that might be established to promote such association. If the benefits associated with a purely voluntary use of either domain are sufficient, then no such entity need exist. But if the affected public requires higher confidence in the association between TLD and content, such an entity may be required, and that entity would be venturing into difficult uncharted waters as it sought to determine whether certain content should or should not be contained within a given TLD. In the case of a .xxx domain, the scope of its responsibility would be to ensure that all sexually explicit material was hosted on a .xxx domain and nowhere else—an entirely daunting task.

13.2 A .KIDS TOP-LEVEL DOMAIN

13.2.1 What Is a .kids Top-Level Domain?

A .kids top-level domain would be reserved for those entities providing material intended and appropriate for children. [9] That is, it would be explicitly designed for the use of children, providing safe, lawful, and appropriate content (e.g., information and entertainment), services, and facilities of especially high interest for them. Further, it would safeguard the privacy and safety of all children accessing .kids domain names.

For example, www.foo.kids would name a site on which such content would be found, and any pages within it (e.g., www.foo.kids/example1) or any subdomains (e.g., www.nature.foo.kids) would be assumed to have similar content as well. In general, use of a .kids domain has been discussed in entirely voluntary terms, and it would make no sense to make it mandatory.

Proponents of a .kids domain argue that it would provide an easy way of recognizing material presumed to be appropriate for children, simplifying the filtering task by simply allowing access only to sites in the .kids domain. As in the case of a .xxx domain, product vendors would have to build software that would provide users with the option of accepting only domain names ending in .kids. Parents, schools, teachers, and other concerned adults would then have to be willing to exercise the options enabled in the software.

13.2.2 How Well Would a .kids Top-Level Domain Work?

Because the use of a .kids TLD amounts to a label to identify content as appropriate for children that is based on the source of that content, all of the conceptual pros and cons of label-based filtering described in Chapter 12 apply to the use of .kids. However, in addition to the baseline question of the extent to which it would help to keep children away from inappropriate materials, a second question particularly relevant to a .kids domain is the extent to which it would succeed in providing appropriate, educational, and informative content and experiences for children.

A .kids domain would be intended to promote access to child-friendly material. To the extent that this occurs, children have less time available to seek out inappropriate material. Thus, a .kids domain alone may help

---

[9]".kids" is pronounced "dot-kids."

to reduce deliberate access to inappropriate material but cannot address the problem of inadvertent access. A browser or Internet service provider restricting access only to .kids Web pages effectively provides the same kind of protection as a content-limited ISP service.

From a filtering perspective, the effectiveness of such schemes depends on the reliability of the assumption that material intended for children will be found on a .kids domain. It can be anticipated that many firms seeking to provide content for children will have incentives to obtain .kids domain names, because such a domain name would guarantee their audience. Today, no Web site owner is forced to use a given TLD, and a Web site operator can post anything on his or her Web site. If this were true in the .kids domain, it could defeat the intent of keeping children away from inappropriate content.

It is unlikely that those in the commercial enterprise of providing adult-oriented, sexually explicit content would choose to place their materials in a .kids domain. Furthermore, other enterprises, especially those operating in the commercial mainstream, would select quite carefully the content they would place in a .kids domain. However, it is easy to imagine that if .kids domain names were as freely available as today's .com domain names, certain parties would place inappropriate content of some kind on a Web site with a .kids domain name.

Thus, the safety of a .kids domain name likely depends on the existence of some mechanism to ensure that the content available from any given .kids site matches the intent of the .kids domain. One such mechanism is an adjudicating body that decides what organizations would be eligible for a .kids domain name (so that .kids domain names would not be as freely available as today's .com or .net names). Further, the body would make decisions about specific content that would be eligible for placement. The effectiveness of a .kids domain would depend, then, on the wisdom of the judgments of the adjudicating body and the extent to which it had the power to enforce its judgments. The body's enforcement power might depend on its ability to take away a .kids domain name from an owner found to be misusing it, or an acceptance of civil liability for false and deceptive advertising or business practices in that event (suggesting a possible role for the Federal Trade Commission).

The second question involves the extent to which a .kids domain would succeed in providing appropriate, educational, and informative content and experiences for children. It is clear that commercial entities that market their products and services to children would make significant use of a .kids domain. But as discussed in Section 10.9, non-commercial entities could also have an important role to play in populating the .kids domain.

13.2.3 Who Decides What Material Should Be Allowed in .kids Web Sites?

In the absence of an adjudicating body for allocating domain names, only the organization seeking a domain name makes decisions about what material is appropriate for children. In the presence of an adjudicating body, the body makes decisions about what should and should not be placed in each domain, thus raising the question of what standards should be used by the adjudicating body and how they would be determined.

An undetermined aspect of a .kids domain would be the developmental or age level that should govern placement. As noted in Chapter 5, what is perfectly appropriate for a 16-year-old may be inappropriate for a 7 year-old. Coupled with the fact that the information needs of small children are generally less than those of older children, it would seem that content for .kids would tend to be oriented toward younger children.

One possibility for definition of Web sites eligible for a .kids domain name is a site that is subject to the requirements of the Child Online Privacy Protection Act (COPPA), that is, a site "directed" to children under 13. To determine whether a site is "directed" toward children, the Federal Trade Commission (FTC) considers several factors, including "the subject matter; visual or audio content; the age of models on the site; language; whether advertising on the Web site is directed to children; information regarding the age of the actual or intended audience; and whether a site uses animated characters or other child-oriented features."[10] If a .kids domain is indeed intended for use by children under 13, the FTC definition of a site directed to children is one reasonable point of departure for a working definition.

13.2.4 How Flexible and Usable Are Schemes Based on a .kids Top-Level Domain?

The usability of schemes based on .kids depends in large part on whether or not domain names with this suffix contain the content implied by the TLD (as described above). As with a .xxx domain, another issue is whether these TLDs receive ICANN endorsement. A number of schemes have been proposed to circumvent ICANN in the establishment of other TLD names, and the discussion above about a .xxx domain in this area applies identically here.

---

[10]See Federal Trade Commission, 1999, "How to Comply with the Children's Online Privacy Protection Rule," November. Available online at <http://www.ftc.gov/bcp/conline/pubs/buspubs/coppa.htm>.

13.2.5 What Are the Costs and Infrastructure Required for a .kids Top-Level Domain?

For mandatory adjudicating bodies to make decisions about content, an effort would be required that is proportional to the volume of information posted by entities with a .kids domain name.

In addition, owners of Web sites in a .kids domain face liability issues. The proposition that a .kids site is appropriate for children is the draw for many users. Content deemed inappropriate by someone that is found in a .kids domain is likely to lead to lawsuits about false and deceptive advertising; if an adjudicating body is involved, it is likely to be named as well. Also, while the intent of a .kids TLD is to make certain material easy to find for children, the existence of a .kids TLD makes it easy to restrict children's access only to Web sites in a .kids domain, even though much other material might be both useful and appropriate for them.

13.2.6 What Does the Future Hold for a .kids Top-Level Domain?

At least one legislative proposal has been offered to support the establishment of a .kids domain.[11] As this report goes to press in May 2002, the prospects of this proposal are unclear.

13.2.7 What Are the Implications of Using a .kids Top-Level Domain?

A Web site can offer users more than passive viewing of content. If a Web site in the .kids domain offers opportunities for a child to interact with other users on the site (e.g., through chat rooms, e-mail, bulletin boards, and so on), adults seeking to interact with children, such as pedophiles, are likely to be drawn to the site as well because of the high likelihood that a user will be a child. This fact is not likely to be reassuring to parents.

A second implication is the following: if a .kids domain consists only of Web sites explicitly designed for children, especially younger ones, it would be highly restricted. In particular, it would not carry sites that provided information for a range of ages (e.g., information found in encyclopedias, which are not designed only for children). Thus, a child restricted only to accessing a .kids domain may not have access to informa-

---

[11]See, for example, David McGuire, 2001, "Bill Would Require ICANN to Create '.Kids' Domain," *Newsbytes*, June 29. Available online at <http://www.newsbytes.com/news/01/167478.html>.

tion necessary to do certain homework assignments. (Indeed, part of the appeal of Internet access is the access that people have to a broader range of information—and so restricting a user to a .kids domain reduces the Internet's appeal.) Such restrictions may be most appropriate for the youngest Internet users.

13.2.8 Findings on a .kids Top-Level Domain

1. A .kids domain may have some appeal for enterprises whose businesses are involved primarily in providing access to child-friendly and appropriate material. Such enterprises are likely to use a .kids domain as a part of their advertising strategies.

2. The use of a TLD to identify child-appropriate content could require software (e.g., Web browsers) that can be configured to accept only content coming from .kids sites. Conceptually, this arrangement is identical to that of filtering based on content, except that the task of developing white lists is made much easier.

3. The use of a .kids TLD would also be useful as an indicator of appropriateness for children even in a non-filtering context, because it would enable parents and other responsible adults to determine a site's appropriateness at a glance.

4. The benefits associated with a .kids domain would depend on the association of a TLD with specific content. This fact raises the question of an institutional entity that might be established to promote such association. If the benefits associated with a purely voluntary use of either domain are sufficient, then no such entity need exist. But if the affected public requires higher confidence in the association of TLD and content, such an entity may be required, and that entity would be venturing into difficult uncharted waters as it sought to determine whether certain content should or should not be contained within a given TLD. In the case of a .kids domain, the scope of its responsibility would be to ensure that the material on Web sites in a .kids domain was in fact child-appropriate.

13.3 AGE VERIFICATION TECHNOLOGIES

Because much of the political debate centers on the access of *children* to inappropriate sexually explicit material on the Internet, it is natural to examine online methods that can be used to differentiate between adults and children. Age verification technologies seek to distinguish adults from children and to grant access privileges only to adults. Age verification technologies seek to accomplish in cyberspace what a clerk checking an ID card or driver's license accomplishes in an adult bookstore.

13.3.1 What Are Age Verification Technologies?

Age verification technologies (AVTs) seek to establish that a given individual is or is not an adult, and based on that determination, an information provider (generally a commercial Web site host) allows/denies access to certain material or allows/prevents a transaction to be completed. The structure of a typical commercial adult Web site is a home page (http://www.adult_site.com) on which are presented a number of sexually explicit "teaser" images that are immediately available to anyone arriving on that page. Other content is accessible only after the user pays for access or enters a special password to gain access.

As a rule, the home page of an adult-oriented, sexually explicit Web site has a number of other options that the user might subsequently choose:

- A "free tour" in which additional teaser images are presented, perhaps on a number of additional pages;
- A "sign-up now" button, which will take the user to a subscription page where he is invited to provide a credit card number; and
- A "provide access code" field, in which the user can enter an access code that has been provided previously or through some other source.

In other cases, the home page may not have any images at all, or have only obscured but suggestive images, with a warning that says, "If you are under 18, please exit by clicking here." In addition, the site may display boilerplate language that seeks to immunize the site owner against charges that he has made sexually explicit adult content available to children (Box 13.1 contains an example); in these cases, the user may enter the site only by passing through this boilerplate language. Clicking the "enter" button is taken to be the user's assurance that he or she agrees with the conditions of use, which include stipulations about age.

As the structure of the canonical adult Web site indicates, the simplest age verification technology is a Web script that asks the user's age, and in many cases, such a request suffices. A similar situation obtains with online forms and profiles that users are often asked to fill out; such profiles often include entries for age. But because young people are sometimes willing to lie about their age, stronger age verification is generally necessary. In general, systems for age verification are based on the technologies described in Chapter 2.

Age verification technologies are implemented by parties who wish to restrict the access of their online products or services to adults. (In addition to limiting access to adult-oriented, sexually explicit materials, AVT infrastructure may also be useful to individuals who sell alcohol,

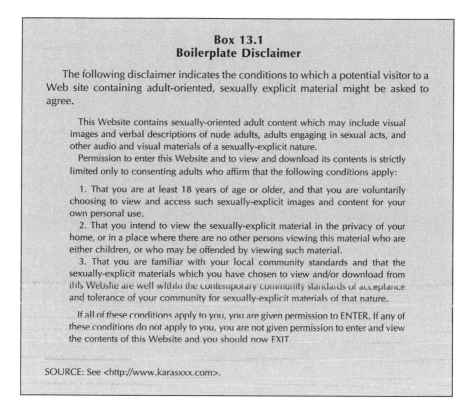

Box 13.1
Boilerplate Disclaimer

The following disclaimer indicates the conditions to which a potential visitor to a Web site containing adult-oriented, sexually explicit material might be asked to agree.

This Website contains sexually-oriented adult content which may include visual images and verbal descriptions of nude adults, adults engaging in sexual acts, and other audio and visual materials of a sexually-explicit nature.

Permission to enter this Website and to view and download its contents is strictly limited only to consenting adults who affirm that the following conditions apply:

1. That you are at least 18 years of age or older, and that you are voluntarily choosing to view and access such sexually-explicit images and content for your own personal use.

2. That you intend to view the sexually-explicit material in the privacy of your home, or in a place where there are no other persons viewing this material who are either children, or who may be offended by viewing such material.

3. That you are familiar with your local community standards and that the sexually-explicit materials which you have chosen to view and/or download from this Website are well within the contemporary community standards of acceptance and tolerance of your community for sexually-explicit materials of that nature.

If all of these conditions apply to you, you are given permission to ENTER. If any of these conditions do not apply to you, you are not given permission to enter and view the contents of this Website and you should now EXIT.

SOURCE: See <http://www.karasxxx.com>.

tobacco, or other adult-only products over the Internet.) However, the deployment of an age verification technology may not indicate a desire to verify age—in particular, consider credit cards that serve the dual function of age verification and payment medium. Because credit cards are today the simplest medium for online exchange of funds, the use of credit cards is just as likely (indeed, far more likely) to indicate a desire to be paid as a desire to restrict adults-only products and services to adults alone.

13.3.2 How Well Do Age Verification Technologies Work?

In general, AVTs protect against deliberate access to sexually explicit material that is being sold. However, they provide no protection against non-commercial sexually explicit material (e.g., an exchange of sexually explicit images between two friends), or against deliberate or inadvertent access to "teasers" on adult Web sites. AVTs also provide benefits both for the owner of an adult Web site (who can operate with less fear of running afoul of the law) and for society (which can reduce the frequency of children coming into contact with adult material or making transactions reserved for adults only).

AVTs protect primarily against deliberate access to sexually explicit material for which adult Web site operators require payment. To be effective, age verification technologies must be deployed in front of any content that is inappropriate for children—in other words, a user must have to pass through an adult verification screening (thus verifying that he or she is an adult) before he or she has access to adults-only content. Material behind an AVT screen is inaccessible to most search engines—and thus cannot be found inadvertently. However, this simple-to-achieve safeguard—placing a "plain brown wrapper" around an Internet adult Web site—is often not implemented even by those sites that require a credit card to get past the teaser pages.

The effectiveness of AVTs is mixed, though they clearly do eliminate some significant percentage of children who would otherwise gain access to sexually explicit material. Factors that reduce the effectiveness of credit cards as AVTs include the placement of highly explicit material before credit card numbers must be submitted, possession of credit cards by children (but see Box 13.2), and the availability of parental credit cards through the rifling of a parent's wallet or purse. On the other hand, the use of credit cards is convenient for both user and vendor, and access can be granted in a matter of a few minutes.

As noted in Chapter 2, AVTs that rely on public records indicating age provide a higher level of assurance regarding age. But the highest level of assurance is provided by coupling these public records with the use of the postal service to authenticate the user's identity, and thus this highest level of assurance is incompatible with rapid initial access. In addition, because not everyone has a driver's license or is registered to vote, vendors that rely on AVTs based on public records have a smaller audience than they would otherwise have. (In other words, these AVTs exclude individuals who would be entitled to gain access.)

AVTs also presume that an adult has not left the access device without logging out. If he or she does not log out, the next user—who may be a child—will automatically have access to all of the content that was accessible to the adult.

Finally, the age of adulthood differs from state to state. Because it is technically difficult to make geographical distinctions among points to which content is delivered, in practice most Web site owners choose 18 as the threshold age above which they will allow access, even if in some states 16 or 17 would be perfectly acceptable and legal. In these cases, those individuals are denied access for no legal reason.

Box 13.2
Visa Buxx Prepaid Visa Cards

Visa Buxx is a prepaid, reloadable Visa card that teens can use everywhere Visa is accepted. Spending is limited to the amount of money parents load onto the card. When a teen makes a purchase with the Visa Buxx card, the purchase amount is deducted from the card balance. At their discretion, parents can add money to the card or can set up a regularly scheduled automatic transfer to the card as they would in giving a child an allowance.

A Visa Buxx card is used in exactly the same manner as a regular Visa card, and transactions with the Visa Buxx card are processed as though it were a credit card. Recognizing that merchants may question a teenager's use of a Visa Buxx card that looks like a Visa card, Visa tells teens that if a merchant asks for identification, they should present their school ID if available; and that otherwise, the merchant should ensure that the signature on the back of the card matches the signature on the sales receipt.

With respect to using the Visa Buxx card at inappropriate places that are online, Visa advises parents to discuss how and where the teen can use the card. Parents are also able to review teen spending online using the Visa Buxx Web site, and Visa can e-mail a parent whose teen uses the card at a merchant associated with a code that indicates the merchant may sell products and services considered inappropriate for teen use. However, not all merchants listed in this designation fit the general description of the category, and so it is up to parents to address with the teen any issues related to the use of the card.

The Visa Buxx card is similar to prepaid telephone calling cards, except that it can be used to pay for any item or service, rather than just telephone service. Visa Buxx purchases are not anonymous, but there is no reason that, in the future, anonymous prepaid cards issued by Visa or Mastercard would not be as available as prepaid telephone calling cards. Moreover, there is no reason for a vendor to discriminate in the sale of these cards on the basis of age, and it will thus be harder to use such cards as an indication of adult status.

SOURCE: Adapted from information on the Visa Buxx card available online at <http://www.visabuxx.com/learnmore/faqs.cfm>.

13.3.3 Who Decides What Is Inappropriate?

The Web site owner is the primary decision maker about whether or not the site contains material that is inappropriate for children. If so, the Web site owner deploys AVTs to prevent access by children. However, there have been legislative attempts to promote the use of AVTs, as described in Chapter 4.

Because it is the Web site owner that makes the decision to use AVTs, many sites containing what some people consider inappropriate material would not see any need for age verification (e.g., Victoria's Secret). As a practical matter, AVTs will be used to differentiate adults and children only when the site contains material that the site operator believes is obscene with respect to minors.

13.3.4 How Flexible and Usable Are Products for Verifying Age?

More rigorous age verification procedures often, but not always, increase the "hassle factor" that users face. For example, the highest degree of reliability is available when public records can be checked and an access code sent to the postal address associated with those records. However, such a requirement also prevents adults from gaining the immediate access that is possible with certain other methods.

13.3.5 What Are the Costs and Infrastructure Required for Age Verification?

Financial Costs

The costs of using AVTs fall primarily on Web site owners and on adult users.

Psychological and Emotional Costs

AVTs may entail a loss of privacy for the adult user, both perceived and real. In a face-to-face transaction with a clerk checking a driver's license, there may be some embarrassment, but as a general rule, the clerk does not make a record of the license and does not record the titles of the material being purchased or rented. As importantly, the user can see that the clerk is not doing so. When an online AVT is used, the reasonable assumption would be that records are being kept (whether or not they are in practice), and so the user has a plausible reason to be concerned that his name is associated with certain types of material.

The privacy problem is exacerbated by how some AVTs work. For example, an age verification system (AVS) often provides a code number certifying age, which the user enters into the age verification field on an adult Web site. Usually, the Web site then contacts the AVS to check the validity of this number (which will expire if the user does not maintain his AVS membership). Thus, the AVS has a complete record of all of the adult sites visited using its age credential.

Furthermore, AVTs that rely on public records generally have access to the age information recorded therein. Thus, the age of a user is made available—even though that provides more information than is needed to satisfy statutory requirements.

Note also that commercial trends are pointing increasingly toward the customization of computer and device behavior and function to specific users (who may be one of many using a particular device). To the extent that this is true, age information may be associated with such functionality. At the same time, for many hosts, there are few incentives and not much of a business case to go to the expense of deploying AVTs.

It should be noted that legislation such as the Child Online Protection Act (discussed in Chapter 4) does not require personal identification—the AVTs specified in the legislation are intended as a way to screen out most minor children, not to obtain the identity of users. However, the transaction between site operator and credit card company inevitably entails some expense for the credit card company, and so the credit card company is not likely to be willing to process such requests if no revenue results from it—therefore, the site operator will submit only transactions that are associated with an actual purchase, rather than a simple age verification request, and purchases are necessarily connected with personal identity.

Infrastructure

The primary infrastructure issue is the deployment of AVTs among host sites. AVTs can play a meaningful role in reducing the access of children to adult-oriented material only to the extent that they are indeed widely deployed. (If they are not, they render only a small amount of content unavailable, and the generic equivalent of that material is almost certainly available elsewhere.)

Depending on the kind of AVTs involved, other cooperating institutions or individuals are necessary.

• AVTs that rely on public records indicating age obviously depend on the availability of those records from public agencies. Given that there is some controversy about the widespread commercial availability of such records, their continued availability from public agencies cannot be taken for granted.

• AVTs are often built into parental controls, and parental controls must be deployed by the adults responsible for youth. In practice, today's infrastructure for Internet access means that all access points (computers) that a given youth might use must have the appropriate parental controls.

13.3.6 What Does the Future Hold For
Age Verification Systems?

Improvements in AVSs depend primarily on the development and deployment of an infrastructure to support age verification, rather than the technologies themselves. For most commercial online transactions, the age of the consumer is not particularly relevant, assuming that the consumer has the ability to pay for the products or services being offered. Thus, there appears to be no general-purpose need for a pervasive infrastructure for age verification.

This suggests that if improved AVSs are to be available for vendors of adult-only services and products, the infrastructure required for verifying age must either be (a) a subset of an infrastructure that can be used for broader purposes, or (b) deployed by those vendors.

In case (a), a number of scenarios are possible. For example, smart-card technology enables a higher degree of security in authentication than do passwords, which are easily compromised. A "smart card" is a small physical hardware device (typically the size of a credit card) containing read-only non-volatile memory and a microprocessor that can be inserted into a card reader attached to a computer. In most scenarios, the individual user carries the card and inserts it into an Internet access point that requires such a device. The memory provided on the device can store information about the user, including his or her age, preferences for material to be blocked, and so on. Software installed on the computer, and on Web sites visited, would check the smart card for dates of birth when necessary, and if the user were underage for certain types of material, would refuse to grant access to that material. However, computing and Internet access technology has not developed in this direction, and the costs of converting to such an infrastructure specifically for this purpose are entirely prohibitive.

If, for other reasons, such technologies become common on personal computers and other devices that can be used to access the Internet, those offering adult-only products or services would be able to require a smart card-enabled age verification as a condition of access. Even today, one firm seeks to offer "smart" library cards on which parents can indicate their preference for their children to have filtered or unfiltered Internet access in the library.[12] Nevertheless, the effectiveness of such an approach depends on the vendor's decision to deny access to those who are unable to present a smart card, for whatever reason (including the lack of a card reader on an Internet access point or a legitimate adult customer who lacks the smart card). Such a decision runs quite counter to business incentives to achieve the maximum exposure of a product or service being sold.

Another scenario is that a vendor's knowledge of a user's age may well provide business benefits and more lucrative marketing opportunities. Routine collection of age information may well occur in the future with tools that provide automated policy preference negotiation (e.g.,

---

[12]See <http://www.libraryguardian.com>.

Passport and similar products[13]). However, age information collected in this manner may well not be verified (as it is surely not when a child is asked online to reveal his or her age).

In case (b), the current "adult check" services available are an example of a vendor-supported infrastructure. However, for the most part, the adult-check services used by those providing sexually explicit material are based on credit cards. (One might argue that credit cards are themselves an infrastructure on which adult check services build.) More effective verification services that are dedicated to serving these vendors are likely to entail additional expense.

Today's credit cards do not distinguish between minor and adult owners. But it is technically feasible for credit cards issued to youth to be tagged with an entry in the credit card company's database saying "do not authorize payment for sexually explicit material." The downside of such an approach is the processing burden that it imposes on the credit card company's systems.

Given widespread concerns for privacy, it may also be possible to develop AVTs that provide a greater degree of privacy for individual users. In particular, the legal requirement that age verification technologies are seeking to meet is not the age of the user but rather whether on a given day he or she is over 18 (or whatever the age of majority is).

Finally, despite the limitations of AVTs based on credit cards, they could be much more effective if they were systematically coupled with "plain brown wrappers" around the content that is inappropriate for children. Chapter 9 described elements of a regulatory approach that can be used to encourage the deployment of AVTs in front of all content that is regarded as inappropriate for children.

13.3.7 What Are the Implications of Using Age Verification Systems?

Widespread AVTs may compromise the privacy of adult viewing. Also, some AVTs enable—indeed require—systematic tracking of all sites

---

[13]Passport (specifically, Kids Passport) is a service offered by Microsoft that is intended to enable parents to decide whether their children can use services provided by participating Web sites that collect and/or disclose personally identifiable information. These services can include newsletters, discussion groups, pen-pal programs, wish lists, and contests. Parents can provide consent for three levels of access—no consent (child can use the Web site but not services that collect or disclose personal information), limited (third party can collect personal information but is not allowed to share or display it), and full (third party can collect and/or disclose personal information according to its privacy policy). For more information, see <http://kids.passport.com> and <http://www.microsoft.com/presspass/features/2000/02-08passport.asp>.

that use a given age certification, thus allowing a dossier of visited adult sites to be compiled.   Thus, they may inhibit free flow of information and create a chilling effect on the freedom of adults who wish to access lawful though perhaps controversial material.

Widespread requirements to present documents certifying one's age raise many of the same concerns that national ID cards raise. In particular, while acknowledging that verification of one's adult status is necessary from time to time, the concern is that a diversity of methods and documents for certifying one's adult status will—in the name of simplicity—lead easily to a single document indicating age, and perhaps other personal information. Once such a document exists, it becomes very easy to insist on the use of this document as the necessary documentation for a wide range of societal benefits, such as employment, health care, gun ownership, and so on. Much as the Social Security number has evolved into a de facto universal identifier, such a document could well become the basis for national databases that track all of the significant activities of all those with this document—and all of the concerns about loss of privacy and government/private sector abuse emerge in full force.

13.3.8 Findings on Age Verification Technologies

One approach to protecting children from inappropriate sexually explicit material on the Internet is based on being able to differentiate between children and adults in an online environment, and AVTs are a tool available for doing that.

1. Those wishing to verify age with very high levels of confidence require that a document with proof of age can be associated clearly and unambiguously with the specific individual in question.[14] Over the Internet, there is no mechanism known to the committee that accomplishes this task on a short time scale (seconds or minutes).[15]

2. As a practical matter, AVTs will be used to differentiate adults and children only when the site contains material that the site operator believes is obscene with respect to minors.

3. Mechanisms that prevent age verification on short time scales are likely to have a significant negative impact on sales and would be an

---

[14]Compared to credit cards, AVTs based on public record databases do provide a somewhat higher level of assurance of an alleged adult status (see Finding #4 in this section). But if these public record AVTs do not also use an offline method to verify identity, they are subject to many of the same problems associated with the teenager use of credit cards that have been pilfered from a parent's wallet.

[15]This finding refers only to the first time the individual needs age verification. In subsequent interactions, the individual can generally use the certification that was previously provided.

impediment for adults seeking commercial adult-oriented products and services.

4. AVTs based on credit cards do provide some significant obstacles to children seeking deliberate access to inappropriate sexually explicit material. However, as credit cards (and prepaid cards usable as credit cards) are increasingly marketed to adolescents as young as 13, such AVTs will become less useful. Furthermore, parents that have explicitly allowed their children to have credit cards or prepaid cards may be more likely to trust the viewing behavior of their children as well.

5. The underlying technology to support widespread, high-confidence age verification does exist, but its implementation could be very expensive, and its use would raise a myriad of important privacy concerns.

13.4 TOOLS FOR PROTECTING INTELLECTUAL PROPERTY

The widespread use of tools for protecting intellectual property may help to reduce the exposure of children to inappropriate sexually explicit materials that may have been taken from subscription adult-oriented Web sites.

13.4.1 What Are Tools for Protecting Intellectual Property?

A variety of technologies have been developed to protect intellectual property. For example, some rights management technologies enable an image to be transmitted to a given user but increase quite substantially the difficulty of printing, forwarding, or saving it.[16] (Box 13.3 describes some rights management technologies.) Other tools compare an image or text found on a Web site to a known and properly owned image or text (presumably the property of its creator or subsequent rights holder), and allow the flagging of near-matches that may indicate improperly derived works.

The primary users of rights management tools would be content providers with proprietary content.

13.4.2 How Well Do Tools for Protecting Intellectual Property Work?

As noted in Chapter 3, the online adult industry is highly stratified—and includes a relatively small number of well-established firms and a much

---

[16]It is of course true that one can always take a photograph of a screen, and then deal with it as one would prefer. But disabling system-provided capabilities for printing, forwarding, and saving goes a long way to protecting content.

Box 13.3
Rights Management Technologies

Rights management technologies fall into two generic categories: technologies to prevent (or increase the difficulty of) an unauthorized use of an information object (e.g., an image, an audio file, a book, a movie), and technologies to facilitate after-the-fact detection of unauthorized use.

Technologies intended to prevent (or increase the difficulty of) an unauthorized use of an information object (prevention technologies) generally rely on encryption techniques. For practical purposes, an encrypted information object bears no resemblance to the original, useful, unencrypted information object. Thus, such technologies rely on the authorized source of the object distributing the encrypted information object to anyone who wants it, but restricting the decryption key (without which the encrypted object is useless) to authorized parties only.

Once the encrypted object is decrypted, it is usable—and if special precautions are not taken, the receiver can distribute it freely. Thus, prevention technologies rely on decrypting the object as close as possible to the point of use, and/or restricting the ability of the user to copy, e-mail, forward, or print the decrypted object. For example, an image viewer might allow the display of an image but disable the functionality of the operating system to copy that displayed image to temporary files.

Technologies to facilitate after-the-fact detection of unauthorized use (detection technologies) embed into the unencrypted information object additional information that allows its creator to be identified. An example of such a technology is a digital watermark—a digital pattern that is inserted into an image that does not alter its quality but is also not easy to remove. Such transparent watermarks have obvious advantages from the standpoint of providing images that lack visible copyright markings and are as visually attractive as possible.

More discussion of these technologies can be found in the CSTB report *The Digital Dilemma.*[1]

---

[1]Computer Science and Telecommunications Board, National Research Council, 2000, *The Digital Dilemma: Intellectual Property in the Digital Age.*

---

larger number of "fly-by-night" operators, many of whom illegally use copyrighted content from established firms. Wide use of rights management technologies could significantly reduce the flow of new content to these firms. There is some reason to believe that these smaller firms and operating entities are also the parties that are least responsible about keeping children away from their adult-oriented content.[17] To the extent that this is true, drying up the supply of new content for these firms will increase the likelihood of a shakeout in the industry that will increase the prominence of the more established firms at the expense of these smaller ones.

---

[17]For example, the smaller ones are likely to derive some considerable fraction of income from raw traffic, thus giving them little incentive to screen out children. See Chapter 3 for more details.

A more mature adult industry (consisting of established firms rather than the "fly-by-nighters") is likely to have more concerns about the protection of intellectual property as well as being more likely to take actions to restrict the access of children to their products. With a reduction in the content available to fly-by-night firms that are less likely to take actions restricting the access of children, certain types of adult content will be less accessible to children. The reduction is likely to mean a lower degree of inadvertent access, but the ease of deliberate access to generic adult content is likely to be unaffected to a significant extent.

Approaches based on tools to protect intellectual property of the adult entertainment industry are relevant only to content originating there, and have no applicability to content for which no intellectual property rights can be legally asserted.

A second benefit of tools that detect possible thefts of intellectual property is in the prosecution of child pornography. As noted in Chapter 4, obscenity and child pornography differ in a number of key respects, and one of the most important differences is that while a legal determination that an image is obscene depends on factors extraneous to the image itself (i.e., on community standards), a legal determination that an image constitutes child pornography does not. Thus, once an image has been determined to be child pornography, images that are substantially identical to it (e.g., cropped images, images with shading superimposed on top) can also be determined to be child pornography. Thus, images suspected of being child pornography can be automatically compared (e.g., by a Web-crawling "spider") to databases of known child pornography.[18] Such a technique will not identify new images of child pornography, but since a substantial amount of child pornography is "recycled," application of this technique is still relevant.

The impact of rights management tools (RMTs) on reducing access of children to adult-oriented material depends on their widespread use, but in any case is an indirect one. The primary purpose of an RMT is to protect intellectual property—and the secondary effect may well be to reduce the volume of adult-oriented materials available to children.

13.4.3 Who Decides What Is Inappropriate?

This question is not applicable in this context.

---

[18]See, for example, testimony of Mark Ishikawa, CEO of Bay TSP to the COPA Commission, on August 4, 2000. Available online at <http://www.copacommission.org/meetings/hearing3/ishikawa.test.pdf>.

13.4.4 How Flexible and Usable Are Products for Protecting Intellectual Property?

From the standpoint of the end user, the primary usability issue is the extent to which different content providers use the same RMTs. If every Web site uses a different "home-grown" RMT, the user interfaces for viewing content are likely to be different—and thus the user will have to use different methods for viewing different Web sites. This limiting case represents the greatest degree of inconvenience for the user.

13.4.5 What Are the Costs and Infrastructure Required for Protecting Intellectual Property?

An approach based on the protection of intellectual property requires client-side software and hardware to perform rights management. While in principle any individual content provider could simply download rights management software to a user to protect its intellectual property, the effort required to do so is large. A widely deployed rights management system would be something on which many content providers could rely to protect intellectual property—and some infrastructure software, such as Windows Media Player, is beginning to incorporate such features. Alternatively, the content providers in the adult industry could develop their own rights management system and require that their content be displayed through it.

An essential element of infrastructure for the use of tools to protect intellectual property is an enforcement mechanism. The enforcement mechanism is technical if the technology prevents content from being improperly copied. However, such systems sometimes affect the user's experience, making systems slower and less convenient to use and to customize for his or her needs. Content providers who insist on using such systems then must deal with customer dissatisfaction that arises as a result. When the technology facilitates or enables the detection of pirated materials, a procedural or organizational or legal mechanism is needed to prevent further pirating and/or to deter others from doing the same. For example, if pirated materials are found on the bulletin board of an Internet service provider, the ISP has to be willing to take down pirated material if intellectual property rights are to be respected.

13.4.6 What Does the Future Hold for Tools for Protecting Intellectual Property?

As of this writing (May 2002), a variety of technology vendors are in the early stages of developing rights management metadata systems, by themselves (e.g., XMCL from RealNetworks and others (http://www.xmlcl.org)) and as part of broader content standards (e.g. MPEG-21). At the same time, peer-to-peer technologies such as Gnutella demonstrate that if a single copy of content can be placed on the network with no rights management wrapping or marked as "unlimited and untracked use by anyone," it can become widely distributed rapidly.

A more detailed discussion of the future of tools for protecting intellectual property is beyond the scope of this report. A report by the National Research Council—*The Digital Dilemma*—addresses this point in greater detail.[19]

13.4.7 What Are the Implications of Tools for Protecting Intellectual Property?

Discussing the implications of tools for protecting intellectual property is beyond the scope of this report. A CSTB study—*The Digital Dilemma*—addresses these implications in substantial detail.[20]

13.4.8 Findings on Tools for Protecting Intellectual Property

1. Purloined content accounts for a significant fraction of sexually explicit material on the Internet, though reliable data on this point is hard to obtain. Tools for protecting such content as the intellectual property of its creators thus have some potential to limit the number of Web sites and channels through which such content might be obtained.

2. To the extent that the rightful owners of this content are firms sufficiently established to be willing to take steps to deny children access to their material, it is in the interest of children that the intellectual property rights of these parties are respected. Owners and operators of adult Web sites will have to take the initiative to enforce intellectual property protection if this approach is to prove viable.

---

[19]Computer Science and Telecommunications Board, National Research Council. 2000. *The Digital Dilemma: Intellectual Property in the Digital Age.* National Academy Press, Washington, D.C.

[20]Computer Science and Telecommunications Board, National Research Council, 2000, *The Digital Dilemma: Intellectual Property in the Digital Age.*

PART III

14

Findings, Conclusions, and Future Needs

14.1 FRAMING THE ISSUE

The Internet has enormous potential to contribute to public welfare and private well-being. One dimension of that potential involves the use of the Internet to enhance and transform education for the nation's youth, and many public policy decisions have been taken to provide Internet access for educational purposes. Easy access to the Internet (and related online services) has many advantages for children—access to educational materials; collaborative projects, publications, online friendships, and pen pals; access to subject matter experts; recreation, hobby, and sports information; and so on.

While such potential for contributing to the nation's welfare in general and to the education of its children in particular is recognized, the Internet also presents to the public a wide variety of concerns. This fact in itself should not be surprising—few powerful and widely deployed technologies have been used solely for socially beneficial purposes. But the Internet poses many challenges for which there are no precedents, and much of the controversy about inappropriate sexually explicit material on the Internet arises because of these differences.

14.1.1 Social Dimensions

What is the issue to be addressed? Although the nominal title of the project was "Tools and Strategies to Protect Kids from Pornography on

357

the Internet and Other Inappropriate Material," a key fact is that "pornography" is a term whose meaning is not well specified. People nevertheless use the term as though it did have a well-specified meaning, and they often fail to recognize that what one may consider pornographic, another may not. For this reason, the committee chose the term "inappropriate sexually explicit material" when in common parlance it might have used the term "pornography." Using the former term keeps in the foreground the question of "inappropriate according to whose standards?"

Internet exposure of children to sexually explicit material is only one dimension of exposure, albeit important, because sexually explicit material and other sexual content exist in a wide variety of other commonly accessible media such as video cassettes, magazines, and cable television. Further, concerns over obscenity may well be a proxy for the desire to suppress access to other sexually explicit or sexually oriented content that would not be judged legally obscene.

Internet exposure of children to inappropriate sexually explicit material is also only one dimension of inappropriate or potentially dangerous activities in which youth may engage. The Internet is also a medium that can facilitate face-to-face meetings between people who do not know each other prior to their Internet contact, and when there is a great disparity of experience and age between these parties, the younger less-experienced person could be more subject to exploitation and physical danger. Other types of material may also be judged by various parties to be inappropriate for children. Some of the approaches to protection from sexually explicit material may be applicable to such other material.

The views of people about "pornography" on the Internet and what to do about it reflect a broad range of values and moral commitments. What is pornographic to some people may be simply mainstream advertising to others; what is morally wrong to some may be entirely acceptable to others; what is legal to show to minors in one community may be regarded as wholly inappropriate by those in another community; and what counts as responsible choice according to one set of values may be irresponsible behavior according to a different set of values. Approaches taken to protect children should be flexible enough to honor that diversity.

14.1.2 Developmental Dimensions

Children from birth to the age of legal majority pass through a wide range of developmental stages as they mature into adults (and furthermore the age of legal majority is not statutorily uniform). The impact of any given piece of sexually explicit material is likely to vary widely with age or, more importantly, level of maturity, and the approaches taken to protect children of a given maturity level should take into account the characteristics of their level of maturity. Moreover, the experiences of individuals can influence how sexual content affects them, especially considering that increasing numbers of adolescents, who are still legally minors, are sexually active. Finally, age usually affects the extent to which children can understand dangers and engage in safe behavior.

The information needs of children that the Internet can and should meet also change with the developmental stage of the child in question. For example, juniors and seniors in high school have a much broader range of information needs (i.e., for doing research related to their education) than do those in the third grade or in junior high school. This, in turn, leads to the question of how to provide older children with access to a broader range of material while preventing younger ones from accessing material that is not deemed appropriate given their developmental level.

14.1.3 Legal Dimensions

As a matter of law, sexually explicit material that is "obscene with respect to minors" must be made available to adults without restriction, though it can be restricted for minors. Certain other sexually explicit materials (obscenity, child pornography) enjoy no First Amendment protection at all. Material that is determined to be obscene or obscene with respect to minors must pass certain tests, including tests related to community standards. For both classes of material, the community standards for making such determinations likely change over time, and in recent years, mores about sex and consumption of sexually explicit material may have changed in such a way as to reduce (but not to eliminate) the scope of both categories.

Thus, there is in practice considerable ambiguity about what should fall into these categories, and the fact that community standards are integral to the application of the law in this area means that material cannot be determined to be obscene or obscene with respect to minors solely on the basis of the material itself. Over the past decade, the number of federal obscenity prosecutions has been very small compared with those in previous years, thus complicating to a significant degree the concept of "community standards." The First Amendment is relevant regarding the extent to which and circumstances under which public institutions of various types can restrict access to particular types of information.

Finally, in the public policy domain, U.S. regulation of sexually explicit material is most likely to have an effect on commercial sources inside the United States, and far less effect on sources located abroad.

14.1.4 Technical Dimensions

Making some material available to adults but not to children requires that providers have a reasonably reliable way of differentiating between them. In the physical world, such differentiation can often be accomplished with reasonable ease (e.g., by checking a driver's license or other identification). But in the Internet context, rules based on age differentiation are highly problematic and technically difficult to enforce. Content providers must also have a clear understanding of the difference between material that is and is not inappropriate for children.

Although many of the issues concerning Internet access to various types of material that may be regarded as inappropriate arise for other media as well, the Internet changes significantly the convenience and anonymity of access, thus reducing certain constraints that may be operative in other media. For example, online chat rooms and instant messages (IMs) have few analogs in the physical world, and these are channels through which a great deal of communication between strangers can occur. For this reason, special attention to the Internet dimensions of the issue may be warranted.

The adult online industry notwithstanding, inappropriate sexually explicit material is available from many non-commercial online sources. Thus, approaches that focus primarily on access to inappropriate sexually explicit material provided by the adult online industry (widely seen as the crux of today's problem) are likely to have limited relevance to problems arising from non-commercial sources.

For a great deal of inappropriate sexually explicit material (specifically, material accessible through Web sites), a reduction of the number of Web sites containing such material, in and of itself, is not likely to reduce the exposure of children to such material. The reason is that a primary method for obtaining access to such material is through search engines, and the likelihood that a search will find some inappropriate material for a given set of search parameters is essentially independent of the number of Web pages represented in that search. That said, if the number of such Web sites is small enough that no Web site operator can flout the rules of responsible behavior with impunity,[1] regulation of their behavior (through public

---

[1]In this context, responsible behavior refers to actions taken to reduce the likelihood that children will obtain access to inappropriate sexually explicit material. To illustrate, one method of inducing Web site operators to act responsibly is to establish codes of behavior to which they must adhere under pain of government enforcement actions (whether civil or criminal). By definition, such an approach requires government action, and with a plethora of operators, the likelihood of being the target of government action is very small—hence the number of operators must be reduced to a "sufficiently small" number. A second illustration of inducing Web site operators to act responsibly is to create disincentives for

policy and/or self-regulatory approaches) becomes significantly easier, and enforceable codes of responsible behavior can have a significant impact on the extent to which operators of Web sites that contain adult-oriented, sexually explicit material make their products and services accessible to children.

14.1.5 Economic Dimensions

The adult online industry is one of the primary sources of sexually explicit images (e.g., on "teaser" home pages) that are accessible without any attempt to differentiate between adults and children. Such teaser pages allow potential customers to sample what would be available with payment, but children have easy access to the free content. The sexually explicit material provided by the adult online industry is available to children through a variety of routes, including mistyped Web site addresses, links returned by search engines in response to search terms with sexual connotations, and spam containing links to adult Web sites.

The revenue models of the adult online industry suggest that broad exposure is needed to attract potential customers, and so the industry engages in tactics that seek to generate the broadest possible audience. Moreover, these tactics to gain exposure cannot be used at low cost if they are to differentiate between adults and children. The result is that children can be "swept up" in the industry's reach for larger audiences of potentially paying customers.

The adult online industry is only one component of supply. The low cost of creating and maintaining a Web site means that the production of sexually explicit material is now within the financial reach of almost anyone. For example, Web cameras can be purchased for under $100, enabling anyone so inclined to produce a video stream of sexually explicit material.

In the Internet environment, an astronomically large volume of material is available for free, including art, literature, science, advertising, and

---

irresponsible behavior. In this method, the key is to associate disincentives with a large number of parties so that irresponsible Web site operators will feel the pressure of those disincentives, for example, by establishing causes of action allowing those affected by irresponsible behavior to take action against such operators. (One example in a different domain is the establishment of liability (and an associated bounty) for junk faxes, an action that dramatically reduced the number of such faxes.) Whether or not these or other actions can in fact reduce the number of Web sites to a "sufficiently small" number is an open question, especially in a context in which U.S. actions are unlikely to affect Web sites operated by foreigners. Note that these illustrations are just that—illustrations—and their inclusion in the report is not intended to signal endorsement or rejection by the committee.

government information, as well as sexually explicit material of every variety. Restricting what any individual may access (or protecting him or her from certain kinds of material) will inevitably impose additional costs on users. Such costs may include denial of access to useful information and loss of privacy for those wishing to access certain kinds of information.

14.2 ON THE IMPACT ON CHILDREN OF EXPOSURE TO SEXUALLY EXPLICIT MATERIAL AND EXPERIENCES

As described in Chapter 6, factors such as certain ethical and legal considerations, an increasing conservatism of university review boards that approve research studies involving human subjects (institutional review boards), and a lack of research funding have contributed to a paucity of research regarding the impact on children of exposure to sexually explicit material. Furthermore, the extant scientific literature does not support a scientific consensus on a claim that exposure to sexually explicit material does—or does not—have a negative impact on children, and there is no adequate research base for understanding the impact of sexually explicit material of various kinds and how different approaches to protection may vary in effectiveness and outcome.

It is important to consider why many young people search for adult-oriented sexually explicit material in the first place. Adolescents go to these sites for many of the same reasons that adults do. Human beings are sexual. Sexuality is a part of identity, and a facet of identity that is a focus during adolescence when youth come of reproductive age. It is not surprising that many children—especially preadolescents and older—are curious about sex, and adolescents who are sexually mature are looking for information about sex and are making choices in this arena. In other earlier eras, they might well be married, but today in Western culture marriage among those in their early and mid-teens is frowned upon. To the extent that adults (parents and families, schools, libraries) provide accurate information and guidance about sexuality in its biological, psychological, emotional, and social dimensions—and information and guidance that is responsive to the situations that their children are facing—it can be argued that young people will be less drawn to searching for adult-oriented sexually explicit material.

This is not to say that parents are wrong to be concerned about their children's exposure to sexually explicit material. There is no reason to suppose that all negative impacts from exposure are necessarily shown or manifested in science-based research studies. The moral and ethical values of parents—whether or not religious in orientation—and a desire to be involved in providing context and guidance for a child exposed to such material are important and understandable drivers of such concerns.

The committee believes that it would not be difficult to come to a consensus on the undesirability of some set of sexually explicit material involving depictions of extreme sexual behavior. That is, such a set could be developed by construction—image after image could be shown to a group of individuals drawn from a broad cross section of the community. (In some ways, the committee consists of just such a group.) Under this procedure, the images that everyone on the committee deemed inappropriate for children would constitute the set—and the set would be substantial in size. Such a consensus would not be based so much on scientific grounds (as the committee knows of no reliable scientific studies that address this point) as much on a sense that such exposure would offend its collective moral and ethical sensibilities. Furthermore, the committee believes that a significant fraction of this set would likely be deemed obscene if prosecuted.

Yet, the fact that such a set could be defined by construction does not mean that it is possible to craft unambiguous rules that define this set without capturing material that would either be protected speech under existing First Amendment precedents or unobjectionable to some number of group members. And, in the absence of such rules, disagreement is inevitable over what else other than "similar" material should be captured in any definition.

The story is quite different for child pornography. In contrast to the diversity of views about what material must count as obscenity or obscene with respect to minors (and hence a diversity of views on what harm might result to children from being exposed to such material), there is a much broader social consensus that child pornography results in harm to the children depicted in such images and that child pornography is morally wrong as well.[2] Over the past decade, the incidence of child pornography has risen as new communications channels such as the Internet have facilitated the exchange of child pornography.

A similar argument applies to sexual predation. By design, the Internet facilitates contact between people who do not know each other. While much that is good and valuable and safe can come from interactions with strangers, parents rightly have some concern when their children talk to strangers in an unsupervised manner. These concerns arise in the physical world, and they are magnified in the online environment—where the range of personality types and intentions is both less known and less

---

[2]The social consensus is strongest when children are used to create sexual imagery. However, the breadth of the legal definition of child pornography has also led to the attempted prosecution of works of art that involve children in various states of nudity (e.g., the works of Jock Sturges), and it is fair to say that there is less of a social consensus around such material.

controllable. Further, the Internet has enabled potential predators to seek out a wider range of vulnerable children.

The committee believes that the issue of face-to-face meetings between children and their Internet acquaintances is very different from that of being exposed to inappropriate material on the Internet because the potential dangers that face-to-face meetings entail are much greater. Furthermore, while the majority of children report that they brush off aggressive solicitation encounters or treat them as a relatively minor annoyance, a significant minority do report being upset or disturbed by them (see Section 5.4.3). In addition, even when children were distressed by such encounters, a large fraction of them did not report the incident to parents or other authorities.

Finally, the committee believes that there is a consensus regarding involuntary exposure to sexually explicit material. Regardless of one's views on the impact of voluntary exposure to sexually explicit material, the committee believes that there is a reasonably strong consensus—indeed, one reflected in its own deliberations—that involuntary Internet exposure to sexually explicit material is inappropriate and undesirable and should not be occurring, and it is particularly inappropriate and undesirable in the context of minors being exposed to such material.[3]

14.3 ON APPROACHES TO PROTECTION

Much of the debate about "pornography on the Internet" focuses on the advantages and disadvantages of technical and public policy solutions.[4] Technology solutions seem to offer quick and inexpensive fixes that allow adult caregivers to believe that the problem has been addressed, and it is tempting to believe that the use of technology can drastically reduce or even eliminate the need for human supervision. Public policy approaches promise to eliminate sources of the problem.

In the committee's view, this focus is misguided: neither technology nor public policy alone can provide a complete—or even a nearly complete—solution. As a rule, public policy aimed at eliminating sources of sexually explicit material can affect only indigenous domestic sources,

---

[3]Are there any circumstances under which involuntary exposure might be beneficial? Perhaps. Consider a situation in which discussions about sex made a child uncomfortable. It might still be a reasonable thing for a concerned parent to have a conversation about sex with his or her child. Needless to say, this kind of situation does not occur frequently in the context of Internet media.

[4]The discussion in this section (Section 14.3) is complementary to the findings and general observations in Chapters 8 through 13, but does not repeat them systematically. Readers are urged to consult those chapters for more specific findings—especially about technology-based tools such as filters and monitoring programs.

and a substantial fraction of such material originates overseas. Nor is technology a substitute for education, responsible adult supervision, and ethical Internet use.

For these reasons, the most important finding of the committee is that developing in children and youth an ethic of responsible choice and skills for appropriate behavior is foundational for all efforts to protect them—with respect to inappropriate sexually explicit material on the Internet as well as many other dangers on the Internet and in the physical world. Social and educational strategies are central to such development, but technology and public policy are important as well—and the three can act together to reinforce each other's value.

Social and educational strategies are a primary focus of the committee because most children are likely to be confronted, on occasion, with material that they—or their parents—regard as inappropriate, or find themselves in online situations that are potentially dangerous. Parents must balance their concerns about exposure to harmful things on the Internet against the benefits gained from exposure to positive things on the Internet, and the question of how children can learn to handle and defend themselves becomes the primary issue. Social and educational strategies that promote and teach responsible decision making are at the core of such defense.

Social and educational strategies are also important for teaching children how to recognize and avoid situations that might expose them to inappropriate material or experiences. Though technology has a role to play here as well, developing "street smarts" about how to avoid trouble is likely to be a far more reliable and robust approach to protection.

In short, a child who responsibly chooses appropriate materials to access and appropriate things to do on the Internet and who knows what to do about inappropriate materials and experiences should he or she come across them is much safer than a child whose parents and school teachers rely primarily on technology and public policy to solve the problem for them. Moreover, social and educational strategies to promote and teach responsible choice have applicability far beyond the limited question of "protecting kids from porn on the Internet," because they are relevant to teaching children to think critically about media messages, to conduct effective Internet searches for information and to navigate with confidence, and to evaluate the credibility of the information they receive.

Social and educational strategies are not quick or inexpensive, and they require tending and implementation. Adults must be trained to teach children how to make good choices on the Internet. They must be willing to engage in sometimes-difficult conversations. And, because social and educational strategies place control in the hands of the youth targeted, children may make mistakes as they learn to internalize the object of these lessons. However, by understanding why certain actions were mistakes, children will more effectively learn the lessons that parents and other adults hope that they will learn. Virtually all of the high school students to whom the committee spoke said that their "Internet savvy" came from experience, and they simply learned to cope with certain unpleasant Internet experiences. They also spoke of passing their newfound expertise down to younger siblings, hence becoming the new de facto educators for younger kids in the "second wave of digital children."

Technology-based tools, such as filters, can provide parents and other responsible adults with additional choices as to how best to fulfill their responsibilities. Though even the most enthusiastic technology vendors acknowledge that their technologies are not perfect and that supervision and education are necessary when technology fails, tools need not be perfect to be helpful—and used properly (an important caveat), they can be an important aspect of comprehensive programs for Internet safety.

First, technology can help to create a child-rearing environment that parents can moderate and shape according to their values and the maturity of their children. In an Internet context, a controlled and moderated environment does not mean that a child's every keystroke and mouse click are preprogrammed forever. But it does mean that the child can exercise choices within safe limits set by parents or other responsible adults—and as a child learns more and develops greater maturity, those limits can be expanded in ways that allow greater freedom of choice and that may at some point entail greater risk taking as well.

An example of a technology-moderated environment for Internet access might call for the provision of Internet access in young childhood that is explicitly limited to child-friendly content (i.e., access based on "white lists"), strongly filtered Internet access in middle childhood (i.e., access based on extensive "black lists"), less filtered Internet access in preadolescence and early adolescence (i.e., access based on a slow reduction in the number of categories deemed inappropriate), and monitored Internet access in middle to late adolescence (i.e., unfettered Internet access but accompanied by warnings about inappropriate material). Parents wishing to provide a more risk-free environment might delay the introduction of less restrictive measures; those wishing to promote a more free flow of information to their children might accelerate the introduction of less restrictive measures.

Second, technology can help to keep parents and other responsible adults informed about what their children are doing online. Of course, the circumstances of obtaining such information matter quite a bit. An intent to provide guidance that helps the child make informed and responsible choices relies on the presence of openness about the presence of monitoring. On the other hand, an intent to "catch" the child in doing something wrong is likely to result in behavior that simply reduces the flow of information to the parent, such as the child obtaining Internet access in a venue that is not monitored.

Third, technology offers many desirable benefits: speed, scalability, standardization, and reduced cost. Because non-technical approaches take valuable time from parents, teachers, and others that is badly needed to address many other issues related to raising responsible young people, it will often be the case that a mix of non-technical strategies and technology-based tools provides the most cost-effective way to protect children on the Internet.

Choosing the right combination of social and educational strategies and technology-based tools depends a great deal on the nature of the problem that parents, teachers, and librarians are trying to solve. For example, recall from Chapter 8 that deliberate access and inadvertent exposure to inappropriate sexually explicit materials pose different protection problems. Recognizing that responsible adults have to deal with both problems, the fact remains that certain tools and certain strategies are more appropriate for the former than the latter, and vice versa. Tools that warn of impending exposure to inappropriate material rather than blocking are better suited to dealing with the problem of inadvertent exposure.

One important point arising from the relative preponderance of males relative to females as consumers of adult-oriented sexually explicit material (Chapter 3) is that adolescent males are probably much more likely to seek out such material deliberately. If so, social and educational strategies that aim at reducing the desire of such individuals to seek out such material may well be more relevant to male children than to female children.

As for the role that public policy can play in protecting children, regulation may help to shape the environment in which these strategies and tools are used by reducing at least to some extent the availability of inappropriate sexually explicit material on the Internet. Public policy can help to influence the adult online industry to take actions that better deny children's access to their material and/or influence others in the private sector to support self-regulatory or self-help measures. Furthermore, through prosecution of violators of existing laws that prohibit the transmission of obscene material, public policy can help to some extent to reduce the number of providers of such materials.

Successful law enforcement depends on many factors, including appropriately formulated statutes, adequate resources, and a willingness to enforce existing law and regulation. In the Internet safety arena, the participation of citizens (e.g., reporting illegal activity) is also an essential element of law enforcement. Proper training of law enforcement person-

nel—including those who take complaints, those who investigate complaints, and those who prosecute cases—at federal, state, and local levels
remains critical to effective law enforcement. Finally, public policy (or
the threat of regulation) can also encourage and promote self-regulatory
efforts that contribute to certain public policy goals, such as Internet service providers taking down materials posted in violation of the terms of
service to which users agree as a condition of use.

Coping with non-commercial sources presents different issues to law
enforcement authorities. In order to attract customers, commercial sources
must draw attention to themselves, which means that their activities are
hard to conceal from law enforcement authorities. But non-commercial
sources such as peer-to-peer file-sharing networks may present no easily
accessible target for legal action (and under many circumstances can operate invisibly to law enforcement). To address non-commercial sources, law
enforcement officials must conduct what amount to "sting" operations.[5]
Such operations are controversial, are personnel-intensive, and may not
offer large leverage, as non-commercial sources are likely to have significantly smaller audiences than commercial sources.

Table 14.1 contains an illustration of how social and educational strategies, technology tools, and public policy can work together.

14.4 TRADE-OFFS AND COMPLEXITY

After more than a year of intensive study of the issue, the committee
was struck by its extraordinary complexity. Such complexity manifests
itself in many ways, but nowhere more prominently than in understanding the trade-offs involved in the development of any comprehensive
approach to protecting children on the Internet from inappropriate materials and experiences.

---

[5]One example of a "sting" operation is an exercise in which a law enforcement official
assumes an online identity corresponding to that of a minor, and engages potential predators seeking to entice a minor for the purpose of initiating a sexual encounter. A second
example is the use of customer lists belonging to an online service that provided child
pornography, lists confiscated after the service itself was convicted of child pornography
charges. In this latter case, known as Operation Avalanche, law enforcement officials continued to operate the online service's Web site and sent e-mail to subscribers offering them
the opportunity to purchase child pornography. Those who responded received controlled
deliveries of child pornography made by investigators, and search warrants were executed
on the residences of those customers immediately after the deliveries were made (see ABC
News, 2001, "An Avalanche of Child Porn: Investigators Use Subscription List to Track
Down Pedophiles," November 14, available online at <http://abcnews.go.com/sections/
business/TechTV/TechTV_Avalanche_Porn_011114.html>).

TABLE 14.1 An Illustration of Mutual Reinforcement

	Impact on Suppliers of Inappropriate Material	Impact on Potential Consumers of Inappropriate Material
Social/ educational strategies	Business decisions and ethics (e.g., ISPs can choose to refrain from carrying USENET newsgroups with a large amount of child pornography)	Teach children to make choices to stay away and to target searches more precisely to reduce chances of inadvertent exposure; teach parents how to educate their children about these strategies and to monitor what their children are doing online
Technology-based tools	Labeling material so that parents and others can easily ascertain the appropriateness of that material for their children	Help guide children to appropriate sites and help to prevent access to inappropriate sites, consistent with parental values and preferences
Public policy	Shape the environment by reducing deceptive practices (e.g., mousetrapping, spam, capturing of misspelled web sites)	Provide support for social and educational strategies (e.g., new standards of learning for K-12, outreach to parents to educate them about the Internet)

The nature of trade-offs is such that doing "better" with respect to one goal implies doing less well with respect to some other goal or goals. In the present instance, any approach that improves protection for children and youth from inappropriate Internet material or experiences is almost certain to have a negative impact on other values or goals that most parents or communities would generally find appropriate and desirable. Note that these latter values and goals may also be associated with children and the Internet.

Two points must be made about the existence of trade-offs. First, the existence of such trade-offs is not an argument, per se, against attempts to "do better" at protecting children and youth from inappropriate Internet material or experiences. Second, the fact that trade-offs exist for any given method suggests that a mix of methods may well be more effective than exclusive or primary reliance on any one method.

To illustrate these trade-offs, the next few sections discuss trade-offs that decision makers must address in considering the use of social and educational strategies, technology-based tools, and public policy actions.

14.4.1 Social and Educational Trade-offs

The committee has identified social and educational strategies to teach children and youth how to make good decisions about using the Internet as foundational for any approach to protection. But socialization and education are inherently processes that operate over a long time scale— thus, they cannot be expected to demonstrate immediate results. Furthermore, they are not simple to implement, and they require forethought, planning, and extensive follow-through. They can be costly, both in terms of dollars and in terms of time.

Perhaps the most important trade-off associated with using social and educational strategies is that they may conflict with other pressing social and educational needs. For example, most K-12 curricula are already overloaded, and information and media literacy curricula must compete for time in the schedule with physical education, art, music, sex education, consumer literacy, and a variety of other pressures on the curriculum. Education in these areas is also important, and passionate advocates can be found for all of them.

Because the amount of time in a curriculum is more or less fixed, there are only three possibilities. One is that something must be removed if something else is added, and the elimination of any given subject area is always controversial, if only because the importance of one subject area must be weighed against the importance of another. A second possibility is that by increasing the efficiency of education in the existing areas of study (so that the same ground can be covered in shorter amounts of time), time can be made available to add information and media literacy. But increasing efficiency is an enormously difficult problem, and in practical terms, it is not clear how to do so. The third logical possibility is to obtain the needed time for information and media literacy by trimming the instructional time devoted to existing subject areas. The risk in this approach is that coverage of those latter areas may become inadequate as a result.

The dilemma is no easier to resolve in the family context, where family time together is at a high premium in many families. Parental efforts to supervise children and youth using the Internet must compete with making sure that children clean their rooms, do their homework, get to the soccer or basketball game on time, avoid unhealthy use of drugs and alcohol, work part-time jobs, and so on. The difference in knowledge about technology and its uses between many parents and their children further inhibits informal candid discussion about issues related to the Internet. Siblings and friends charged with providing peer assistance may also play tricks on children to get them into trouble.

Finally, educational strategies to teach children and youth to refrain from seeking out inappropriate sexually explicit materials face a powerful challenge in that many adolescents, especially boys, are highly motivated to seek out such materials. Some children do let educational efforts "roll off their backs" and are not influenced by them, and although education and socialization are the only approaches that have the chance of reaching all or most children or that have any chance of reducing a child's desire for such materials, the expectations for such education and socialization should not be unrealistic.

14.4.2 Technology Trade-offs

One technology trade-off is illustrated in the balance that users of technology-based tools must strike between two concerns—shielding the child from inappropriate material and experiences against enabling child-centered control over the flow of information to him or her. One can increase shielding—but only at the expense of reducing a child's discretionary control over and access to information.

A related trade-off is the issue of false positives and false negatives. While false positives and false negatives in general trade off against each other, even when human beings are actively involved in making judgments about the appropriateness of material to be shown to children, the trade-off is most stark when technology is used to assess appropriateness, and a fundamental reality of technology is that it does not provide an accurate and inexpensive way to assess content. As a general rule, increasing the probability that a device or system will identify inappropriate sexually explicit material as such also increases the probability that some not-inappropriate material will also be improperly identified as inappropriate. If false positives are generally tolerable (i.e., one is generally willing to pass up useful information as the price of protecting against inappropriate material, as might be the case for many risk-averse parents), then the automated assessment of content does have significant utility.

Still another technological trade-off arises because of tensions between flexibility and ease of use. Products that are flexible can be customized to the needs of individual users, and most people say that they want flexible products. Yet, a highly customizable product involves many decisions for a user to make, and many users find the actual exploitation of a product's flexibility to be a chore. As a result, the most common use of any technology tool is in its default "out of the box" configuration. Thus, for practical purposes, it is fair that any assessment of a tool place great weight on what the tool does out of the box. Against that standard, many tools for protecting children from inappropriate Internet material and experiences place a far greater emphasis on labeling Internet material and experiences as inappropriate than on carefully selecting whether appropriate material might be labeled as inappropriate. That is, if it *might* be inappropriate, it is labeled and flagged as such. Filters thus favor overblocking rather than underblocking, while monitors are likely to flag more material as questionable rather than less.

This systematic bias in favor of overcaution provokes anxiety in many people. For example, to the extent that technology-based tools are preferred instruments of government policy, concerns arise that government may be implicitly endorsing a lesser degree of information flow to the public—and to children—than would be the case in the absence of technology-based tools. It is also an empirical observation about many tools on the market identifying certain kinds of information as inappropriate for children that their supporters and advocates are perceived as supporting an underlying political agenda. Finally, political pressures and mandates to deploy technology-based tools distort the market, in the sense that they create artificial demand for solutions to problems that communities do not perceive to exist to a significant degree (if they did, they would deploy these tools without such a mandate).

Even the protection itself that technology offers with respect to protecting children and youth from inappropriate material involves a potential trade-off. To the extent that technology-imposed limits on choice work as intended (i.e., to block rather than discourage access to material that may be inappropriate), children and youth lose an opportunity to exercise responsible choice, and hence an associated chance to learn how to make responsible decisions. For younger children—who tend to be less good at decision making than older children—the consequences of bad choices may be more serious, because of their relative inexperience about life and their greater impressionability; for such children, opportunities for unconstrained decision making and choice are not appropriate under most circumstances.

On the other hand, children who develop internal standards of appropriateness can be safer in those situations in which they—or their parents and guardians—cannot rely on technology to protect them. This is important given the increasing ubiquity of Internet access points in many venues. When responsible and respected adults and mentors talk with these older children about responsible decision making and establish sanctions for inappropriate choices, they create an environment that encourages and supports responsible choice, which in turn is likely to be conducive to the development of positive habits. Such habits are most important as adolescents reach the age of majority, when they will have the rights of adults and no constraints relative to Internet access. On this point, parents must decide how to proceed.

14.4.3 Public Policy Trade-offs

As noted in Chapter 9, the viability of many public policy proposals depends on how policy makers make certain trade-offs between the goal of helping to shield children and youth from inappropriate sexually explicit material on the Internet and other desirable societal goals. For example, the committee believes that spam containing material that is obscene for minors should not be sent to children. But laws banning such e-mail to minors are potentially problematic in an online environment in which it is very difficult to differentiate between adults and minors. (Indeed, regulation that depends on regulating a certain type of content (namely, sexually explicit speech) is inherently more suspect on First Amendment grounds than are proposals that regulate speech independent of content.) On the other hand, a ban of all spam regardless of content may be seen as too broad because it affects many other interests— for example, those parties with a commercial interest in using e-mail channels to advertise non-sexual goods and services.

The committee also believes that it would be desirable for adult Web site operators who exhibit material that is obscene for minors to use age verification systems so that children would not be able to access such material. However, in an online environment in which it is very difficult to differentiate between adults and minors, it is not clear whether denying access based on age can be achieved in a way that does not unduly constrain the viewing rights of adults. Thus, as one illustrative example from Section 9.3.2, the government might offer a grant of immunity from prosecution under obscenity laws to Web site operators that use age verification systems to prevent minors from accessing such material.[6] In this instance, the trade-off is helping to protect children from exposure to certain kinds of inappropriate sexually explicit material (such a measure would help to reduce the inadvertent discovery of such material from commercial Web sites) in return for limitations on possible obscenity prosecutions.

Aggressive enforcement of obscenity laws also presents trade-offs. Increased prosecution of obscenity would likely require increased re-

---

[6]More specifically, immunity for adult Web site operators from prosecution under obscenity laws would be granted if (a) they take actions to prevent their content from being indexed by search engines, and (b) they provide a plain-text front page that warns users that the site they are about to enter has adult-oriented content and an "exit" button to a child-friendly site if the user acknowledges being under 18.

sources, and those resources must be taken from some other activity. If, as is likely, the other activity represents prosecutions of other crimes, policy makers must make the judgment that it would be wise to pursue more obscenity prosecutions rather than other criminal prosecutions, or that more prosecutions for obscenity would necessarily be the best use of additional resources—if such resources are available. Such judgments are complex and require a careful weighing of many competing factors well beyond the scope of this report.

14.5 TAKE-AWAY MESSAGES FOR DIFFERENT PARTIES

In the committee's judgment, the bottom line on reducing the exposure of children to inappropriate material and experiences on the Internet is that those who rely exclusively, or even primarily, on technology and public policy will find that the resulting protection will rest on uncertain and shifting ground—and is likely to fail their children when exposure to inappropriate material or dangerous situations occurs. If one installs tools and/or passes legislation in the hope that they will "take care of the problem," and that in doing so one's responsibilities will thus be adequately discharged, children are highly likely—eventually—to encounter inappropriate material or experiences on the Internet in some venue, whether by accident or on purpose. And such an encounter will come as a disturbing surprise to the parent, teacher, librarian, or public policy maker who feels that he or she has done all that needed to be done. In the end, responsible choice—which is foundational for safe Internet use by children—is closely tied to the values that parents and communities wish to impart to their children, and that influence judgments about the proper mix of education, technology, and public policy to adopt.

Box 14.1 describes some of the behavioral aspects of Internet safety for children that families, schools, and libraries might wish to teach.

14.5.1 Parents

Parents have a primary responsibility for guiding children into maturity. They have responsibilities to their children in the physical world, and they have corresponding responsibilities in cyberspace. With respect to Internet usage, developing maturity implies the ability to make safe, responsible, and morally appropriate choices about what to do and what to see on the Internet and a facility for coping constructively with inappropriate or objectionable experiences.

Box 14.2 describes one possible "best practices" scenario focused on the home. In addition, parents might wish to keep the following points in mind.

Box 14.1
Some Aspects of Internet Safety for Children

There are a variety of sources of good advice for children about Internet safety.[1] The following points summarize some of the most important things to keep in mind.

• Don't give out personal information without parental permission to anyone that you know only from the Internet. That includes your real name, your address, telephone number, parents' work address and/or telephone number, or the name and location of your school. It also includes your picture, which is information that is in fact about as personal as you can get. If you need to give out a name, make one up, or use your login or screen name. Don't use your real name as a login or screen name.

• Report to your parents, a responsible adult, or an older sibling anything that makes you uneasy or uncomfortable. Don't wait to look around or explore—report it immediately. There's nothing wrong with seeking out help for an experience that makes you feel uncomfortable.

• Never meet anyone in person that you first met through the Internet without parental permission *and* their accompanying you to a face-to-face meeting. If you do meet the person (even with parental permission and presence), do it in a public place.

• Realize that many people in real life are very different from how they seem online. Many people find it easier to lie in an online environment, are very good at it, and rely on the fact that you have no way to check on what they say. Someone who claims to be 5' 4", blond, and female and sends you a picture to "confirm" that could be a 6' 2" black-haired male who happened to have a picture of a girl that he found online.

• Talk with your parents (or teachers) about their expectations and group rules for going online. Establish mutually agreeable rules for when and how long you can be online, and identify appropriate areas and helpful Web sites for you to visit. If you want to do something that is not covered by these rules, talk to your parents or teachers about it.

• Don't talk to or engage with people that you don't know. If you get e-mail from an address you don't recognize, delete it without opening it. If you get an instant message from someone whose name you don't recognize, cancel it. Stay away from chat rooms without having an adult present.

• Treat others respectfully in an online environment. One good rule to follow is that you should not say or do anything with someone that you would not want your parents to find out about. Teasing, hurting, threatening, or being mean to someone else is inappropriate and wrong, whether it is online or in person—and is wrong even if you are anonymous to the other person.

---

[1]See, for example, <http://disney.go.com/legal/internet_safety.html>, <http://www.safekids.com/kidsrules.htm>, and <http://www.getnetwise.org/safetyguide/>.

Box 14.2
An Illustrative "Best Practices" Scenario for the Home

In a "best practices" scenario focused on the home, parents provide instruction and supervision about Internet use. In particular, computers would be located in public family areas rather than in rooms that are conducive to private use (e.g., a child's bedroom). Parents would have gone beyond their work experiences with the Internet and learned about the materials and experiences to which their children might plausibly be exposed, keeping in perspective a balance of the Internet's positive and negative aspects. For example, they would have spent some time sitting by their children's sides surfing the Internet or exploring their online service with them. They would have educated themselves about appropriate and useful Web sites and consulted their children's teachers about how Internet use could support their children's education. They would also have spent time without children in attendance surfing the Web so that they could experience firsthand some of the "not-so-desirable" content in instant messages and chat rooms and on Web sites. They would have talked with their children about both the benefits and the dangers of the Internet, and provided clear guidance about what material and activities were inappropriate and explanations for what made them inappropriate. They would ask their children to report any experiences that made them (the children) feel uncomfortable or in which they encountered an inappropriate experience or unsuitable material, and promise to refrain from being upset with their children should such happen. They would also keep that promise, and when their children reported inappropriate material or experiences, they would counsel rather than punish them. Parents would also set time limits for how much time a child may spend online. When time is constrained, people are more likely to concentrate on the activities that they value most highly. To the extent that children seek out inappropriate material out of idle curiosity, these are the activities that are most likely to be curtailed in the presence of time limits. Parents would be willing to learn about technology from their children and would not feel awkward about asking their children technology-related questions. Furthermore, older and more experienced siblings would be encouraged to supervise, encourage, and guide younger siblings.

- When children are young, a wider and more extensive range of precautions and a limited range of choices are appropriate. However, as children mature, precautions can generally be relaxed and the range of choices expanded. If technology is used to limit access, consider the age-appropriateness of the limits you wish to impose.
- Interactive dialog (whether through e-mail, instant messages, voice and/or video, chat rooms) with strangers is a much greater potential threat to a child's well-being than other things that he or she is likely to encounter on the Internet. Account for the fact that children often overestimate their ability to make good judgments about the intentions of people whom they do not know.
- An environment in which your child will feel comfortable talking to you is more likely to result in conversation about potentially serious

issues. If they are afraid of your reaction to what they tell you, they will be less likely to tell you when they encounter things that might make you uncomfortable. Thus, think in advance about what you will say and do when your child is exposed to material that you regard as inappropriate.

• For most people (children included), instant messages and chat dialogs are no different than telephone conversations, mail, or diary entries. Reading logs of chat room or IM dialogs is likely to be seen in the same way as listening in on a child's telephone conversations or reading a child's diary. For some parents, the cost of violating a child's privacy is worth the gain of learning what is on a child's mind. For others, the cost of violating a child's privacy is too high a price to pay under most ordinary circumstances. A related question is that of the extent to which a child's rights to information go beyond what a parent is willing to grant. Some parents are willing to state explicitly that their children should be able to obtain information on certain subjects, even if it would make them (the parents) uncomfortable, while others find such a notion to be unacceptable. Thus, consider your own philosophy regarding privacy and information rights for your children.

• The policies of your child's school, library, and friends' families regarding Internet use and access have an effect on your child's Internet experience. Coordinate the Internet experiences available at home and at school, the library, or at the homes of friends (if you approve of those policies), or provide an alternative for your child (if you disapprove of them).

• Children often copy what their parents say verbally and actually do behaviorally. If you believe that the viewing of sexually explicit material is inappropriate for your children, explain to your children why such behavior is inappropriate for them and set a good example in your own household.

• Illegal or inappropriate behavior or material can be reported to the responsible authorities. For example, the National Center for Missing and Exploited Children provides one-stop reporting to law enforcement authorities of child pornography found online by the general public (http://www.cybertipline.com or 1-800-843-5678). Local law enforcement agencies (e.g., state or town police) are often recipients of complaints related to online solicitations of children for sexual purposes, and the Federal Bureau of Investigation and the U.S Customs Service have authority in this matter as well. Certain online services provide mechanisms for reporting inappropriate activity. For example, AOL provides a way for users to notify AOL's "Community Action Team," which has the responsibility of enforcing AOL's terms of service. Among other things, AOL's terms of service forbid vulgar language and disruptive behavior in chat rooms or instant messages and e-mail and instant messages that contain requests from strangers for passwords, credit card numbers, or other personal information.

Finally, the committee believes that a parental lack of knowledge about Internet culture and the diversity of possible Internet experiences has been—and continues to be—a source of both complacency (because some do not know what on the Internet may be of concern to them and their children) and excessive fear (because they do not know enough to be able to place these dangers in proper perspective). For this reason, parental education about the Internet continues to be an important part of a comprehensive program of Internet safety education for children.

14.5.2 Teachers and Librarians

Teachers have a responsibility for educating students and for providing a safe environment in which learning can occur. Libraries have a responsibility for providing the communities they serve with a broad range of useful materials appropriate for their needs. Box 14.3 and Box 14.4 describe possible "best practices" scenarios for schools and libraries, respectively. In addition, teachers, school administrators, and libraries might wish to keep the following points in mind.

• The educational and informational needs of young people at various ages—from kindergarten to the seniors in high school—vary enormously, and the Internet content that is made available to students at

---

Box 14.3
Illustrative "Best Practices" Scenarios for Schools

In a "best practices" scenario for schools, the Internet and information technology are used to support learning and are integrated into the regular curriculum as tools for learning. Students—and parents—would actually read acceptable use policies (AUPs). Discussions about AUPs between students and parents would occur. Some instructional time would be spent on teaching students what it meant to comply with AUPs. Enforcement of AUPs would be sufficiently flexible that inadvertent violations would be seen as teaching opportunities rather than automatically being considered occasions for punishment. Internet safety instruction would be a prerequisite for school-provided Internet access. Some instruction in media literacy would be integrated into the curriculum at all levels as an essential dimension of scholarship and learning. Selected older students would serve as computer and Internet tutors and guides for younger students. Teachers would be offered professional development opportunities by their school district to understand the importance of media literacy on the Internet and how to teach it. The PTA would offer programs to parents or guardians wanting to know more about Internet safety and guidance on maintaining open communication between parents and adolescents.

> **Box 14.4**
> **Illustrative "Best Practices" Scenarios for Libraries**
>
> In a "best practices" scenario focused on the library, libraries offer Internet safety instruction to both parents and children. Software would be installed to "clear" browser histories and caches so that a new user would not be able to view anything seen by the previous user. Libraries would also offer users a variety of choices regarding filtered or unfiltered access. Internet access points inside children's areas would ask the age of the child—young children (e.g., those below 10, although this age is arbitrary) would receive a notice that they were being given filtered access, while older children would be offered an unbiased choice of filtered and unfiltered Internet access. (In this context, "unbiased" means that neither filtered nor unfiltered access is the default. Instead, prior to Internet use, a user would specify—in private—an explicit choice of filtered or unfiltered access. In this way, a user who wishes to gain private and unrestricted access to information could do so without having to be embarrassed or feel uncomfortable about having to ask for unfiltered access, and a user who wished to not be exposed to certain kinds of material could do so without having to acknowledge to someone that he or she might be uncomfortable with such material.) In any event, information on the filtering policy would be conspicuous and available so that users would have a general idea of what was blocked.

these various stages of development must be matched to their needs, skills, and maturity. Furthermore, teachers and librarians have an important role in educating parents about the Internet—its benefits and its dangers—and they are sources of advice about how to cope with the dangers that the Internet may pose.

• Transparency is a virtue, both for adult supervisors and child Internet users. Transparency can include an understanding of why a given site is or is not regarded as inappropriate, access to detailed information about what is deemed inappropriate, knowledge of instances when actions are being monitored or influenced, and the ability for on-site adult supervisors to override non-local decisions about inappropriateness.

• The total cost of technology solutions, rather than just the initial deployment costs, must be evaluated. Specifically, technology generally entails continuing costs of maintenance and upgrade, as well as human staff members to ensure that the technology is being used appropriately and is serving its intended functions. For example, staff may be needed to process requests for filtering overrides (if filtering is in place) or to process parental complaints (if filtering is not in place).

• Efforts to provide educational outreach to parents must account for busy family schedules as well as, perhaps, a certain resistance among some to deal with technology-based issues with which they are unfamiliar. For example, outreach activities requiring parents to go far out of their way tend to be poorly attended; conversely, parents would be more inclined to attend programs that are conveniently located and scheduled consistently with the community's work hours. One program described to the committee during the first workshop involved taking computers to venues that had little to do with technology such as a gardening class or music festival. By demonstrating how the technology could have useful applications even in such venues, a context arises naturally in which it is possible to raise issues related to young people, the Internet, and parenting. Also, coordination with volunteer organizations outside schools and libraries may make more resources available for these outreach efforts. PTA organizations, for example, are well suited to provide such outreach efforts.

14.5.3 Industry

Various components of industry can make a major contribution to the Internet safety of children. The segments of industry relevant to the issue include ISPs and online service providers, makers of access devices such as personal computers, software vendors, content providers, and the adult online industry.

- ISPs and online service providers could:
— Provide easily understood and implemented parental controls. As noted in Chapter 11, flexibility is often not used because presenting a range of options is confusing to the parent trying to configure a system. On the other hand, a single "one-size-fits-all" approach does not take into account the needs of individual children. One approach to simplifying parental controls, implemented by some service providers, is to set default measures depending on the age of a child, while giving the parent the ability to adjust these defaults appropriately.

— Design and provide educational and child-friendly areas. Chapter 10 discusses a number of means to concentrate child-friendly and compelling content that would attract children's online attention. To achieve critical mass, such content would be designed to be broadly appealing over a wide variety of topics, including information on relationships, sexual health, and other topics of interest to adolescents.

— Provide a uniform channel for user complaints about child pornography and/or obscene material. Such a channel (which could be as simple as a link to the CyberTipline) could easily be placed on the complaints or customer service page of the service provider.

— Refrain from carrying material that they believe to be illegal, such as suspected child pornography. (As discussed in Chapter 4, the "Good Samaritan" provisions of the Communications Decency Act remain in force and largely immunize providers exercising such control over content from liability for failures in such control.) For example, on their own authority, ISPs could refrain from carrying Usenet newsgroups known to carry large amounts of child pornography.

- Makers of access devices such as personal computers could:
— Provide in-the-box Internet safety tips and best practices. Many such brochures published by reputable organizations are available for free, and "out-of-the-box" information relevant to Internet safety could be a valuable route to greater publicity for such efforts.
— Provide configuration options for children in a household. At greater cost, the initial machine-setup configuration process could be modified to ask the device owner or administrator if children are expected to use the device. If so, the process could guide the owner or administrator through a setup process for specifying parental controls for the use of the device. (For example, the setup process might specify certain limits on Internet access if a child logs into the device.)

- Software vendors could:
— Develop software to prevent mousetrapping. Recall that mouse-trapping (discussed in Chapter 3) refers to the phenomenon in which a user who tries to leave a sexually explicit site is automatically forwarded to another such site. Some programs are available today to block "pop-up" advertisements, and these work to prevent mousetrapping as well. However, these programs must be invoked before the pop-up ad or mousetrapping occurs, and they also disable some useful features of Web sites. A "panic button" could be installed that is always available on the user's screen, and if a user is mousetrapped, clicking on the "panic button" should close all current browser windows.
— Develop software to help configure computers to be child-friendly. Such software would operate in lieu of the child-oriented setup routines described above.
— Integrate label-based filtering options into Web browsers (see below).
— Include in software regularly used by adults tips for their children's Internet safety. For example, upon initial installation of a software product, the software setup program could ask if the user wanted to view a screen of Internet safety tips for children, and if so, could display such tips or direct him or her to an appropriate Web site.
— Provide content creation tools that have been adapted to speed the process of content developers creating labels that can be used by PICS-based filtering schemes.

- Content providers could:
— Participate in labeling schemes. As discussed in Chapter 12, the

success of a labeling scheme depends primarily on its widespread adoption. In October 2001, AOL Time Warner, Yahoo, and Microsoft Network announced their adoption of the content labeling system of the Internet Content Rating Association.

— Integrate educational and entertainment value into content developed for children. If children are to use content voluntarily, such integration is likely to enhance its appeal for both children and parents.

— Add links to age-appropriate sexual and emotional health content to Web sites visited by older youth. As noted in Section 14.2, many older youth are interested in information that relates to their sexuality. Given this fact, it makes some sense to provide reliable and appropriate information to meet this need, rather than leaving them on their own to find unvetted information that may be of questionable value or to seek out adult-oriented, sexually explicit content that depicts sexual behavior in ways that are demeaning or disturbing.

• The adult online industry could:

— Take more effective steps to keep children from accessing their products. For example, operators of adult Web sites could set up their home pages without sexually explicit material (i.e., the cyber-equivalent of a brown paper wrapper around an adult magazine), and use the robot.txt protocol (described in Chapter 2, Box 2.3) to prevent indexing of pages (even free teaser pages) that contain such material. Thus, children searching the Web would never find the sexually explicit material directly (though they might be directed to an adult site's home page).

— Stop the practice of involuntary mousetrapping. For example, it would be simple to offer a user seeking to leave a Web site a choice about whether or not to be redirected. Such a simple step could do much to reduce the perception of irresponsible behavior on the part of the adult online industry.

— Use contracts to require more responsible behavior among affiliates that use content provided by commercial sources of adult-oriented, sexually explicit imagery. For example, a contract between a content provider and an affiliate might require that the affiliate would have to put its content behind plain brown wrappers and so on, and the firms that supply content would be in a position to penalize them if they did not (by cutting off a content source).

Finally, the information technology industry should not be discouraged from undertaking serious technology-based efforts to help parents and other responsible adults to improve and enhance the safety of their children's Internet experiences and to reduce the amount of inappropriate material to which they may be exposed. Indeed, as a primary beneficiary of the Internet age (as well as being instrumental in creating it), the information technology industry arguably has a special responsibility to help safeguard children on the Internet. Developing more discriminating filters, enabling parental controls, supporting research of the type described in Section 14.6, and adopting and promoting labeling schemes are a few of the ways that the IT industry has sought to discharge its responsibilities in this area, and a further enhancement and strengthening of these types of effort can only expand the range of options that parents and other responsible adults can exercise.

14.5.4 Makers of Public Policy

Public policy—at the local, state, and federal levels—helps to shape the environment in which Internet access occurs. But because the scope of public policy actions are—by definition—pervasive throughout the community to which those actions are relevant, public policy makers must proceed judiciously.

Public policy actions are most effective when they are based on reliable science rather than anecdote, and when they reflect a strong social, ethical, and moral consensus. For example, the sentiment that child pornography and sexual molestation of children are wrong is shared by people among a very broad spectrum of political views. Thus, it is reasonable to say that these are serious national problems, and addressing them continues to be an important task for the nation. Furthermore, the scale of these problems—already large—is increasing, and in any event outstrips the resources available to deal with them.

By contrast, public policy makers should tread lightly when it comes to other areas in which a consensus is not so apparent. For example, the committee heard from parents who did not trust the federal government to take actions to reduce children's Internet exposure to inappropriate materials. The striking aspect of this sentiment was that it was expressed by both conservative and liberal parents.

Public policy makers should also be wary of cheap, easy, or quick solutions. As the discussion in Chapter 12 on filtering demonstrates, such "solutions" may not fix the problem that they seek to solve—at least not to the extent that they would enable resources and attention to be turned elsewhere. It is true that the cost of social and educational strategies tends at first blush to be considerably larger than the costs of protective technologies—but the benefits that accrue are also correspondingly higher. Students will be more able to avoid problematic experiences and material of their own volition, and will be better able to cope with them when they occur.

Finally, it is necessary to underscore the fact that public policy can go far beyond the creation of statutory punishment for violating some ap-

proved canon of behavior. Certainly, legal sanctions are one possible public policy option, and such sanctions act both to punish those who behave
in a way contrary to law and to deter others from conducting themselves
in a similar way. Options such as more vigorous prosecution of existing
obscenity laws are discussed at length in Chapter 9. But public policy can
be used much more broadly and can shape the Internet environment in
many ways. For example, public policy can be used to:

• Reduce uncertainty in the regulatory environment. Uncertainty in
the regulatory environment is often inhibiting to business plans. For
example, prior to the enactment of the "Good Samaritan" section of the
Communications Decency Act (discussed in Section 4.2.3), at least one
court case (*Stratton Oakmont v. Prodigy*) had suggested that an ISP exercising editorial control over messages posted on its bulletin boards in accordance with its acceptable use policy was subject to liability as a publisher
for content available through the ISP that was inconsistent with its acceptable use policy. This precedent gave ISPs incentives to refrain from exercising editorial control, and the Good Samaritan provisions of the Communications Decency Act—never overturned in the courts—eliminate
such liability.

• Promote media literacy and Internet safety education. Promotion
can include:

— Funding the development of model curricula for media literacy
and Internet safety. There are political sensitivities related to the federal
government's role in education, which is a local responsibility, but developing models and giving grants are both well-accepted federal practices
in the area of education.

— Encouraging and supporting professional development for teachers on Internet safety and media literacy. Professional development for
teachers seeking to use the Internet for pedagogical purposes is sparse
compared with the need,[7] but Internet safety and media literacy do not
account for more than a very small fraction of the sparse support that is
available.

— Supporting outreach to educate parents, teachers, librarians, and
other responsible adults about Internet safety education issues. Grants
could also be made available to non-profit and community organizations
to run Internet safety programs. In addition, given the gap in knowledge
between adults and their children, a media-based educational outreach
campaign has some potential for reducing this gap. For example, public

---

[7]U.S. Department of Education. 2001. *Teachers' Tools for the 21st Century: A Report on Teachers'
Use of Technology.* Available online at <http://nces.ed.gov/pubsearch/pubsinfo.asp?pubid=
2000102>.

service announcement campaigns could help to inform parents of online issues related to their children (TV ads, enclosures in phone and/or Internet bills). Another part of media outreach might be the creation of a national "children's safety day"—a day in which the media would highlight all that can be done to improve children's safety and well-being, and adults would take concrete steps to review safety issues with children. Internet safety education could well be one aspect of such a day.

• Support the development of and access to high-quality Internet material that is educational and attractive to children in an age-appropriate manner. Public support for the development of PBS programming has a long tradition of providing such material in the TV medium, and with the dearth of comparable material for children on the Internet, such support could have a substantial impact. In addition, educational portals that organize existing safe and educationally appropriate content (see comments under Section 14.5.3) would improve the accessibility of that content to diverse audiences.

• Support self-regulatory efforts by private parties. For example, public policy can provide financial or legal incentives for ISPs and content providers to behave in responsible ways. It can also coordinate and facilitate private efforts to self-police the Internet environment (analogous to the rating efforts of the music and game industry). Such self-policing relies on the public at large to report possibly illegal material or behavior, ISPs to take actions consistent with their terms-of-service provisions, and information exchange mechanisms to ensure that all parties have the information needed to take appropriate action.

• Support research in areas that are relevant to the issue of Internet safety. Some of the relevant areas are the impact of exposure to sexually explicit material on children at various ages; the Internet use patterns of children; and the in-practice effectiveness of various social and educational strategies, technology-based tools, and public policy at federal, state, and local levels at increasing the safety of children's Internet experiences. Of special interest is the possibility of research and development into technologies specifically designed to accurately identify sexually explicit material and thereby enhance and improve the effectiveness of tools that can help to reduce the exposure of children to inappropriate Internet materials and experiences.[8] As discussed in Chapter 2, the general information-retrieval problem is a very difficult one to solve. However, research intended to focus on the identification of sexually explicit material may progress more rapidly than work on the more general problem. The

---

[8]Non-industrial support for such research may be justified on the grounds that, as discussed in Chapter 12, there is little market incentive for more accurate methods for identifying sexually explicit materials (and hence for more accurate filtering).

reason is that in seeking to identify sexually explicit material (rather than arbitrarily selected material), one might be able to make use of heuristic methods and clues signaling the presence of sexually explicit content that are not available for use in the general case.[9]

• Support efforts to enable families and other private parties to exercise greater latitude of choice in the Internet experiences of the children for whom they are responsible. For example, parents and others lack a good evaluative guide to technology-based tools and must assess the claims of vendors on their own. This report helps to provide a framework for understanding how to think about such tools but does not provide specific product guidance. Publicly available assessments of specific tools rated multidimensionally according to common criteria could help parents and others select tools that are appropriate for their own situations.

Finally, makers of public policy must keep in mind the international dimensions of the Internet. This does not mean that U.S. actions should not be undertaken, or that they will be wholly ineffective, but expectations for the impact of such actions must necessarily be moderated compared to the case in which the United States is the only significant actor.

14.6 RESEARCH NEEDS

As the length of this report suggests, the problem of protecting children from inappropriate material and experiences on the Internet is complex. Reliable information in a number of areas is needed. Indeed, throughout its work, the committee was concerned about the lack of reliable and valid science-based information for many dimensions of the problem it was addressing. Such information would have helped to strengthen committee deliberations.

• The effectiveness of technology-based tools and social and educational strategies in practice should be examined and characterized. Chapter 12 discusses one aspect of evaluating the performance of filters, based on a "head-to-head" comparison of how filters performed in blocking inappropriate materials. But protection of children is a holistic enterprise that must account for the totality of their Internet experience—which suggests the need for an examination of all of the tools in all of the venues in which children use the Internet. The same is true for understanding how social and educational strategies affect the behavior of children "on the ground."

---

[9]Note that more effective technology in this area could be used for the benefit of those who want to block such material and of those who want to search more precisely for it.

• Given the inadequate scientific basis for understanding how media exposure to sexually explicit material affects children, more research in this area is needed. Systematic research on U.S. children may not be possible, for all of the reasons described in Chapter 6, but cross-national longitudinal studies in countries similar to the United States may shed some light on these issues. In addition, it may be possible to conduct research to study exposure to such material that occurs in the course of children's use of the Internet (which is likely to include both accidental and deliberate exposure). A further dimension of media research is the impact of media exposure on the development of personal character in youth.

• It seems reasonable that providing high-quality, age-appropriate information about sex and sexual health addressing the physical, emotional, social, and psychological issues on the minds of children would have a dampening effect on the urge of many adolescents to search for inappropriate sexually explicit materials. To test this proposition, longitudinal studies of children and adolescents who receive such information would be helpful.

• There is a need for research and development directed toward a comprehensive curriculum that provides in detail what parents need to know in order to handle the issue of Internet safety with their children. Such a curriculum would provide specifics on what a parent might do operationally.

• A better understanding of the population of online sexual predators might help government efforts to prevent sexual predation. If, for example, a large percentage of online sexual predators were already-convicted child molesters, that fact might argue for longer prison terms for such felons, closer supervision of their activities after release, and/or prohibitions on their use of online resources.

14.7 CONCLUSION

The Internet offers enormous potential to enhance the intellectual, educational, social, and personal development of children. Those who take actions to address the concerns described above must bear in mind the potential benefits that the Internet offers. Thus, any "appropriate" mix of actions should be seen as balancing competing goals and values rather than endorsing the absolute supremacy of any one goal or value.

Furthermore, evolution with respect to technology and the e-business environment, as well as possible changes in community standards governing obscenity, means that there are no foreseeable technological "silver bullets" or single permanent solutions to be crafted. Rather, any approach adopted to protect children must adapt to changing circumstances. While technology and public policy have important roles to play, social and educational strategies that impart to children the character and values to exercise responsible choices about Internet use and the knowledge about how to cope with inappropriate material and experiences is central to promoting children's safe Internet use.

APPENDIXES

A

Information-Gathering Sessions of the Committee

PLENARY MEETING OF JULY 17-19, 2000

National Research Council
2001 Wisconsin Avenue
Green Building
Washington, D.C.

Monday, July 17

Presentation of Charge
Dean Hoffman, U.S. Department of Justice
Linda Roberts, U.S. Department of Education

Panel: Considering the Extent of the Problem
David Finkelhor, University of New Hampshire
Michael Marshall, Microsoft (retired)
John Rabun, National Center for Missing and Exploited Children
Jeff Richards, Internet Alliance

Primer on the First Amendment
Geoffrey Stone, University of Chicago

Panel: First Amendment Perspectives
Bruce Taylor, National Law Center for Children and Families
Robert Flores, National Law Center for Children and Families

Elliot Mincberg, People for the American Way
Marvin Johnson, American Civil Liberties Union
Paul McMasters, The Freedom Forum

Tuesday, July 18

Panel: Technological Issues
Milo Medin, Excite@Home
Paul Resnick, University of Michigan
Bhavani Thuraisingham, MITRE

Panel: Library Perspectives
Marilyn Mason, Independent Consultant
Carol Roddy, Ohio Public Library Information Network
Judith Krug, American Library Association
Walter Minkel, Cahners Business Information
Caroline Ward, Ferguson Library and outgoing president of Ameri-
can Library Association Services for Children

Panel: School Perspectives
Lynne Schrum, University of Georgia
Linda Braun, LEO: Librarians and Educators Online
Carrie Gardner, Milton Hershey School
Maribeth Luftglass, Fairfax County Schools

Panel: Community Perspective
Robin Raskin, Family PC
Parry Aftab, Cyberangels
Bruce Watson, Enough Is Enough

PLENARY MEETING OF OCTOBER 18-20, 2000

Georgetown Holiday Inn
Mirage Room II
2101 Wisconsin Avenue, N.W.
Washington, D.C.

Wednesday, October 18

Panel: Perspectives on Child Development
Jeff McIntyre, American Psychological Association
Mary Anne Layden, University of Pennsylvania

Demonstrations: Sexually Explicit Material on the Internet (closed session)

Panel: Understanding the Obscenity Statutes

Governmental Perspectives
Terry Lord, Child Exploitation and Obscenity Section, U.S. Department of Justice
Kenneth Neu, Federal Bureau of Investigation
Daniel Armagh, National Center for Missing and Exploited Children

Nongovernmental Perspectives
Rob Showers, Gammon & Grange
Beth Farber, Federal Public Defender
Robert Peters, National Obscenity Law Center, Morality in Media
Jon Katz, Marks & Katz, LLC

Questions for the Panels

• Given a policy to prosecute obscenity cases, what factors determine whether or not to pursue a case? How does the exposure of a minor to obscene materials affect a decision to prosecute?
• How are community standards for determining obscenity set?
• Would a case of Internet obscenity be prosecuted differently from one associated with a neighborhood bookstore? Why or why not?
• How has policy regarding enforcement of obscenity laws changed over the years at the local, state, and federal level?
• What approaches would be most effective in dealing with online obscenity? (to include but not be limited to any or all of the following: technological tools such as filters, community practices, legislation or regulation)

Thursday, October 19

Panel: Perspective of ISPs (general purpose, family friendly)
Steve Ensley, American Family Online
Mike Chilton, Dotsafe
Ginny Wydler, America Online

Questions for the Panel

• How do you decide what is appropriate material for minors to access? How does this differ by age?

- Please comment on the exposure of minors to sexually explicit material online by source, i.e., explicitly sought, inadvertently accessed, or pushed actively by another party.
- How do you limit exposure for minors to sexually explicit material online? What strategies or tools appear most successful? What strategies or tools have limited success? Why?
- Is there a "range" for access for minors? How is it determined?
- What approaches would be most effective in limiting the exposure of minors to sexually explicit material on the Internet?
- Unsolicited or bulk e-mails are sent to minors' accounts but may contain links to sexually explicit sites. How might these mailings be eliminated or better targeted to adults?

Panel: Perspectives of Education Associations
Julie Underwood, National School Boards Association
Arthur Sheekey, Council of Chief State School Officers

Questions for the Panel

- What are your primary concerns about the exposure of minors to sexually explicit material online?
- How are your members responding to the issue?
- How should the risk of exposure to inappropriate sexual content be balanced against the risk of denying access to helpful or educational material that might be inappropriately blocked?
- What approaches to limit the exposure of minors to online sexually explicit material are appropriate for schools, communities, libraries, and families?

Panel: Perspective of Teenagers
Brittany and Yves, Teenangels, New Jersey, with Parry Aftab, Cyberangels
Alex, Thomas Jefferson High School for Science and Technology, Alexandria, Virginia

Questions for the Panel

- Do you think that adults (parents, teachers) understand enough about the Internet to provide supervision?
- How easy is it to circumvent actions intended to prevent someone from reaching sexually explicit material online?
- What do you think are the best ways to protect minors from inappropriate Internet content?

- Have you ever seen pornography online? How did it happen? For instance, was it sent to you? Did you accidentally access a message containing a link? Did you mistype a URL and get an adult site?
- What have you done when you have gotten sexually explicit material online? Have you told anyone? Who? What happened?
- Do you think you get a lot of bulk or unrequested e-mails containing sexually explicit material?
- Have you ever been made uncomfortable by someone in a chat room or by an Instant Messenger message? What happened? What did you do?
- Do you know how to protect yourself when you go online? Where did you learn these rules?

Discussion of COPA Commission Report (closed session)

Friday, October 20

Panel: Adult Entertainment Industry Representatives
    Danni Ashe, Danni's Hard Drive
    J.T. Edmond, Flying Crocodile
    Gloria Leonard, Free Speech Coalition
    Larry Lux, Playboy Online
    Gerard Van der Leun, Penthouse.com

Questions for the Panel

- What is your perception of the issue of minors' exposure to sexually explicit material online? How are your members/clients responding to the issue? How broad is your membership base compared to the universe of providers of such material?
- What are the most appropriate means for distinguishing between adults and minors in an online context?
- How should/can the current regime of limiting the exposure of minors to sexually explicit print and TV and movies be extended to the Internet domain?
- What are the most appropriate approaches to limit the exposure of minors to online sexually explicit material? What strategies or tools appear most successful? What strategies or tools have limited success? Why?
- Unsolicited or bulk e-mails are sent to minors' accounts but may contain links to sexually explicit sites. How might these mailings be eliminated or better targeted to adults?
- What approaches would you like to see adopted or developed to limit the exposure of minors to online sexually explicit material?

• What technologies might better target likely audiences for adult entertainment?

Overview of Bertelsmann Report, Protecting Our Children on the Internet
    Jack Balkin, Yale University

PUBLIC WORKSHOP OF DECEMBER 13, 2000

Georgetown University Conference Center
Salon H Meeting Room
3800 Reservoir Road, N.W.
Washington, D.C.

> Note: The proceedings of this workshop are summarized in an NRC report entitled *Nontechnical Strategies to Reduce Children's Exposure to Inappropriate Material on the Internet: Summary of a Workshop* (National Research Council and Institute of Medicine, Board on Children, Youth, and Families and Computer Science and Telecommunications Board, Joah G. Iannotta, ed., National Academy Press, Washington, D.C., 2001).

Non-Technical Strategies That Can Be Used to Protect Children on the Internet: What Are the Roles of Policies, Parents, Schools, Libraries, and Communities?
    Linda Roberts, Director, Office of Educational Technology and Senior Adviser to the Secretary, U.S. Department of Education
        Anne Thompson, Program Commissioner, National PTA

Questions for Discussion

• How does one define non-technical strategies for protecting kids from inappropriate material on the Internet?
• What non-technical approaches are used in the home, classroom, and community settings?
• What is the role of parents in making non-technical strategies effective, and what do parents need?
• How effective have current policies been in encouraging schools and communities to develop non-technical strategies?

An Extended Panel on Bringing Developmental Considerations to Bear on the Impact of Inappropriate Material on the Internet
    Part I: Effects of Exposure to Pornographic and Other Inappropriate Material on the Internet
        Jane Brown, Professor, School of Journalism and Mass Communications, University of North Carolina at Chapel Hill

Joanne Cantor, Professor, University of Wisconsin, Madison

Ed Donnerstein, Dean and Professor, Department of Communication, University of California, Santa Barbara

Moderator/Discussant: Sandra Calvert, Committee Member and Professor of Psychology, Georgetown University

Issues for Discussion

• What types of inappropriate material do young people encounter, and how do they come in contact with it?

• What is the potential impact on children of viewing sexually explicit and other forms of inappropriate material in the media?

• Is impact dependent only on the type of material or also on the source (e.g., static image on the Internet, picture from a magazine, active images from television)?

• What are the limits of this research, and to what extent can we make comparisons among the effects of viewing different types of inappropriate material (e.g., sexually explicit vs. violent vs. hate speech)?

Part II: Developmental Considerations for Determining Appropriate Internet Use Guidelines for Children and Adolescents

Patricia Greenfield, Professor, Department of Psychology, University of California, Los Angeles

James Youniss, Professor, Life Cycle Institute, Catholic University of America

Dorothy Singer, Senior Research Scientist, Department of Psychology, Yale University, and Co-director, Yale University Family Television Research and Consultation Center

Issues for Discussion

• How are emotional, cognitive, social, and moral development affected by the media landscape created by children's access to and use of the Internet?

• What types of material may be harmful according to children's growth and developmental needs, and how may harmful effects change with age and developmental milestone?

• How do parents and educators balance giving young people the responsibility of exploring the Internet with protecting them from material that may be disturbing?

• How should developmental issues shape non-technical strategies to protect kids from inappropriate material, and what non-technical strategies will most benefit children's development?

Push and Pull on the Internet: Children's Use and Experiences
Don Roberts, Thomas More Storke Professor, Department of Communication, Stanford University
Sarah Keller, Assistant Professor, Health Communication, Department of Communication, Emerson College
Moderator/Discussant: Janet Schofield, Committee Member, Professor of Psychology and Senior Scientist at the Learning Research and Development Center, University of Pittsburgh

Questions for Discussion

• How are children using the Internet, in what settings are children logging on, and are there differential patterns of use according to age, gender, and ethnicity?
• What are children's experiences while online, both positive and negative?
• How are children pulled into material that they might not otherwise view, and what effect might this have?
• How are young people driving their experiences on the Internet, and how can young people be encouraged to stay in charge of their online experiences?

Innovative Approaches and Existing Efforts to Use Non-Technological Strategies to Protect Children on the Internet
Laurie Lipper, Director, The Children's Partnership
Kathy Boguszewski, Instructional Technology Consultant, Wisconsin Department of Public Instruction
Mary Dempsey, Commissioner, Chicago Public Library
Nancy Willard, Director, Responsible Netizen Research, Center for Advanced Technology in Education, University of Oregon
Eileen Faucette, Founder and Coordinator, PTA Live Online
Moderator/Discussant: Winnie Wechsler, Committee Member

Questions for Discussion

• What are some of the non-technological strategies that might be used by educators, librarians, parents, and local communities to ensure children's safe and appropriate use of the Internet?
• What types of inappropriate material do these strategies address, and how do they protect against the potential harm this material might cause?
• Who has been responsible for implementing and monitoring these approaches?
• How can these approaches be tailored to different venues (e.g., home, school, library)?

Bridging Research, Policy, and Practice
Ellen Wartella, Dean and Professor, College of Communication, University of Texas, Austin
Laura Gurak, Associate Professor, Rhetoric; Faculty Fellow, Law; and Director, Internet Studies Center, University of Minnesota
Betty Chemers, Deputy Administrator, Office of Juvenile Justice and Delinquency Prevention

Questions for Discussion

• What research is needed to develop new non-technical strategies for protecting children from inappropriate material on the Internet?
• Are regulations needed to protect children on the Internet, and what policies might encourage children to use the Internet in safe and appropriate ways?
• How should nonprofit organizations, educational institutions, government agencies, and parents be working together to create a safe environment for kids to use the Internet?
• How should we be thinking about linking research, policy, and practice?

PLENARY MEETING OF MARCH 7-9, 2001

Excite@Home
450 Broadway
Redwood City, California

Wednesday, March 7

Basic Concepts in Information Retrieval
Nick Belkin
David D. Lewis
Hinrich Schutze, Center for the Study of Language and Information, Stanford University
David Forsyth, University of California, Berkeley
Ray Larson, University of California, Berkeley, School of Information Management and Systems

Issues for Discussion

• Stability of content categorization
• Automatic text categorization
• Machine-aided text understanding

- Vision and image recognition
- Search engine technology

Filters
Susan Getgood, Surf Control Inc.
James Wang, Pennsylvania State University
Bennett Hazelton, Peacefire

Questions for Discussion

- What techniques can be used to identify sexually explicit material?
- How do filter vendors select the content they screen?
- What flexibility do their products offer?
- What is involved in circumventing the filtering provisions?
- How is the performance of a product measured? (rates of false positives, false negatives)

Authentication and Age Verification
Eddie Zeitler, Lambert and Associates
Fred Cotton, Search.org
Deirdre Mulligan, University of California, Berkeley

Business Models

Models for Kid-Friendly and Kid-Safe Internet Businesses
Brian Pass, MediaOne
Irv Shapiro, Edventions Inc.

Questions for Discussion

- What are the primary challenges of building a business based on the idea of attracting kids to safe and appropriate Internet content?
- What is the business case for firms operating in this space?
- What role do responsible adults (parents, teachers, librarians, and so on) play?
- How do you deal with the issue of inappropriate material?

Business Models Based on Advertising and Ad Tracking
Chris Kelly, Excite@Home

Questions for Discussion

- How do business models based on the sale of Web advertising work?
- What techniques are used to filter out those with a low probability of buying from those with higher probabilities of buying?
- What drives the cost structure of such businesses?

Thursday, March 8

Rights Management Technology
  David Maher, Intertrust Inc.
  John Blumenthal, @Stake Inc.

Issues for Discussion

- The technology of digital rights management systems
- Infrastructure needed to support rights management systems
- Application of rights management systems to restricting distribution of material

Usenet Newsgroups and the World Wide Web
  Dan Geer

Developmental Progression and Sexuality
  John Gagnon, SUNY Stony Brook
  Pepper Schwartz, University of Washington
  Elizabeth Casparian, Independent Consultant

Questions for Discussion

- How does developmental progression affect the appropriateness of exposing a minor to sexually explicit material?
- What types of material may be harmful according to children's growth and developmental needs, and how may harmful effects change with age and developmental milestone?
- How should developmental issues shape efforts to protect kids from inappropriate sexually explicit material?

Approaches to Regulating Sexually Explicit Material on the Internet
  Larry Lessig

.xxx domains (by videoconference)
Donald Eastlake, Motorola

Public Testimony from Birds of a Feather Session with the 2001 Conference on Compters, Freedom, and Privacy, by Videoconference

SITE VISIT TO AUSTIN, TEXAS, APRIL 3-4, 2001

Attendees from the National Research Council
Linda Hodge
Marilyn Mason
Herb Lin (staff)
Daniel Llata (staff)

Tuesday, April 3

Pflugerville: John Connally High School
Session with teachers, administrators, school librarians, and technologists
Session with students

Cepeda Branch Library
Session with librarians and technical managers
Session with youth group leaders, teachers, and program directors

Open Session at the Courtyard Marriott Hotel North
Parents and PTA members
School board members
Other adults

Wednesday, April 4

Visit to Settlement Home
Panel session with students
Panel session with teachers and school administrators

SITE VISIT TO GREENVILLE, SOUTH CAROLINA, APRIL 17-18, 2001

Attendees from the National Research Council
Father William J. Byron
Linda Hodge
Bob Schloss
Herb Lin (staff)
Daniel Llata (staff)

Tuesday, April 17

Mauldin Middle School
   William Harner, District Superintendent
   Session with students
   Session with teachers and school administrators

W. Jack Greer Library of Mauldin
   Beverly James, Executive Director of Greenville County Library System
   Session with librarians and technical managers

Phillis Wheatley Association
   Session with youth group leaders
   Session with students

Open Session at W. Jack Greer Library of Mauldin
   Boards of Trustees, Greenville County Library System
   Representatives of School District of Greenville County
   PTSA representatives

Wednesday, April 18

Greenville Senior High Academy of Academic Excellence
   Ginger Stuart, Interim Principal
   Session with students
   Session with teachers and school administrators

SITE VISIT TO SALT LAKE CITY, UTAH, APRIL 26-27, 2001

Attendees from the National Research Council
   David Forsyth
   Geoffrey Stone
   Gail Pritchard (staff)
   Joah Iannotta (staff)

Thursday, April 26

Utah Education Network (UEN)
   Sessions with UEN administrators and technologists

Meeting with Paula Houston, Complaints Ombudsman, Obscenity and Pornography, Office of the Utah Attorney General

Salt Lake City Library
    Session with librarians and technical managers
    Session with Library Teen Advisory Panel

Open Session at Salt Lake City Library

Friday, April 27

Tooele High School
    Sessions with students
    Session with teachers and school administrators

SITE VISIT TO SAN DIEGO, CALIFORNIA, MAY 2-3, 2001

Attendees from the National Research Council
    Linda Hodge
    Janet Schofield
    Winnie Wechsler
    Herb Lin (staff)
    Gail Pritchard (staff)

Wednesday, May 2

Rancho Bernardo High School
    Session with students from the high school
    Session with students from Bernardo Heights Middle School
    Session with high school teachers, school administrators, and school librarians

Casa Familia Community Program
    Session with Casa Familia staff
    Session with Casa Familia students
    Session with Casa Familia youth group leaders, instructors, and technical managers

El Cajon Library
    Session with librarians and technical managers

Open Session in El Cajon Library Community Room

Thursday, May 3

Lincoln High School
    Session with high school students

SITE VISIT TO BLACKSBURG, VIRGINIA, MAY 8-9, 2001

Attendees from the National Research Council
Dick Thornburgh
Sandra Calvert
Linda Hodge
Robin Raskin
Herb Lin (staff)
Gail Pritchard (staff)

Tuesday, May 8

Blacksburg Middle School
Session with students
Session with teachers and school administrators

Christiansburg High School
Session with librarians and technical managers
Session with instructional supervisors and teachers of technology courses

Blacksburg Electronic Village
Discussion with director

Wednesday, May 9

Blacksburg High School
Session with teachers and school administrators
Session with students

SITE VISIT TO CORAL GABLES, FLORIDA, MAY 31-JUNE 1, 2001

Attendees from the National Research Council
Nick Belkin
Herb Lin (staff)
D.C. Drake (staff)

Thursday, May 31

Coral Gables High School
Session with students (mostly juniors and sophomores)
Session with teachers and school administrators

Boys and Girls Club, Kendall Branch
    Session with students
    Session with administrators and instructors

Open Session at Coral Reef Senior High School
    PTA representatives
    Other parents

SITE VISIT TO REDDING, SHELTON, BRISTOL, KENT, AND HAMDEN, CONNECTICUT, JUNE 1-2, 2001

Attendees from the National Research Council
    Dan Geer
    Linda Hodge

Friday, June 1

Joel Barlow High School in Redding, Connecticut
    Panel session with parents and community members

Shelton Intermediate School in Shelton, Connecticut
    Session with teachers, school administrators, librarians, technical managers, and resource officers
    Session with middle school students

Bristol Board of Education Offices in Bristol, Connecticut
    Session with principals, teachers, public librarians, students, and technical managers

Open Session at Kent Center School in Kent, Connecticut
    Session with local education policy makers and parents

Saturday, June 2

Connecticut State PTA Office
    Session with parents

B

Glossary and Acronyms

Acceptable use policy (AUP) is a set of guidelines and expectations about how individuals will conduct themselves online.

Adolescent is generally an individual older than 13 but younger than the age of majority or 18, whichever is smaller.

Adult is an individual who has attained the age of majority. Note that "adult" is a term with legal significance and also with social significance. The age of majority varies by state and even by context (e.g., a 19-year-old can vote but not drink alcohol in many states).

Adult verification service is a service provided to businesses that validates the adult status of certain customers. Often, but not always, a credit card is used to provide assurance of one's adult status.

Algorithm is a step-by-step problem-solving procedure, especially an established computational procedure for solving a problem in a finite number of steps.

Authentication is the process of confirming an asserted identity with a specified, or understood, level of confidence. The mechanism can be based on something the user knows, such as a password, something the user possesses, such as a smart card, something intrinsic to the person, such as a fingerprint, or a combination of two or more of these.

AVI is a format for online video. A file named "example.avi" is likely to be a full-motion video that can be played on a computer.

Bandwidth refers to the amount of data that can be transmitted in a fixed amount of time. For digital devices, bandwidth is usually expressed in bits per second (bps) or bytes per second. A standard dial-up connection to the Internet, for example, typically has a bandwidth of around 56 k (or 56,000 bits per second).

Binary refers to a number system that has just two unique digits. Computers operate on the binary numbering system (binary code), which consists of just two unique numbers, 0 and 1 (or, as some like to think of it, "on" and "off").

Bit (or binary digit) is the smallest element of computer storage. It is a single digit in a binary number (0 or 1).

Black list, in Internet filtering technology, is a list of Web sites (or URLs) to which access from a given workstation or user has been specifically forbidden. Contrast with *white list*.

Boolean logic refers to a system of logic based on operators such as AND, OR, and NOT. In many search engines, search terms are linked with these Boolean operators to formulate more precise queries.

Broadband is a term used commonly to refer to communications or Web access that is faster than dial-up (56 k). Such access would include cable modems and digital subscriber lines.

Browser software is the actual computer program used to view documents on the World Wide Web (e.g., Netscape's Navigator or Microsoft's Internet Explorer).

Bulletin board is a computer system used as an information source and forum for a particular interest group. The bulletin board typically holds postings made by various participants and replies to those postings from other participants.

Byte is the common unit of computer storage. It is made up of eight bits (or binary digits). A byte holds the equivalent of a single character, such as the letter A, a dollar sign, or a decimal point.

Cache refers to a place to store files locally for quicker access. Caches are used to speed up data transfer and may be either temporary or permanent. Memory and disk caches are used in every computer to speed up instruction execution and data retrieval.

CERT is the Computer Emergency Response Team based at Carnegie Mellon University.

Chat is real-time conferencing between two or more users on the Internet. Chatting is usually accomplished by typing on the keyboard, not speaking, and each message is transmitted directly to the recipient.

Chat room is a virtual room where a chat session takes place. Technically, a chat room is really a channel, but the term "room" is used to promote the chat metaphor.

Child is used in the report to denote a broad category of individuals who are younger than adult.

Click (or mouse click) is a way of making a selection online.

Client is an application that runs on a personal computer or workstation and relies on a server to perform some operations. For example, an e-mail client is an application that enables one to send and receive e-mail.

Client-server model is a network architecture in which each computer or process on the network is either a client or a server. Servers are powerful computers or processes dedicated to managing disk drives (file servers), printers (print servers), or network traffic (network servers). Clients are PCs or workstations on which users run applications. Clients rely on servers for resources, such as files, devices, and even processing power.

Client-side refers to any operation that is performed at the client workstation. Contrast with server-side.

Content provider is an organization or individual that creates information, educational, or entertainment content for the Internet. A content provider may or may not provide the software or network infrastructure used to access the material.

Cookie is a message given to a Web browser by a Web server. The browser stores the message in a file (generally called cookie.txt). The message is then sent back to the server each time the browser requests a page from the server. Cookies are often used by Web sites to track users and their preferences.

Cost per acquisition (CPA) refers to an advertising model in which an advertiser pays a Web site operator for displaying an ad based on the number of new subscriptions the ad generates.

Cost per click (CPC) refers to an advertising model in which an advertiser pays a Web site operator a certain amount (e.g., $0.05) each time a user clicks on one of the advertiser's ads on the operator's Web site.

Cost per mille [thousand] (CPM) refers to an advertising model in which an advertiser pays a Web site operator each time the advertiser's ad is displayed (e.g., $3 per 1,000 displays).

Crawler—see *spider* or *Web crawler*.

Cybersex referes to online real-time dialog with someone (usually text-based) that interactively describes sexual behavior and actions with one's online partner for erotic purposes and expression.

Cyberspace is a term—coined by William Gibson in his 1984 novel *Neuromancer*—that refers to the Internet or to the online or digital world in general.

CyberTipline is the program operated by the National Center for Missing and Exploited Children for reporting child abuse and child pornography.

Database is a collection of information organized in such a way that users (often both people and computer programs) can quickly select desired pieces of data.

Dial-up is the most common method for accessing the Internet. It involves making a connection from a user's computer (by using a modem) over a standard phone line to an Internet service provider. Contrast with "always-on" access methods such as cable modems or DSL lines.

Digital subscriber line (DSL) is a term used to denote a class of technologies that use copper phone lines to establish high-speed Internet connections between telephone switching stations and homes or businesses (a so-called "last-mile" technology).

Domain name service (DNS) is an Internet service that translates domain names into IP addresses. For example, the domain name "www.national academies.org" might translate to "198.105.232.4."

Download refers to the act of copying data (usually an entire file) from a main source to a peripheral device. The term is often used to describe the process of copying a file from an online service to one's own computer.

E-mail is short for "electronic mail," the transmission of messages over networks.

Encryption is any procedure used in cryptography to convert plain text into cyphertext to prevent anyone but the intended recipient from reading the data.

File attachment is a method by which users of e-mail can attach files to messages (e.g., one might send a relative a digital picture of a newborn in an e-mail announcing his or her birth).

Filter (or filtering) is a type of technology that allows Internet material or activities that are deemed inappropriate to be blocked, so that the individual using that filtered computer cannot gain access to that material or participate in those activities.

Gnutella is file sharing system on the Internet that lets users search for software and documents on the GnutellaNet, a loose federation of users and organizations that make a wide variety of information available to the world at large. Gnutella is also an example of peer-to-peer networking.

Graphics file is a file that holds an image. JPEG and GIF are two popular formats for image files.

Hard disk is a computer's primary storage medium, and it is usually a fixed component within the computer itself. Contrast with "floppy" disks, which are temporary, disposable, and removable.

Harvester is an automated program that is designed to collect e-mail addresses by scanning Web sites, bulletin boards, and chat rooms (among other things).

History file refers to the list most Web browsers maintain of downloaded pages in a session so that users can quickly review everything that has been retrieved. However, history files can be cleared or altered easily.

Hypertext markup language (HTML) is the authoring language used to create documents on the Web. Web pages are built with HTML codes (usually called "tags") embedded in the text; these tags define page layout, fonts, and graphic elements, as well as hypertext links to other documents on the Web.

Hypertext transfer protocol (HTTP) is a communications protocol used to connect clients and servers on the Web. HTTP's primary function is to establish a connection with a Web server and transmit HTML pages to the client browser.

ICQ ("I Seek You") is a conferencing program for the Internet. Much like AOL's Instant Messenger service, ICQ provides interactive chat and file transfer, and can alert users when someone on their predefined list has come online.

ICRA is the Internet Content Rating Association (www.icra.org).

Image recognition/analysis (or "recognition") is the process through which a computer can identify an image (e.g., this graphics file contains an image of a naked woman).

Information retrieval refers to the processes, methods, and procedures used to selectively recall recorded data from a database.

Instant message (IM) is a two-way, real-time, private dialog between two users. A user initiating an IM sends an invitation to talk to another (specific) user who is online at the same time. Instant messaging is very popular today, because unlike participation in chat rooms, one tends to talk to people whom one already knows. Note also that IMs are often used in conjunction with chat rooms—a user in a chat room can send an IM to someone else in the chat room (because he or she sees the other party's screen name or "handle"), thus establishing a private communication.

Intellectual property refers to the ownership of ideas and control over the tangible or virtual representation of those ideas.

Internet is a decentralized global communications network connecting millions of individual users and machines.

Internet protocol (IP) is a part of the TCP/IP suite of protocols that allows the various machines that make up the Internet to communicate with each other.

Internet relay chat (IRC) is another conferencing system used on the Internet. However, unlike in instant messaging, users do not communicate directly with each other; rather, the server broadcasts all messages to all current users of a particular channel.

Internet service provider (ISP) is an organization or company that provides access to the Internet. Examples of national-level ISPs include America Online (AOL), Earthlink, and Microsoft Network (MSN).

Internet telephony refers to two-way transmission of audio over the Internet. Internet telephony allows users to employ the Internet as the transmission medium for telephone calls. It is also commonly referred to as voice-over-IP (VoIP).

IP address is an identifier for a computer or device on a TCP/IP network. Networks using the TCP/IP protocol route messages based on the IP address of the destination. The format of an IP address is a 32-bit numeric address written as four numbers separated by periods. Each number can be zero to 255 (e.g., "1.160.10.240" could be an IP address).

Keystroke log is a method for recording each keystroke made by a user on a given computer.

Link (or hyperlink) is a reference or pointer to another document. Clicking on (or selecting) a link on a Web page generally takes one to the document being referenced (e.g., clicking on a link to the NRC's home page will open the NRC's home page document in the user's browser).

Local area network (LAN) is a computer network that spans a relatively small area. Most LANs are confined to a single building or group of buildings. However, one LAN can be connected to other LANs over any distance via telephone lines and radio waves.

Log is a file that lists actions that have occurred. For example, Web servers maintain log files listing every request made to the server. See also *keystroke log*.

Login refers to the way that computers recognize users. Logins are also commonly referred to as user names. Generally, the combination of a correct login (or user name) and password is required to gain access to networked computers.

Megabyte (MB) is the term used to denote 1 million bytes (or, more precisely, 1,048,576 bytes).

Meta tags are elements within HTML code that allow page creators to describe the content of Web pages. Meta tags are often read and indexed by search engines.

Metadata is component of data which describes the data. It describes the content, quality, condition, or other characteristics of data. For instance, in the HEAD section of most HTML documents, many Web page creators encode information about the title, author, date of creation or update, and keywords relating to or descriptions of the document's content.

Minor is a term generally used in a legal context to denote individuals who are younger than adults.

Modem is a device that enables a computer to transmit digital data over analog telephone lines.

Moderated newsgroup is a mailing list in which all postings are "moderated" by a specific individual with the authority and power to reject individual postings that he or she deems inappropriate.

Mousetrapping is a technique that forces a user to remain on a specific Web site by not allowing the user to leave the site. Whenever the user tries to leave the site by closing the browser window or going to a new URL, the site that is mousetrapping will automatically open a new browser window with its URL or not allow the browser to go to the new URL.

MPEG is a term that refers to the family of digital video compression standards and file formats developed by the Motion Picture Encoding Group (hence, MPEG). The term is also often used to refer to the files of digital video and audio data available on the Internet.

Multimedia refers to applications that combine text, graphics, full-motion video, and/or sound into an integrated package.

Napster was initially an application that gave individuals access to one another's music (MP3) files by creating a unique file-sharing system over the Internet.

Net is a short term for Internet.

Newsgroup is an online discussion group. On the Internet, there are literally thousands of newsgroups covering every conceivable interest (e.g., see <http://groups.google.com>).

Offline refers to the time that a user is not connected to the Internet. Contrast with *online*.

Online refers to the time that a user is connected to the Internet. Contrast with *offline*.

Overblocking refers to a situation where Internet filtering software blocks access to resources that authorities did not intend to block. Contrast with *underblocking*.

Password is a secret series of characters that enables a user to access a file, computer, or program. On multiuser systems, each user must enter his or her correct user-name/password combination before the computer will respond to commands.

Peer-to-peer network is a communications network that allows all computers in the network to act as servers and share their files with all other users on the network. Gnutella is one example of peer-to-peer networking on the Internet. Contrast with *client-server*.

Pixel is the smallest discrete element of an image or picture on a computer monitor (usually a single-colored dot).

Platform for Internet content selection (PICS) is a system for rating the content of Web sites that has been endorsed by the World Wide Web Consortium.

Plug-in is an auxiliary program that works with Internet browser software to enhance its capability (e.g., RealNetwork's RealPlayer or Microsoft's Media Player).

Portal is a Web site or service that offers a broad array of resources and services, such as e-mail, search engines, subject directories, and forums. Yahoo! is an example of a portal.

Precision is a measure of the effectiveness of information retrieval and is often expressed as the ratio of relevant documents to the total number of documents retrieved in response to a specific search. For example, using a Web search engine, if a search retrieves 100 documents, but only 30 of them are truly relevant to the search, the precision would be 30 percent. Contrast with *recall*.

Probabilistic algorithm is an algorithm that works for all practical purposes but has a theoretical chance of being wrong.

Proxy server is a server that sits between a client application, such as a Web browser, and a real server. It intercepts all requests to the real server to see if it can fulfill the requests itself. If not, it forwards the request to the real server. Proxy servers can also be used to filter requests to prevent users from accessing specific Web sites.

Push transfer refers to a form of data delivery in which data is automatically delivered to the user's computer without the user's having to make a request for the data.

Real-time audio/video refers to communication of either sound of images over the Internet that occurs without delay in real time, much like a telephone conversation.

Recall is a measure of the effectiveness of document retrieval expressed as a ratio of the total number of relevant documents in a given database (or on the Web) to the number of relevant entries or documents retrieved in response to a specific search. However, determining a search's recall can be problematic because it is often very difficult to determine the total number of relevant entries in all but very small databases. Contrast with *precision*.

Remote viewing is the capability of system administrators (whether they be information technology "helpdesk" personnel or teachers in a classroom) to view what is being displayed on a given workstation or computer from their own location.

Scanner is a device that can copy text or illustrations printed on paper and translate that information into a form a computer can use.

Screen name is an alias (or short nickname) chosen by a computer user to employ when accessing his or her online service or network account. See also *login*.

Search engine is program that searches documents (or indexes of documents) for specified words or phrases and returns a list of the documents where those items were found.

Server is a computer (as well as the software that is running on that computer) that delivers (or serves up) Web pages.

Server-side refers to any operation that is performed at the server. Contrast with *client-side*.

Smart card is a small physical hardware device (typically the size of a credit card) containing read-only non-volatile memory and a microprocessor that can be inserted into a card reader attached to a computer. In most scenarios, the individual user carries the card and inserts it into an Internet access point that requires such a device. The memory on-board the device can store information about the user, including his or her age, preferences for material to be blocked, and so on. Software installed on the computer, and on Web sites visited, would check the smart card for dates of birth when necessary, and if the user were underage for certain types of material, would refuse to grant access to that material.

Spam generally refers to unsolicited e-mail, particularly unsolicited e-mail of a commercial nature.

Spider is a computer program that automatically retrieves Web documents. They are often used to feed pages to search engines for indexing. Another term for these programs is *Web crawler*.

Streaming media refers to a technique for transferring data in such a way that it can be processed as a steady and continuous stream (as opposed to the user's needing to download the entire file before being able to view or listen to it).

Surfing (or Web surfing) is a metaphor for browsing the contents of the Web.

TCP/IP (or Transmission Control Protocol/Internet Protocol) is the suite of communications protocols used to connect machines on the Internet. TCP/IP allows different hosts on the Internet to establish a connection with each other and exchange streams of data.

Teaser refers to Web pages or portions of Web sites that are intended to entice users to spend more time at a given Web site or become paying customers.

Thumbnail is a miniature display of a page or image. Thumbnails enable users to see the layout of many items on the screen at once.

Top-level domains are the major subdivisions within the Internet's domain name service (DNS). Examples of top level domains include—among others—.com, .gov, and .edu.

Traffic refers to the load on a given Web site or resource. A high-traffic Web site, for instance, receives many visitors or requests for data.

Traffic forwarding is the practice whereby one Web site forwards traffic to another Web site and may receive a fee for doing so.

Underblocking refers to a situation whereby Internet filtering software does not block access to resources that authorities intended to block. Contrast with *overblocking*.

Uniform resource locator (URL) is the address of documents and other resources on the World Wide Web. The first part of a URL indicates what protocol to use to access the document (e.g., "http" or "ftp"), while the second part specifies the domain name where the resource is located (e.g., www.example.com) as well as the directory and the name of the requested document.

Usenet is a worldwide bulletin board system that can be accessed through the Internet or through many online services. It contains more than 14,000 forums, called newsgroups, that cover almost every imaginable interest group.

V-chip is an electronic circuit or mechanism in a television that parents can use to block programs they consider inappropriate for their children. V-chips can be configured to block all programs of a given rating.

Virtual hosting refers to the ability of Internet service providers or Web site operators to "host" Web sites or other services for different entities on one computer while giving the appearence that they exist on separate servers. For instance, with virtual hosting, one might have Web sites from two separate, distinct organizations residing on and being served from one particular server (with one particular IP address).

Web is a shortened form of World Wide Web (WWW).

Web crawler is a computer program that automatically retrieves Web documents. They are often used to feed pages to search engines for indexing. Another term for these programs is *spider*.

Web page hosting refers to the ability of Internet service providers, companies, or other organizations to act as a server of Web pages.

Webcam is a video camera that is used to capture periodic images or continuous frames to a Web site for display.

WebTV is a service that makes a connection to the Internet via a user's telephone service and then converts the downloaded Web pages to a format that can be displayed on a television.

White list, in Internet filtering technology, is a list of Web sites (or URLs) to which access from a given workstation or user has been specifically approved. Contrast with *black list*.

Workstation refers to a computer connected to a network (often the Internet).

World Wide Web (WWW) refers to the set of all the information resources that can be accessed via HTTP.

World Wide Web Consortium (W3C) is one of the main standards bodies for the World Wide Web. The W3C works with the global community to help establish international standards for client and server protocols that enable communications on the Internet.

C

Selected Technology Issues

C.1 INFORMATION RETRIEVAL TECHNOLOGIES

Information retrieval, a function that supports people who are actively seeking or searching for information, typically assumes a static or relatively static database of digital objects against which people search. These digital objects may be documents, images, sound recordings, and so on.

The general information retrieval problem is one of making a decision about which objects in the database to show to the user. Systems for information retrieval seek to maximize the material that a person sees that is likely to be relevant to his or her information problem, and to minimize the material that is not relevant to the problem.

An information retrieval system works by representing the objects in a database in some well-specified manner, and then representing the user's information problem ("information need") in a similar fashion. The retrieval techniques then compare needs with objects.

A key aspect of object representation is the language used to describe the objects in question. Typically, this language (more precisely, a "metalanguage") consists of a vocabulary (and sometimes precise grammar) that can characterize the objects in a form suitable for automated comparison to the user's needs.

The representation of information objects also requires interpretations by a human indexer, machine algorithm, or other entity. When people are involved, the interpretation of a particular text by one person is likely to be different from that of someone else, and may even be different for one person at different times. As a person's state of knowledge changes, his or her understanding of a text changes. Everyone has experienced the situation of finding a document not relevant at some point, but quite relevant later on, perhaps for a different problem or perhaps because we, ourselves, are different. Such subjectivity means that decisions about representation will be inconsistent. An extensive literature on interindexer consistency indicates that when people are asked to represent an information object, even if they are highly trained in using the same meta-language (indexing language), they might achieve 60 to 70 percent consistency at most in tasks like assigning descriptors.[1]

Machine-executable algorithms for representing information objects or information problems do give consistent representations. But any one such algorithm gives only one interpretation of the object, out of a great variety of possible representations, depending on the interpreter. The most typical way to accomplish such representations is through statistically based automatic indexing. Techniques of this sort index (represent) documents by the words that appear in them, deleting the most common (articles, prepositions, and other function words), conflating different forms of a word into one (e.g., making plural and singular forms the same), and weighting the resulting terms according to some function of how often they appear in the document (term frequency—the more occurrences, the greater the weight) and how many documents they appear in (document frequency—the more documents, the lower the weight).

A consistent result in information retrieval experimentation is that automatic indexing of the sort just described gives results that are at least as good as human indexing, and usually better. Performance is evaluated by a pair of measures, *recall* and *precision*.[2] This result is often stated as meaning that automatic indexing is better than manual indexing, because manual indexing is so much more expensive than automatic. But it is important to keep in mind another consistent information retrieval result, that the sets (or lists) of documents that are retrieved using one technique

---

[1]L.E. Lawrence, 1977, *Inter-indexer Consistency Studies 1954-1975: A Review of the Literature and summary of study results*, University of Illinois, Graduate School of Library Science, Urbana-Champaign; K. Markey, 1984, "Interindexer Consistency Tests: A Literature Review and Report of a Test of Consistency in Indexing Visual Materials," *Library and Information Research*, 6(2): 155-177; L. Mai-Chan, 1989, "Inter-indexer consistency in subject cataloging," *Information Technology and Libraries* 8(4): 349-357.

[2]"Recall" measures how complete the search results are, and is the proportion of relevant documents in the whole collection that have actually been retrieved. "Precision" measures how precise the search results are, and is the proportion of retrieved documents that are relevant.

are different from those retrieved by another technique (both relevant and non-relevant documents).

Having constructed representations of both the information objects and the person's information problem, the information retrieval system is in a position to compare these representations to one another, in order to identify those objects that match the information problem description. Technologies for accomplishing this are called *search* or *retrieval techniques*. Because people in general cannot specify precisely what it is that they do not know (that for which they are searching), because people cannot represent accurately and completely what an information object is *about*, and because relevance judgments are inherently subjective, it is clear that such techniques must be probabilistic, rather than deterministic. That is, any decision as to whether to retrieve (or block) an information object is always a guess, more or less well informed. Thus, in information retrieval, we cannot ever say with confidence that an information object is (or is not) relevant to an information need, but can only make judgments of probability (or belief) of (non)relevance.

It can be easily seen that many of the problems that information retrieval faces are also problems that information filtering must face. Although filtering aims to *not* retrieve certain information objects, it still must do so on the basis of some representation of those objects, and some representation of the person for whom the filtering is done. Filtering works by prespecifying some information object descriptions that are to be excluded from viewing by some person or class of persons. Thus, it depends crucially on having an accurate and complete representation of what is to be excluded (this is analogous to the query or information problem representation), and also accurate and complete representations of the information objects that are to be tested for exclusion. Just as in information retrieval, making the exclusion decision in information filtering is an inherently uncertain process.

C.1.1 Text Categorization and Representation

Automatic text categorization is the primary language retrieval technology in content screening. Text categorization is the sorting of text into groups, such as pornography, hate speech, and violence. A text categorizer looks at a text-based information object and decides the proper categorization for this object. Applications of text categorization are filtering of electronic e-mail, chats, or Web access; and indexing and data mining.

The principal problem with text categorization is that text is ambiguous in many ways: polysemy, synonymy, and so on. For example, a bank can be either a financial institution or something on the side of a river (polysemy). The context matters a lot in the interpretation.

Efficient automatic text categorization requires an automated categorization decision that identifies, on the basis of some categorization rules, the category into which an object falls. (Note that if the rules are separated from the decision maker, the behavior of the decision maker can be changed merely by changing the rules, rather than requiring the rewriting every time of the software underlying the decision maker.) The decision-making software examines the text in the information object, and on the basis of these rules, categorizes the object. The simplest decision rules might base the decision on the mere presence of certain words (e.g., if the word "breast" appears, the object is pornographic). More sophisticated rules might search for combinations of words (e.g., if the word "breast" appears without the word "cancer," the object is pornographic), or even weighted combinations of different words.

Decision rules are developed by modeling the kinds of decisions that responsible human beings make. Thus, the first step in automated rule writing (also known as "supervised learning") is to ask a responsible individual to identify, for example, which of 500 digital text objects constitute pornography and which do not. The resulting categorization thus provides a training set of 500 sample decisions to be mimicked by the decision rules.

Of course, the selection of the persons who provide the samples is crucial, because whatever they do becomes the gold standard, which the decision rules then mimic. Everything depends on the particular persons and their judgments, but the technology does not provide guidance on how to define the community or whom to select as representatives of that community.

Research indicates that supervised learning is at least as good as expert human rule writing.[3] The effectiveness of these methods is far from perfect—there is always a high error rate—but sometimes it is near agreement with human performance levels. Still, the results differ from category to category, and it is not clear how directly it applies to, for example, pornography. As discussed below, there is an inevitable trade-off between false positives and false negatives (i.e., attributing an item to a category when it should not be; not attributing an item to a category when it should be), and categories vary widely in difficulty. Substantially improved methods are not expected in the next 10 to 20 years.

---

[3]Fabrizio Sebastiani. 2002. "Machine Learning in Automated Text Categorization," *ACM Computing Surveys* 34(1): 1-47.

It is not clear which text categorization techniques are most effective. The best techniques are not yet used commercially, so there may be incremental improvements. Nor is it clear how effective semiautomated categorization is, or whether the categories that are difficult for automated methods are the same as those that most perplex people.

The simplest machine representation of text is what is known as the "bag-of-words" model, in which all of the words in an object are treated as an unstructured list. If the object's text is, "Dick Armey chooses Bob Shaffer to lead committee," then a representative list would be: Armey, Bob, chooses, committee, Dick, lead, Shaffer. (A slightly more sophisticated version associates a count of the number of times each word occurs with the word itself.) Note that in such a representation, the structure and context of the text are completely lost.

Thus, one weakness in the representation is due to the ambiguity of language, which is resolved in human discourse through context. For example, the word "beaver" has a hunter's meaning and a pornographic meaning. Other words, such as "breast" and "blow," may be less ambiguous but can be used pornographically or otherwise. When context is important in determining meaning, the bag-of-words representation is inadequate.

The bag-of-words representation is most useful when two conditions are met: when there are unambiguous words indicating relevant content, and when there are relatively few of these indicators. Pornographic text has these properties; probably about 40 or 50 words, most of them unambiguous, indicate pornography. Thus, the bag-of-words representation is reasonably well suited for this application, especially if a high rate of false positives is acceptable. However, in many other areas, such as violence and hate speech, the bag-of-words representation is less useful. (For example, while a pornographic text such as the text on an adult Web page often can be identified by viewing the first few words, one must often read four or five sentences of a text before identifying it as hate speech.)

When fidelity of representation becomes important, a number of techniques can go beyond the bag-of-words model: morphological analysis, part-of-speech tagging, translation, disambiguation, genre analysis, information extraction, syntactic analysis, and parsing. For example, a technique more robust than the bag-of-words approach is to consider adjacent words, as search engines do when they give higher weight to information objects that match the query and have certain words in the same sentence. However, even with these technologies, true machine-aided text understanding will not be available in the near term, and there always will be a significant error rate with any automated method. Approaches that go beyond the bag-of-words representation improve accuracy, which may be important in contexts apart from pornography.

C.1.2 Image Representation and Retrieval

Images can be ambiguous in at least as many ways as text can be. Furthermore, there is no universal meta-language for describing images. People who are interested in images for advertising purposes have different ways to talk and think about them than do art historians, even though they may be searching for the same images. The lack of a common meta-language for images means that special meta-languages must be developed for images for use in different problem domains.

The process of determining whether a given image is pornographic involves object recognition, which is very difficult for a number of reasons. First, it is difficult to know what an object is; things look different from different angles and in different lights. When color and texture change, things look different. People can change their appearance by moving their heads around. We do not look different to one another when we do this, but we certainly look different in pictures.

Today, it is difficult for computer programs to find people, though finding faces can be done with reasonably high confidence. It is often possible to tell whether a picture has nearly naked people in it, but there is no program that reliably determines whether there are people wearing clothing in a picture.

To find naked people, image recognition programs exploit the fact that virtually everyone's skin looks about the same in a picture, as long as one is careful about intensity issues. Skin is very easy to detect reliably in pictures, so an image recognition program searching for naked people first searches for skin. So, one might simply assume that any big blob of skin must be a naked person.

However, images of the California desert, apple pies, and all sorts of other things are rendered in approximately the same way as skin. A more refined algorithm would then examine how the skin/desert/pie coloring is arranged in an image. For example, if the coloring is arranged in patterns that are long and thin, that pattern might represent an arm, a leg, or a torso. Then, because the general arrangement of body parts is known, the location of an arm, for example, provides some guidance about where to search for a leg. Assembling enough of such pieces together can provide enough information for recognizing a person.

A number of factors help to identify certain pornographic pictures, such as those that one might find on an adult Web site. For example, in such pictures, the people tend to be big, and there is not much other than people in these pictures. Exploiting other information, such as the source of the image or the words and links on the Web page from which the image is drawn, can increase the probability of reliable identification of such an image.

But it is essentially impossible for current computer programs to distinguish between hard-core and soft-core pornography, because what constitutes "hard-core" versus "soft-core" pornography is in the eyes of the viewer rather than the image itself. Consider also whether the photographs of Jock Sturges, many of which depict naked children, constitute pornography. Furthermore, in the absence of additional information, it is quite impossible for computer programs to distinguish between images that contain naked people in what might be pornographic poses, which are considered "high art" (e.g., paintings by Rubens), and what someone might consider a truly pornographic image.

What computer programs can do with reasonable reliability today (and higher reliability in the future) is to determine whether there might be naked people in a picture. But any of the contextual issues raised above will remain beyond the purview of automated recognition for the foreseeable future.

C.2 SEARCH ENGINES AND OTHER OPERATIONAL INFORMATION RETRIEVAL SYSTEMS

Information retrieval systems consist of a database of information objects, techniques for representing those objects and queries put to the database, and techniques for comparing query representations to information object representations. The typical technique for representing information objects is *indexing* them, according to words that appear in the documents, or words that are assigned to the documents by humans or by automatic techniques. An information retrieval system then takes the words that represent the user's query (or filter), and compares them to the "inverted index" of the system, in which all of the words used to index the objects in the collection are listed and linked to the documents that are indexed by them. Surrogates (e.g., titles) for those objects that most closely (or exactly) match (i.e., are indexed by) the words in the query are then retrieved and displayed to the user of the system. It is then up to the user to decide whether one or more of the retrieved objects is relevant, or worth looking at.

From the above description, it is easy to see that "search engines" are a type of information retrieval system, in which the database is some collection of pages from the World Wide Web, which have been indexed by the system, and in which the retrieved results are links to the pages that have been indexed by the words in the user's query.

The basic algorithm in search engines is based on the "bag-of-words" model for handling data described above. However, they also use some kind of recognition of document structure to improve the effectiveness of a search. For example, search engines often treat titles differently from the body of a Web page; titles can often indicate the topic of a page. If the system can extract structure from documents, then this often can be used as an indicator for refining the retrieval process.

Many search engines also normalize the data, a process that involves stripping out capitalization and most of the other orthographic differences that distinguish words. Some systems do not throw this information away automatically, but rather attempt to identify things such as sequences of capitalized words possibly indicating a place name or person's name. The search engine often removes stop words, a list of words that it chooses not to index—typically quite common words like "and" and "the."[4] In addition, the search engine may apply natural language processing to identify known phrases or chunks of text that properly belong together and indicate certain types of content.

What remains after such processing is a collection of words that need to be matched against documents represented in the database. The simplest strategy is the Boolean operator model. Simple Boolean logic says either "this word AND that word occur," or "this word OR that word occurs," and, therefore, the documents that have those words should be retrieved. Boolean matching is simple and easy to implement. Because of the volume of data on the Internet, almost all search engines today include an automatic default setting that, in effect, uses the AND operator with all terms provided to the search engine.

All Boolean combinations of words in a query can be characterized in a simple logic model that says, either this word occurs in the document, or it does not. If it does occur, then you have certain matches; if not, then you have other matches. Any combination of three words, for example, can be specified, such that the document has this word and not the other two, or all three together, or one and not the other of two. However, if the user does not specify the word *exactly* as it is stored in the index, then it will not be processed appropriately, and in particular the word cannot be a synonym (unless you supply that synonym), an alternate phrasing, or a euphemism.

Another strategy is the vector space model. A document is represented as an N-dimensional vector, in which N is the number of different words in the text, and the component of the vector in any given direction is simply the number of times the word appears in the text. The measure of similarity between two documents (or, more importantly, between a document and the search query similarly represented) is then given by the cosine of the angle between the two vectors. The value of this param-

---

[4]Note that the stop list is a likely place to put a filter. For example, if "bitch" was included in the stop list, no Web site, including that of the American Kennel Club Web site, would be found in searches that included the word "bitch."

eter ranges from zero to 1.0, and the closer the value is to 1.0, the more similar the document is to the query or to the other document. In this model, a perfect match (i.e., one with all the words present) is not necessary for a document to be retrieved. Instead, what is retrieved is a "best match" for the query (and of course, less good matches can also be displayed).

Most Web search engines use versions of the vector space model and also offer some sort of Boolean search. Some use natural language processing to improve search outcomes. Other engines (e.g., Google) use methods that weight pages depending on things like the number of links to a page. If there is only one link to a given page, then that page receives a lower ranking than a page with the same words but many links to it.

The preceding discussion assumes that the documents in question are text documents. Searching for images is much more difficult, because a similarity metric of images is very difficult to compute or even to conceptualize. For example, consider the contrast between the meaning of a picture of the Pope kissing a baby versus a picture of a politician kissing a baby. These pictures are the same in some ways, and very different in other ways.

More typically, image searches are performed by looking for text that is associated with images. A search engine will search for an image link tag within the HTML and the sentences that surround the image on either side—an approach with clear limitations. For example, the words, "Oh, look at the cute bunnies," mean one thing on a children's Web site and something entirely different on Playboy's site. Thus, the words alone may not indicate what those images are about.

C.3 LOCATION VERIFICATION

Today, the Internet is designed and structured in such a way that the physical location of a user has no significance for the functionality he or she expects from the Internet or any resources to which he or she is connected. This fact raises the question of the extent to which an Internet user's location can in fact be established through technical means alone.

Every individual using the Internet at a given moment in time is associated with what is known as an IP address, and that IP address is usually associated with some fixed geographical location. However, because IP addresses are allocated hierarchically by a number of different administrative entities, knowing the geographical location of one of these entities does not automatically provide information about the locations associated with IP addresses that it allocates. For example, the National Academy of Sciences is based in Washington, D.C., and it allocates IP addresses to computers tied to its network. However, the Academy has employees in California, and also computers that are tied to the Academy network. The Academy knows which IP addresses are in California and in Washington, D.C., but someone who knew only that an IP address was one associated with the Academy would not know where that IP address was located.[5]

Under some circumstances, it can be virtually impossible to determine the precise physical location of an Internet user. Consider, for example, the case of an individual connecting to the Internet through a dial-up modem. It is not an unreasonable assumption that the user is most likely in the region in which calls to the dial-up number are local, simply because it would be unnecessary for most people to incur long distance calling costs for such connections. Furthermore, the exchange serving dial-up modem access numbers can, in principle, employ caller-ID technology. However, the exchange associated with the telephone from which the dial-up call originates may not be technologically capable of providing caller-ID information; this would be the case in some areas in the United States and in much of the world. Or the user might simply suppress caller-ID information before making the dial-up modem call. In these instances, the number through which the individual connects to the Internet does not necessarily say anything about his location at that time.

Internet access routed through satellites can be difficult to localize as well. The reason is that a satellite's transmission footprint can be quite large (hundreds of square miles?), and more importantly is moving quite rapidly. Localization (but only within the footprint) can be accomplished only by working with a detailed knowledge of the orbital movements of an entire constellation of satellites.

However, those connecting to the Internet through a broadband connection can be localized much more effectively, though with some effort. For example, while a cable Internet ISP may assign IP addresses to users dynamically, any given address must be mappable to a specific cable modem that can be identified with its media access control address. While such mapping is usually done for billing and customer care reasons, it provides a ready guide to geographical addresses at the end user's level. Those who gain access through DSL connections can be located because the virtual circuit from the digital subscriber line access multiplexer is

---

[5]While location information is not provided automatically from the IP addresses an administrative entity allocates, under some circumstances, some location information can be inferred. For example, if the administrative entity is an ISP, and the ISP is, for example, a French ISP, it is likely—though not certain—that most of the subscribers to a French ISP are located in France. Of course, a large French company using this ISP might well have branch offices in London, so the geographical correspondence between French ISP and French Internet user will not be valid for this case, though as a rule of thumb, it may not be a bad working assumption.

mapped to a specific twisted pair of copper wires going into an individual's residence. Also, wireless connections made through cell phones (and their data-oriented equivalents) are now subject to a regulation that requires the network client to provide location information for E-911 (enhanced emergency 911) reasons. This information is passed through the signaling network and would be available to a wireless ISP as well.

In principle, the information needed to ascertain the location of any IP address is known collectively by a number of administrative entities, and could be aggregated automatically. But there is no protocol in place to pass this information to relevant parties, and thus such aggregation is not done today. The result is that in practice, recovering location information is a complex and time-consuming process.

To bypass these difficulties, technical proposals have been made for location-based authentication.[6] However, the implementation of such proposals generally requires the installation of additional hardware at the location of each access point, and thus cannot be regarded as a general-purpose solution that can localize all (or even a large fraction of) Internet users.

The bottom line is that determining the physical location of most Internet users is a challenging task today, though this task will become easier as broadband connections become more common.

C.4 USER INTERFACES

The history of information technology suggests that increasingly realistic and human-like forms of human-computer interaction will develop. The immediately obvious trends in the near-term future call for greater fidelity and "realism" in presentation. For example, faster graphics processors will enable more realistic portrayals of moving images, which soon will approach the quality of broadcast television. Larger screens in which the displayed image subtends a larger angle in the eye will increase the sense of being immersed in or surrounded by the image portrayed. Goggles with built-in displays do the same, but also offer the opportunity for three-dimensional images to be seen by the user. Virtual reality displays carry this a step further, in that the view seen by the user is adjusted for changes in perspective (e.g., as one turns one's head, the view changes).

---

[6]See, for example, Dorothy E. Denning and Peter F. MacDoran, 1996," Location-Based Authentication: Grounding Cyberspace for Better Security," in *Computer Fraud and Security*, Elsevier Science Ltd., February. A commercial enterprise now sells authentication systems that draw heavily on the technology described in this paper. See <http://www.cyberlocator.com/works.html>.

Speech and audio input/output are growing more common. Today, computers can provide output in the form of sound or speech that is either a reproduction of human speech or speech that is computer-synthesized. The latter kind of speech is not particularly realistic today but is expected to become more realistic with more research and over time. Speech recognition is still in its infancy as a useful tool for practical applications, even after many years of research, but it, too, is expected to improve in quality (e.g., the ability to recognize larger vocabularies, a broader range of voices, a lower error rate) over time.

Another dimension of user interface is touch and feel. The "joystick" often used in some computer-based video games provides the user with a kinesthetic channel for input. Some joysticks also feature a force feedback that, for example, increases the resistance felt by the user when the stick is moved farther to one side or another. Such "haptic" interfaces can also—in principle—be built into gloves and suits that could apply pressure in varying amounts to different parts of the body in contact with them.

Finally, gesture recognition is an active field of research. Humans often specify things by pointing with their hands. Computer-based efforts to recognize gestures can rely on visual processing in which a human's gestures are viewed optically through cameras connected to the computer, and the motions analyzed. A second approach is based on what is known as a dataglove, which can sense finger and wrist motion and transmit information on these motions to a computer.[7]

Product vendors of these technologies promise a user experience of extraordinarily high fidelity. For example, it is easy to see how these technologies could be used to enhance perceived awareness of others—one might be alone at home, but through one's goggles and headphones, hear and see others sharing the same "virtual" space. (In one of the simplest cases, one might just see others with goggles and headphones as well, but the digital retouching technologies that allow images to be modified might allow a more natural (though perhaps less realistic) depiction.)

---

[7]See, for example, <http://www.ireality.com/Wireless_announce.html> for a 1997 product announcement by the General Reality Company.

D

Site Visit Synthesis

D.1 BACKGROUND

The committee conducted site visits in a number of places, including Austin, Texas (April 3-4, 2001), Greenville, South Carolna (April 17-18, 2001), San Diego, California (May 2-3, 2001), Blacksburg, Virginia (May 8-9, 2001), Coral Gables, Florida (May 31, 2001), and various towns in Connecticut (Redding, Shelton, Bristol, Kent, and Hamden in the period June 1-2, 2001). During these site visits, members of the committee spoke with students in junior and senior high school, as well as school teachers, administrators, librarians, and technologists. In addition, the committee spoke with public librarians (branch managers, children's librarians, reference librarians) and technical managers from library systems. When possible, the committee also visited after-school programs and other venues in which young people had Internet access, and spoke with both children and responsible adults. Finally, the committee held a number of open sessions in which parents and other interested parties could talk to the committee.

D.2 RECURRING THEMES

Though the individuals to whom the committee spoke cannot be taken as being drawn from a representative population, a number of themes did occur repeatedly during the various site visits.

- Pornography was a concern of many students and school personnel, but only one of many. Teachers were more concerned about inaccurate and misleading information on the Internet, and with keeping students in school "on task." Both students and responsible adults were quite concerned about violence (especially "how-to" sites) and hate.

• Meeting people face-to-face that one had encountered first online in a chat room or through instant messaging was a standard practice. While only a small a number of students acknowledged having done so, all thought it was an unremarkable, commonplace occurrence. In general, they recognized in an abstract manner the dangers of doing so, but thought that they could tell if they were dealing with an untrustworthy individual—and said that they would never provide personal information to an individual they regarded as untrustworthy.

• High school students expressed a number of common sentiments, including the following:

—They often needed for research purposes information on Web sites that were blocked by the school filter ("improper blocking").

—They rarely or never complained to teachers about such blocking because they could get information anyway through home access.

—Many of the sites improperly blocked by the school were needed for senior high school purposes, but may have been appropriately blocked at the junior high school and elementary school levels.

—They had been exposed to Internet pornography, especially through spam mail, but had no interest in receiving such mail and deleted it as fast as they could get it.

—They were not particularly affected by Internet pornography because the entire media environment in which they live is highly sexualized. However, a number of students noted that what was upsetting about pornography was not so much the material itself as the likelihood that their parents would "freak out."

—They were frustrated by losing control of their computers, mentioning especially spam mail and mousetrapping.

• Most of the schools that the committee visited had installed filters, and many libraries had done so as well. However, when asked what benefit filters offered their schools and libraries, teachers and librarians invariably pointed to the political and management benefits—not a single teacher or librarian said that his or her students or patrons were better off with filters in place. The primary political benefit of filters was that they eliminated parental complaints, while the primary management benefit was that they eliminated the need for teachers and students to constantly monitor student and patron usage.

In schools, acceptable use policies (AUPs) were also common. However, students received little or no instruction in how to comply with them. Students signed AUPs (sometimes with parental signatures required as well), but they noted that the AUPs were just one more form to be filled out at the beginning of the year, and they were not given much attention, were often not even read carefully, and generally were not internalized in any meaningful way. In practice, AUPs seemed to be a tool with which a school could discipline a student for some behavior that was not explicitly forbidden but that nevertheless was inconsistent with school policy.

In no school were media literacy and Internet safety part of the formal curriculum. Librarians did note that they spent some time teaching students how to evaluate sources and credibility, but they were unable to spend more than a class period on this subject in the course of a year.

- Most libraries with filters noted that the filters solved problems caused by adults accessing pornography on the Internet on public access terminals and making a nuisance of themselves. Furthermore, they made staff more comfortable, because staff were no longer forced to confront patrons about violations of posted AUPs. Librarians were also concerned with staff having to make value judgments about what is and is not pornography, particularly when it comes to deciding what a customer can print and receive; they don't want to be "policemen" in the library; they believe the library should be used for educational purposes; and, they don't want to formally monitor what people are doing online.

- Both parents and students commented on the gap in knowledge between them. For example, many students reported that they can change their parents' parental preferences (on AOL) for themselves and have access to their parents' accounts, or that their parents don't know what privileges are associated with their screen names. In general, those students with home access have the most expertise, and hence the most knowledge about how to circumvent adults, know what is available on the net, and know where to find what they should not see. Parents acknowledged the knowledge gap as well, pointing out that they were uncomfortable working in an area in which they could not presume superior knowledge and experience and thus did not know how to properly instruct their children in this area. Moreover, many did not know much about the nature of the issues their children face on the Internet (apparently because of the significant differences between using the Internet as a social medium (the experience of their kids) and using it as a business medium (their own experience).

In general, the parents to whom the committee spoke understood the responsibility they had as parents to provide supervision. However, they were also aware to some extent that providing supervision does not necessarily mean that a child will absorb the lessons that such supervision is intended to impart. They understood the time-intensive nature of appropriate supervision and knew that they (and especially other parents) were unable or unwilling to provide supervision; nevertheless, they generally expressed considerable hesitation to involve the government in this problem (a view that was expressed by both liberal and conservative parents).

E

Biographies

E.1 COMMITTEE MEMBERS

Dick Thornburgh, *chair*, served as governor of Pennsylvania, attorney general of the United States, and undersecretary-general of the United Nations during a public career that spanned more than 25 years. He is currently counsel to the national law firm of Kirkpatrick & Lockhart LLP, resident in its Washington, D.C., office. Elected governor of Pennsylvania in 1978 and reelected in 1982, Thornburgh was the first Republican ever to serve two successive terms in that office and was named by his fellow governors as one of the nation's most effective big-state governors in a 1986 *Newsweek* poll. After his unanimous confirmation by the U.S. Senate, Thornburgh served 3 years as attorney general of the United States (1988-1991) under Presidents Reagan and Bush. Thornburgh took vigorous action against racial, religious, and ethnic hate crimes, and his office mounted a renewed effort to enforce the nation's antitrust and environmental laws. During his tenure as attorney general, Thornburgh twice personally argued and won cases before the U.S. Supreme Court. All told, Thornburgh served in the Justice Department under five presidents, beginning as a United States Attorney in Pittsburgh (1969-1975) and Assistant Attorney General in charge of the Criminal Division (1975-1977), emphasizing efforts against major drug traffickers, organized crime, and corrupt public officials. Thornburgh was educated at Yale University, where he obtained an engineering degree, and at the University of Pittsburgh School of Law, where he served as an editor of the Law Review.

Thornburgh served as director of the Institute of Politics at Harvard's John F. Kennedy School of Government (1987-1988) and was a visiting lecturer at the George Washington University Law School (1995). Thornburgh is a member of the board of directors of Elan Corporation, plc and serves on the boards of the Urban Institute, the National Museum of Industrial History, the DeWitt Wallace Fund for Colonial Williamsburg, and the National Academy of Public Administration. He is chairman of the State Science and Technology Institute and vice-chairman of the World Committee on Disability. He also chairs the Legal Policy Advisory Board of the Washington Legal Foundation. He is a member of the American Bar Foundation, the American Judicature Society, and the Council on Foreign Relations.

Nicholas J. Belkin is a professor at the Rutgers University School of Library and Information Science. His research involves the development of theory, design principles, and systems that will lead to effective and humane information support for human problem management. Such a program entails understanding people's problem situations, and how they attempt to resolve them, in a variety of contexts; the nature and functions of information support communication; and information representation, retrieval, and presentation appropriate to such contexts. These factors lead to specific research goals, which currently include characterization and classification of human information-related problems; description and an analysis of human-human information interaction and design of human-computer information interaction; and classification of human information-seeking strategies and interactions with texts.

The Reverend William J. Byron, S.J. teaches "Social Responsibilities of Business" in the McDonough School of Business at Georgetown University, where he holds an appointment as Distinguished Professor of the Practice of Ethics and serves as rector of the Georgetown Jesuit community. From 1982 to 1992, he was president of the Catholic University of America. Prior assignments include service as president of the University of Scranton (1975 to 1982), dean of arts and sciences at Loyola University of New Orleans (1973 to 1975), and various teaching positions in his field of economics and social ethics. Father Byron is the author of several books, including *Quadrangle Considerations* (Loyola, 1989; winner of the Catholic Press Association's 1990 Best Book Award in Education), and *Answers from Within: Spiritual Guidelines for Managing Setbacks in Work and Life* (Macmillan, 1998); he also edited *The Causes of World Hunger* (Paulist, 1982) and *Take Courage: Psalms of Support and Encouragement* (Sheed & Ward, 1995). He is a trustee of CareFirst Blue Cross Blue Shield, Loyola College in Maryland, and the University of San Francisco; he was a founding director and past chairman of Bread for the World, a public member of the board of commissioners of the Joint Commission for the Accreditation of Healthcare Organizations, and an original member of the board of directors of the Federal Commission on National and Community Service (now the Council of Independent Colleges' Academic Leadership Award). Father Byron grew up in Philadelphia, where he attended St. Joseph's Preparatory School. After service in the Army's 508th Parachute Infantry Regiment in 1945 to 1946, he attended Saint Joseph's University in Philadelphia for 3 years before entering the Jesuit order in 1950. He was ordained a priest in 1961.

Sandra L. Calvert is director of the Children and Media Project at Georgetown University. She received her Ph.D. in developmental and child psychology from the University of Kansas in 1982. Dr. Calvert is a professor of psychology, an associate member of the linguistics department, and a core member of the communication, culture, and technology program at Georgetown University. Her research involves how information technologies, such as television and computers, influence children's attention, memory, and comprehension. She is particularly interested in how the forms of media (i.e., features such as action, sound effects, and language) interface with how children think (e.g., visually or verbally) at different points in their development. Her recently published book, *Children's Journeys Through the Information Age* (McGraw Hill, 1999), provides a critical synthesis of the research on children's social and cognitive development in relation to information technologies.

David Forsyth is associate professor of computer science at the University of California, Berkeley. He is a renowned researcher in the area of object recognition; several of his papers describe systems for identifying humans and their activities in single images. He holds a B.Sc. and M.Sc. in electrical engineering from the University of the Witwatersrand, Johannesburg, and a D.Phil. from Balliol College, Oxford. He has published more than 60 papers in computer vision and computer graphics. He is currently co-authoring *Computer Vision—A Modern Approach*, a graduate textbook in computer vision; some 20 chapters are currently available on the Web. He has served as a referee for all the main professional journals in the area, and he is currently program co-chair for the IEEE Computer Vision and Pattern Recognition conference and a member of the program committee for the European Conference on Computer Vision.

Daniel Geer is chief technologist officer for @Stake Inc., a privately held confidential e-commerce consulting firm. Dr. Geer previously served as vice president and senior strategist for CertCo, as director of engineering at Open Market Inc., and as chief scientist, vice president of technology, and managing director for OpenVision Technologies. He has served as a technical director within Digital Equipment Corporation's research division and was for a number of years the manager of systems development for MIT's Project Athena, where he was the responsible manager for all technical development, including the X Window System, Kerberos, and others. He holds a B.S. in electrical engineering and computer science from MIT and a Sc.D. in biostatistics from Harvard University.

Linda Hodge of Colchester, Connecticut, is National PTA president elect, 2000-2003. Prior to becoming president-elect, Hodge was National PTA Vice President for Programs, 1999-2001. She is a former National PTA Region 7 director, which included representing the states of Alaska, Hawaii, Idaho, Montana, Oregon, Washington, and Wyoming. She has also chaired the National PTA Bylaws, Technology/Safety, and Membership Committees and is a former member of the Executive, Budget, and Leadership Committees, and the IOD Cultural Arts Subcommittee. Hodge is a past president of Hawaii State PTA. Hodge is a National PTA honorary life member as well as an honorary life member of fourteen state PTAs. Included among her awards are the California PTA Honorary Service Award, the California PTA Continuing Service Award, and the Vallejo School District Award Recognizing Outstanding Parent Volunteers. Outside of the PTA, Hodge serves on the board of directors of the Flock Theatre, a regional theater group serving Connecticut, New York, and Massachusetts. Her volunteer activities have included serving on the boards of local Girl Scouts, Boy Scouts, Little League, and youth center organizations. Hodge holds an A.S. degree in computer science and is currently taking courses at Eastern Connecticut State University in business administration.

Marilyn Gell Mason has more than 25 years of management experience with 20 years as a chief executive in complex and highly political organizations. She has served as director of two major urban library systems (Cleveland Public Library and Atlanta Public Library) and of the 1979 White House Conference on Library and Information Services. She has a demonstrated track record of providing the leadership and management expertise needed to bring about institutional innovation and change in short periods of time. She serves on the board of trustees of the Council on Library and Information Resources and the board of directors of Data Research Associates Inc., and has served on numerous national and international advisory committees. She has also directed research and management consulting projects and has published widely, most recently in the areas of strategic management and the integration of print and electronic information. She received her M.P.A. from Harvard University's Kennedy School of Government in 1978.

Milo Medin is senior vice president of engineering and chief technology officer of Excite@Home. Mr. Medin oversees the development of Excite@Home's high-speed backbone. @Home's performance-engineered scalable network removes Internet "traffic jams" and enables true end-to-end management. In addition, the network employs replication and caching technologies that dramatically improve network efficiency. Prior to joining Excite@Home, Medin served as project manager at NASA Ames Research Center. During his tenure, he directed the NASA National Research and Education Network project that, in combination with partners at the Lawrence Livermore National Laboratory, deployed a high-speed national ATM infrastructure connecting major supercomputing and data archiving centers. He also supervised the primary West Coast Internet interconnect network. In addition, he pioneered the global NASA Science Internet project, providing network infrastructure for science at more than 200 sites in 16 countries and 5 continents, including Antarctica, and initially helped establish the TCP/IP protocol as an industry standard. Before working at NASA, Medin held various positions at Science Applications Inc., programming supercomputers for defense program activities at the Lawrence Livermore National Laboratory and Los Alamos National Laboratory, under contract to the Defense Nuclear Agency. Medin has a B.S. in computer science from the University of California, Berkeley.

John B. Rabun was a founder and has been the vice president and chief operating officer of the National Center for Missing and Exploited Children since April 1984. He administers the national clearinghouse, a nonprofit organization in Alexandria, Virginia, with five branches throughout the United States, a staff of 154, and an annual budget of $38.5 million, two-thirds of which comes from Congress via the Department of Justice. Mr. Rabun received a B.A. from Mercer University in 1967, an M.S.W. from the University of Louisville in 1971, and membership in the Academy of Certified Social Workers in 1973. From 1973 to 1984, he was a sworn juvenile officer, founded and managed the Louisville-Jefferson Co. Kentucky Exploited and Missing Child Unit as the first police/social work special investigations team on child sexual exploitation. Immediately before that, he was the executive director for the Kentucky affiliate of the American Civil Liberties Union. Mr. Rabun has provided consultation and technical assistance as a member of the international Expert Network on Self-Regulation of Internet Content for child protection for the Bertelsmann Foundation, Gutersloh, Germany, and INCORE (Internet

Content Rating for Europe), Munich, Germany, over the last 2 years. Mr. Rabun has authored numerous publications and frequently makes guest appearances on national TV and radio specials and news programs.

Robin Raskin is a technology consultant with Ziff Davis Media specializing in consumer technologies. She is regarded as one of the leading authorities on today's family and how they cope (or not) with technology. The former editor in chief and founder of *FamilyPC* magazine, Raskin has been writing, lecturing, and consulting in the consumer technology arena for the past 20 years. Prior to launching *FamilyPC*, Raskin was the editor of *PC Magazine*. Her work as a freelance writer appeared in such magazines as *PC World*, *PC Week*, *InfoWorld*, *Working Mother*, *Working Woman*, *Child*, and *Newsday*. Raskin has authored six books about parenting in the digital age and is a frequent guest on many of the morning news shows. Raskin writes a syndicated column for USAToday.com and for the Gannett News Services, which appears in more than 150 newspapers around the country. She is also the on-air host for a "connected family" TV broadcast that is distributed nationally, reaching 4 million to 6 million viewers monthly. Raskin resides in New York City and Hudson Valley with her husband, three children, and a pile of ever-changing computer equipment.

Robert J. Schloss is research senior software engineer at IBM's Thomas J. Watson Research Center. He holds an A.B. from Yale University in Mathematics and Computer Science. His work on digital endorsement, annotation, and reputation data as strategies for on-the-fly information quality assessment, on personalization strategies for Web content, and on modular data interchange vocabularies began in the early 1990s. Mr. Schloss was a major contributor to the World Wide Web Consortium's PICS (Platform for Internet Content Selection) recommendation (now implemented in major browsers, proxies, and Web servers), including the ability to filter using metadata provided by third-party rating/labeling agencies instead of, or in conjunction with, the metadata provided by the content owner. (PICS was one technology considered by the courts in ruling that the Communications Decency Act section of the telecommunications reform bill was unnecessary.) Mr. Schloss co-chaired the W3C's follow-on effort on metadata interchange frameworks, the Resource Description Framework Data Model and Syntax (RDF), which became a recommendation in 1999. His work includes content sharing strategies across broadband, Web, and wireless systems. His work (with others) on XML Schema Language is a base for the Data Description Language adopted for the MPEG-7 standard for description of multimedia content. He has been on the program committee of the WWW conferences, teaches tutorials on metadata strategies at WebNet and XML conferences, and is an IEEE senior member and a member of Computer Professionals for Social Responsibility and ACM. Schloss resides in Westchester County, New York, with his wife and teenage son.

Janet Ward Schofield is a professor of psychology and a senior scientist at the Learning Research and Development Center at the University of Pittsburgh. She is a social psychologist whose research during the last 25 years has explored the impact of social and technological change in educational settings. This work has led to the publication of over 50 papers and three books, the most recent of which is *Bringing the Internet to School: Lessons from an Urban District* (Jossey-Bass, New York, 2002). Professor Schofield received a B.A. from Harvard University, where she was elected to Phi Beta Kappa, in 1968. She received her M.A. and Ph.D. degrees in social psychology from Harvard University as well. She currently serves as a member of the Board on International Comparative Studies in Education of the National Research Council. She recently also served as a member of the governing body of the American Psychological Association, the Council of Representatives.

Geoffrey R. Stone is University of Chicago Provost and Harry Kalven, Jr. Distinguished Service Professor of Law. Professor Stone received his undergraduate degree in 1968 from the Wharton School of Finance and Commerce of the University of Pennsylvania. He then attended the University of Chicago Law School, where he served as editor-in-chief of the Law Review, was awarded his degree cum laude, and was elected to membership in the Order of the Coif. Following graduation in 1971, Mr. Stone served as law clerk to Judge J. Skelly Wright of the U.S. Court of Appeals for the District of Columbia Circuit. He spent the next year as law clerk to Justice William J. Brennan, Jr. of the Supreme Court of the United States. Mr. Stone was admitted to the New York Bar in 1972 and has been a member of the faculty since 1973. From 1987 to 1993, Mr. Stone served as dean of the Law School. Mr. Stone has served on the board of governors of the Chicago Council of Lawyers, on the board of directors of the American Civil Liberties Union, Illinois Division, as a fellow of the American Academy of Arts and Sciences, an ex-officio member of the American Law Institute, a member of the Executive Committee of the Association of American Law Schools, a member of the Board of Advisers of the National Association of Public Interest Law—The Public Service Challenge, a member of the Advisory Board of the Legal Aid Society, and a member of the Advisory Board of the Chicago Volunteer Legal Services Foundation. Mr. Stone has taught courses in constitutional law, civil procedure, evidence, criminal procedure, contracts, and regulation of the competitive process. Mr. Stone has written a casebook with Mr. Sunstein in the area of constitutional law. He has also written numerous articles concerning such matters as the freedom of speech and press, freedom of religion, the constitutionality of police use of secret agents and informants, the privilege against self-incrimination, the Supreme Court, and the FBI. Mr. Stone is the editor, with David Strauss and Dennis Hutchinson, of the *Supreme Court Review*.

Winifred B. Wechsler has been operating Internet businesses targeted to children and families since 1995. Most recently, she was executive vice president and general manager of Internet and broadband services for Lightspan Inc., an educational software and Internet services company. Prior to that, she was with the Walt Disney Company for 14 years, where she held various management positions. In 1995, she was one of the founders of Disney Online and was responsible for the launch and growth of Disney.com, which is currently the most visited destination for children and families on the Web. She was also senior vice president of Buena Vista Internet Group (now Walt Disney Internet Group), where she set strategic direction, both internationally and domestically, for all of Disney's Internet properties. Throughout, she has been concerned with the ways that commercial enterprises can create responsible methods for advertising and marketing to children on the Web. Prior to working in the Internet industry, she was a senior executive with the Disney Channel for 10 years. She holds an M.B.A. from the Wharton School of the University of Pennsylvania and a B.A. from Wellesley College.

E.2 PROJECT STAFF

Herbert S. Lin is senior scientist and senior staff officer at the Computer Science and Telecommunications Board, National Research Council of the National Academics, where he has been the study director for major projects on public policy and information technology. These studies include a 1996 study on national cryptography policy (*Cryptography's Role in Securing the Information Society*), a 1991 study on the future of computer science (*Computing the Future*), a 1999 study of Defense Department systems for command, control, communications, computing, and intelligence (*Realizing the Potential of C4I: Fundamental Challenges*), and a 2000 study on workforce issues in high-technology (*Building a Workforce for the Information Economy*). Prior to his NRC service, he was a professional staff member and staff scientist for the House Armed Services Committee (1986 to 1990), where his portfolio included defense policy and arms control issues. He also has significant expertise in math and science education.   He received his Ph.D. in physics from MIT in 1979. Avocationally, he is a long-time folk and swing dancer, and a poor magician. Apart from his CSTB work, a list of publications in cognitive science, science education, biophysics, and arms control and defense policy is available on request.

Gail Pritchard was a program officer at the Computer Science and Telecommunications Board, where she contributed research and administrative skills to help produce such reports as *Cryptography's Role in Securing the Information Society, Being Fluent with Information Technology,* and *Building a Workforce for the Information Economy.* Within the Center for Education, Ms. Pritchard has contributed to the reports *Developing a Digital National Library for Science, Mathematics, and Engineering Education* and *Transforming Undergraduate Education in Science, Mathematics, and Engineering Education.* She also served as study director of two committees charged with reviewing drafts of the most recent K-12 mathematics and technology standards, and is currently a program officer with the Committee on Undergraduate Science Education and the Committee on Science Education K-12.   Prior to joining the NRC, Ms. Pritchard was a program specialist in the offices of the Secretary and the University and Science Education Programs at the U.S. Department of Energy.   Ms. Pritchard received a B.A. in liberal arts from St. John's College and an M.Ed. from the University of Virginia.

Joah G. Iannotta is a Ph.D. candidate at the University of Minnesota and a research assistant for the Board on Children, Youth, and Families of the Institute of Medicine and the National Research Council of the National Academies.   Since joining the board, Ms. Iannotta has been involved in the development of a wide range of projects on topics including adolescent risk and vulnerability, children's development and computer technology, and the social and economic benefits and losses of family leave.   She edited a report entitled *Nontechnical Strategies to Reduce Children's Exposure to Inappropriate Material on the Internet* and is a co-editor of *Adolescent Risk and Vulnerability: Approaches to Setting Priorities to Reduce Their Burden,* published by the National Academy Press. Prior to her position on the board, Ms. Iannotta was a research fellow at the University of Minnesota's Tucker Center for Research on Girls and Women in Sport. In addition to conducting analyses of the social and cultural impact of sport on issues of equity, Ms. Iannotta coordinated the Tucker Center's "Image Is Everything" program. This educational workshop introduced high school female athletes to a critique of the media's often highly sexualized portrayal of female athletes and encouraged them to develop their own action plans for addressing issues of equity in sports within their schools and communities. Ms. Iannotta is finishing her doctoral work at the University of Minnesota in the Department of Kinesiology with a concentration in sport sociology and a minor in feminist studies. Her dissertation work uses qualitative research methodologies to uncover strategies collegiate coaches use to address issues of equity (e.g., racism, sexism, and homophobia) within women's athletics in order to create tolerant and cohesive climates on their teams in which all athletes can thrive and develop.

Janice M. Sabuda joined the Computer Science and Telecommunications Board in August 2001. Currently, she is focusing on two projects, Privacy in the Information Age, and Tools and Strategies for Protecting Kids from Pornography on the Internet and Their Applicability to Other Inappropriate Content. She began her term with work on the Global Networks and Local Values project (2001). Prior to joining the National Academies, Ms. Sabuda worked as a customer service representative at eContributor.com, an online fundraising company, and as a product trainer and research associate at a Fairfax, Virginia, prospect research firm. She received her B.S. in business administration from the State University of New York College at Fredonia.

Index